P9-DIG-930

BY GENE FOWLER & BILL CRAWFORD

Texas Monthly Press, Inc.
P.O. Box 1569
Austin, Texas 78767

A   B   C   D   E   F   G   H

Library of Congress Cataloging-in-Publication Data

Fowler, Gene, 1950—
   Border radio.

   Bibliography: p.
   Includes index.
   1. Radio broadcasting—Mexican-American Border Region.   2. Radio sta-
tions—Mexican-American Border Region.   I. Crawford, Bill, 1955—
      . II. Title.
HE8699.M4F68   1987   384.54′53′09721   87-17975
ISBN 0-87719-066-6
Book design by David Kampa

*To all our friends in radio-land,
in beautiful Mexico, Canada and
the good old U.S.A. especially
Gyla McFarland and Diana Borden*

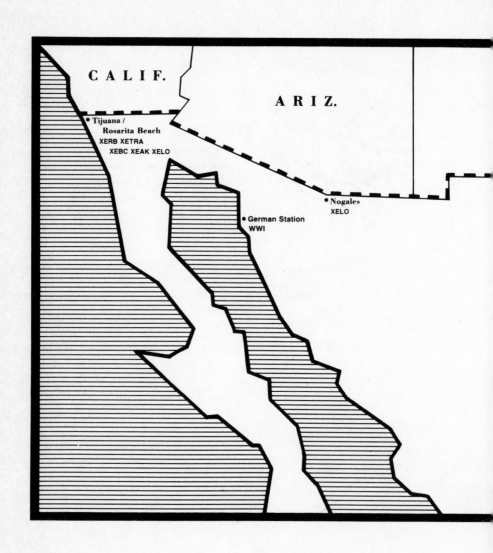

CALIF.

ARIZ.

• Tijuana /
  Rosarita Beach
  XERB XETRA
    XEBC XEAK XELO

• Nogales
  XELO

• German Station
  WWI

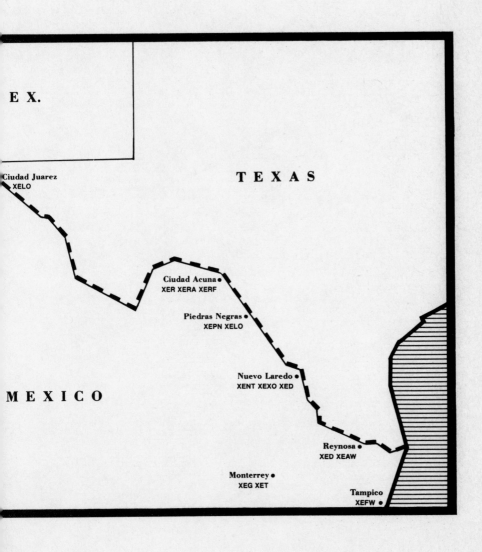

N. MEX.

TEXAS

Ciudad Juarez
XELO

Ciudad Acuna ●
XER XERA XERF

Piedras Negras ●
XEPN XELO

Nuevo Laredo ●
XENT XEXO XED

MEXICO

Reynosa ●
XED XEAW

Monterrey ●
XEG XET

Tampico ●
XEFW

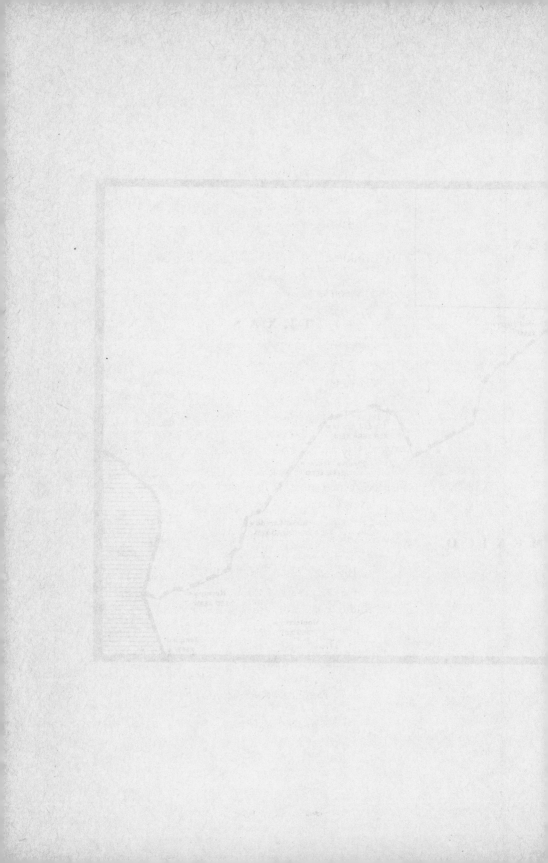

First off, if it wasn't for border radio, I doubt very much if there ever would've been a Wolfman Jack. At least not the Wolfman Jack you and I have come to know.

It was those 250,000 watts, baby, each and every one of 'em making their way across the continent, getting into every city, every little town and hamlet, cuttin' through the night like a knife through a thick fog.

We will probably never again see the likes of it. Times have changed, and it's hard to imagine anyone like Dr. Brinkley over the airwaves again. Or the voices of Reverend Ike and—well, even the Wolfman has never really been the same as back in the days of XERF and XERB.

Border Radio succeeds in its attempt to explain to you not only how this phenomenon of broadcasting affected the industry but also how it influenced a whole generation of people. People like George Lucas. Border radio inspired his motion picture *American Graffiti*, which took me outta the shadows and gave a whole new dimension to my career.

In this book you'll get quite a vivid picture of outlaw broadcasting, so to speak. And you'll realize how something like this could only have happened when it did, with the characters it did.

But most of all, *Border Radio* reminds us all of the magic that went on when hundreds of thousands of watts were let loose into the air, and all of us involved were allowed to shuck and jive and explore new areas of broadcasting. And you'll learn how the magic was destroyed by everyday forces like politics and greed.

Ya know it's a fact that everything ever broadcasted stays out there in the stratosphere, and sometimes, through some fluke of transmission, old sounds return exactly as they were originally heard. So if one night you're cuddled up in bed with the radio on and the moon gleaming through your window, and suddenly you hear a strange static followed by a howl, or a plea to get a goat gland operation, or a voice tellin' you to send a few hard-earned bucks for a reverend's down-home church, listen closely . . . you are most likely in tune with the magic that was border radio.

WOLFMAN JACK

Turn Your Radio On

"Turn your radio on,"
And you'll hear music.
Turn your radio on,
And you'll be free.

—"Turn Your Radio On," hymn sung by
Rhubarb Red and His Rubes, and adapted from song written by Albert E.
Brumley, and broadcast over XEG, Monterrey, Mexico, 1940's

For centuries *la frontera*, as the border between the United States and Mexico is called, has attracted freethinking individuals who chafed under the collar of established society. Coronado, Sieur de La Salle, Bigfoot Wallace, Judge Roy Bean, Jim Bowie, Sam Houston, and Pancho Villa were among the independent frontiersmen who ventured into this sparsely populated semiarid desert area, searching for the freedom they believed they needed to achieve their individual destinies. The broadcasters who built the superpowered radio stations just south of the United States-Mexico border stood in this great tradition of border renegades. The men and women who created border radio were frontiersmen of the ether, imaginative experimenters who came to the Southwest seeking freedom from the restrictive rules of the American media establishment. By building huge transmitters and testing new and untried formats, these pioneers created a proving ground for many of the technical, legal, and programming aspects of today's broadcasting industry, and they managed to be quite entertaining as well.

At the turn of the century, America's airwaves were a virgin communication wilderness, barely touched by Guglielmo Marconi's recent discovery, the wireless. The transmission of voices through the North American airwaves began on Christmas Eve, 1906, when Reginald

Aubrey Fessenden fired up his experimental radio station at Brant Rock, Massachusetts. Wireless operators on ships off the East Coast, listening on their headsets for the short electronic burst of messages in Morse code, were astounded to hear a woman singing. They called in ship's officers and other technicians to experience the wireless miracle and thrilled to the sound of a violin soloist performing "Oh, Holy Night." With this successful experimental broadcast of his own violin performance, Fessenden displayed one of the most important capabilities of Marconi's invention, the capability of sending the human voice out through the heavenly ether.

Following the lead of this media trailblazer, hundreds of amateur radiophiles leapt into the world of the wireless, which soon became known as radio—short for radiotelegraphy. They filled their attics with wires, Leyden jars, and the other paraphernalia necessary to transmit and receive the magical radio signals. They watched sparks flash brilliantly across homemade receivers and tweaked tuning crystals with thin wires called cat's whiskers, as they strained to hear the secrets of the airwaves. When one devoted band of radio enthusiasts heard a musical broadcast for the first time, they called in the neighbors just to make sure "that not a single one of us was having a daydream." Some spent their evenings searching the electromagnetic spectrum, trying to make contact with ships at sea, while others tuned in faraway time signals and marveled "at the ability of man to conquer distance." In 1912 the U.S. government passed the first laws concerning radio broadcasting. Within five years, more than 8500 transmitting licenses had been issued, and a chorus of radio voices was creating an "amateur clamor" in the American heavens.

World War I brought an end to the squawking, as the Navy ordered all transmitters off the air to keep the airwaves clear for the vital function of ship-to-shore communication. At the close of the war, the Navy tried to maintain control of all broadcasting, arguing that the medium was too important to be managed by private commercial interests. But when the doughboys returned from France, radio amateurs returned to the ether, and federal officials decided to let free enterprise determine the fate of American broadcasting.

America's fascination with radio soon turned into an obsession. In the first issue of *Radio Broadcast* magazine, published in 1920, the editors commented on the growth of the new medium, writing that "the rate of increase in the number of people who spend at least part of their evening listening in is almost incomprehensible." Colleges, churches, newspapers, department stores, radio manufacturers, hundreds of enterprising individuals, and even stockyards started their own stations. Jazz bands, poets, starlets, and elephants broadcast live in a rush of largely unrehearsed programming. The number of stations mushroomed from just 8 in 1921 to 564 in 1922, and investment in radio equipment zoomed from $60 million in 1922 to $358 million in 1924.

It is difficult for our video-glutted generation to imagine what radio meant to Americans in the twenties. Radio was the housewife's companion, the friendly voice of consolation that brightened the world of cooking, washing, and child rearing with music, romance, and understanding conversation. Radio became the center of the family entertainment circle, as children, parents, and grandparents gathered by the Grebe, Radiola, or Aeriola set in the radio room and marveled at the sounds they heard transported mysteriously from faraway lands.

Radio was hailed as the world's greatest source of knowledge, the creator of international harmony, and the invention that would stop all wars. Those who had radio sets spent the better part of their days and evenings tuned in to the voices from the ether. Those who wanted to buy sets, according to a contemporary chronicler, often "stood in the fourth or fifth row at the radio counter waiting their turn only to be told when they finally reached the counter that they might place an order and it would be filled when possible." By the mid-twenties America was truly a country crazy for radio.

Listeners who brought radio sets were sometimes disappointed, though. Shrieks, grunts, groans, and cross talks ruled the airwaves, which were described by some as a hertzian bedlam. Broadcasters jumped frequencies and boosted power in their efforts to be heard over the broadcasting babble. Farmers complained that the conflicting radio waves caused their cows to give sour milk. As early as 1923, Secretary of Commerce Herbert Hoover found the chaos of the air intolerable, froze the issuance of licenses, and assumed the power of allocating different frequencies to different radio stations. He was not able to restrain the runaway radio broadcasters, however, until passage of the Radio Act of 1927, which established the Federal Radio Commission, forerunner of the Federal Communications Commission. In 1934, Washington legislators passed the more far-reaching Communications Act and created the Federal Communications Commission, which managed to rein in the radio stampede and to this day regulates the American airwaves.

While Hoover was trying to bring order to the radio mayhem, broadcasters were trying to figure out how to make money out of it. Advertising was not considered to be a particularly lucrative use of the new medium and was actually opposed by powerful figures in the broadcasting world, who saw radio as nothing more than an extension of telegraphic services. A national radio conference in 1922 recommended that "direct advertising in broadcast radio service be absolutely prohibited." Critics compared radio advertising to "a grotesque, smirking gargoyle set at the very top of America's skyscraping adventure in acquisition ad infinitum." Secretary of Commerce Hoover declared, "I believe the quickest way to kill broadcasting would be to use it for direct advertising." In 1924 more than 400 of the 526 existing radio stations refused to accept sponsors, and as late as 1927 most of the radio stations in America served as publicity vehicles for newspapers like the *Detroit News*, retail stores like Gimbel's and John Wanamaker, and hotels and manufacturers. AT&T viewed radio as an extended telephone system with limited potential and put the operation of its radio stations under the direction of its by-products services division.

In 1926 three of the nation's biggest equipment manufacturers—Radio Corporation of America, Westinghouse, and General Electric—joined forces to bring some order to the cluttered market arena of radio programming. To do that, they created the National Broadcasting Company, or NBC, and established two radio networks, the Red and the Blue, for the dissemination of programming. The networks were groups of stations that were joined by telephone lines and agreed to play programs produced at flagship stations WEAF and WJZ in New York City. According to *Fortune* magazine, NBC began its broadcasting network merely to sell radios, figuring that "if it could stimulate the sale of radios perhaps it would not be necessary for it to make any profit at all on broadcasting." The magazine added, "This stimulation of sales was done on a very high ethical plane."

NBC projected a highbrow aura, building for itself a reputation as a defender of enlightened cultural programming. *Fortune* magazine explained that the company viewed itself as "the guardian of radio, the Great Red and Blue Father, a 'service' organization interested in the dissemination of culture to the masses." That philosophy was clearly expressed in the advertising for the debut of the NBC networks, which was billed as "the most pretentious broadcasting program ever presented." Network executives provided their listeners for the most part with live performances of conservatory music, described by one program director as "potted palm" music. Tin Pan Alley tunes that found their way onto the networks had to undergo the close scrutiny of censors. "Whatcha doin', honey? I feel so funny," a line of the song "Pettin' in the Park," was changed to "Dad and Mother did it, but we admit it" before network officials would allow it to be performed on the air. Action series like *Gangbusters* and serials such as *Stella Dallas* and *Just Plain Bill* eventually came along to brighten up the orchestral format somewhat, and comedians such as Jack Benny, Fanny Brice, and Eddie Cantor tried to spice up their audiences' listening hours, but broadcasting executives, joined later by federal government officials, kept a tight rein on programming directors. During the first decade of radio some stations took themselves so seriously that they refused to broadcast saxophone music, saying that it had an immoral influence on its listeners.

At first, the networks showed some discrimination as to the products they advertised, in tune with their highbrow progile. NBC, for example, turned down a massive contract from one of America's largest manufacturers of toilet paper, refusing to advertise a product so intimate. That sensitivity soon gave way to the bottom line, however. A November 1932 issue of *Broadcasting* magazine ran the headline Taboo on Delicate Ads Removed by Networks: Ex-Lax Signs With CBS. Network officials lured advertisers with statements like quickest way to a woman's lips are her ears, pointing out that drug and cosmetic radio programs constitute the largest group of advertising on the air today. In 1934, radio grossed $72,887,000 in advertising, more than 80 percent of which went to the advertising of drugs, foods, and other convenience items. Stations sold Marmola, a fat reducer composed of thyroid extract and bladder wrack, which caused headache, delirium, and fever in some unfortunate overeaters. Many other stations sold Kolorbak, a lead-salt type of hair dye that caused lead poisoning in overusers anxious to restore their health. Koremlu, another big radio advertiser, was a depilatory made from thallium acetate, a rat poison that caused abdominal pain, nausea, and blindness as well as the loss of all body hair, sightly or unsightly. Radio stations in the United States touted Lysol as an effective and safe douche, and stations ran hundreds of hours of ads for Bromo-Seltzer, even though medical experts at the time warned the Bromo-Seltzer if used frequently may lead to serious physical and psychical disturbances, not the least of which are sexual impotence and bromide intoxication.

The explosion of advertising brought with it a tidal wave of public criticism of broadcasters and their practices. The U.S. Senate considered a resolution that would limit advertising to a simple mention of a product as a program's sponsor. Dr. Arthur J. Cramp of the American Medical Association published a book on dangerous personal products entitled *Nostrums and Quackery*, in which he maintained that the public is much less likely to be carried away by false or fraudulent claims made in cold type than it is when similar claims are made by a plausible radio announcer. Under Secretary of Agriculture Rexford Guy Tugwell tried to introduce a bill to force the listing of all ingredients on labels. The Proprietary Association, a group of patent medicine manufacturers, called the bill grotesque in its terms, evil in its purposes, and vicious in its possible consequences and fought hard to maintain the American people's constitutional right to self medication. The broadcasting establishment was also firmly opposed to such a bill and lined up powerful friends in Congress to work against the impending legislation. Josiah Bailey of North Carolina became known as the Senator for Vick's Vapo-Rub, and James Mead of New York became the Congressman for Doan's Kidney Pills. Despite the opposition of the radio industry, legislators managed to pass a food and drug law in 1938 that increased the effectiveness of the Food and Drug Administration, which in 1931 employed a mere 65 inspectors to monitor more than 110,000 products.

The radio industry also ran afoul of consumers and government bureaucrats in its promotion of radio stargazers. CBS featured astrologer Evangeline Adams, a seer who could solve any personal problem sent to her by mail, as long as it was accompanied by a Forhan's boxtop. *The Voice of Experience*, sponsored by Haley's M-O and Musterole, was another extremely popular CBS program. The Voice, alias M. Sayle Taylor, used a system of numbered prescriptions to take care of 10,000 to 20,000 correspondents a week who wrote of all kinds of emotional and physical distress. The Voice went so far as to operate the Voice of Experience Investigation Bureau, which looked into cases further to make sure they had a satisfactory outcome.

In 1937 the National Association of Broadcasters, an industry group originally created to win broadcasting concessions from the American Society of Composers, Authors, and Publishers, first distributed a pamphlet entitled "Standards of Practice for Radio Broadcasters of the United States of America." In the publication, the radio industry addressed the issue of appropriate programming for the American ear, stressing that radio should be used to promote "spiritual harmony and understanding of mankind" and urging that broadcasters limit advertising sales to individuals and firms who "comply with pertinent legal requirements, fair trade practices, and accepted standards of good taste." The pamphlet added, "The advertising of fortune-telling, occultism, spiritualism, astrology, phrenology, palm reading, numerology, mind-reading or character-reading is not acceptable."

The self-regulation of the industry by the NAB was evidence that the radio industry had matured. By the thirties the radio world was no longer a wide-open free-for-all inhabited by wild-eyed individuals with big ideas and intense motivation. Rather, the broadcasting industry was controlled by large corporations working closely with federal regulators to maintain orderliness. Tasteful advertising and potted-palm programming was the order of the day, sounds that were uncontroversial and profitable but decidedly unadventuresome.

Border radio blasted like a blue norther across the American airwaves, inspiring radio pundit Walter Winchell to comment that the border stations offered the best entertainment available in the wee hours. The men who first moved to the border began their broadcasting careers when the federal regulatory agency was but a twinkle in Herbert Hoover's eye. These media trailblazers deeply resented the monopolistic power of the networks and the increasing government interference in their activities. They traveled from the hinterlands of Iowa, Kansas, and Brooklyn to a territory beyond the pale of American law, a sparsely populated land of ocotillo, grapefruit, and Angora goats—*la frontera*, the border.

Border radio operators came up with a unique method of sidestepping United States broadcasting restrictions. They built their stations just across the border, in Mexican territory, and worked out special licensing arrangements with the broadcasting authorities in Mexico City, whom they found to be much more agreeable than the stuffed shirts at the Federal Radio Commission. Like all radio stations licensed in Mexico, the border stations were given call letters beginning with *XE*, a brand that added to their mystique. To compete with the wide coverage of the established multistation networks, these operators created what were essentially single-station networks, stations with such extraordinary power that their signals could cover the entire United States and, in some cases, most of the world. Border radio operators accomplished this feat by hiring expert engineers to build special transmitters. While most radio stations in the United States broadcast over transmitters with about 1000 watts of power, border radiomen boomed their programming across America with transmitters humming at as much as 1,000,000 watts.

The sky wave, or ozone skip effect, enabled the signals of these superpowered stations to travel incredible distances. AM radio waves bounce or skip off the atmosphere surrounding the globe in much the same way as a rock skips across a smooth pond. Because of the sky wave phenomenon, listeners in Dallas, San Francisco, and even New Zealand could tune in to the border stations, oftentimes with astonishing clarity. Thus, over the years border radio developed an international reputation, and the sounds of the big X stations became familiar to listeners in Ulysses, Kansas, as well as Uppsala, Sweden.

At sunrise every morning in the mid-thirties the Pickard Family greeted radio listeners tuned to the border radio stations located just south of the silvery Rio Grande, "the center of romance in America." Bub, Ruthie, Charlie, and the rest of the family asked their sleepy-eyed listeners the musical question, "How many biscuits can you eat this morning?" Accompanied by the Hillbilly Boys, W. Lee O'Daniel, the future governor of Texas, described the cure for the country's economic woes and sang, "I've said skiddoo to the hard-time blues, And from

here on in I'm smiling through. . . . I've got that million-dollar smile."
Brother Bill introduced AP, Sarah, Maybelle, Jeanette, Helen, June and
Anita—the original Carter Family—who admonished those listening to
"Keep on the sunny side, Always on the sunny side, Keep on the sunny
side of life." Cowboy Slim Rinehart and "America's number one singing
cowgirl," Patsy Montana, assured their audience that they were "happy
in the saddle again," and Doc Hopkins shouted out, "Cornstalk fiddle
and a hickory bow, Take your honey and around you go" to the tune of
"The College Hornpipe." Russ Pike and the Modern Pioneers, Mainer's
Mountaineers, and Doc and Carl, among others, joined in for the *Good
Neighbor Get-together*, "four hours packed solid with fun and music,"
while Paymaster Pete Malaney and the Riders of the Rio Grande let out
whoops and hollers to the fiddle tune "Whoa, Mule, Whoa."

Listeners to border radio stations could find a solution to almost any
ailment—physical or spiritual—that could possibly be imagined. Bub
Pickard exhorted his listeners, "Don't let gray hair cheat you out of your
job and cause you a lot of worry. . . . Get a bottle of Kolorbak from your
nearest drug or department store." On other mornings, Bub told his
extended radio family about "a fine and dandy offer we know each of
you will want to take advantage of." Bub offered listeners "a liberal test
bottle of the famous Peruna Tonic, which folks everywhere are now using
to help build cold-chasing resistance to knock out the torture of colds."
And the liberal bottle was sent absolutely free, along with "valuable information on colds."

Another authoritative voice from the border informed listeners of some
basic biological facts: "Water is the greatest of all cleansers. . . . It fur-
nishes the medium by which impurities in the body may be carried
away. . . . A man may live without food for forty, sixty, or even eighty
days, but deprive him of water for five or six days and he'll die a horrible
death." The speaker went on to describe the "many people in the world
who are troubled with some condition that was caused or being made
worse by a sluggish system," and he offered a solution, provided by
"kind Providence." "If you'll add a teaspoonful of Crazy Water Crystals
to about a large glass of water, preferably warm, and drink it thirty
minutes before breakfast for the next three weeks, I'm just confident that
it will help you."

The lavender-suited and velvet-tongued Norman G. Baker offered
talks on the mind, the digestion, and the benefits of driving on Tangley
tires, while noted specialist Harry M. Hoxsey, N.D., promoted his surefire cancer cure developed by his great-grandfather, a well-known horse
doctor. Other healers, like the famous goat gland specialist Dr. John R.
Brinkley, were a regular feature of border radio, offering long-suffering

radio listeners cures for everything from hemorrhoids to cancer. "Just because you're not seriously sick does not make it so," warned Dr. Brinkley. He described his special "x-ray and microscopical as well as chemical examinations" designed to diagnose properly "the disease that's in your body, the disease that's destroying your earning power, the disease that's causing you to keep your nose to the grindstone and spend every dollar that you can rake and scrape." He pleaded with those listening, "You men, why are you holding back? You know you're sick, you know your prostate's infected and diseased. . . . Well, why do you hold back? Why do you twist and squirm around the old cocklebur . . . when I am offering you these low rates, this easy work, this lifetime-guarantee-of-service plan? Come at once to the Brinkley Hospital before it is everlastingly too late."

Those in need of spiritual insight listened to Rose Dawn, Marjah, Koran, Rajah Rayboid, and other spooks who migrated to the border. M. N. Bunker, president of the American Institute of Grapho-Analysis, made startling predictions based on his listeners' penmanship. "Remember, friends, your future is written in the stars," intoned Dr. Ralph Richards, Ms.D., Ps.D., a metaphysician and the Friendly Voice of the Heavens. "Send me the date of your birth and one dollar, and I will search the stars to learn your future." Other border radio fans tuned in to a soft female voice cooing, "Maybe one of you big, strong, handsome men would want to meet me and love me and maybe spend the rest of your days with me? I'm just one of thousands of beautiful, warm, affectionate women who are members of the Hollywood Four Hundred Club."

For those more interested in the Bible than the needs of the flesh, the Wilburn Family sang familiar hymns, sweetly coaxing listeners to tune the radio receivers in their souls to "radio station S-A-V-E-D. . . . Direct from heaven, from the glory land on high, where there is no interference, no static in the sky." The Reverend Sam Morris, the Voice of Temperance, preached his most famous sermon, entitled "The Ravages of Rum." "Young men start takin' nips and totin' flasks to be smart and show they're regular fellas," he said. "They often show up behind bars or in the gutter without friends or a future." The fate of young girls who sampled alcohol was just as bleak: "Often they end up as social outcasts, unmarried mothers, gangster molls, and pistol-packin' mamas."

As America entered World War II, Mexico and the United States signed a broadcasting agreement that many thought would mark the end of border radio. It did not. Some stations shut down temporarily, and others changed ownership and frequency, but when the dust settled along the Rio Grande, the stations were still there, as popular as ever with listeners who still tuned in to them for hope. The Bell Family promised in high-pitched harmony to "keep 'em flyin'," declaring that "Uncle Sam is with us, and God above, We'll keep 'em flyin' for the land we love." Arnaldo Ramirez, the future mayor of Mission, Texas, hosted *La Hora del Soldado* (The Soldier's Hour), which was aimed at the Spanish-speaking workers who came to the factories and bases in the Southwest to assist in the war effort.

In the boom times after the war, border radio became the most important national outlet for the emerging genre of country-and-western music. The deep rich voice of Paul Kallinger, "your good neighbor along the way," introduced Webb Pierce, Eddy Arnold, Ernest Tubb, Hank Thompson, Red Foley, Jimmie Wakely, and other country greats who entertained audiences with songs like "The Wild Side of Life," "There Stands the Glass," and "Filipino Baby."

Border radio advertising companies in the fifties was nothing short of *amazing*, as companies like All-American Radio Program Sellers and Federal Home Products tempted listeners with incredible bargains. The Blade Man offered "an amazing free gift offer" of a "slim, streamlined, modernistic pocketknife" for each order of one hundred of the "finest-quality, extra-sharp double-edged razor blades for only one dollar." Announcer Randy Blake offered "an amazing easy way for every man, woman, and child to earn lots of spending money"—motto cards. "These mottoes sparkle like diamonds in the daylight, and they glow like stars in the dark," Blake declared, "and contain popular verses such as the Lord's Prayer, 'Mother of Mine,' and 'Kneel at the Cross.'" Entrepreneurs pitched oil wells, real estate deals, lottery tickets—all spectacular opportunities for enrichment, and 100 percent guaranteed. Other advertisements told of "the most amazing family life insurance offer ever made" and the "amazing fountain pen" that "writes almost fifty miles of words without a refill" complete "with an amazing lifetime guarantee." And for those whose nerves suffered from the overabundance of amazement, the golden-throated Del Sharbis had the answer. "In this age of atomic weapons, worry, and stress," he explained, "scientific research has produced a substance to help calm and soothe worried and nervous people. Such a substance is in the sleep aid Restall."

"Wherever ya are, and whatever ya doin', I wancha to lay ya hands on da raydeeooo, lay back wid me, and squeeeze ma knobs. We gonna feeeel it ta-nite. . . . OOOOOOWWWWWWOOOOooooooooo." Wolfman Jack slamdunked border radio into the sixties with his fast-talking, sly jive and his taste for white-hot rhythm and blues. From midnight till dawn, the Wolfman sat below the Rio Grande and filled the heavens with the sounds of James Brown, Freddie King, and other sizzling comets of soul. Amid tequila parties, shoot-outs, and high-level diplomatic negotiations, Wolfman and his cohorts pitched sex pills, diet pills, record packages, even Wolfman roach clips, guaranteed to make the intrepid insects easier to handle.

In the sixties and seventies, border radio became a mecca for electronic evangelists who broadcast, in the words of one station's jingle, "From early evening till late at night, The gospel voices to help you think right." The Reverend A. A. Allen played tapes recorded live at his Miracle Restoration Revival services, specially designed for those "who are tired and disgusted with cold, dead religious form and tradition" and who sought "salvation for the soul, healing for the body, salvation from demon powers, nicotine, alcohol, dope, witchcraft, spirits, and the curse of poverty." Dr. C. W. Burpo, director of *The Bible Institute of the Air*, told listeners, "Our heavenly Father loves you. Yes, he does, and I do too." The Bishop A. H. Holmes, "your man of God," told the mothers listening to "sit back, relax, and put the pot on low simmer while the Bishop walk that walk and talk that talk this morning." "Right now there's a plague has hit this nation," shouted Brother David Terrell. "Minnesota is being eaten up by caterpillars, and Canada is five inches deep in caterpillars." The Reverend Frederick Eikerenkoetter II, better known as Reverend Ike, told his audience that "the lack of money is the root of all evil. Don't be a hypocrite about money," he urged. "Admit openly and inwardly that you like money. Say, 'I like money. I need money. I want money.' If you know you're a lost ball in high grass," he said, "if you're tired of short stakes and bad breaks, write me a letter." For decades, border radio was full of the spirit, supported by the love offerings of those who found hope in the prayer cloths, holy oil, and bacteriostatic water treatment units offered by the border preachers.

Like the tales of southwestern gunfighters, drifters, and cattle rustlers, stories of the border radio desperadoes have fascinated listeners for decades. Writers have penned numerous articles about border radio's preachers, healers, and hucksters. Filmmakers have told the border story on celluloid, and musicians from Asher Sizemore to ZZ Top have sung about the exploits of the great superpowered broadcasters. This book is a collection of just some of these tales, the chronicles of a few amazing individuals who made their way to the tall antennas rising from the rugged countryside of northern Mexico and left their mark on the mysterious, elusive and always entertaining sliver of the American electromagnetic spectrum designated by the letter *X*.

Del Rio's Dr. Brinkley:
The Big Daddy of Border Radio

"A man is only as old as his glands."
—John R. Brinkley, M.D., Ph.D., M.C., LL.D.,
D.P.H., Sc.D.; Lieutenant, U.S. Naval Reserves;
member, National Geographic Society

A young couple, living on the dust-blown plains of West Texas in the depths of the Great Depression, woke up one morning after a long night of howling winds and stared out at a world of dust. The weathered barn, the fence posts, the old pick-'em-up truck—everything was covered with thick layers of dust. They started out into the dull, gray void, as though the land they had owned and worked on for so many years had simply vanished.

"Del Rio," said the young woman to her bewildered husband. "Del Rio," spoken as if it were a drink of water that would save them from perishing. They had heard of the magic oasis on their radio, an old RCA table model, in between Mexican sopranos, fiddling hillbillies, and commercials for Kolorbak. They marveled at the descriptions of the San Felipe Springs, where 60 million gallons of "lovely mineral springwater" gushed forth every day. "Just think of drinking that lovely springwater," a melodious voice invited over the radio, "right out of the spring, just as God gives it to you, and it does not cost you a cent." As the world around them dried up and blew away, they dreamed of the watery wonderland named Val Verde, ("Green Valley"), the site of the Queen City of the Rio Grande, "where flowers are in bloom and everything is pretty and green," where "thousands of fertile acres await development," and where "fruits of all kinds thrive in the kindly climate." They loaded up the truck, left their dusty homestead to the tumbleweeds, and headed for the Mexican border, seeking the source of the magic voice, radio station XERA, The Sunshine Station Between the Nations.

Arriving in Del Rio, the couple discovered a fantasyland beyond their imaginations. Sparkling hotels and rooming houses graced the shady avenues. Leafy gardens were nourished with a canal system fed by the San Felipe Springs. Well-fed families gathered in the park for band concerts, as cadres of elegant elderly gentlemen strolled through town with a lively fire in their eyes.

The voice that lured this couple and so many others to the Texas border belonged to Dr. John R. Brinkley, a well-dressed physician. Stories of his medical exploits had appeared in papers nationwide, often accompanied by photographs that depicted him gazing scientifically through small round spectacles. There was something exotic and experimental about his image, highlighted by his goatee, his glittering diamonds, "a statuesque head that a phrenologist would admire," and light blue eyes "with a shrewd and friendly twinkle in them." Shrewd, indeed, for it was this same Dr. Brinkley who made a fortune with a simple surgical procedure.

The jazz age of the twenties could have also been called the age of rejuvenation. Americans, following in the footsteps of Ponce de León and other early explorers who commanded high prices for pepper, cinnamon, cloves, and other spices thought to be aphrodisiacs, sought the restorative powers of royal jelly, herbal brews such as pego palo cocktails distilled from a plant known as the vitality vine, and glandular overhauls. Even the future governor of Louisiana, Jimmie Davis, sang about the phenomenon of sexual rejuvenation in a rendition of "Organ Grinder Blues," "Gonna get me some monkey glands, Be like I used ta wuz." As rejuvenation fever swept the nation, thousands of fountain-of-youth seekers swarmed into Dr. Brinkley's hospital desperate and willing to hand over large sums of money or mortgage the farm to feel the restorative power of Brinkley's skillful hands. They sought the "goat gland proposition," the transplantation of thin slivers of billy-goat gonads into the human scrotum. Brinkley announced his discovery of the capric performance additive in 1917 and for the next quarter of a century was known around the world as the goat gland man. Praised by some as "the Kansas Ponce de León" and scorned by others as a "loquacious purveyor of goat giblets," he was undoubtedly one of the most remarkable figures of his time. A millionaire, yet in his own estimation "just as easy as an old shoe," Dr. Brinkley was, above all else, the father of border radio.

Born in the North Carolina mountains in 1885, John Romulus Brinkley dreamed of greatness as a young boy. According to the author he paid to write his biography, Clement Wood (a practicing dream analyst who also produced biographies of Henry VIII, Norman Baker, and Jehovah) the young Brinkley picked out three men to pattern himself after ". . . Abraham Lincoln. Thomas A. Edison. William McKinley," and spent long hours pondering great things to come. "John Brinkley freeing the slaves . . . John Brinkley illuminating the world . . . John Brinkley healing the sick." He chose to pursue the latter dream, following barefoot in the steps of his father, a country doctor. Earning enough money as a mail carrier to pursue his dream, he tried to gain admittance to Johns Hopkins University. Wearing overalls and a torn shirt, he met with the dean of the medical department, who advised him, "You're probably a good mail carrier. I advise you to stick to that."

Undaunted, Brinkley pursued his degree at the somewhat less well-known Bennett Eclectic Medical School in Chicago and worked for the Southern Railroad Company and Western Union at the same time to support his young wife and family. Although Brinkley "personally denied himself everything," according to his biographer, college life was rough on the family. The aspiring physician was forced to drop out and flee with his daughter to Montreal while seeking a permanent divorce from his unsympathetic wife. Remarried to Minnie Telitha Jones, the daughter of a wealthy Memphis physician, Brinkley managed to acquire a certificate from the National University of Arts and Sciences in St. Louis and worked for some time in Greenville, Tennessee, as an "electro medic doctor." Patients at the clinic were shown startling sculptural renditions of ailments due to sexual indiscretion and then were treated by the doctor.

After he ran into legal difficulties with his practice and had his father-in-law pay some outstanding bills, Brinkley decided to further his formal education. He enrolled in the Eclectic Medical University in Kansas City and earned his degree in less than a month. The Eclectic course of study focused on herbal healing, homeopathy, and naturopathy. While the degree was recognized in eight states, the head of the university was later to boast that he never granted a diploma "for less than $500."

Brinkley was given a license to practice medicine in Arkansas, and through reciprocal arrangements, he acquired medical licenses in Kansas, Tennessee, Missouri, Texas, and Connecticut. He took a job as the plant surgeon with Swift and Company in Kansas City, stitching up cuts and taking advantage of the unparalleled opportunity for studying the diseases of animals. One observation in particular was to prove pivotal in Brinkley's future work. When asked what was the healthiest animal that was slaughtered at the plant, almost everyone agreed that it was the goat. Having gained this useful bit of knowledge, the doctor moved on, stirred by the conviction "that he was placed in this world for a definite purpose." He decided on a central location and settled down in little Milford, Kansas, in October 1917, a tiny crossroads community located near the geographical center of the United States. When Minnie, also a graduate of the Eclectic Medical University, saw the meager metropolis her husband had chosen to call home, she burst into tears.

Doctor (Brinkley often referred to himself by this simple generic distinction) must have felt called by destiny to that isolated spot in the heartland. The supersurgeon opened an office and a small drugstore stocked with patent medicines and whipped a flu epidemic that was plaguing the locals. Whipping the flu was a minor skirmish compared with the major medical victory he would accomplish within a month, one that Doctor felt certain would change the course of human history and place the name "Brinkley" above those of Pasteur, Curie and Hippocrates.

No one will ever know for sure what really happened on the Day of Discovery in Milford. The Brinkley-authorized version recorded that a local farmer, Mr. S., walked into his country doc's office one day and described his manly problem. "Yep, there is something wrong with me," the farmer confessed, "though to look at me you wouldn't judge it. I do look husky, don't I?" He then explained that he was 46 and that although he had an eighteen-year-old son, he had been unable to sire any further offspring. "I'm all in," he continued. "No pep. A flat tire. I've been to plenty of doctors about it, and spent wads of money on 'em too—and not a one of 'em has done me a mite of good. Now I know you've been in the army. I figured the government might have taught you something about it, there, that might be good for a man who was what they call sexually weak."

Doctor explained that he had treated cases like this before with "serums, medicines, and electricity" and that nothing had proven effective, that medical science simply had no remedy for such a condition. The talk then drifted on to farming and rams and buck goats. Doc joked to the farmer that he "wouldn't have any trouble if you had a pair of those buck glands in you."

"Well, why don't you put 'em in?" the farmer inquired. "Why don't you go ahead and put a pair of goat glands in me? Transplant 'em. Graft 'em on, the way I'd graft a Pound Sweet on an apple stray."

According to Clement Wood, "The doctor half closed his eyes and considered. . . . And then he shook his head, slowly. The code of ethics his father had drilled into him forever forbade him from any conduct, especially with relation to healing, except the utterly honest and straightforward." Doctor said no—he couldn't do it. Mr. S. grew more desperate. He begged. He pleaded. He offered to pay any price. He finally threatened to ruin the physician's reputation, to drive away potential patients just as the hardworking Brinkley was getting a foothold in the small community.

So Doctor relented to the strange request, striking out for the untamed frontiers of medical science under cover of darkness by performing the operation in secret in the middle of the night for $150.

A few seasons rolled by over the Kansas plains, and Mrs. S. gave birth to a healthy goat-gland baby boy. The youngster, appropriately nicknamed Billy by his father "in honor of the assistance we had received from our four-footed friend," told the *Kansas City Star* decades later that Brinkley had talked his father into the operation with the promise of paying the farmer handsomely for participating in the experiment.

No matter which version of the story was true, word of the goat gland miracle spread around the community, and Doctor operated on several libido-lagging locals. One became "a regular billygoat—twice as good as any man around Milford." Another gave birth to a healthy boy who was scientifically named Charles Darwin. In order to better serve humanity, Doctor hired an advertising consultant. When Brinkley told the adman about the goat gland proposition, the jubilant executive exclaimed, "Dr. Brinkley, you've got a million dollars in your hands and you don't even realize it!" Brinkley sent news of his discovery to medical societies and newspapers and began to attract well-known personalities to the tiny town. Dr. J.J. Tobias, chancellor of the Chicago Law School, underwent the Brinkley operation with great success. "I left the hospital feeling twenty-five years younger," he told newspaper reporters, "and I seem to grow still younger every day!" The plucky chancellor awarded Brinkley an honorary degree of Doctor of Science and introduced him to politicians, society women, and business moguls, many of whom were transformed by the skillful hands of the trailblazing medico. As wire stories reported the success of the revered scholar's rejuvenation, Doctor's success was in the bag.

Soon Brinkley was attracting a steady stream of pilgrims to his remote Kansas kingdom. He refined his surgical technique, using only glands from Toggenburg goats after two "society men" from California demanded Angora goat glands, which resulted in great potency but a horrible odor. At first, patients were encouraged to bring their own goats to the small clinic, but when Doctor built a brand new hospital, he also constructed adjoining pens to hold the livestock he was having shipped in weekly from Arkansas. Transplant recipients could stroll among the frisky bucks and take their choice.

Doctor hired Sydney B. Flower, editor of *Hypnotic Review*, to assist in expounding on his theories of rejuvenation, and soon an endless stream of treastises in the form of books, pamphlets, mail-outs, and advertisements came forth from the "dupligraphs" of the Kansas physician. "All energy is sex energy," Brinkley theorized. "A man is only as old as his glands." Doctor tipped his professional hat to Dr. Serge Voronoff of France, who experimented with a "monkey gland operation" and ignited a rejuvenation frenzy in Europe. While Voronoff acknowledged that he had experimented with monkey and human glands, the pioneering physician maintained that "the superiority of Dr. Brinkley's method . . . is apparent to the reasoning mind." The glands, Doctor's literature testified, would actually feed into and grow into the human body. He maintained that a "certain anastomotic technic" was required in working with the gland, "so that its energy is 'on tap' . . . just as the starting battery in your automobile is unused except when you need it for lighting and starting purposes." Deriding the pessimistic medical establishment for being "either brainless or lazy," Doctor boldly declared that "all diseases are curable" and that the Brinkley operation would restore conjugal vigor, cure everything from diabetes to dementia praecox, and turn an otherwise weak patient into "the ram what am with every lamb."

Doctor was one of the first masters of modern public relations, and he managed to place stories about his discoveries in some of America's most prestigious news outlets. Headlines from papers in the Midwest screamed, GOAT GLANDS REJUVENATE DECREPIT KANSAS VILLAGE and JAPAN MAKES GOAT GLAND TRANSPLANTATION COMPULSORY, and stories told of His Highness the Maharajah Thakou of Morvi in India, who visited New York to receive the Brinkley treatment. One large spread that appeared in New York City papers featured a billy-goat head in its center. Sprouting out from the head in the shape of horns were the words "Preaches Fundamentalism—Practices Goat Gland Science." Above the horned slogan, the lead-in began, "How a Famous Surgeon Combines Old-Time Religion and New-Fangled Operations on a Strange Medico-Gospel Farm." Beneath graphic depictions of Doctor, Billy (the world's first goat gland kiddo), Mrs. Brinkley holding two frisky Toggenburgs, and the Reverend Dr. Charles Draper (the Brinkley Institute's resident preacher, who "doesn't believe in scientific evolution"), a rambling text invited the gentle reader to "meet the most unusual scientist-fundamentalist in the whole world, Dr. John R. Brinkley of Milford, Kansas, who saves souls with the word of God and repairs human bodies with glands from lively goats." Readers learned that goat glands were used because bull glands were found to be "too strenuous" and ape glands were "too short-lived and prone to disease." Toggenburg goats were described as the ideal battery charger because they were "practically diseaseless and their glands strongly resembled those of *Homo sapiens,*" a lesson Doctor had learned from his days at Swift and Company.

More notable Americans contacted Brinkley. He performed a goat gland operation on Senator Wesley Staley of Colorado, who described Doctor and his wife as "two of the finest people and the greatest benefactors to mankind on earth." Doctor traveled to China to perform his medical miracles. Although the trip was not an outstanding financial success, the *China Press* hailed the goateed physician as "the Burbank of Humanity." Doctor acquired an honorary degree from the Royal University of Pavia, Italy, founded in 1321, and was licensed by the Medical Board of London. He was invited to California by Harry Chandler, owner of the *Los Angeles Times.* The *Times* heralded Brinkley's arrival with the headlines NEW LIFE IN GLANDS—DR. BRINKLEY'S PATIENTS HERE SHOW IMPROVEMENT—MANY VICTIMS OF "INCURABLE" DISEASES ARE CURED—TWELVE HUNDRED OPERATIONS ARE ALL SUCCESSFUL. With a special California medical license, obtained through the good offices of Mr. Chandler, Doctor performed $40,000 worth of operations, perking up the managing editor of the paper, a U.S. circuit court judge, and a lucky individual who was much improved after the operation, "the swelling of the body having disappeared, and the drooling being much less."

Doctor was impressed with Chandler's new radio station, KHJ, one of the first in the Los Angeles area. Upon his return to Milford, Doctor decided to build a radio station of his own for the entertainment of his patients and was granted a broadcasting license on September 20, 1923, by Secretary of Commerce Herbert Hoover. A few months later, Brinkley began to preach his goat gland gospel electromagnetically over the first radio station in Kansas, his own KFKB ("Kansas First, Kansas Best" or "Kansas Folks Know Best"), nicknamed the Sunshine Station in the Heart of the Nation.

Methodist Episcopal church services, Masonic lectures, light music from the Ninth Cavalry-U.S. Army Orchestra, French lessons from Kansas State College's College of the Air—these and other uplifting and inspiring performances went forth from the broadcasting towers of KFKB, at 1050 kilocycles on the radio dial. Doctor himself gave medical lectures over the station three times a day, telling of his success in the field of goat gland research. He urged those "disgusted with being below par" to listen to his broadcasts, and he became a warm and well-trusted radio personality as he described the symptoms of nephritis, arteriosclerosis, and paralysis agitans. Doctor spoke conversationally with a well-oiled country accent, blending flat midwestern intonation and a Smoky Mountain drawl. Building on the faith and sympathy of his largely rural audience, the radio physician combined earthy country language with just enough Latin medical terminology to impress and confuse most anyone. According to one listener, "His voice would just wound you." The *New York Times* described him as having a "soothsayer's mysterious voice" and listeners from all over the Midwest agreed with the fan who said, "There's something about Dr. Brinkley that gets close to your heart."

Doctor had an impact on other parts of his listeners' anatomy as well, as patients flocked to Milford to undergo the goat gland experience. Brinkley charged $750 for the operation, a princely sum for the times, but as Doctor put it, "If you have a beer pocketbook, do you expect champagne to be served?" Payment was on "a strictly cash basis and no terms," for, under Doctor's care, patients were not required to subsidize "what some 'deadbeat' secured and did not pay for."

Soon men and women began to "cross all oceans" to reach the "little village of Milford in quest of the Fountain of Youth." Milford became "a veritable mecca for thousands of men and women broken in body and spirit," and the Kaaba of this mecca was the Brinkley Hospital. Doctor increased his staff, hiring specialists such as Walter A. Marshall, "who studies your 'innards' under a microscope and knows lots of your secrets," according to Brinkley literature. Brinkley constructed a "Brinkley Block" in downtown Milford, put in a sewage system and sidewalks, paved the highways, installed electricity, a bandstand, and park benches, and built a $100,000 brick sanitarium, as well as apartment houses and bungalows, for his patients and employees. Doctor could well afford those services to the community. "If I had accommodations for 1,000 patients, I could be performing that many goat gland transplantings a month," Doctor boasted to a reporter from the *Kansas City Star*. As it was, the rejuvenator's annual income ran well into six figures.

The communications infrastructure of Milford strained under the deluge of response to KFKB. More than three thousand letters a day came into the small town, and Brinkley built a new post office to handle the load. Doctor hired a stenographic staff to help respond to the overwhelming number of requests, and then he devised a scheme for answering the mail in a more efficient manner by using the radio. Doctor called the new program *The Medical Question Box*. During the broadcasts, he read letters from his listeners and prescribed medicine for their ailments, medicine that they could get from one of the more than 1500 pharmacists who belonged to the Brinkley Pharmaceutical Association. After giving news of his current patients over the air ("O.O. Robb has been sitting up all day. Alfred Nash sends greetings home"), Doctor started to dig into the question business: "Sunflower State, from Dresden, Kansas. Probably he has gallstones. No, I don't mean that. I mean kidney stones. My advice to you is to put him on prescription numbers eighty and fifty for men, also sixty-four. I think that he will be a whole lot better. Also drink a lot of water." To another supplicant, Doctor responded, "For three months take Doctor Brinkley's treatment for childless homes. Of course, doctors say it is vulgar for me to tell you about this, but we are taking a chance and we don't think it is obscene down here. . . . If this lady will take numbers fifty and sixty-one and that good old standby of mine, number sixty-seven, for about three months, and see if there isn't a great big change taking place." To a person with exactly the opposite problem, Doctor responded, "I suggest that you have your husband sterilized and then you will be safe from having more children, providing you don't get out in anybody else's cow pasture and get in with some other bull." Doctor charged $2 per inquiry to handle stenographic costs and received $1 for every bottle of medicine that was sold, resulting in a tidy income in addition to the charges for surgery.

As the dizzy decade slipped away and America's good times turned to soup lines, Dr. Brinkley was lord of Milford. An honorary admiral in the Kansas Navy and sponsor of the winning Little League team the Brinkley Goats, Brinkley looked with pride on KFKB, which in 1929 won a gold cup as the most popular radio station in America, according to a survey conducted by the Chicago-based *Radio Times*. Doctor seemed invincible, but his position was soon to be assailed by the U.S. medical and broadcasting establishments, "jealous oligarchs" in his view.

Dr. Morris Fishbein, representing the American Medical Association, spearheaded a drive to revoke Brinkley's medical license. Doctor was affronted by the very thought and told his listeners to be wary of anyone connected with "Fishy" Fishbein and the "Amateur Meatcutters Association." When KFKB won the privilege to boost its power to 5000 watts, a privilege that was denied a radio station owned by the powerful newspaper the *Kansas City Star,* the paper began running an exposé of Doctor's activities. Soon the U.S. government joined the fray. The Federal Radio Commission threatened to revoke KFKB's license unless Brinkley could show that the station was operating in "the public interest, convenience and necessity." Brinkley counterattacked, filing suits against the AMA, Morris Fishbein, the head of the Kansas State Board of Medical Examiners, and the *Kansas City Star.* When the *Kansas City Journal Post* published a similar exposé, Doctor displayed his sense of humor by sending the reporter a live goat, free of charge.

At first it seemed as if officialdom had Doctor by the glands. Although Brinkley's attorneys filed 211 affidavits of support, the FRC voted three to two to revoke Doctor's license to operate KFKB. The commission charged that Doctor was engaged in point-to-point communication for commercial purposes, which was prohibited by international treaty, that he broadcast obscene and indecent material, and that *The Medical Question Box* was contrary to the public interest. The courts later upheld the revocation in a landmark decision, which drew a distinction between censorship and review of past broadcasts. "By their fruits, ye shall know them," quoted the judges in regard to Brinkley.

A few months later, the Kansas State Medical Board revoked Doctor's license to practice medicine, after hearing goat-gland patients confess strange postoperative urges "to chew sprouts." Although one board member who witnessed a Brinkley operation called it "as skillful and deft a demonstration of surgery as I have ever witnessed," the board as a whole voted against Doctor and was later upheld in its decision by the Kansas Supreme Court, which wrote, "The licensee has performed an organized charlatanism . . . quite beyond the invention of the humble mountebank."

Defeated in the courts, Doctor fought back with a brilliant strategic move that almost worked. He tossed his hat into the Kansas governor's race in 1930 as a write-in candidate on the Independent ticket using the slogan "Let's Pasture the Goats on the Statehouse Lawn." Launching a vigorous populist campaign that later served as a stylistic model for Louisiana's Huey Long and Jimmie Davis and for Texas' W. Lee "Pappy" O'Daniel, Brinkley visited every county in the state in his plane, *The Romancer*. As nurses from Milford distributed balloons and lollipops to the children in the crowd, Brinkley, sporting a huge sunflower in the lapel of his conservative business suit, imbued his rallies with a curiously entrancing aura of evangelism, complete with warm-ups for the audience by KFKB cowboy singer Roy Faulkner and a Brinkley-worshiping preacher. Often introduced as the "modern Moses", Brinkley addressed his crowds: "The men in power wanted to do away with Jesus before the common people woke up. Are you awake here?"

His voice filled the airwaves from KFKB, which was still operating under appeal of the FRC's ruling. "If I am a quack," he told his hushed listeners, "Dr. Luke was a quack too, for he did not belong to the American Medical Association." On another broadcast he made his martyrdom even more apparent. "I, too, have walked up the path Jesus walked to Calvary," he said. "I have spent much time in Palestine and Jerusalem. I stood in the Savior's tomb. I know just how Jesus feels." Brinkley promised to "turn Kansas into a modern Canaan" with free schoolbooks, free auto tags, and lower taxes. He pledged "to put a microphone in the governor's office and his bed chamber in the executive mansion so he could tell the people day and night the goings-on at the seat of government," according to the *New York Times*. His opponents, mild-mannered members of the American Legion, became concerned over the popularity of their flamboyant opponent and obtained a ruling from the Kansas attorney general that invalidated any write-in ballots that did not have the specific name "J.R. Brinkley" written on them. While Dr. Brinkley received the largest number of intended votes for governor of Kansas and even carried several counties in Oklahoma, more than 50,000 Brinkley ballots were voided by election officials, and rumor had it that thousands more floated away down the Kansas River. Doctor's luck in the Sunflower State had run out.

Defeated in politics as well as the halls of justice, Brinkley knew deep in his heart that there had to be another way for him to continue his important healing work. Stroking his goatee and gazing out the window of his airplane, his yacht, or one of his numerous Cadillacs, Doctor pondered the problem. Soon a masterful plan took shape. Why not build a new station in a foreign country—like, say, Mexico—beyond the long arm of the FRC and that demon's den of organized doctordom, the AMA? After all, as Doctor observed, "Radio waves pay no attention to lines on a map."

Brinkley sold KFKB for $90,000. Biographer Clement Wood wrote that his patron's last broadcast from Kansas was fraught with emotion: "Tears were running down the cheeks of most of his hearers, as the courageous little fighting doctor told them . . . that he would come back, greater than ever." Brinkley headed south, but not to disappear like so many renegade Kansas rustlers. Doctor wanted to let his accusers know exactly where he was. Early in 1931 Brinkley paid a visit to Mexican government officials and inquired about the possibility of constructing a broadcasting facility somewhere along the Rio Grande. Mexican authorities were very cooperative, as Brinkley's proposition could help them develop a new industry and get even with the United States and Canada for dividing up the North American long-range radio wavelengths between themselves and allowing none for their southern neighbors. Mexican papers explained, "No arrangement has been made between Canada, Mexico and Cuba in regard to the limitation of wavelengths to be used in each country. There is an arrangement of this nature between Canada and the U.S." Doctor returned to Kansas with a "blanket concession, covering everything," as reported in the press, allowing him to build a 50,000-watt station anywhere along the border. The press began to speculate where the station might be—Matamoros, Reynosa, Juárez.

Young, ambitious A .C. Easterling, newly inducted secretary-manager of the Del Rio Chamber of Commerce, was one of those who read about Dr. Brinkley's predicament. The local area known as the Wool and Mohair Capital of the World had recently witnessed the failure of the Del Rio Bank. Easterling was eager to rejuvenate the borderland economy, and Brinkley's station meant business. The secretary-manager immediately dispatched a letter to the famous physician, inviting him to visit and inspect the Queen City of the Rio Grande. Though he probably didn't realize it at the time, Easterling's invitation would bring publicity to Del Rio beyond the wildest dreams of any border booster and open the door to one of the strangest chapters in the history of mass communications.

Doctor remembered having heard the glorious words "Del Rio" while sipping a cold beer on a train bound for El Paso, where he had served briefly as an Army physician. He responded quickly to Easterling's kind invitation, asking if Del Rio had a place to land his private plane. Easterling replied that Del Rio had a "splendid flying field" and that an arrow on the roof of the Roswell Hotel pointed to it. He assured the famous gland man that the town was 100 percent behind him, that the chamber of commerce would see to it that all red tape was dispensed with and all concessions granted. Easterling was also able to report that the *presidente* of Villa Acuña had been so gracious as to grant ten acres of land for construction of the radio station.

Sometime in the spring or summer of 1931, ground was broken just outside of Acuña for Dr. Brinkley's border blaster. Doctor contracted a firm from Salina, Kansas, to erect a $30,000 broadcasting building, and he hired Will Branch, an engineer who had built the first transmitter for Fort Worth's WBAP, to draw up plans for a powerful $175,000 transmitter. When Brinkley's engineers told him that special tubes for the transmitters would have to be built at a cost of $36,000, Doctor reached into his pocket, pulled out a wad of greenbacks, and peeled off 36 $1000 bills. News of the famous surgeon's radio move to the border spread like a range fire. The Texas State Medical Association made a halfhearted attempt to revoke Doctor's Texas medical license. Doctor remarked nonchalantly to the Del Rio Chamber of Commerce that he had lost so many licenses that losing his Texas medical license wouldn't make much difference.

As the three-hundred-foot towers of XER rose on the Mexican desert, the United States government kept a wary eye on Doctor's international activities. Official memos and State Department dispatches flew back and forth between Mexico and Washington, D.C. Materials for the monster transmitter had barely been picked up at the Del Rio train station across from the mohair warehouse when an official at the American embassy in Mexico City notified the State Department in Washington that "what is said will be the world's largest radio broadcasting station is being erected at Villa Acuña, Coahuila, Mexico, on the Rio Grande, opposite Del Rio, Texas." The report said that the Villa Acuña Broadcasting Company would operate station XER at 75,000 watts, 25,000 watts higher than the maximum power allowed in the U.S. at that time. The station's license was said to give the company "absolute freedom in the control of the station." The Villa Acuña Broadcasting Company could even use its airwaves to instigate a revolution if it so desired.

While the United States government kept up a stakeout on Doctor's south-of-the-border maneuvers, the radio surgeon began to experience the pitfalls that were to plague border blasters for the next fifty years. It seemed that some Mexican officials supported the activities of the renegade radiomen, while others worked to end them. Officials in Villa Acuña, only too happy to see their tiny isolated village turned into a media haven, were firmly behind Doctor's efforts, but some federal authorities in Mexico City were not so supportive. The Department of Health told the Mexican public about the background of the rich gringo perched on its northern border. At the department's urging, the Ministerio de Gobernación suddenly issued an order to prohibit the radio star's crossing the international bridge to visit XER.

Brinkley had used his first station, KFKB, to keep his political contacts well greased, allowing politicians of any party to trumpet their views over his airwaves. The surgeon never missed a chance to collect on that multilateral investment. When he was denied a visa to enter Mexico, he promptly went straight to the Executive Branch, wiring an urgent plea for assistance to fellow Kansan and vice president of the United States Charles Curtis. In the lengthy telegram Doctor asserted that the U.S. ambassador to Mexico had asked the Mexican government to pull the plug on the long-winded people's friend. "I am trying to find out why I am being hounded in a foreign country," the telegram read. "All I have asked was to be left alone. . . . I feel someone in the administration is responsible and I feel that our president's good name and office is being used to pull somebody's chestnuts out of the fire." Doctor went on to say that he was having an investigation made in the Mexican capital to "uncover the prime movers in this plot coming from Washington and expose the whole sordid mess."

Vice President Curtis, mindful of Brinkley's influence over many Kansas voters, delivered a request to the Secretary of State that the department not place any additional obstructions in Doctor's path. Curtis knew that Brinkley's resourcefulness should not be underestimated, as it had been by many Mexican bureaucrats who thought they could keep him off the airwaves merely by keeping him out of the country. A remote studio was set up in the Roswell Hotel in downtown Del Rio, and a special telephone hookup to XER allowed Dr. Brinkley to deliver his message to humanity over his new superpowered radio station.

As Longhorns, Horned Toads, and Del Rio Rams squared off on gridirons across the state for the 1931 football season, Del Rioans celebrated their border town's rising star. When test broadcasts began in early October, the mysterious electric creature on the Rio Grande lit up the desert sky with luminous green emanations—called coronas—from the antennas, and music mingled with the screeches of nighthawks in the chilly desert night. "It was like the angels," remembered one Acuña resident. "It was very beautiful."

Beginning October 21, XER blasted into regular operation as Del Rio fandangoed through a cavalcade of merriment during XER Gala Week. A special Radio Edition of the *Del Rio Evening News* recounted the Cinderella story that had brought the famous Kansan and his pioneering communications empire to the banks of the Rio Grande. MEXICO PRAISED FOR AIDING XER PLANS, announced the banner headline. XER DEDICATION WILL ATTRACT THRONG. The chamber of commerce welcomed the Sunshine Station Between the Nations with a large splashy advertisement, as did most every business concern in the area, including Marathon Oil, Piggly Wiggly, De Los Santos Music Store, Electric Bakery, the Border Grocery, and the Roswell Hotel and Cafe. Boosters in Villa Acuña got into the act too. One full-page ad extending "Greetings and best wishes to the staff members of the Acuña Broadcasting Company" was sponsored by a group of Coahuila concerns, including Crosby's Cafe, customs broker Raymundo Riviera, and Lou Mohr Novelty Entertainment. Like the department stores, jewelers, auto dealers, insurance firms, and lumber companies across the river in Del Rio, the leaders of commerce in Acuña recognized the opportunity in the airwaves and jumped on the radio bandwagon. As a border booster told the *Saturday Evening Post* after the gland boom went bust, "He was going to set up shop somewhere, and we could use the money he'd bring."

The streets of Del Rio were festooned like the Fourth of July to kick off the border blaster jubilee. A banquet was held by the chamber of commerce in honor of Dr. and Mrs. Brinkley. Doctor himself was traveling through the near heavens in his private plane, on his way to the dinner on the Rio Grande. Not long after crossing the Red River, the plane experienced problems, and the physician was forced to land and spend the night at the oil boomtown of Ranger, Texas. Down on the border the festivities went on without the main attraction. Mrs. Brinkley, who once announced she might run for governor of Kansas just as Ma Ferguson had done in Texas, gave a brief speech praising the hospitality found in Del Rio, and her sister, Lillian Munal, treated the South Texans to a sampling of classical ballet. A telegram was read from Dr. Brinkley to the 150 people in attendance. Miss Rosa Dominguez, appearing on behalf of the Eagle Pass Junior Chamber of Commerce, premiered the beautiful soprano voice that earned her a job as Mexico's Nightingale on XER. A tenor performance and dancing for all completed the entertainment at the San Felipe Country Club.

Many of Doctor's entertainers and radio personalities from his defunct Kansas station made the trip to the border to perform on XER. Singing Cowboy Roy Faulkner was on hand to favor listeners with traditional western tunes and yodeling. Uncle Bob, champion fiddler of Arkansas, smoked his bow in the new border blaster studios. H.L. Munal, Brinkley's brother-in-law, known to radio land as Bert the Sunshine Man, became managing director of XER. The Bluebird Trio, a female singing group, arrived in Del Rio on the Sunset Limited passenger train, followed by operatic vocalist Mrs. Osborn. Psychologist-astrologer Mel Roy was in town with his police dog, preparing for a "strenuous routine" of XER appearances. Accordionist Fenoglio was also on hand to delight radio listeners. Other performers on the brand-new border blaster included the Old-timer, the Baxter Melody Method Entertainers, and the Red Peppers. Mexican music was provided by the Studio Mexican Orchestra and the Sabinas Orchestra. Doctor employed Isaias Gallo, former inspector of radio and telegraph for the Republic of Mexico, as the official engineer of XER. Gallo relied heavily on the brilliant young engineer from KFKB, James Weldon, who came down to the border to keep the pioneering electromagnetic hardware functioning as smoothly as possible.

After the festivities of XER Gala Week, the station settled into its unusual pattern of business-as-usual—an intricate kind of political chess that Doctor and his associates played with the Mexican and U.S. governments. The *Del Rio Evening News* reported, "Dr. Brinkley may aptly be styled the mystery man of the Rio Grande. People along the border do not understand him. Here is a man of strange ideas and methods. To some, he is a rich doctor but a novice in business." Engineer James Weldon described Doctor as having an "inferiority complex; he did not enjoy meeting people for the first time." Weldon added that Brinkley "was an easy mark for the sales pitches of others." Some local wiseacres felt that the whole enterprise was foolhardy, since some pocket-padding Mexican official would sooner or later confiscate the property.

Most of the citizens of Val Verde County had complete faith in Doctor's enterprise. "He is the smartest businessman we ever have seen," said one admirer. "He is too big for them. His station is too valuable a concession for Mexico to refuse to cooperate with him," said another booster, fully aware of the international situation allowing the Queen of the Air, as Doctor called his giant transmitter, to blanket the land with "scientific information." Dr. Brinkley maintained that Mexican officials had been straight shooters with him, that he had not paid "one cent of graft." Furthermore, he stated expansively, one of XER's primary missions would be the improvement and strengthening of relations between the two nations and assistance in development of Mexican industry and tourism.

Back in the Sunflower State, Doc's associate physicians kept administering the goat gland whammy at the Brinkley Hospital, while its namesake remained on the border, cooing into the radio ears of sufferers nationwide. "Life offers few sights more tragic than that of a splendid, successful man, keen of mind, robust of body, transformed into an old weakling, tottering on the brink of senility, his mental powers wanting, his body constantly fatigued." Doctor used graphic comparisons to emphasize the necessity of his glandular operations. "Contrast the castrated animal, of any species, with the natural male or female. Note the difference, for instance, between the stallion and the gelding. The former stands erect, neck arched, mane flowing, chomping the bit, stamping the ground, seeking the female, while the gelding stands around half-asleep, cowardly, and listless . . . with no interest in anything."

Doctor challenged his listeners: "You people who are all the time grunting and groaning, never fit for anything, you are entirely to blame for your condition . . . you have probably used poor judgment." He prayed that his audience not be "deranged by the psycho-bunko" of the medical establishment and lamented the state of the universe. "The great trouble with the world today is a shortage of thinkers—men who can stand on their own feet. . . . If you are a red-blooded 'he-man' with a real backbone, we will hear from you." He continued, questioning the integrity of his audience: "When asked, 'What class of people get the least value from your operation?' I reply, 'Idiots and fools!' This is literally true. . . . Delay is, oh, so dangerous." Doctor urged his listeners to come to his clinic "before the last ride. The cold undertaker's slab may be your portion prematurely. . . . Many untimely graves have been filled with people who put off until tomorrow what they should have done today. . . . It is, you know, your health or your funeral." In closing, Doctor left the choice to his listeners: "Dr. Brinkley is anxious to help you if you are man enough to help yourself. You only can make the answer. What is it, please?" Even the healthiest radio listener felt a bit queasy after listening to Doctor's scientific lecture, and many rushed straight to the depot to catch a train bound for the shrine of miracles.

Located at 735 kilocycles on the radio dial, XER muscled in between two popular American stations, WSB in Atlanta and WGN in Chicago. American broadcasters complained of the border blaster interference, and Congress moved to pass legislation to stop U.S. broadcasters from creating their "wall of noise." If Brinkley heard the congressional saber rattling, he brushed it off as another minor nuisance, and his messages to humanity continued to be phoned across the river from his Del Rio studio and beamed back northward by the station's mighty towers.

Shortly after New Year's Day in 1932, a report tabulating the power of XER's personalities as "mail pullers" indicated that the radio solicitations resulted in 27,717 pieces of mail in one week. According to the postmarks, XER was being enjoyed in every state of the United States and at least fifteen other countries. Even with that powerful reach, Doctor felt the need to turn up the juice and announced that he hoped to increase the power of the station to 150,000 watts. The Mexican press, incorrectly citing Brinkley's specialty as monkey gland surgery, noted that such an increase would make XER only 8000 watts less powerful than the world's strongest station in Warsaw, Poland.

Political circles in Kansas were taking the Brinkley presence seriously in the spring of 1932. Months before Doctor returned from Del Rio to campaign once again, a *Wichita Beacon* poll showed him to be a four-to-one favorite for governor. The anticipated hat toss came in May. Doc Brinkley would be an independent candidate for governor of Kansas in 1932. Brinkley Clubs throughout the state rallied round their persecuted leader returned from the Southwest frontier. And once again the medical maverick took his cause to the voters of Kansas. Enormous crowds greeted the radioman as he campaigned in all 105 Kansas counties, sometimes arriving in his plane and other times pulling up in a sixteen-cylinder Cadillac to meet the assembled throngs of faithful believers. Often he traveled in a motorcade, the lead vehicle being an attention-getting sound truck dubbed Ammunition Train #1. Though it did not inspire an Ammunition Train #2, the sound truck delivered healthy doses of cowboy singing and Methodist preaching, warming up the crowd for the appearance of the master.

Before the election, Brinkley anted up for a special $10,000-a-month phone line from Milford to XER. This staggering expenditure enabled him to remain in Kansas and keep a watchful eye on his hospital employees while piping reports of surgical breakthroughs a thousand miles to the border. His rhetoric blasted back across the continent, easily blanketing Kansas, where voters heard a candidate for the highest office in the state campaign from a radio station in a foreign country. Using the slogan "Clean Out Kansas, Clean Up Kansas, and Keep Kansas Clean," Brinkley led his supporters in singing his own campaign song, "He's the Man," which ended with the chorus, "He's the man we want to guide us, Dr. Brinkley!" The tune failed to catapult the gland man into the Topeka governor's mansion, however. Doctor ran a close third, receiving about 250,000 votes.

During the campaign, Doctor instructed his representatives to seek a huge increase in power from the Mexican authorities, and once again the Brinkley lobby proved successful in the land of the Aztecs. On August 18, 1932, the Mexican government authorized XER to increase its power to a whopping 500,000 watts, making it the most powerful radio station in the world. *Radio Stars* magazine, in a report heavily biased in favor of the beleaguered broadcaster, alleged that Mexico's chief executives asked Dr. Brinkley to soup up his transmitter to match the power planned for station WLW in Cincinnati.

News reports of XER's impending boom in power circulated around the U.S., noting that the increase would pose a greater interference threat to a dozen or more big-city American stations and make it difficult to receive favorite programs like *Amos and Andy* or *Charlie McCarthy*. While State Department memos flew from the American consulate at Piedras Negras to Washington, the U.S. government tried to come to some kind of a regulatory agreement with Mexico, but to no avail. Mexican negotiators decided to keep Brinkley in their front pocket, as a 500,000-watt bargaining chip in future negotiations. When asked by reporters what he thought of the conference, Doctor issued a threat that he was to make several times throughout his career. The surgeon announced that if he were denied his broadcast facilities, he would equip his yacht with a monster transmitter and broadcast from the high seas beyond the twelve-mile range of American control. And then, he warned, what he would have to say about his persecutors "would be a-plenty."

Doctor must have daydreamed of such an arrangement during the summer of 1933. He cruised on the yacht the entire season, recharging his personal batteries and musing upon the great mystery of his medical discovery. Upon his return to Kansas in early September, Doctor announced a brand-new improved scientific breakthrough. "It isn't necessary to transplant glands anymore," the surgeon declared, "because we have commercial glandular preparations that we can buy on the market and inject to take the place of the glandular transplantation." Brinkley was bold in his support of the new technique: "What is the use of pussyfooting on the subject? Why not drag it out in the open?" The new surgical method depended upon a "change of relationship between the epididymus and the gland itself," with "the replacement of decreased sex hormones." Not only would the new techniques restore a weakened male patient, but it would also satisfy the loving wife who "panteth for the running brook." Dr. Brinkley realized that his new treatment would not receive universal acceptance. "We have always had our doubters," he said. "Do you remember poor old Thomas who did not believe until he had seen and placed his hands in the wounds of our dear Savior?" To those who asked how long they could live after the Brinkley treatment or other "foolish questions of similar nature," Mrs. Brinkley answered, "Until Gabriel blows his trumpet on Judgment Day, and then they'll have to knock you on the head with a mallet."

While Doctor was pioneering surgical science, his once-loyal employees were performing surgery on the Brinkley clinic in Milford. Several former colleagues opened a clinic of their own in the small Kansas town, offering what they said was the Brinkley treatment at a substantially reduced rate. Shortly after discovering this dramatic breach of loyalty, Doctor announced that the Brinkley Hospital would soon leave Milford for Del Rio. As his reasons for moving, Doctor cited the prohibitive costs of broadcasting from the Sunflower State and said he had "nothing but the kindliest feelings toward the people of Kansas." Despite his kindly feelings, Doctor found it necessary to raze his hospital, his home, and several other of the buildings he had added to the Milford skyline, in much the same way that Caesar ordered that salt be plowed into the fields of Carthage. Citizens of Milford responded by chiseling the name "Brinkley" from the lintel of the drugstore built by their former benefactor.

A caravan rolled toward the border, trucks filled with hospital and office equipment and an auto convoy of thirty families of Brinkley employees. Doctor leased several floors of the Roswell Hotel in downtown Del Rio to house the new medical facility and leased the entire basement for x-ray equipment. As the ever watchful American consul at Piedras Negras reported, "The most prominent judge of Del Rio gave a very big reception and tea honoring Doctor and Mrs. Brinkley at his home on Saturday, Nov. 4. It was attended by a great majority of the people of Del Rio. There is great enthusiasm in the town for him and apparently everyone is happy except the doctors. The report concluded by observing that Doctor was reciprocating for his royal welcome by taking care to broadcast the charms of Del Rio and of the general locality over the world."

Villa Acuña welcomed the Brinkley presence in royal border style as well. Even before the hospital went south, Bert the Sunshine Man, XER's managing director, wrote to Doctor that the Acuña Chamber of Commerce had "passed a resolution to show you a big time when you come down here again." The director continued, "They want to meet you and your family at the end of the Mexican bridge with a brass band and escort you to the Mayor's office. This is in appreciation of what you have done for Villa Acuña."

Not all Mexicans were so enchanted with the wealthy American radio physician. The Mexican Health Department slapped Brinkley with a series of fines for broadcasting by remote facility in English and for breaching health department regulations in the content of *las transmisiones*.

Brinkley ignored the minor irritation and kept pouring on the juice. The Mexican officials, however, meant business this time. On February 24, representatives of the Department of Communications, accompanied by federal troops, seized the Sunshine Station Between the Nations and stopped its transmission. Some reports maintained that a violent confrontation was narrowly avoided between the federal troops and local citizenry loyal to Doctor. The Villa Acuña police, wearing new uniforms purchased for them by the magnanimous surgeon, were understandably reluctant to join the revolt against their gringo benefactor. Dr. Brinkley once again performed the role of persecuted martyr, asserting that he closed the station voluntarily to avoid potential bloodshed. In a statement to the *Del Rio Evening News,* he attributed the shutdown to interference in Mexico by the chairman of the Federal Radio Commission, Judge E.O. Sykes, and by troublemakers from the *Chicago Tribune* and WGN, a Chicago radio station that felt the interfering sting of XER's marauding wave.

"Conditions became so acute Friday night," Doctor reported, "that I ordered the station closed until legal procedures could iron out the conditions. We don't anticipate being off the air long; business will be carried out in the usual manner. Patients will be received at the Roswell Hotel: all advertisers of XER will remain in Del Rio and their mail will be received and taken care of as usual." He said he regretted shutting down his station, because XER helped support 3000 Acuña residents and 83 employees living in Del Rio. Gesturing expansively toward the foreign capital to the south and bristling at the challenge of a good ol' international scrap, Doctor said, "I desire an amicable settlement with the Mexican government. In closing the largest and most powerful broadcasting station in the world, the Mexican people will suffer."

Less than a week later the Villa Acuña Broadcasting Company was dissolved. In its place was formed Cia. Mexicana Radiofusora Fronteriza. Mrs. Esther O. de Crosby, owner of the most popular dining spot in Villa Acuña, was the titular head of the new corporation, but it was still Doctor who controlled the border blaster, now brooding silently in the stillness of the Mexican desert.

Brinkley was not to be undone by the bandit raid on his airwaves. During the time that XER was closed, he bought time on radio stations KVOD in Denver, KVOR in Colorado Springs, KFEQ in St. Joseph, Missouri, and, oddly enough, on KFBI in Milford, Kansas, formerly Doctor's own KFKB. Brinkley managed to maintain his presence on the border as well, offering his messages of medical salvation over XEPN, another border blaster located conveniently near the American consul in Piedras Negras.

Doctor's attorneys and agents appealed the government's actions in the courts, and a lengthy investigation followed. After twenty months the federal district judge at Piedras Negras ruled in favor of the wealthy American, stating that the fines had been assessed on the old company that owned XER and the new owners of the station were not liable for them. The Mexican supreme court eventually upheld the decision, and Doctor was free to go on the air once again. Made cautious perhaps by the recent government actions, Brinkley decided to acquire a backup border blaster, and one week after his victory at Piedras Negras, he purchased station XEAW, down the Rio Grande from Del Rio in Reynosa, Tamaulipas.

On the American side of the river, in McAllen, Texas, business leaders were breathless over the news. The *McAllen Daily Press* reported that Brinkley planned to boost the power of the relatively small station to 500,000 watts and to invest $100,000 in a new branch of the Brinkley Hospital, a move that business leaders felt would be "a rapid stride forward for the city from a health standpoint." Doctor opened the rejuvenated border blaster in September 1935, with a special 72-hour prize giveaway. Eight months later he opened a new hospital in nearby San Juan, Texas, which specialized in the "surgical and nonsurgical treatment of piles, fistulas, fissures, colitis, and diseases of the female and male rectum." In a letter of announcement, he urged the nearly 20,000 people on his mailing list to "please get this thought into your mind— that we are offering guaranteed treatment for your two sewers . . . your water works and your garbage." To avoid confusion among his radio listeners, Doctor often repeated the simple phrase, "Remember, Del Rio for the prostate and San Juan for the colon."

As Christmas season of 1935 drew near, Dr. Brinkley instructed his staff to prepare holiday baskets for the less fortunate of Val Verde County and northern Coahuila, and he began broadcasting once again from XER, now reborn as XERA. Brinkley's brilliant engineer James Weldon had repaired the sleeping behemoth and added a new directional antenna that kicked the unique signal northward with an effective transmitting power of 1,000,000 watts—"the world's most powerful broadcasting station," according to Doctor's literature, booming "way above the timid voices of ordinary radio stations." Promotional pamphlets explained that "it takes a station like XERA, with its million watts of power, to do justice to Doctor Brinkley's messages of Health and Happiness and to carry them to the millions of men and women who listen daily to this great healer and disciple of health." People living near the station did not even need a radio to enjoy the great healer's messages. Del Rio residents talking on the phone heard Doctor's mellifluous voice asking such questions as "How many of you suffer from gas, indigestion, bloat, and belching . . . and chronic appendicitis?" Ranchers were startled to find their fences electrified by the high-powered broadcasts of hillbilly performers. Some residents even said they picked up the station with the fillings in their teeth. At 840 kilocycles, powerful XERA brushed aside the signals of WWL in New Orleans and KOA in Denver as if they were 98-watt weaklings. A *Variety* reporter in New York said that he could hear XERA regularly, and a Philadelphia resident said he had trouble getting anything but Dr. Brinkley's station on his family's radio set.

As the state of Texas entered its centennial year, 1936, Dr. Brinkley was rolling nothing but sevens. He must have felt a great sense of satisfaction as he snuggled up before the microphone twice every evening, gazed out at a palm tree or two silhouetted in the borderland moonlight, stroked his goatee, and began his broadcasts. "My dear, dear friends— my patients—my supplicants," he said. "Your many, many letters— many hundreds of them since yesterday—lie here before me, touching testimonials of your pain, your grief, the wretchedness that is visited upon the innocent." Oftentimes Doctor recorded his messages on sixteen-inch records called electrical transcriptions, which he made either in his home or in a studio near his rectal clinic in San Juan. Brinkley was one of the pioneers in the use of these transcriptions, which were played from the inside groove out at 33⅓ rpm. Relatively cheap and easy to make, electrical transcriptions became a radio industry standard in the thirties. Attentive listeners could hear a click during Doctor's transcribed lectures, marking the point at which the attending engineer had to clean the purple "goon fuzz" from under the recording needle. Villa Acuña residents found that the aluminum-based disks discarded from the station made excellent shingles, and soon the roofs of homes near the station glinted with Doctor's messages of mercy.

Del Rio basked in the sweet radio waves of the Sunshine Station Between the Nations. The town grew steadily in population as Doc filled the land with a siren song about the seductive charms of the enchantress known as the Queen City of the Rio Grande. "We are apt to think of Del Rio as a backward little border town," stated Dr. Brinkley, in *The Doctor Book*, available for only a quarter. "Not so." Besides Del Rio's offering golfers "one of the sportiest, most picturesquely beautiful courses in America," Doctor pointed out, "rich, natural gas deposits are being developed near Del Rio that may interest you." Doctor billed the seat of Val Verde County as "America's last big game frontier," offering "deer, bear, mountain lion, coyote, fox, 'coon, possum and javalin ('wild hogs')." Anglers could hook into "robalo ('ever hear of that one?'), sardine, catfish, trout, eel, seabream, needlefish, goldfish," and other forms of exotic aquatic life. "Over there in the hills," Doctor mentioned for the benefit of the more adventuresome, "you'll find Indian villages where the redskins live entirely by hunting and fishing just as they did a thousand years ago."

The wonders of Del Rio did not distract Doctor from his lifesaving work, and he began to develop new theories of medicine that, according to this literature, "made his name stand out in bold relief among the great luminaries of this generation." Doctor had determined that the prostate gland was the "glandular brain" in the male body. Citing "the older editions of Gray's Anatomy, Von Bergman & Bull's Surgery, Sajous' Encyclopedia of Medicine," among others, Doctor maintained that "a man undergoes changes of life like a woman, with the enlargement of the prostate." Noting that "65% of men past the age of 40 have some disease or dysfunction of the prostate," Doctor urged those suffering to "remove the short from your batteries and note the change." During the winter months, he spoke over XERA to his long-suffering listeners: "Now that it is getting cold up there, ice and sleet, this is the time of year that that old prostate will give you a lot of trouble. Yes, I know it is hurting a lot. You are sitting down there squirming, squirming, and squirming around on that old cocklebur and yet you won't come and have that old prostate treated." He told his listeners to "stop letting your doctor two-dollar you to death" and warned a patient in a personal letter, "If you go ahead to the doctors there and have your prostate gland removed you will be just the same as a castrated man or an old steer and good for nothing. . . . Wishing you a merry Christmas and a prosperous New Year."

The new prostate fixer was marketed by Doctor for any size pocket-book. The popular Average Man's Lifetime Guaranteed Treatment was "not an operation. It is medical and it is designed for . . . softening your prostate, reducing it in size, and making its removal unnecessary." The $750 price included round-trip train fare to Del Rio, as well as free "personal consultation with Dr. Brinkley by mail," a urine examination "every six months free," and "the privilege of returning at any time for further treatment if needed without one cent charge for it." The Business Man's Treatment included "the Compound Technique, the 'Rock of Gibraltar' of Dr. Brinkley's work," performed with the personal services of the master surgeon himself. Priced at $1000, it was designed for men who owned "the finest automobiles, the finest homes, the best horses, best diamonds, best works of art." To provide healthful salvation for those less fortunate, the menu included the Poor Folks' Treatment. For as little as $125, patients could receive "a complete examination and one complete prostate treatment." No round-trip train fare or payment for living expenses was included in the Poor Folks' treatment, but as Doctor

Brinkley warned, "Cheap treatments are very expensive at any price."
And for the truly destitute sufferers, Doctor offered to diagnose symptoms by mail for just $2, "which barely covers the cost of postage, steno-
graphic hire, office rent, and so forth."

The years in Del Rio marked the acme of Doctor's career. He was
bringing in "eleven hundred thousand dollars" a year, as he so humbly
put it, at a time when most doctors were earning $3000 to $3500 a year.
While Brinkley's income was tremendous, his expenses were lavish as
well. The operating costs of his radio stations, his hospitals, and his advertising and promotions staff, as well as his legal and advisory fees, ran
into the hundreds of thousands of dollars. Ever mindful of his prestige
and his image in the community, Doctor was an insatiable joiner, and at
one time or another was a member of the Masons, the Odd Fellows, the
Shriners, the Modern Woodmen of America, the Methodist Episcopal
Church, the National Institute of Social Sciences, and the National Geographic Society, a distinction he earned by subscribing to the publication. Doctor was also a fervent Rotarian. He described the organization
as "shot to the core with the sunshine of love" and donated time on
XERA and XEAW for the promotion of the Rotary Club. The thankful
Rotarians elected Doctor president of the Del Rio chapter. Despite his
work for the organization, Doctor received a far-from-enthusiastic greeting when he attended an international Rotarian convention in Europe.

His civic involvement was matched by the flamboyance of his personal
lifestyle. Whenever he entered his clinic at the Roswell Hotel, John R.
Brinkley, M.D., Ph.D., M.C., LL.D., D.P.H., Sc.D., sparkled as the
numerous glittering diamonds he routinely wore glinted in the Texas sun-
light. On his left hand was a thirteen-carat diamond ring; on his right,
another. He sported two diamond-studded fraternal emblems on his la-
pels, and his cuff links were also set with the valuable jewels. A huge
pear-shaped diamond adorned a tiepin, resting just above a tie clip set
with a dozen or more precious stones, while diamond-encrusted Rotary
and Mason emblems hung from a heavy watch chain. Doctor rolled
through the streets of Del Rio in his custom Cadillac, one of eight—or
was it nine? Doctor had a hard time keeping count, although he had his
name emblazoned on each vehicle in thirteen different places from hub-
cap to trunk.

Lord of his own eccentric empire, Brinkley purchased a mission-style
mansion a short distance from the Rio Grande and remodeled it to meet
his specifications. Large wrought iron gates bore the words "Dr. Brinkley" molded in the grillwork, announcing the owner of the fantastic palace. Biting geese and three huskies guarded the entrance to the paradise
built by goat glands and border radio, while peacocks strutted, Galápa-

gos tortoises munched celery tops, and penguins suffering sunstroke roamed the lavishly landscaped acreage. Sometimes maintaining the household menagerie proved vexing to the busy physician. "How he would fret," Minnie Brinkley remembered, "when he would drive in and have to wait while three-hundred-pound tortoises slowly crossed the driveway."

Doctor installed elegant water fountains in a blue-tiled lily pond on the spacious grounds and lit the liquid sculpture with multicolored floodlights. He built a parti-colored tile swimming pool described as having "the cubic content of a small volcanic crater" and put his name on it in three places. Neon lights spelled the name "Doctor Brinkley" between a bronze depiction of Romulus and Remus suckling at the teat of a wolf and a marble rendition of the Three Graces. Doctor's mansion featured a large mahogany ballroom from which the master spoke to his radio audience, furnished with a mammoth pipe organ that occupied an entire wall and bore the name of Dr. Brinkley in several places. Ultramodern in its thirties designer glamor, a sweeping staircase with wrought iron rails again preserved the mantra "Doctor Brinkley" and led to the second floor, with round-walled, bird's-eye maple bedrooms and bathrooms finished in bright red and deep purple tile. The massive living room fireplace was surrounded by framed photographs of Doctor on several of his worldwide jaunts. Items picked up during these travels filled the home—a Chinese tapestry, a perfume collection, and cut glass crystal bearing the words "Dr. Brinkley." The total environment changed color as workmen painted and repainted the mansion's exterior and the Brinkley auto fleet in a bright monochrome of pink, apple-green, or fire-engine-red, depending on Doctor's mood.

Texas Centennial Magazine described the Brinkley Mansion as the "showplace of the Southwest." Vacationers in the thirties filled their scrapbooks with snapshots of their families posed at the Grand Canyon, Judge Roy Bean's Jersey Lily, Old Faithful geyser, and the Brinkley Mansion in Del Rio, Texas.

In the spring of 1937 Doctor staged what the *Del Rio Press* called the Southwest's largest party. Billed as a "Bon Voyage Garden Reception, a farewell gesture" before the Brinkleys' vacation cruise to Europe, the affair was dedicated "to the Del Rioans who have shown friendliness to the Brinkley organization." Thirteen hundred guests were treated to a huge feast, served by twenty lucky Del Rio High students dressed up as geisha girls, wafting between colored lights and lanterns designed to fit the Japanese theme. Pupils from the Mary Rose Jones School of Dance presented terpsichorean treats throughout the evening, with dance master Jones performing a solo entitled "Grecian Illusion." The Gunter

Hotel Orchestra from San Antonio, complete with house blues singer, was hired to provide music for the fiesta. Two "wise seers" divined guests' fortunes by reading palms and cards, while a "specialist from Dallas" periodically dazzled partygoers with stunning pyrotechnic displays that one observer said rivaled "that of the Centennial display in Dallas last year."

In the Texas of Brinkley's day it was bad form for a rich man not to have at least one oil well, and the famous surgeon took to the oil fields at Luling in Central Texas. He rounded out his portfolio with a healthy spread of citrus groves in the Rio Grande Valley, a Del Rio lumber company, a good patch of land over in Mexico, a six-thousand-acre estate in North Carolina, a goat farm in Oklahoma, and twenty accounts in ten banks located in five states and one foreign country. Doctor even owned a gravestone company, which sold customized memorials by mail from Del Rio—for those who were not able to receive Doctor's treatment, and maybe even for some that did.

During the summer months, when broadcasting reception was at its poorest because of solar interference, Doctor took a vacation and recommended the same for his patients. An admiral in the Kansas Navy, Doctor's preferred form of vacation was a long, rejuvenating cruise, either on one of his personal yachts or on one of the finest ocean liners. Wherever he landed his yachts, christened the *Brinkley 1* and the *Brinkley 2*, the radio star was hailed by the press. The *Washington Times* noted the arrival of "one of the most luxurious yachts ever to come up the Potomac." The *Liverpool Advance* printed an enthusiastic greeting upon Brinkley's arrival in Great Britain: "Thrice welcome, Dr. and Mrs. Brinkley, you are more welcome than the flowers in May." A home movie recorded one of the treks of the 115-foot-yacht around the watery globe. Del Rioans who later saw the film at the Princess theater downtown marveled at the Panama Canal, the Galápagos Islands, and the wonders of the deep that were landed by the intrepid Doctor. The greatest thrill was watching their famous neighbor hook a Texas-size tuna fish off the coast of Nova Scotia. This particular 788-pound catch made Doctor the undisputed holder of the Western Hemisphere Tuna Record, a title that had been held by western author Zane Grey for the previous dozen years.

The philanthropist-surgeon had his champion tuna stuffed, and he presented the specimen to the Del Rio High School. Doctor had previously assisted borderland education with gifts of typewriters, desks, and a hefty cash donation for the founding of a public library. The last gift bore the stipulation that the house of books be named—what else?—the Dr. Brinkley Library.

Programming on Brinkley's border blasters underwent gradual changes as the thirties wore on. Hillbilly musicians and Mexican balladeers, as well as astrologers, numerologists, and fortune-tellers—collectively known as spooks—became the staple of XERA's repertoire. This type of programming proved to be the most popular among the rural listeners in the heart of America who formed the core of Dr. Brinkley's listening audience. Unlike entertainers on the radio networks, who relied on the questionable "Hooper ratings" to determine their audience size and their popularity, border performers were judged on their ability to "pull mail." A good mail puller was someone who generated numerous inquiries for products and services offered on the air, sometimes as many as several thousand per day. As long as a performer pulled mail, he or she was assured border stardom and job security.

One of the most successful mail pullers in border radio history was Rose Dawn, a lady whom *Time* magazine referred to as a "blondined uplifter." Advertised as the Star Girl of Radio Station XERA, Rose Dawn was Dr. Brinkley's personal astrologer. In addition to divining the signs of listeners' horoscopes, Rose Dawn would pray for a particular radio fan or give advice on matters of the heart for the small fee of $1. In fact, everything on her mystic menu seemed to cost a buck—books that could make one's personality "blossom like a flower," special vials of exotic perfume. Rose Dawn, also known as the Patroness of the Sacred Order of Maya, an esoteric organization she founded during the Texas centennial, was married to Koran, an equally enigmatic radio personality who sat in the XERA studios, adjusting his turban, and pulling mail from devotees in radio land. The couple were an ethereal sight on the streets of Del Rio as they glided past gawking onlookers in their pink Chrysler with orchid wheels.

Despite competition from such otherworldly healers, Dr. Brinkley remained the most popular performer on XERA. "You can spot a man every time with prostate gland trouble," Doctor lectured. "Disturbance of this kind acts like a narcotic." He encouraged his listeners to be open with him: "I know men, being a man. I know men sow wild oats. . . . Ninety percent of the men in this country and of all civilized nations have had gonorrhea or mumps at some time in their lives." He spoke to the women in the audience, recommending lamb stew for those who "do not eliminate sufficiently." As he put it, "What is better than a good lamb stew with nice carrots and onions? I got hungry myself after I talked the other night about lamb stew." Mrs. Brinkley broadcast on Sunday nights, focusing her talks on colon and rectal disorders, and even Johnnie Boy got into the radio act. His mother proudly pointed out that even at his young age, her son did not stumble over words like "tonsillectomy" and "hemorrhoids."

The Brinkley presses also rolled at full speed. Form letters told recipients, "YOU HAVE BEEN SELECTED FROM YOUR PARTICULAR LOCALITY: NOW GRAB THIS OPPORTUNITY OF A LIFETIME." He warned insincere correspondents, "If you think you can trick me, do not write. You will be exposing your 'innerself', which you CANNOT conceal from me." He continued to deride the advice of "jealous doctordom" and informed one patient, "If your son is taking a diet to cure his epilepsy, it is to laugh." He scoffed at letters from patients who went to other doctors, refusing to "pull their chestnuts out of the fire," and he published an updated version of *The Doctor Book*, complete with carefully drawn "Actual X-Ray Photographs" and a retelling of the sad tale of Paw and Maw. In the illustrated fable, Paw felt poorly, visited official doctordom, and was "brought home in a wooden box. But if Paw had listened to station XERA," the story continued, "if Paw had only taken the train to Del Rio . . . Paw, like thousands of others would have returned home a well and happy man." The publication ended with Brinkley's commandment, "Find God and be happy. It is the only way."

In those high-flying times, Doctor did not limit his talks to medical subjects. The radio lectures, later published in a work entitled *Roads Courageous*, included philosophical musings on "Highway Safety," "The Mormons," and "Idiosyncracy." Doctor often waxed poetic on the topic of his adopted state. "Her sunsets are as glorious," he purred over the radio, "as those that kiss the bounding billows of the Mediterrean into a flame of gold. Her landscapes are painted with the broken ends of the rainbow and thrown across a thousand purple hills. Her prairies burst into unforgettable fields of royal bluebonnets." Texas to Doctor was "an empire of opportunity glistening before our eyes like a crystal palace bathed in the glory of the morning . . . a land of treasured memories, with history running through the mists and glamor of centuries . . . An agricultural domain, the wildest on the continent . . . a cattle region so extended that the morning and evening sun plays upon a million horns . . . an oilfield producing liquid gold from bound to bound." And then, in a burst of reverence, Doctor exclaimed, "TEXAS IS IMPERIAL!"

It was about that time that Doctor experimented with a new promotional medium and produced a motion picture to advertise his latest medical breakthroughs. Staring whimsically at the camera from behind an oak desk, the surgeon began, "Hello, my friends in Texas, Kansas, and everywhere. This is Dr. Brinkley speaking to you from my lovely home in Del Rio, Texas, where summer spends the winter." He told of the new dental department in the Brinkley Hospital: "You know, you'd better go to my dental clinic if we recommend it. I had a pain in my shoulder once, and it didn't stop until I had my tooth pulled." Tiring of dentistry, Doctor expounded on the effects of high blood pressure: "If you have high blood pressure, watch your diet. Eat no salt at all. . . . You know, most people with high blood pressure die during sexual intercourse. . . . Remember, clean up, clean out, and keep clean."

Doctor continued his message, relaxed, intimate, yet stern and sprinkled with just enough technical jargon to make it difficult to understand his exact meaning. Soon Minnie stepped into the picture, as Doctor did his utmost to add a touch of realism to the performance. "Oh, look who's here," he said, looking stage left.

Minnie gave Doctor a peck on the cheek and addressed the camera: "You'd better listen to Doctor, or you'll be much worse off than you are now. . . . But excuse me, I have to go off to the kitchen to cook our Sunday dinner." Doctor looked fondly after his wife as she left the picture. He turned to the camera, stroked his goatee, and, with a slight smile, spoke: "You can trust what Minnie says, folks. After all, she just came from communion."

By that time, Del Rio was getting used to the unusual, maybe even a bit weary of the attention. Humorists began chuckling in their columns about "Dollar Rio, Texas." Local jokesters took out full-page ads with taunting remarks about "Ye Olde Prostate Shoppe," which were later mentioned in a scathing article about Dr. Brinkley in the *Saturday Evening Post*. The article described an even more vexing challenge to Doctor's medical empire: "What happened was that a well-established Del Rio surgeon suddenly went off the ethical rails and started advertising over the border station XEPN." The surgeon, James R. Middlebrook, M.D., asserted that he could perform Brinkley's infamous "compound operation" at a considerable discount and offered a "Special Prostate Package for Home Treatment" for just $5. Aggressive field reps for the upstart bargain prostate specialist began to scout out disembarking train passengers headed for the Brinkley clinic in the Roswell Hotel, and the salesmen smooth-talked them into saving money by going to the cut-rate competitor. According to the *Saturday Evening Post*, "Another group of touts began to rally round the Del Rio station to rescue backsliders as they left the train. They say that platform was pretty lively back then, with all the pulling and hauling and the embarrassment of elderly through passengers who had stepped off the train to stretch their legs when perfect strangers rushed up and wanted to know if they were suffering from the less decorous ills that Doctor specializes in. Several times these hostile puller-inners got into gang fights. Some went heeled in the traditional Texas style, in case things got even more serious."

Dr. Brinkley was so upset that the Del Rio power machine allowed the rival surgical swami to muscle in on his bidness, that he decided to move his medical empire once again. Telling his fellow Rotarians and other former Del Rio boosters that he was fed up with paying train fare and needed a more central location, Doctor picked Arkansas as a likely spot, particularly since it was one of the few states that still recognized the Eclectic degree. Doctor shopped around and selected two locations in Little Rock, a small in-town hospital and a deluxe site fifteen miles south of town. The latter was the former home of the Shrine Country Club, a picture-book group of large stone buildings beside a hundred-acre lake. Doctor advertised it as the "Most Beautiful Hospital in the World," complete with an eighteen-holer billed as the South's Sportiest Golf Course. Brinkley took to the commuter skies once again, spending Monday through Thursday in Little Rock taking care of business at the hospital, then returning to Del Rio Friday through Sunday to broadcast live and make transcriptions for the next week.

Doctor was in something of a bad mood when he opened his Arkansas fix-up shops in the spring of 1938. Earlier that year his archnemesis, Dr. Morris Fishbein and the "Amateur Meatcutters Association" had been up to their old tricks. "Fishy" had written a series of articles entitled "Modern Medical Charlatans" for the AMA-sponsored journal *Hygeia*, in which he gave the famous radio surgeon a rough going-over, saying that "in John R. Brinkley, quackery reaches its apotheosis."

Dr. Brinkley was indeed offended. He described the American Medical Association as "the biggest bunch of grafters and the biggest bunch of crooks and the biggest bunch of thieves on the top side of this earth." He filed suit against old "Fishy" for $250,000, claiming that the libelous article had injured his reputation so adversely that his income had dropped to about $800,000 per year. The trial began in March 1939 in the Spanish-style federal courthouse in Del Rio. The jury of twelve area citizens consisted of several ranchers, some of whom were as intimately acquainted with goat glands as Doctor himself. Students in the civics class at Del Rio High School were present during the trial, causing some to comment that the vocational class in agriculture should be attending the proceedings as well.

Fishbein's attorneys, selected from law firms in Chicago, San Antonio, and Del Rio, gave Dr. Brinkley a difficult time on the witness stand. But the radio Doc came to court with a full tank of gall. "I am the man who originated the goat gland operation," he stated during his two days of testimony on the stand while the jury blinked at the $100,000 worth of diamonds he wore to court. Brinkley's lawyers winced at the pronouncements of their outspoken client. They objected to any mention of goat glands, insisting that they were not relevant to the case. Fishbein's lawyers gave the radio medic a hard time about his biography *The Life of a Man.* They established that Doctor had paid Clement Wood $5000 to compose the tome in 1934 and that Wood was one of Brinkley's paid publicists. They quoted from the text, paying particular attention to one chapter immodestly titled "The Most Learned Doctor in America." Brinkley's attorneys were planning to rely on the testimony of former patients. Described by one observer as "the friskiest bunch of old roosters you ever saw in your life," the witnesses were not allowed to testify because of a rule of evidence prohibiting a layperson from expressing a medical opinion.

The trial attracted national attention. XERA offered a cash prize to the person who could best complete the sentence, "I consider Dr. Brinkley the world's foremost prostate surgeon because ———." Supportive Del Rioans ran ads in the local paper saying that they believed Dr., Mrs., and Johnnie Boy Brinkley to be "good, clean, Christian folks . . . regardless of the outcome" of the trial. According to veteran Texas newsman Millard Cope, most Del Rioans were hoping for a victory for Dr. Brinkley. They remembered how their town had prospered when Doc brought his medical magic to the border, and they rooted for the long-suffering surgeon even though he had moved most of his operation to the Ozarks. They remembered the crowds of randy old-timers staying at the Roswell Hotel, dancing to music in the city park, dining at Ma Crosby's Cafe, and testing their new vigor in Acuña's active Boys Town, or red light district. The local folks had heard that even Huey Long had an appointment at the Brinkley Hospital in Del Rio, but an assassin's bullet had cut short his travel plans back in 1936.

Seven days after the trial began, the jury of Doctor's peers returned a verdict in favor of Dr. Fishbein. Brinkley boosters felt sure that the radio wizard would recover from that legal setback as he had so often in the past, but they underestimated the effect of the defeat on Doctor's health and his bankbook. The Del Rio jury's verdict, sustained after appeal in the higher courts, unleashed a tidal wave of lawsuits that daunted even the litigious Doctor. Disgruntled former patients crowded into Little Rock law parlors to file more than $1,000,000 in lawsuits for everything from carelessness to "criminal negligence in permitting a patient to bleed to death on the operating table." While Mrs. Brinkley, who had never approved of the move to Arkansas, suggested to the ladies of the Oklahoma City League of Democratic Women that "we must keep America nice," the Internal Revenue Service filed a Texas-size claim against Doctor for back taxes. And just after Christmas in 1939, Mexico finally ratified the provisions of an international agreement with the United States, clearing the way for definite action against XERA.

The sting of his reverses inspired Doctor to chase again the laurels of elected office. Back in the spring of '38 the scuttlebutt in Del Rio maintained that Brinkley was ready to jump into the Texas gubernatorial contest but changed his mind when fellow radio star W. Lee O'Daniel announced his candidacy. Shortly after the libel trial verdict, Brinkley consulted astrologer Rose Dawn about his chances of winning the presidency of the United States in 1940. In May 1941 the surgeon took action on his political impulse and filed his application with the Texas Secretary of State to get his name on the ballot as candidate for the U.S. Senate. One of Doc's archenemies from his Kansas days, William Allen White (the Sage of Emporia), quipped, "He may win. He is irresistible to the moron mind, and Texas has plenty of such."

Prior to his candidacy, Brinkley had filed for bankruptcy in the Texas courts. He took the stand and stated that he would pay all claims in full, but clever shuffling of his far-flung holdings left the bankruptcy examiners frustrated and left Brinkley relatively free to pursue his political goals. Doctor sent a promo letter to his mailing list in which he stated, "I am bankrupt and have no money to contribute to my campaign. If I am to be elected, it must be a free-will offering from the people of Texas who love and trust me." The slim response to the mailing convinced Brinkley to withdraw from the race, and he threw his support to another candidate—radio personality, Governor O'Daniel, with a letter stating, "Mrs. Brinkley and I have made a private poll of 50,000 of our friends in Texas and found them overwhelmingly in favor of you as their next Senator."

Frantically looking for a way to shore up his crumbling empire, Brinkley announced plans to move the Brinkley Hospital back to the Roswell Hotel "in sunny Del Rio, Texas, near the silvery Rio Grande and romantic Old Mexico." He had the support of Del Rio community leaders who wrote in an open letter in the paper, "Knowing the good you have done and are doing suffering humanity, we invite you back to Del Rio to resume your valuable services to the sick and needy."

The move never took place, however, as President Manuel Ávila Camacho, the newly elected leader of the Mexican republic, ordered the expropriation of XERA. As reported in the Mexican newspaper *Excelsior*, the president asserted that the station had transmitted "news broadcasts unsuitable to the new world" and was controlled by "foreigners sympathetic to the Nazi cause." Although William Dudley Pelley, leader of the anti-Semitic Silver Shirt organization, testified before Congress that he had received $5000 from Brinkley, it is doubtful that Doctor was a Nazi sympathizer. Nevertheless, the *federales* closed in on the tall radio towers outside Villa Acuña and silenced XERA.

After learning the sad fate of his station, Doctor sent Minnie a handwritten letter that would have misted the eyes of his old enemy Morris

Fishbein. "Honey," he wrote from the Hotel Bellerive in Kansas City. "It seems my heart will break since you phoned XERA was being torn down. As long as this did not happen I had a faint hope. . . . But now the patient is dead. 'The Sunshine Station Between the Nations' is gone. The world's most powerful broadcasting station is silent."

The thrill of speaking into a microphone and knowing that his voice was booming across the land was John R. Brinkley's life-force. Without the healing power of his radio voice, Doctor felt the strain of his battles more intensely. A short time after XERA went off the air, he suffered a severe heart attack. In August 1941 a blood clot formed in his leg. Gangrene set in, and it became necessary to amputate. While Doctor was convalescing in Kansas City, he was arrested by a United States marshal on a charge of using the U.S. mails to defraud. "I guess there isn't any danger of my running away," he joked, displaying the strength of character that had enabled him to fight so many bureaucracies for so many years. Dr. Brinkley never stood trial for mail fraud. He spent several months at a second family home in San Antonio, growing continually weaker, and on May 26, 1942, John R. Brinkley, M.D., Ph.D., M.C., LL.D., D.P.H., Sc.D., and member of the National Geographic Society, passed away.

After his death, the legend of the "mystery man of the Rio Grande" lived on in Val Verde County and across the country. His photograph hung on the walls of Del Rio High School as late as 1946. Even today, if you ask an old-timer if he remembers Dr. Brinkley, the response will likely be "Oh, you mean the goat gland man." And whenever and wherever performers and fans gather together to reminisce about the good old days of radio, someone whose eyes sparkle as if viewing a photograph of long-remembered youth will tell the familiar joke: What's the fastest thing on four legs? A goat passing the Brinkley Hospital.

Purple Shadow on the Rio Grande:
Norman Baker in Nuevo Laredo

Phone 666 upon arrival in Laredo, Texas.
—From Norman Baker's pamphlet "Cancer Is Curable"

It is doubtful that Norman G. Baker had planned it that way, but many who followed his career, particularly members of the American Medical Association, would have found it appropriate that the phone number of his Laredo office was identical to the number described as the mark of the beast in Revelation 13:18. Postal inspectors, communications officials, physicians, and radio listeners round the country echoed those sentiments, calling Baker a "human corn borer" and "a disgrace to the entire broadcasting fraternity." The cause of all the uproar was Baker's own style of medico-broadcasting "quackery," border-blasted to the public in the form of miracle cures appealingly dangled before those suffering from cancer. Dr. John Brinkley's nemesis Morris Fishbein reserved the sharpest barbs from his pen for Baker and his associates. "Of all the ghouls who feed on the bodies of the dead and dying," he wrote, "the cancer quacks are the most vicious and the most unprincipled." And he awarded top honors in the field to Norman Baker.

There were many similarities in the careers of Baker and Dr. Brinkley. Baker also had a radio station and hospital in the heartlands, was hounded by medical and communications authorities, sought vindication through high office and obsessive, self-righteous defense of his practices, and hightailed it south of the Rio Grande to operate a high-powered Mexican border blaster.

Above all, Norman Baker was a superb showman. His smooth gift of gab was so persuasive that thousands of radio listeners and cancer sufferers gave their hearts and savings to his claims of persecuted genius. The natural-born salesman had a flair for the dramatic, accented by his penchant for purple clothing and the fervent manner in which he raved at his enemies in print and on the air.

The "wild and woolly Norman Baker from the cornfields of Iowa," as the press in the nation's capital once referred to him, was born in the Mississippi River town of Muscatine in 1882. Anxious to get ahead on his own terms, the future broadcasting pioneer left high school after eighteen months and took up work as a machinist. Baker had an agile, restless mind and easily acquired skill as a mechanic. He followed that line of work for a couple of years, wandering in and out of jobs at machine shops in Illinois, Ohio, and Indiana.

Shortly after the turn of the century, the lure of the footlights cast its spell on young Norman Baker. It was showbiz fever, and the ambitious mechanic had it bad. The man he most admired was a vaudeville hypnotist named Professor Flint. Baker set out to emulate and surpass his theatrical hero. Trading his grease-stained overalls for a boiled white shirt and a silk plug hat, he quickly assembled a mental suggestion act. The novice trooper booked his first show at Coal Valley, Illinois. The telepathic demonstration was to be preceded by a lecture on mental suggestion by Baker. Experiencing the pangs of virgin stage fright, the young mentalist fortified his thespian inspiration with a big snort of firewater. Stepping out onto the stage to face the imposing glare of theater lights and the sea of waiting faces, Baker froze. Though he had rehearsed the twenty-minute talk endlessly, he could not remember a word of it. At that moment, Norman Baker discovered his spellbinding talent, the ability to speak extemporaneously and hold the rapt attention of large audiences. He simply started talking, telling the folks his views on mental suggestion in down-to-earth terms. His authorized biographer, Clement Wood, reported that the crowd went wild. Baker's first venture into show business was a success.

The man from Muscatine kept up the act for a dozen years, refining the scheme and performing all over the country. At one point he changed the name of the show to "Madame Pearl Tangley—The Mental Marvel." The big show began, as usual, with a talk by Baker on the mysteries of controlling the subjective mind. Then the curtain went up on a stage outfitted with a panoramic drop depicting the interior of an Egyptian temple. Madame Tangley, the Priestess of the Temple, robed in exotic mind-reading attire, assumed her position on a platform at the front of the stage. Occasionally the mystic from the Nile appeared to levitate before her audiences, suspended in midair with a metal rod while a powerful Tesla coil onstage emitted crackling blue bolts of light. Brave volunteers from the audience mounted the stage and wrote questions on a blackboard behind Madame. The mystic lady not only divined the question but also gave the volunteer its answer.

"Never forget that Madame Tangley is not a pretender," showman Baker, using the stage name Charles Welch, reminded the awestruck crowd. "She does not claim to possess any supernatural powers; she is merely a skilled and scientific deductionist. Her performance is offered for purposes of amusement only. Notice how she is blindfolded, with a ball of cotton over each eye, and a towel firmly fastened over that, so that there is absolutely no opportunity for her seeing a thing." Baker never revealed the exact nature of Madame's skill, but the sound of words like "scientific deductionist" convinced many Tangley fans that this was serious stuff.

Over the years there were a number of Madame Tangleys, all possessing the rare power to control the subjective mind. Baker married one of those ladies, the daughter of an ivory-tinkling preacher, but the union was annulled after five years.

By 1914 the showman had learned to resist the lure of the vaudeville circuit, and he landed back in Muscatine, where he began a variety of new enterprises. First, though he had never studied music, he applied his mechanical expertise to the task of inventing a musical instrument that could be played outdoors for advertising purposes. Calling the invention the Tangley air calliope and later the calliaphone, the instrument was an air-powered version of the calliope, which was normally powered by steam. The invention paid off, as the units started selling as quickly as Baker's Muscatine firm could produce them. The Tangley Company advertised that "any energetic person" could earn $5000 yearly by renting its "Calliaphone Outfit to Merchants, Theatres, Celebrations, Fairs, Shows, Rinks, Church Socials, Sales, Auctions, and numerous enterprises. The world is your field. You can travel from Coast to Coast, doing outdoor advertising in each city you visit." Custom calliaphone jobs were also available, with some of the larger outfits having built-in living quarters. Bakeries, candy companies, cake makers, and gum factories advertised with calliaphones built to resemble loaves of bread, Domino mints, layer cakes, and five-cent gum packs. "They compel the attention of all," marveled Tangley.

As the political situation in Europe deteriorated and North Americans began to realize the horrors of modern warfare, Baker addressed a letter to the Canadian Minister of Militia, offering to alleviate the suffering of shell-shocked doughboys through the power of mental suggestion. But Baker was never called on to perform his psychic miracles in the trenches, and as the twenties began to roar, a fire wiped out the Tangley Company. Approaching age forty, Baker hung around a Muscatine photography studio and pondered his reverses, searching for an angle to use to get back on top. One day a hobo artist wandered into the photo shop and offered to teach its proprietor the arts of oil painting and photo tinting for $10. Baker observed the technique with interest, and the idea for another big money-maker sprouted in his mind. The Tangley Art School was soon advertising that anyone, "even though unequipped with especial artistic talent," could learn oil painting by mail in ten easy lessons. For three years would-be Rembrandts across the country received their inspiration by mail from Muscatine. As an incentive, the Tangley studios offered not only to train the artists but also to sell their creations, in the form of oil-painted pillow tops that Baker sold along with the lessons and instruction books. Women eager to earn a little extra money jumped at the scheme. According to one of his former protégés, Baker was "raking in something like $30,000 a month out of suckers who couldn't afford to buy the salt to go into their mush." With profits like those, the Muscatine entrepreneur was soon able to close the Tangley Art School and revive the Tangley Calliaphone Company.

Clement Wood, commissioned by Dr. Brinkley to write his propagandistic biography, was also hired by Norman Baker to chronicle his life story. Entitled *The Throttle: A Fact Story of Injustice, Confiscation and Suppression* (later reissued under the title *Doctors, Dynamiters and Gunmen*), the book concluded with the prediction that Baker would be elected president of the United States and Mexico at the same time. Wood, a noted man of letters who had attended Yale Law School and worked for a brief time as Upton Sinclair's secretary, wrote the Baker biography under the pen name Alvin G. Winston but attached a foreword under his own name in which he showed his libertarian leanings by declaring, "I don't like the canned programs of the chain radio bunch, I know already what inefficient asses most doctors are." Throughout the Baker biography, Wood reminded the reader that his subject was a genius. The distinction was not entirely undeserved: Baker's lawyer, testifying before Congress on a radio bill, described his client as an "eccentric genius." Wood also pointed out that many of Baker's actions sprang directly from his uncommonly keen intuitive powers. His entrance into the radio industry was born of just such a moment's hunch. Early in 1924 some of Muscatine's business leaders were talking about starting up a radio station for the town. After considerable piddling, they settled on a weekly Muscatine Night on a station at nearby Davenport. Noting local disappointment, Baker suddenly proclaimed that he would build a radio station for his hometown. "I'll lift Muscatine from being a little burg lost in the Mississippi cornfields to a city the whole world knows about," he told the local banker.

As Secretary of Commerce, fellow Iowan Herbert Hoover headed the agency in charge of U.S. radio affairs at the time, and he approved the application for a license to operate a 500-watt radio station. Baker, believing that his instructive broadcasts to humanity would shake up the entrenched social order, decided that the call letters of his station would be KTNT. "Know the Naked Truth" became the station's slogan. KTNT was constructed on the highest hill in Muscatine with a sweeping view of Mark Twain's river down below. The architectural style combined "a bit of America, a dash of Moorish, a gob of Spanish, an ort of Egyptian," and so on. Large oil paintings of Egyptian desert scenes hung above the interior doorways, recalling the Middle Eastern theme of the Madame Tangley performances, and even the radiators in the building were adorned with Egyptian motifs. "The nation's most beautiful radio station," Baker said, would be a "monument to the radio industry."

Throughout his carrer, the showman insisted that he was fighting the "vested interests" and watching out for the rights of the helpless masses. In the struggle to enact his radio dream, Baker found himself up against the rapidly expanding power of the "radio trust," a small group of companies that Baker accused of monopolizing station ownership and the manufacture of radio equipment. The Big Five, as Baker called them, consisted of RCA, General Electric, Westinghouse, AT&T, and the United Fruit Company. Many small independent broadcasters sympathized with Baker's dislike of the large radio companies. In the mid-twenties, broadcasters needed two permits to begin operations, one from the Department of Commerce in Washington for a frequency and one from AT&T's subsidiary Western Electric to build a radio transmitter. Baker refused to pay the $4-per-watt annual fee that AT&T demanded from anyone who used one of its transmitters. Instead, Baker acquired part of the transmitting equipment from a different patent holder and built the rest of the equipment himself.

Baker asked Senator Smith W. Brookhart of Iowa to complain to the Secretary of Commerce about the monopolistic activities of the radio trust and traveled to Washington, D.C., himself in 1925 to attend the Fourth National Radio Conference, which had been organized to discuss future radio legislation. Baker publicly put the big boys on notice at the conference, calling for chain programming to be broadcast on the same frequency and attacking AT&T as "a giant octopus seeking entire control of the air." Baker saw a bleak future for conciliatory broadcasters, warning that "the radio monster that suckles them now" planned "only to devour them later on."

Baker was successful enough to get KTNT on the air, and the first broadcast from America's Most Beautiful Radio Station went out on Thanksgiving Day, 1925. Broadcasting from "Calliaphone Studio KTNT, Muscatine, Iowa, the storm-proof city with cheap electricity for factory and home," Baker dedicated his station to "farmers, laborers, and the common folks." He declared that the melodious sound of the calliaphone enabled KTNT to go on the air "with absolutely the first change in a radio program that has been heard in the radio world." From the start, the "wild and woolly" broadcaster vowed to "keep the air free" and launched attacks against the radio electric trust and a host of other monopolizing evildoers he thought were out to get him. Bankers, public utility companies, merchants, newspapers, and soon the Federal Radio Commission and the American Medical Association all felt the sting of the radio Robin Hood of Muscatine, Iowa.

In addition to revelations of corruption among the powers-that-be by the "champion of fair play," KTNT featured the whistling toots of the calliaphone, choral numbers, piano duets, orchestras, and bands. A slapstick duo named Daffy and Gloomy and an old-time fiddler's group, the Plough Shoe Cronies, were part of the lineup. Political speeches, agricultural debates, homemaking tips, and a singing canary named Jim also wafted forth from the hill above the Mississippi. As Baker explained it, "Our programs are arranged like a vaudeville program—you don't know what is coming next when the curtain goes down." KTNT even ventured into international service when an official of the Mexican consulate spoke over the station, addressing the midwestern audience on "The Religious Controversy of Mexico." The public was invited to visit the station, marvel at its inner workings, and purchase snacks and souvenirs.

No doubt Baker found the radio stage even more gratifying than the vaudeville houses. He was also proving wrong the chain station owners who had snickered that a radio station could never succeed in the cornfields and open spaces of Iowa. Not only did the showman-entrepreneur succeed and prosper, but he also diversified even more and expanded his empire nearly to the limits of consumer imagination. He opened the KTNT Gas Station, the KTNT Cafe, the KTNT Stores, and the Western Drug Company. On the air and through a mail-order catalog he sold a variety of goods that competed with Sears and Roebuck and Montgomery Ward, and listeners who became members of the Tangley Association enjoyed a 5 percent discount on all their purchases. From tires to brassieres, canned fruit to storage batteries, cigars to alarm clocks, radios, coffee, and mattresses—almost any item one could name was available from the Baker Sales Company, even Baker's Iowa Pig Meal and his special-formula hay balancer.

In 1927 KTNT was named official mouthpiece for the Farmer's Educational and Cooperative Society of America and fought the compulsory testing of cattle for tuberculosis, a stance that was popular with midwestern farmers who resented the government inspectors and suffered heavy financial losses because of the program. The station was also endorsed for its devotion to agricultural issues by the Corn Belt Federation, the National Farmers Union, and the Iowa Farmers Union. Baker was proud of the public service role performed by his station. "We give the day's news and other items of interest to the farm folks who do not have access to the daily papers until they are a day old." KTNT also served the personal needs of its rural listeners with the *Corresponding Club*, a radio meeting place for lonely souls that was so successful, it resulted in an on-the-air marriage.

Still, not all who received the KTNT signal were pleased with its programs. In a complaint to Secretary of Commerce Hoover, one listener wrote, "These monotonous programs are broadcasted during some of the good chain programs and listeners in that area have called this station by telephone requesting them to remain off the air, but at times have been reprimanded over the radio by Mr. Baker." Another dissatisfied listener accused Baker of broadcasting "Russian Bolshevik propaganda," while still another wrote, "It is very unfortunate that a person of Mr. Baker's policies and nature should have been able to secure a station."

The "eccentric genius" behind KTNT, like Dr. Brinkley, did not hesitate to appeal to the highest powers. Baker testified several times in both houses of Congress about the problems in the radio industry as he saw them. He spoke out in favor of hard-sell advertising, a practice still frowned upon in those days of radio's commercial innocence. "What's the difference," Baker wrote in an informational brochure, "between describing an article in detail, like the chains do, and refusing to mention the price, or to describe the article in the same way and give the price?" Baker opposed government regulation of the prices paid for broadcasting stations, a controversial position at that time but one that is the first commandment of modern broadcasting. "If you have an automobile, a Ford, and you can find a sucker to give you a half million dollars for it, take the half million dollars," Baker said.

Baker's main concern was the monopolizing of his industry by the "radio octopus," and he sought help on several occasions from Herbert Hoover, as Secretary of Commerce and, later, president of the United States. Once, he wrote Secretary Hoover that a film company had contacted him, wanting to make a picture entitled *Stranglehold*, which would "picturize the doings and the activities of the Radio business and showing up that 'Giant Octopus' as they really are. And personally, Mr. Hoover, I think it would be the right step in the right direction to educate the public as to what is taking place."

Baker formed his own pressure group, the American Broadcasters Association, to fight for the interests of the smaller, independent radio stations. About 25 broadcasters joined the association, perhaps the most colorful being W. K. "Hello World" Henderson, the owner of station KWKH in Shreveport, Louisiana, who used his powerful radio platform to castigate the chain stores. The ABA disbanded in 1927 when the Federal Radio Act was passed, creating the Federal Radio Commission and incorporating a few watered-down suggestions from Baker's group about the limitation of chain station dominance and prevention of radio monopolies.

Not all the radio stations that received Baker's informational form letters appreciated his zeal. A Des Moines station manager wrote to the Secretary of Commerce and called Baker "an agitator of the worst sort." After receiving material from KTNT's American Broadcasters Association, Amon G. Carter, president of the *Fort Worth Star-Telegram* and its radio station, WBAP, sent copies of it to Texas senators and congressmen with letters that stated, "We are pioneers in broadcasting and we have, therefore, had an opportunity to observe the regulations of the Department of Commerce and they have certainly handled a most vexing problem in an efficient manner. The party who is trying to create an agitation is just a newcomer in the radio game and really understands none of its problems."

Several broadcasters in New York were even more concerned about Baker, as KTNT's signal interfered with their programming. The New Yorkers asked the FRC to lower the power of Baker's station, but they were rebuffed by the commission. The commission also turned down a request to turn Baker's frequency over to the *Sioux City Journal*. Several Republican senators, including Smith Brookhart of Iowa, Gerald Nye of North Dakota, and William McMaster of South Dakota, lobbied successfully on Baker's behalf, noting that "his programs are popular in the farming region and no good reason has been given . . . why they should be discontinued."

In 1929 another weapon was added to the Baker arsenal with the publication of *TNT Magazine*, a monthly that reached a circulation of 30,000 before it was discontinued in 1931. In the first lavender-covered issue, Baker explained the journal's name: "In the age of canned goods and canned opinion, everything wears a label. A lot of truths and errors, often unrelated are grouped together and called some kind of an 'ism' and one is supposed to swallow it whole as a truth, or reject all of it as a lie. A tremendous and dangerous confusion exists. Men and women have come to think in terms of names and labels rather than about facts and conditions. . . . As a matter of fact, we usually don't know what we are talking about. . . . The time has come to see and study FACTS instead of DOCTRINES—to see THE NAKED TRUTH, instead of some doctrinal in"terpretation of the truth. Hence, our name—TNT—which means THE NAKED TRUTH."

Alert for causes to champion, Baker noted press reports that Dr. Charles Ozias of Kansas City claimed to have discovered a cure for cancer. Baker contacted the physician, who was a member of the American Association for Medico-Physical Research and the Defensive Diet League of America, and arranged for a test of the treatment on several persons afflicted with the disease. Convinced that he had found a true miracle cure, Baker soon added a cancer hospital called the Baker Institute to his Muscatine dynasty. A converted roller rink, the institute featured walls covered with "fine lavender linenette paper," and prospective patients were assured that those "with odors stay in sealed rooms away from other patients." As the first stream of patients flooded into town, the December 1930 issue of *TNT* announced to the world, "Cancer Is Conquered!"

Muscatine began to boom because of the hospital and Baker's other industries, and the town felt few effects of the Depression. But townfolk were not uniformly enthusiastic. Not only was the purple-suited wunderkind beginning to monopolize local mercantilism, but his patients also roamed around Muscatine with open sores that contaminated town drinking fountains with blood. The hospital began to take in as much as $100,000 a month, and the cash was taken out in suitcases under cover of night. Some reports contended that deceased patients were similarly discharged from the palace of healing.

Not long after the hospital opened, Baker acquired an associate named Harry Hoxsey. A gruff man from rural Illinois, Hoxsey at various times had worked as a coal miner, a taxi driver, an insurance salesman, a semipro baseball pitcher, and a human fly. When Hoxsey was just a young boy, his father, a veterinarian, had given him the secret ingredients for a cancer cure discovered by Hoxsey's great-grandfather in collaboration with a horse. Hoxsey had begun to treat cancer at the Hoxide Institute in southern Illinois with great support of local residents who at one point celebrated a Hoxsey Day, complete with parades and high school bands. Soon, however, the American Medical Association forced the unlicensed physician to cease his activities and flee to Iowa and the lavender-colored walls of KTNT.

The Illinois medicine man broadcast side by side with the inventor of the calliaphone. "We are not willing to accept any patient," the duo professed, "unless we know we can help them more or less." Sometimes the physicians resorted to scare tactics to draw in patients: "Isn't it a terrible condition to think you got a cancer inside of you, a tumor eating day by day, getting larger and larger day by day and soon going to cause your death?" Before long, as many as three hundred patients a day were treated for cancer at the Baker Institute, although doctors in the area later testified that many of the sufferers did not even have the dread disease.

In May 1930 Baker used his vaudeville training to further his medical efforts, and he teamed up with Hoxsey to stage a medical show and cancer-curing exhibition on the lawn of KTNT. "Thirty-two thousand people attended—twice as many people as the entire population of Muscatine," wrote *The Throttle*. "They covered the hillside, which was a hundred and sixty five feet high; thousands of cars from places as distant as Kansas City had to be parked in a space surrounding the radio station a mile long, and extending along the side streets in each direction for several blocks. Such a crowd could not possibly all see the demonstration; some of them had to be content with listening to the remarks and explanations broadcast from various points below the hill's summit by loudspeakers. After introductory remarks by Baker, a score of cancer patients from the Baker Institute, representing every stage of the disease, from the most malignant on which treatment had just begun, to definitely cured cases, appeared on the platform. Wherever possible, these exhibited the effects of the treatments, and each made a speech testifying to the remarkable results of the treatment. The Baker treatment was administered to one patient. A cancer was lifted from the face of another patient before the astonished eyes of the vast multitude. . . . As a climax, the entire top portion of the skull of a patient almost in the last stages of cancer was removed and held up for exhibition by the physician before the gasping throng, exposing the brains of the entire top of the patient's head. It was the most remarkable demonstration of healing ever held in the history of man, in any land in the world."

When patient Mandus Johnson's skull top was "pried off," many within viewing range fainted. The AMA contended that the exposed anatomy was actually just the medullary portion of the skull. Whatever it was, it made for grisly photographic reproductions that had a strong impact on readers of *The Throttle* and *TNT Magazine*. Norman Baker, the consummate performer, capped the exhibition by swallowing a bottle of the secret nostrum that could effect such dramatic cures. *The Throttle* contended that "the meeting turned into an ovation to this living human savior, who could heal those that were sick and restore sight to the blind and cure the halt and the lame."

A second open-air cancer cure show was held a few weeks later. This time the governor of Iowa, John Hammill, graced the stage on the banks of the Mississippi. *TNT Magazine* estimated the crowd at about 50,000. The governor, running for reelection, later received a great deal of criticism for his appearance at the spectacle. Like most politicians, however, he doubtless realized that a crowd is a crowd, and a microphone is a microphone.

While Baker was displaying his curative abilities on the stage, the licensed physicians of Iowa and the rest of the country were working hard to close down the Baker Institute. The attack was led by Dr. Morris Fishbein, editor of the *Journal of the American Medical Association.* "All the other wicked medical fakes, firing hope and darkening it to despair, pale beside the savagery of the cancer charlatans," poeticized Dr. Fishbein. "They look like men, they speak like men, but in them, pervading them, resides a quality so malevolent that it sets them apart from others of the human race. Even in this time of scientific and social progress they brazenly dare the daylight. With Stone Age lures, they call. The credulous believe. They slay their patients as if they knifed them in the heart."

Asserting that the organized doctors were simply against innovation and progress, Baker erected a sign over his hospital door proclaiming, "A Quack is one who thinks and does things others can't." On the air he went after his opposition with sharper barbs, instructing his audience to avoid regular physicians at all costs. He echoed Dr. Brinkley, calling the AMA the "Amateur Meatcutters Association," and invented his own term for organized doctordom, the "American Mummy Association." The abbreviation "M.D.," he said, stood for "More Dough." When an investigator from the Iowa State Health Department began snooping around the hospital, Baker went on the air and called the official "a dirty cur . . . lower than a rattlesnake in a ditch." He called a state health official a "bloodsucker" and referred to the State University of Iowa Hospital as "that slaughterhouse." He encouraged his followers to shun vaccinations, even while a smallpox epidemic ravaged Muscatine, saying the serums used were nothing more than "cow pus which will cause syphilis." Baker accused doctors of the worst kind of immorality, asking rhetorically, "Is it not a fact that many of these men use their profession as an excuse to fondle and gaze upon the nude parts of innocent children?" If a radio fan suffered from appendicitis, Baker told the patient to "rub the abdomen downward with a hot onion poultice, and if the appendix is kinked, it will straighten out." For lockjaw, Baker had a simple solution: "Heat common turpentine and put it on the sore. That's all there is to it." Unsympathetic members of the press were dismissed as "immoral drunkards, contemptible curs, scoundrels, and cowards."

According to one of the commissioners, the Federal Radio Commission received more complaints about KTNT than about any other station in America. An FRC examiner recommended the removal of KTNT's broadcast license, stating that Baker used the station primarily to advance his own personal interests and that KTNT created too much civil strife and turmoil. The commission took the less drastic step of placing KTNT on probation.

Vowing that he was "in this fight for humanity against the medical trust" to the bloody finish, Baker quickly filed a brief with the FRC, detailing his exceptions to the examiner's report. He went so far as to appeal directly to President Hoover and met with him in the White House for almost half an hour in September 1930. According to Baker, the president promised to investigate the alleged cancer cure. The Iowa radio medic left the meeting with high hopes that Hoover "would see the necessity of not believing everything some doctors say but will get some broad-minded and commonsense men with ordinary horse sense to investigate the remarkable treatments going on every day at the Baker Institute, Muscatine, Iowa, and which is going to make Muscatine the cancer center of the world." The president, however, did not fulfill the promise.

Nor was Baker the least bit hesitant to rebuke his adversaries with a gentlemanly duel on the courtroom floor. Taking offense at the mildest criticism, he instructed his lawyers to demand retractions on a regular basis. A small rural newspaper, after a visit to KTNT, reported to have "found everything running with a wide open and gracious hospitality which you paid for at so much per, just the same as at any other money-making institution. We didn't notice that anything was sold cheaper than elsewhere. We saw Norman himself; also his gold and purple KTNT Franklin sport model car, and we wondered why he had Goodyear tires on it, since he advertises the Tangley tires so extensively." Baker filed suit against the paper for this gentle verbal poke in the ribs. The offending country journalist, obviously amused at the incident, reported that his paper "got Borman Naker's [sic] goat, and believe me it's some cross nanny. Why, he's fit to be tied all the time. And he needs to be tied outside at that!" Baker may have kicked and snorted at the newspaperman, but he eventually dropped his suit.

Many freethinking radio listeners enjoyed the Baker style and appreciated his attacks on the big-time professional fat cats. That Baker's own bank account was growing fat never entered the picture. "You're a real he-man," wrote a listener who picked up KTNT in Philadelphia. "I glory in your spunk in talking and saying what you did last evening. You and your station, I think, is one of the greatest in America." Referring to an interference problem the Muscatine station was having with WCAU of Philadelphia, the Baker fan offered to write letters on behalf of KTNT to senators and congressmen he knew personally. "This WCAU reminds me of the road hog with an automobile," he continued, "only WCAU is an air hog. There are all kinds of hogs in this world."

A shadowy episode that became known as the KTNT Shoot-out dramatically illustrated the controversial nature of Baker's Muscatine empire. On the still side of midnight on a Friday in April 1930, Norman Baker and Harry Hoxsey sat talking on the second floor of the KTNT building and looking down on the Mississippi through a large window. According to the Baker-authorized version of the story that appeared in *The Throttle*, the office phone rang suddenly at one o'clock. Hoxsey answered the phone.

"Mr. Baker'd better not come down," rasped an excited Baker employee, calling from the KTNT Cafe. "There are three tough-looking guys parked across the street, in front of the American Savings Bank, in an old model Buick, with a foreign license plate. We're worried about him."

Five to ten minutes later, Baker and Hoxsey started to leave the station for a late snack. From the darkness next door, a little dog began to bark. As *The Throttle* described it, "The sound sliced the brittle stillness; it was so clear, so definite, that they could picture the whole scene: some intruder was outside the building." The cancer specialists killed the lights in the radio station. Then they saw "three men skulking on the lawn outside." Hoxsey pulled out his own revolver, and hot lead flew through the darkness.

"The shooting awakened all the patients in the hospital," according to *The Throttle*. "Wild excitement dominated the place. Some insisted on going home at once, and could hardly be pacified. One hysterical patient started the wild rumor that, if the prowlers could not get Baker, they would return and blow up the hospital."

GUN FIGHT CLIMAXES FIGHT WITH DR. FISHBEIN, read the Associated Press headline the following day. "Hoxsey told police he jumped to the window on hearing the shots and fired at the three men whom he could dimly see on the ground below, wounding one of them," wrote the AP. "The other two dragged the wounded man around the building, supposedly to a waiting automobile, and made their getaway. Bob Hunter, first officer to arrive on the scene, found blood on the grass where the attacker had fallen."

Baker quickly turned the KTNT compound into a fortress. A reporter visiting the station not long after the shoot-out stated, "The radio station on the hill gleamed a dazzling white under a glare of electricity which flooded the extensive grounds. No one could approach the place unseen. At the Institute, there were two guards standing on the porch as I went in. Since then Mr. Baker has procured and set up machine guns."

Shortly after fortifying his empire, Baker had a falling-out with the sharpshooting Hoxsey over financial matters. In the beginning of their six-month partnership, Baker offered to pay Hoxsey a salary of $75,000 a year, a goodly amount at a time when agricultural workers made about 30 cents an hour. It wasn't enough for Hoxsey, who reportedly demanded a percentage of the receipts from the institute as well. Baker wouldn't budge. Hoxsey accused Baker of breach of contract and talked a Baker employee into stealing the institute's records. Hoxsey then had Baker arrested for searching the employee's house without a warrant. Baker presented Hoxsey with a claim for an unpaid note and attacked his former partner over the air, saying that "prohibition officers have his name as a frequenter of roadhouses in this vicinity." Hoxsey sued Baker for slander, started his own Muscatine institute, and testified against KTNT's owner in a Muscatine trial, where he and Baker were codefendants being sued by the State of Iowa for practicing medicine without a license. The court was not able to convict Baker or Hoxsey because of a technicality, and the two dedicated healers competed fiercely on the streets of Muscatine for cancer sufferers.

Baker did not spend his entire fury on his former partner but saved some of his bile for another enemy, the press. In a radio address Baker attacked a particular newspaper publisher "who is bald because he lies so much." His favorite target, however, were those who wrote and published the *Muscatine Journal,* a newspaper that Baker maintained was conspiring with the AMA to discredit his institute and communications empire. In one radio broadcast Baker suggested that the editors of the *Journal* "stay home with their own wives and not visit other men's wives." On another occasion Baker said that the publisher of the paper and his associates "get stewed to the gills and get drunk as a loon, and they are not satisfied and they start after more booze." In May 1930 Baker made a frontal assault on his enemy by means of a "radiothon." He spoke out against the paper "from 12:30 until 23 minutes past seven, the longest radio talk ever given in the world," according to his own estimation. During the talk, Baker encouraged townfolk to cancel their subscriptions to the *Muscatine Journal* and invited listeners to call him and report their cancellations over the air.

Another bombshell that Baker delivered during his talkathon was the announcement that he would soon begin publishing his own newspaper, the *Midwest Free Press*. Like all of the enterprises in his Iowa Kingdom, the paper achieved rapid success, with thousands of subscriptions coming in during the first month of publication. President Herbert Hoover, sitting in the White House, pressed a gold telegraph key that started the rotary presses in Baker's Muscatine printshop. Puzzling over this publicity coup, the *Journal of the American Medical Association* noted, "As an engineering feat, the demonstration must have given joy to the presidential cerebrum. As a demonstration of presidential judgement and a sense of the fitness of things, it gave acute pain to the press." An official of the AMA's Bureau of Investigation expressed further indignation in a note to the director of the Food and Drug Administration. "It is an unfortunate fact in the Baker matter," he wrote, "that this outrageous mountebank seems to wield a good deal of political influence."

Dr. Brinkley also helped the KTNT man. As the radio bureaucrats turned up the pressure on his station, KFKB, Doctor wrote to Baker that he was "privately informed that KTNT is to be taken off the air as well as KFKB, providing the American Medical Association can do it. I understand that as soon as they get through with me they are going to fight you. I presume if I lose they will fight you and if I win they won't cite you. Therefore, it would seem that any help you can throw my way would be helping yourself." Brinkley also threw some aid Baker's way by providing tips on effective affidavit-gathering techniques for battling various medical associations and government agencies.

The Brinkley strategy notwithstanding, KTNT came under a fierce attack from Ellis A. Yost, chief examiner for the Federal Radio Commission, who recommended that KTNT be denied a license for broadcasting. Baker dug in his heels and got Congressman Harold McGugin from Kansas' third district to file a brief with the FRC supporting the position of independent radio stations. "Freedom of speech in America is already dead," the brief stated in part, "except for the voices of KWKH and the small independent radio stations of the country." Baker's attorneys also filed their own brief in defense of the station, objecting to Yost's assertion that radio outlets should display "proper respect for the rights, privileges and opinions" of others. Baker's brief called the phrase a "trite and meaningless platitude" that if followed "would prohibit and bar the discussion of any public or controversial question over a radio station and forbid the playing of any particular type of music." Baker's brief declared, "No objectionable programming is shown to have been broadcast, certainly nothing so unreasonable as that with which the Commission must be familiar such as promising women a means of retaining their 'perfect figure' by smoking So and So's cigarette. . . . Why are all station owners not on trial here?"

In a last-ditch effort, Baker himself appeared before the commission in mid-May 1931. Stating that he took "this broadcasting matter as seriously as" the commissioners did, Baker pointed out that he cut off KTNT's receipt of chain programming when ABC radio scheduled a "fortune-teller and clairvoyant" on the lineup. "I immediately sent back the message over their private wire," the former vaudeville mentalist continued, "that positively, under no circumstances, would I ever think of letting any fortune-teller, astrologist, phrenologist, or any other man or woman who attempted to prophesy the future, do over my station, or any other kind of faker." The FRC was grumbling loudly at the time about radio mystics on American air, and Baker obviously hoped to win points with his denunciation. He did, however, stick by his cancer treatments, adding that his hospital was curing "16% of external cancer and 6% of internal cancer," though these estimates of success were much lower than his advertising boasted.

Less than a month later, on June 5, 1931, the Federal Radio Commission voted not to renew KTNT's license. The commission held that the principal issue was that of "the public interest, convenience and necessity in view of the character of the station's operation." Among the reasons given for its decision, the commission cited its view that KTNT programs "included personal and bitter attacks upon individuals, companies, and associations." Furthermore, it noted that "station KTNT has been operated in such a manner as to subordinate the interests of the listening public to those of the licensee, in that the programs have been composed largely of direct selling and price quoting of applicant's merchandise." As the straw that broke the camel's back, the commission also complained of "the use of obscene and indecent language" on KTNT. "Though we may not censor," the commissioners wrote, "it is our duty to see that a standard of refinement fitting our day and generation is maintained."

Like the Kansas goat gland martyr, Iowa's persecuted son resented the action deeply. Having been branded as a radio outlaw, he decided to become one. Shadowing the moves of Dr. Brinkley, Norman Baker lit out for the broadcasting badlands south of the Rio Grande.

After scouting the border and choosing Nuevo Laredo for his new high-powered station, Baker made arrangements to address the Laredo Chamber of Commerce early in 1932. Surely, he thought, his charismatic presence would win Laredoans over, just as Brinkley's had the Del Rioans upriver. Addressing the border-town chamber, Baker told the business leaders of his plans to build XENT, the largest commercial broadcasting station on the North American continent. He said the station would cooperate with the Mexican government to promote "the beauty, the art, the wonders of Mexico" in order to attract tourists and increase commerce in that section of the borderlands.

The American side was promised superwatt publicity as well. Laredo would be mentioned frequently on the station, and its glories exploited far and wide. All Baker wanted the Laredo business concerns to do was spend $5000 on an eight-mile power line to run from the city to XENT, south of Nuevo Laredo. He said that he was spending $250,000 to bring his media giant to the remote border town. It seemed only natural to him that Laredo's commercial leaders would be eager to pitch in and make the small investment that would provide such glamorous rewards to an area so isolated that it was the only place in the United States where peyote grew wild.

The members of the chamber of commerce, however, were not impressed. The town's power elite was composed mainly of family dynasties with two hundred years of tradition and wealth behind them. They could not understand how a Mexican border blaster owned by a purple-suited sharpie from Iowa could possibly improve the quality of life they enjoyed on *la frontera*. After all, Laredo had once been the capital of an independent nation, the Republic of the Rio Grande, and though they whipped up huge fiestas each year to celebrate George Washington's birthday, these descendants of Laredo revolutionaries remained opposed to any appearance of Yankee or Mexican domination. Baker told the president of the chamber of commerce that his associates lacked vision and progressive drive and that many of Laredo's choice retail locations sat boarded up and empty because of such a lack of foresight. Then he set about to raise all the needed funds on his own. One scheme he devised took him back to Muscatine.

Baker's fundraising strategy evolved from his litigious paranoia. Months earlier he had filed a suit against the AMA, seeking $500,000 in damages resulting from Dr. Fishbein's alleged slander in the *Journal of the American Medical Association*. Among other things, Fishbein had blasted Baker for his "obscene mouthings and pernicious promotions." The trial began in Muscatine on February 9, 1932. Each side presented its own expert witnesses and depositions from former patients who said they had been maimed or healed at the Baker Institute. Witnesses for the AMA alleged that many patients were admitted to the Muscatine hospital and treated for cancer without even having the disease. A young man from Maquoketa, Iowa, testified about his visit to the institute. He had visited his own doctor, who had diagnosed his annoying skin condition as ringworm. But the fellow had kept listening to Norman Baker's discussions of cancer on KTNT. The more he listened, the more the slow-healing sore began to take on ghastlier proportions in his mind. He finally decided to visit the Baker Institute and was treated there by a physician who also diagnosed his condition as ringworm. Then, according to the young man's testimony, Harry Hoxsey examined him. Hoxsey concluded that the other doctors were mistaken. "That's a full-fledged cancer," he declared. "Absolutely, we can cure it." Since the patient was in a hurry, Hoxsey administered a "double treatment" for $250. "Well, old boy, we got it the FIRST time," he said after dumping a quantity of yellow powder into the open sore just inside the man's lip. The next day, the patient returned home. By the time he arrived, his mouth was painfully swollen, and he returned to his small-town doctor, who asked him about the curious treatment he had received for ringworm.

Testimony also disclosed that the Baker Institute did not contain a miscroscope. The hospital's namesake did not understand why he needed one. "Please tell me," he inquired of his associates, "how in the hell any surgeon with a patient on the table and his belly laid open can get a microscope in the wound or his belly to test all the surrounding tissue from where they cut out the first bunch." An investigation of the Baker medicine alleged that the personnel at the institute treated external cancer with arsenic powder. For internal cancer, institute employees administered a mixture of carbolic acid, glycerin, alcohol, and a trace of peppermint oil, samples of which were obtained from former patients who had managed to survive. Baker himself refused to hand over his secret treatments to the AMA, saying the "amateur meatcutters" would steal his closely guarded formulas. Another medicine from the Muscatine hospital was alleged to be a mixture of watermelon seeds and cornsilk boiled in water. Occasionally Baker's prescriptions made sense, such as his belief that a good diet and a healthy mental attitude were factors that could help prevent cancer. At other times he was wildly errant, scoffing at doctors' suggestions that too much exposure to rays of the sun increased the risk of skin disease.

Baker became impatient with his attorneys during the trial, believing that they were not going after the doctors with enough venom. He issued long memos telling them how they should handle the case. The attorney who could prove the doctors to be lying, Baker said, "would be heralded throughout the world as a wizard, but none have done it as yet merely because their lives are spent in law and they refuse suggestions from a layman whose years of life have been spent in cancer reading on the 'other side.'" He lumped doctors and lawyers together, calling them both "educated fools."

One of Baker's attorneys might have been more effective if he had not been in fear for his life each time he drove to the courthouse. The at-

torney had the honor of giving his client a lift every morning to the proceedings. Unfortunately, the memory of the KTNT Shoot-out was fresh in
Baker's mind, and the former vaudevillian cradled a submachine gun in
his arms as he rode in the attorney's car. When traffic passed, the eccentric medical man followed the cars in the sights of the weapon, scanning
the barrel right past his attorney's perspiring face. Later, a U.S. marshal
removed a .38 from Baker's pocket in court. Baker's personal protection
did not protect him from the opinion of the jury, which returned a verdict
in favor of the American Medical Association. Baker would get no funds
for XENT from the pocket of Morris Fishbein.

The deposed medico-broadcaster managed to hold onto enough cash
from his various Muscatine investments to purchase a 75-acre ranchero
eight miles south of Nuevo Laredo on the highway to Monterrey. There he
began the long process of constructing his giant radio station while extolling the virtues of his newfound homeland. "All should see Mexico,"
Baker wrote in his lavender-colored pamphlet "Cancer Is Curable."
"Tourists are safer in Mexico than in the U.S. Don't be afraid to stop your
car anywhere on the highway. You don't experience the 'holdups' as you
do in the States. The paved highways are of the finest, and most pictur-
esque." Photos of the Pyramid of the Sun, Mexico City's cathedrals and
Sunken Gardens, and other tropical wonders graced the pamphlet to attract tourists and cancer sufferers to the getaway land of miracles.

After Baker's return to Mexico, a warrant was issued in Muscatine for
the broadcaster's arrest on a charge of conspiracy to violate the medical
laws of Iowa. Muscatine lawmen traveled down to Texas and presented
the warrant to Governor Ross Sterling. Some Texas Rangers were dispatched to Laredo, but Baker could not be lured back across the border
and the Rangers failed to get their man. Iowa newspapers reported that
the purple iconoclast was hiding out in Mexico, a fugitive from justice.

While building his Mexican radio station, Baker kept his Iowa cancer
hospital and his *Midwest Free Press* in full operation. The newspaper
came in handy when he ran for governor of Iowa on the Farmer-Labor
ticket in 1932. The ticket was supported by the United Farm Federation of America, an organization Baker founded to promote his candidacy. Conducting the entire campaign from the shelter of his outpost
on the Rio Grande, the candidate was represented to the voters by a purple sound truck. "TNT Baker" was printed in gold on each side of the
truck over a broom and the slogan "Vote for Baker and Clean Up the
State Grafters." TNT Baker received only five thousand write-in votes.

Will Branch, the Cowtown engineer who built XER, was hired to set
up XENT. It took him more than a year to construct the buildings, the
dual three-hundred-foot towers, the 150,000-watt transmitter, and the

1340-horsepower diesel engines. The international bridge from Laredo cracked under the weight of the massive radio equipment, much of which had been trucked down from Muscatine. The delay was caused in large part by Baker's attempts to take shortcuts. When a certain gasket needed replacing, the station owner attempted to substitute a rubber inner tube. The rubber soon exploded, destroying several expensive parts of the transmitter and adding to the delay. Meanwhile the U.S. State Department and the American Medical Association kept a stakeout on Doc Brinkley's downriver copycat. The secretary of the Nuevo Laredo chamber of commerce wrote the AMA, asking whether Baker would "make a desirable citizen" and if "his business will be obnoxious."

Laredo newspapers, though less cool to the broadcasting carpetbagger than the chamber of commerce was, reported the station's birth with little enthusiasm. The *Laredo Times*, under the headline BIG RADIO STATION TO OPEN HERE SOON, gave a rather indifferent summary of the showman's past. But the story did note that the station was being extensively landscaped, as Baker planned "to make it the leading amusement place of northern Mexico and western Texas." The main studio was designed for both indoor and outdoor broadcasting, and a large patio was constructed for dancing. The planned hotel and entertainment complex was never developed. "I am glad that organized medicine and others closed my station at Muscatine for their opposition inspired me to build XENT, the largest station on this continent," Baker told the *Laredo Times*. "We shall strive to arrange our programs to make them different from the average program."

The *South Texas Citizen* mustered a little more excitement, reprinting the XENT press release verbatim. "The XENT programs," the paper reported, "will be like the KTNT ones, homey, rather than highbrow: the voice of the mellow Calliaphone, The Bells of St. Mary, Beautiful Isle of Somewhere, O Sole Mio, A Hawaiian medley, Mother Machree, a medley of old songs, Negro spirituals, stirring marches, My Mother's Bible . . . the Kiddie's Hour, the recipes, the stirring talks by Baker, impressive talks by others, the Calliaphone, taps. . . . No advertising or fake stocks and bonds, or fake or shoddy material of any kind; nothing against the interest of the people, and enough against their enemies." Baker also pledged that he would use his new station as a mouthpiece for international peace.

XENT finally went on the air shortly after Christmas in 1933. Station offices were set up in downtown Laredo to handle American advertising sales. A Baker Hospital was opened in the border town, and "Cancer Is Curable" pamphlets soon appeared in a bilingual format. The Muscatine hospital was leased to a succession of Baker-controlled physicians and remained in operation under his name, publicized by the far-reaching Mexican radio station.

The "eccentric genius" wrote to Texas governor Miriam "Ma" Ferguson and implored her to investigate his claims of a cure for cancer. Baker asked Ferguson to select thirty test patients for a treatment at his expense and to appoint a committee of a dozen Texas citizens to judge the success or failure of the results. After Texas' only female governor ignored the request, Baker's publicity stated that she had received so many calls and letters begging her to investigate the cure that other gubernatorial matters suffered a lack of attention. When Ma was not reelected the following year, Baker boasted that his thousands of Texas followers had played a substantial role in her defeat.

Much of the evidence suggests that the cancer-fighting layman truly believed in the value of his treatments. He made his same plea for investigation to numerous other political figures, including President Hoover and the governor of Iowa. Institute publicity offered to pay $5000 "to any person who furnishes evidence proving that Norman Baker misrepresents when he stated cancer is being cured at the Baker Hospital, Muscatine, Iowa." Two days after Christmas in 1935 he even wrote to Dr. Morris Fishbein, in a "spirit of fairness," and requested that the AMA official help administer a test of the Baker treatment. "I am very sincere in this matter," Baker wrote to the man he had unsuccessfully sued for $500,000 on a charge of slander, "and ask that you put aside any prejudice, or malice and put the matter to this test. The world will be convinced of two things; namely, that Norman Baker is a fraud and the Baker treatment useless and should be condemned and that they should stop the treatment, or that the Baker treatment is a cure for cancer and tumor and for both external and internal cancer. . . . Can there be a need of anything more valuable than a cure for cancer? With every good wish for the holiday season and hoping to have an answer to my offer, I remain . . . Yours truly, Norman Baker." But there was no response, and the treatment was never tested under scientifically controlled conditions.

Baker, whom Harry Hoxsey once described as a "handsome, wavy-haired, middle-aged, aggressive personality with hypnotic eyes," became something of a mysterious playboy in Nuevo Laredo. Border-radio legend has it that he kept a bed in the XENT studio and would often broadcast his thoughts and feelings on politics and medicine while having sex with his mistress.

Another, more shadowy picture of the maverick broadcaster was furnished by M. N. Bunker, president of the American Institute of Grapho-Analysis of Kansas City, who visited Baker in Mexico in 1934. Baker had contacted Bunker about a handwriting analysis program for XENT.

Arriving in Laredo, Bunker checked into a hotel and then proceeded across the bridge and down the Pan-American Highway to the station. The XENT buildings were unmistakable, the mission-style exteriors all done in a brilliant shade of purple.

"A huge police dog was giving sufficient warning that we had arrived so that shortly a sloppy woman leaned over a back bannister on a stair landing" and asked Bunker what he wanted, the graphologist wrote a few years later in *American Freeman* magazine. "Explaining my business and that I had traveled from Kansas City to the radio station under the impression that they wished me to handle a series of programs, the slattern backed off with a grunt" and told Bunker to come upstairs.

"We climbed the rickety pair of stairs and were given seats in a room that was a conglomeration of books, junk, this and that, old printed matter, and almost everything that a junk heap might have in it. In a tiny office adjoining, a white-haired man sat with his shirt open to the top of his trousers, exposing a rather expansive stomach. 'Set down,' he yelled.

"Puzzled, intrigued, even fascinated by the finesse of the reception as compared with radio stations on this side of the border, I 'set.' After a few minutes the Flowing White Hair and Belly got up and waddled out and thrust out a hand.

"'I'm Doctor Baker. I've had an awful day, and I can't be bothered with you now. You can go back into town; you can find the Europa Cafe, and go in there and wait for me and don't go across the border because. . . .'"

The handwriting expert was interested and a little frightened, but he waited at the Nuevo Laredo cafe. "Finally a lavender car, two women, and the doctor (all dressed up) came in, the belly shaking vigorously, and under the apparent impression that noise made learning. He sat with us, and told us what foods to select."

Baker asked Bunker what he knew about radio. Bunker related his fair amount of experience. "The Belly was emphatic and the white hair shook. 'Well, I know more about radio than any (son of a bitch) living. You stick by me and I'll make you.'"

Baker then launched into a treatise on his cancer cure and a résumé of all his Tangley activities. Bunker decided to give it a try and stuck it out at the border blaster for four days. But the job did not pan out. According to Bunker, Baker wanted him to state on his program "that a woman in California has written you and that you can see from her handwriting that Upton Sinclair is going to carry the State of California by the greatest majority in the history of the world or the state." Bunker did not comply. Next, Baker insisted that he pretend to analyze a letter from a female listener who wondered what was wrong with her: "I was supposed to tell her from her handwriting that she had cancer, and that by going to one of the Baker hospitals she could be cured of this disease." Shortly afterward, Bunker returned to Kansas City.

Other specialists adjusted better to Baker's unorthodox managerial style. Dr. C. T. Betts was a dentist from Toledo who was particularly concerned about the dangers of using aluminumware as cooking utensils. He began his association with Baker by writing an antialuminum column in *TNT Magazine,* and soon the broadcaster himself took up the fight, urging his listeners to "throw all aluminumware out of the kitchen. Throw it away. I don't care what you paid for it." Many responded to Baker's insistence that "one half of the cancers in the U.S. are caused by eating out of vessels made with aluminum." One listener thanked Baker for his warning, testifying that "if it hadn't been for Mr. Baker we probably would be using aluminum as yet." When Baker moved to the border, he and Betts established the American Medical Associates to distribute medical talks to stations across the country. Betts forwarded all inquiries from listeners to Baker, who sent the anxious respondents advertisements for his hospitals, courtesy of the "AMA."

Members of the other AMA did not believe that Baker's strudent testimonials and medical activities were really undertaken "for the sake of humanity." Officials of the Texas State Board of Medical Examiners wrote to the national doctors' club, requesting information about the broadcaster's unsuccessful libel suit. "We are doing our best to stop Baker's broadcasting in Mexico, as we finally succeeded with Brinkley, who is now on the high seas," the board's secretary wrote overconfidently to the medical investigators in 1934.

A letter from a doctor at the prestigious Scott and White Clinic in Temple, requesting information about the Baker hospitals, reveals the effectiveness of Baker's radio pitch. "Last night while returning from Laredo, Texas," the doctor wrote in 1936, "I heard a radio program with Doctor Baker discussing the Baker Cancer Treatment with positive statements that the cancer treatment which he had instituted in 1929 was still showing six year cures. . . . He further stated if his treatment had not proved up as he had said, the United States Government would certainly not allow him to continue in operation. . . . It is certainly difficult for a great many people not to believe what he says when they hear such programs in such clear English and given so convincingly." Another XENT listener was shocked to hear Baker deliver vicious anti-Semitic slurs. The listener told the AMA that Baker had accused Jews of "killing people by their claiming to have a cure for cancer" and had recommended that "all of them ought to be taken back to Germany and let Hitler do to them what he wants to."

The doctor who took Baker's presence most personally, however, was Dr. Albert Cook of Laredo. A member of the American Medical Association, Dr. Cook was inspired to action when he read in the association's journal that "if this Mexican practice is to continue without interference, American users of the radio may well anticipate for the coming years as the dominating theme of the broadcasts to which they may listen the lamenting and feeble baa-baa of the castrated goat and the blatant charlatanism of Norman Baker. Oft in the still night will come the voices from over the Rio Grande beseeching the use of the liver pill, the kidney pill and the woman's pill."

The Laredo doctor wrote to Dr. Fishbein in Chicago, urging prompt action against the Baker enterprise. "He came here almost broke," Dr. Cook noted, "having spent his ill-gotten gains in a series of court fights in Iowa. He is now well along toward the accumulation of another million dollars for his War Chest. A million dollar breakwork in Mexico that cannot be beaten down with nickel bullets."

Failing to receive the desired assistance from the AMA, Dr. Cook started "a one-man revolution against Baker. . . . I may not have conducted the fight according to the rules of Sherlock Holmes and Philo Vance but I have put more fleas in Baker's hair than he has been able to scratch with ten fingers."

Dr. Cook did engage in a bit of detective-style intrigue, establishing relationships with several former XENT employees and paying the informants out of his own pocket. Labor relations had never been Baker's specialty. Once when he needed a good engineer, he phoned Emilio Azcárraga at the Radio Department in Mexico City. Sitting in Azcárraga's office was Nestor Cuesta, a knowledgeable young engineer who had worked with James Weldon at Dr. Brinkley's radio station in Villa Acuña. Cuesta accepted the job and moved to Nuevo Laredo. When the first payday rolled around, he discovered that Baker had quoted his salary in pesos—not dollars, as Cuesta had been led to believe. The engineer stayed at XENT only six months before moving on to another border blaster in Reynosa.

After Cuesta left Nuevo Laredo, an engineer told another employee that he planned to wreck the XENT transmitter and installed pieces of equipment that would quickly destroy the powerful apparatus. Almost immediately, Baker realized that something was wrong and ordered loyal employees to detain the fleeing engineer and his fellow mutineers. The rebels galloped across the border, racing toward the home of Dr. Cook. Baker called the Laredo sheriff and urged him to cut the saboteurs off at the pass. The sheriff did not manage to catch the culprits, and XENT was off the air several weeks for transmitter repairs. According to the revised edition of Baker's biography, *Doctors, Dynamiters and Gunmen*, the station returned to the airwaves and shortly thereafter broadcast a special two-hour program produced for the Mexican government and "especially dedicated to the United States," with a lengthy address by Ambassador Josephus Daniels.

Stanley Baker, the broadcaster's nephew, commented that he had worked at the Nuevo Laredo station for "a couple of years but finally on his big ranchero in Tamaulipas the snakes, tarantulas, bugs, and the terrible summer heat and humidity of the Rio Grande Valley got to me so I left in the fall and never went back." Like his nephew, Norman Baker grew homesick in the foreign land and kept up with his contacts in the Hawkeye State. In 1935 he applied to the federal government for a permit to operate a new station in Muscatine. Predictably, the application was denied. The following year he celebrated the Texas centennial by running for U.S. Senator in Iowa. This time he did campaign in person, touring the state with a calliaphone and a caravan of three purple cars with "XENT" gilded on the doors. The candidate handed out campaign literature printed in orchid and purple and always wore his famous lavender suits and purple ties on the stump. "I like those beautiful colors," Baker told the press, "and if I was to do as Mark Twain did, instead of wearing a white full dress suit it would be lavender and purple—just to be different." Baker emphasized the uniqueness of his campaign by adopting the slogan "So Different." Different as he was, the radioman lost the nomination, though he did receive an impressive 27,000 votes. Having aimed his campaign at the constituency that supported the populist movements of Dr. Francis Everett Townsend and Father Coughlin, Baker told the Iowa press after the race that he planned to form a Bull-Moose Progressive party in the state.

While Baker was shaking hands and kissing babies in the corn belt, he and two employees were indicted by a federal grand jury in Laredo for violating a section of the Federal Communications Act of 1934—Section 325(b) to be exact, commonly known as the Brinkley clause. Baker was accused of exporting sound recordings for the purpose of broadcasting them back into the United States in violation of federal legislation that had been passed specifically to stop the activities of border radio operators. Baker alleged that Dr. Cook had instigated this new harrassment by feeding information to the feds and that the Texas State Board of Medical Examiners was also conspiring to get him. The board had recently threatened several of the physicians in Baker's Laredo hospital with revocation of their licenses unless they left his employ.

Baker and the employees, E. R. Rood and Roy Richardson, stood trial in Laredo federal court in April 1937. All three were found guilty.

Baker received the heaviest sentence, six months in jail and a $2000 fine, and he quickly appealed the decision. In a rare victory for Baker, the appeals court overturned the decision and ruled in favor of him. The court's ruling spelled out the limitations of actions under the Brinkley clause, maintaining that the exporting and rebroadcasting of electrical transcriptions and phonograph records did not come under the purview of the legislation.

While Baker spent time on the campaign trail and in the courtroom, XENT continued to broadcast its unique sound across the continent. A typical programming day began at six in the evening, when the 150,000-watt signal could reach the farthest. A Mexican orchestra spiced up folks' suppertime, followed by variety programs called *Tune Corral*, *Memory Lane*, and *Mexican String Orchestra* and an address by Norman Baker. Programs such as *The Islanders, Popular Dance Orchestra, Helping Hand, Grab Bag, Cuban Orchestra*, and *Hit Parade* entertained audiences throughout the evening, punctuated every ninety minutes with "stirring talks by Baker." The Hillbilly Boys, led by future Texas governor W. Lee O'Daniel, were one of the most popular acts on XENT and advertised O'Daniel's Hillbilly Flour with a lively blend of hillbilly and sacred music. The Mexican Típica Orchestra greeted the sun's return to the banks of the Rio Grande, re-creating the romance of Old Mexico until the station signed off at seven-thirty in the morning.

Baker finally decided to clear his record of the Iowa medical conspiracy charge that had tracked him to the border five years earlier. Found guilty, he served one day in the Muscatine jail and paid a small fine. Several hundred supporters and a brass band greeted Baker as he stepped out of the jail to freedom. "I went to jail for you!" he screamed triumphantly. His hospital advertising shouted the same refrain, beneath a photo of the martyr emerging from behind the iron bars.

When Doc Brinkley bought the beautiful Shrine Country Club south of Little Rock and moved his hospital from Del Rio, Baker watched with envious approval. Even though the *Laredo Times* wrote in 1937 that Baker "has done, perhaps, more than any other individual to make the name of Laredo known throughout the world," many Laredoans had remained consistently cold to the cancer battler's presence on the border, and problems continued at the Muscatine hospital. Besides, Arkansas had traditionally allowed Hippocratic methodology and innovation that most other states shunned. The state was one of a handful that still provided licenses to doctors with the Eclectic degree. It must have given Baker insomnia to hear Brinkley advertising his new medical mecca as the Most Beautiful Hospital in the World. So he fired up the purple-mobile and went hunting for real estate.

Baker found what he was looking for in Eureka Springs, in the northwest corner of Arkansas, where the Ozarks begin to seduce a traveler's senses. Motoring into Eureka Springs, Baker found a little town strung through a beautiful wooded area of deep gulches and towering hills. Long before white men came to the area, the natural mineral springs had been known for their curative power by the Cherokee, Sioux, and Osage. One of the many names later bestowed upon the town was Indian Healing Spring. In 1854 Alvah Jackson, a pioneer doctor, became the first white man to discover the springs. A short time later, a product called Dr. Jackson's Eye-Water appeared on the market.

As news of the "wonder water" spread, health-conscious settlers started an aqua rush into Eureka Springs. The healing waters, flowing from more than sixty springs in the area, were reputed to cure at least 25 diseases, ranging from cancer to baldness. Eureka became a bustling health resort, the City That Water Built. Known by a variety of names, including the Little Switzerland of America, and Siloam of the Afflicted, the resort's peak of popularity lasted from 1885 to 1910.

The real estate that Baker purchased in Believe-It-Or-Not-Town was the Crescent Hotel. A magnificent five-story structure perched on a mountain high above the town, the hotel became known as The Grand Old Lady of the Ozarks. Formally opened in 1886, the Crescent was constructed of Arkansas limestone from the White River quarry in a style that has been described as a mixture of Victorian, French Gothic, and Italian Renaissance. The cost of construction was a staggering $294,000. With its turrets, spires, balconies, and sumptuous interior, the hotel well deserved its title Castle in the Wilderness.

The combination of the town's legendary history and the eccentric grandeur of the Crescent Hotel appealed to Norman Baker. In July 1937 he picked up the huge edifice at a bargain, since the hotel had operated at a loss since the Depression. Purists of Victorian architecture in Eureka Springs had fits when Baker began his renovation of one of the town's most cherished landmarks. He removed all the interior doors in the hotel and painted most of the walls his favorite color. The grand lobby suffered a technique called polychroming and was redone in a bright but gaudy combination of red, yellow, orange, and black. Baker's purple office was sealed off from the lobby by bulletproof glass. And just in case the American Medical Association or the Federal Communications Commission launched an armed assault on Crescent Mountain, the hotel's proprietor kept two submachine guns on the wall within arm's reach of his desk. From the roof, of course, a calliaphone blasted out over the Ozarks.

Though many Eurekans probably advocated running Baker out of town on a rail, some of the business people hoped that the cancer clinic would rejuvenate the town's commercial scene. As the hospital readied for its first patients, the *Eureka Springs Daily Times Echo* noted that Baker would be singing the praises of the Gem of the Ozarks far and wide. "Mr. Baker is owner of the broadcasting station XENT," the paper noted, "the second most powerful radio station on the North American continent— heard in two Americas and in other nations of the world. Let us not lose sight of the fact that as long as Norman Baker prospers in Eureka Springs, likewise the city and every property owner and businessman."

Publicity began to gush out of the World's Most Beautiful Health Resort. Pamphlets extolled the virtues of the perfected Baker cancer treatment. "We cure cancer and tumors without operations, radium or X-rays. We treat all ailments. We do not cut out any organ." The hospital was the place "Where Sick Folks Get Well." The Castle in the Air was advertised as being two thousand feet above sea level, "above the malaria line. . . . Mosquitos rare." Baker urged those in need of treatment or anyone who would come to "bring your knit bag, books, music, fishing tackle, golf outfit and your fiddle—WE ARE JUST LIKE ONE BIG FAMILY living in a mansion like plain folks."

The hospital began to prosper, aided by its founder's harangues on the airwaves from the Rio Grande. "Norman Baker is one of the most interesting speakers on the radio," his booklets modestly informed, "and can be heard nightly from XENT, in Nuevo Laredo, Mexico, on 910 kilocycles, in a series of interesting health and commonsense talks."

But the cancer clinic was not to last long in America's Most Unique City. The "interesting health and commonsense" information that Baker sent out in promotional mailers caught the attention of postal inspectors, after strenuous efforts by a newly elected prosecutor whom Baker had attacked on XENT. Early in 1940, about the same time Little Rock lawyers were preparing malpractice suits against Dr. Brinkley (and not long after Baker had turned 57 at the largest birthday party ever held in Arkansas), a grand jury in that city returned an indictment charging Norman Baker with mail fraud. The trial was held in federal court in Little Rock and lasted fourteen days, breaking the record for the longest court proceeding in Arkansas history. Throughout the trial, Baker wore his lavender suits and his purple ties, perhaps believing that they would magically protect him.

His luck ran out late in January when a guilty verdict was returned and a sentence of four years' imprisonment and a $4000 fine was handed down. The jury had apparently listened to the prosecutor, who charged that the Baker physicians "gave the same treatment to everyone, whether for a broken pelvis or a wart on the nose." Baker took the case to a higher court, basing his appeal on a claim that the jury had been drunk. The appeal was denied.

The sartorially resplendent cancer wizard and radio star traded his tailored purple suits for prison grays and entered Leavenworth prison on March 23, 1941. No record survives to settle the issue, but it's doubtful that the warden allowed Baker to purplefy his new residence.

Nor would prison officials allow him to cut transcriptions for broadcast on his border blaster. Without its master, XENT limped along in a state of flux. Baker signed a power of attorney allowing a trusted employee to sell the station's property in Laredo and Nuevo Laredo. Some reports say the Texas Quality Network paid a handsome sum to obtain the hardware and real estate. Another border radio legend contends that the associate sold XENT to a pair of drunk soldier boys she met in a Nuevo Laredo bar. In Eureka Springs the Crescent Hotel sat ghostly and empty through World War II. Then some new investors purchased the property and began the arduous task of undoing the Grand Old Lady's peculiar renovations.

After his release from Leavenworth, Baker returned to Muscatine and attempted to open the Baker Research Foundation, but Iowa officials blocked the effort. Though his prime money-making scheme had been effectively destroyed, the notorious Baker still had plenty of his profits stashed away. Eventually he retired to Florida, where he lived aboard a luxurious yacht called the *Niagara*, formerly owned by financier Jay Gould. He played the stock market, fought for impeachment of the judge who had sentenced him to prison, and puttered with pipe dreams of a national health center.

Baker died on the yacht in 1958. His passing added a bleak dimension of irony to his career, as his death was reported to have been precipitated by cancer of the liver. A rebel to the end, the dying man refused to seek treatment because he still did not trust doctors.

Upon his death, two of his most trusted associates set fire to the archives of the Baker hospitals and XENT. Many still believed that Baker had been unjustly persecuted. "The fact remains," said border radio personality Dallas Turner, "that I myself have talked to people who claim they were cured of cancer by Norman Baker. So if it would only work in one case out of ten thousand, I don't think they should have crucified the man like they did. They should have just let him lay in bed and broadcast and make love at the same time. Don't you think so?"

Down on the Rio Grande, tall tales continue to infuse the legend of this unusual man, just as they do Doc Brinkley's. Rumor has it that Norman Baker cached $1 million somewhere in Mexico before he died. Dreaming of Sierra Madre, many a fortune seeker from Muscatine and the two Laredos has gone hunting for the fabled stash. But like most stories of lost gold and buried treasure, as common in the Southwest landscape as prickly pear cactus, the mythic loot has never been found. Perhaps it waits in the desert still.

Border Blaster at Black Rock

Down in old Piedras Negras That's where it all began; To a great broadcasting station Came a young and handsome man. Just a smiling Texas cowboy, Few could ride and rope with him . . . . His name was Nolan Rinehart, But they called him Cowboy Slim . . . . He was loved by countless millions Who heard his nightly show From the big broadcasting stations In romantic Mexico. Cowboy Slim, the master pitchman, Soon was rollin' in the dough . . . . He could have sold an icebox To a freezin' Eskimo.

—From "Cowboy Slim Rinehart," by Dallas Turner

While Del Rio and Villa Acuña celebrated XER Gala Week in October 1931, residents of Eagle Pass and Piedras Negras 56 miles downriver watched the dizzy festivities with envy. Even before the Acuña border blaster's official opening, the *Eagle Pass Daily Guide* featured regular updates on the progress of the "wonderful radio station" that pledged to give the borderlands "an aerial voice which can be heard from Del Rio to far-off Australia and New Zealand."

The business community of Eagle Pass saw Dr. Brinkley grabbing national publicity for Del Rio and realized that it was about to fall further behind in the race for tourism and industry. Just ten days after local talent returned from performing at the XER fandango, the *Eagle Pass Daily Guide* declared that the town needed publicity. The secretary of the chamber of commerce, on the defensive after the coup his Del Rio counterpart had pulled off, denied that Eagle Pass was being "discriminated against." The reason more travelers were going to Laredo and Del Rio, he said, was because residents of his town needed to "get busy and tell folks what we have." Eagle Pass was founded as a coal mining town in the 1880's; hence the name for its sister city across the Rio Grande—Piedras Negras, or "black rocks." As industries substituted oil for coal, the mine lost its importance. The city began to bill itself as the Gateway to Mexico and looked for its future in the tomatoes, cabbages, and cauliflower produced by farmers in the area. Eagle Pass proudly served as the hub for what became known as South Texas' Winter Garden District, and it boasted of fishing, hunting, prospecting, and one of the few paved roads all the way from the border to San Antonio.

Additionally, the secretary pointed out that Eagle Pass offered visitors the chance to "see the greatest irrigation project in the history of the State of Texas." The Quemado Valley development, about twenty miles northwest of Eagle Pass, was a 12,800-acre irrigation project developed at a reported cost of more than $5 million. The first 1000 acres were sold shortly before XER's initial broadcast, and the sale marked the opening of the area to settlers. The majority of the land was to be developed into large irrigated citrus farms.

Eagle Pass boosters took the secretary's words to heart and soon decided they needed a little ol' border blaster of their own. Two weeks after XER began regular broadcasts, the *Daily Guide* announced, GIANT RADIO UNIT PROPOSED FOR PIEDRAS NEGRAS. Though the chambers of commerce of Eagle Pass and Piedras Negras heartily endorsed the project, the idea was initially proposed by two promoters from San Antonio. Fort Worth engineer Will Branch, who built XER and other border stations coast-to-coast, came on board as part owner and contractor. The San Antonio promoters had been part of the Pan-American Good Will Flight of 1930, a tour of Mexico and Central America for U.S. businessmen. In addition to publicizing the charms of Eagle Pass, the Winter Garden District, and the Quemado Valley, the proposed station was to be used for "rebroadcasting chain programs originating on low wave in Central American countries," referred to by radiophiles as the banana band. The Pan-American Highway was under construction at the time, and a radio relay starting from as far south as Panama was recommended to inform Americans of tourist attractions on the long international roadway.

The Eagle Pass Lions Club endorsed the proposed border blaster, and a subscription drive was begun to fund the project with advance advertising sales. A Maverick County judge agreed to hold the funds in escrow until the station was ready to go on the air. Business concerns on both sides of the Rio Grande anted up to get things started and tried to top one another in border-blasting enthusiasm. The mayor of Eagle Pass said it would "mean new life" for his border town. Buck Taylor, sales director for the Quemado Valley irrigation project, believed that the "resultant publicity will give these cities a burst of life such as they have never yet dreamed of." The owner of Riskind's Department Store said, "The station will put our towns on the map, modernize them, keep them abreast of the times. We must keep up."

The Winter Garden Railway kicked in $3875 for the radio fund. Landowners south of the Rio Grande vied for the honor of donating land for the station site. The chairman of the Piedras Negras Chamber of Commerce was dispatched to Mexico City to apply for the broadcasting license. Pablo Valdez, senior senator from the state of Coahuila who handled negotiations for XER's permit, came out in favor of the new station named XEPN, after Eagle Pass-Piedras Negras. Two days before Christmas the application was approved via telegraph from the Secretary of Communications in Mexico City. The Compañía Radiofusora de Piedras Negras was officially in business, though it would still be nearly a year before XEPN began to blast its "clarion call through the ether."

Meanwhile Buck Taylor was talking up the Quemado Valley irrigation project to the Brinkley organization, and he established a Del Rio office early in 1932 to handle land buyers arriving from the North. A few days later, the *Eagle Pass Daily Guide* noted the magic of radio with a report on two potential Quemado investors who had come down from the Panhandle after hearing Minnie Brinkley advertise the project on XER. And her husband stated that the Acuña station was receiving 30,000 letters a week inquiring about the Del Rio-Eagle Pass area.

At the end of January a grand dream of Doctor's seemed destined to come true. Three hundred people from the two border towns gathered on the banks of Las Moras Creek, in the heart of the sprawling Quemado irrigation project, for speeches and ground-breaking ceremonies for a brand-new Texas metropolis to be named Brinkley.

As newsreel cameras recorded the historic occasion, Doctor (whom the *Eagle Pass Daily Guide* called the Wizard of Station XER) extolled the virtues of the extensive Quemado Valley. Real estate dealers from Kansas and Del Rio assured rapid development of the new town, initially offering twenty lots for business concerns and thirty lots for private homes. People wishing to homestead in the model city were told that all buildings must be constructed of fireproof materials. Streets in the brave new burg were to be named after Dr. Brinkley's associates. The fabulous vision of Brinkley City, however, sank into the muddy canals.

Work began on XEPN early in the spring of 1932 and continued through the summer and fall. The stuccoed building that housed the massive transmitter was located nine miles northwest of Piedras Negras, directly across the Rio Grande from the local power plant. Broadcasting studios were established in the Yolanda Hotel in Eagle Pass and the Casino Club in Piedras Negras. The American studio was later moved to the Eagle Hotel, and the Mexican studio was moved to the International Hotel, a building that housed General Venustiano Carranza's troops during the 1910 Mexican Revolution. Will Branch said the Yolanda studio, beautifully furnished with a $3000 grand piano with room for a thirteen-piece orchestra, was "one of the best hotel studios on the border." XEPN was the first station in which border radio veteran Branch had a personal stake. He pledged that his "showplace of engineering" would present "programs" and not "hum-drum, hurdy-gurdy affairs with canned music."

To back up his pledge, Branch sent broadcast supervisor Dan Hosmer to Chicago and other big cities on a talent safari. In September came the announcement that 42 radio stars had been signed. Programming on XEPN followed the eclectic variety format generally found on most thirties border stations. In addition to a "snappy jazz orchestra," the hub of the Winter Garden welcomed rural comedians Ma and Pa Smithers, a pair of blind harmony singers sponsored by Willard's Tablets, an operatic contralto, Houston blues singer Ora Starnes, and the Original Uncle Buster and His International Hot-Timers, a six-piece old-time fiddlers' band that also did humorous skits. From WFAA in Dallas came a fellow named Peg Moreland, "an old stage driver who croons the ditties of the camps and the songs of the trail." His broadcasts were said to be "different from the general type of cowboy yodelers." From East Texas came Shorty Malone, a "dandy clarinet player."

XEPN was due to begin test broadcasts in early September, but its maiden flight was postponed half a dozen times that autumn as torrential floods roared down the Rio Grande. In the interim, pitchmen polished their routines and musicians played the cabarets of Piedras Negras.

But the citizens of Eagle Pass and Coahuila were radio-happy and could not restrain their enthusiasm much longer. Store windows were adorned with the XEPN motif. The Aztec Theatre paid tribute with new pictures by Will Rogers and the Marx Brothers. A deluxe radio edition of the *Eagle Pass Daily Guide* was announced. When it hit the streets on November 5, 1932, the front page shouted, STATION XEPN TO CLAIM ATTENTION OF WORLD NEXT WEEK.

The 100,000-watt broadcast facility was dubbed the Voice of the Western Hemisphere. The special radio issue of the *Daily Guide* was well stocked with ads welcoming XEPN, just as the *Del Rio Evening News* had welcomed XER. The Eagle Pass chroniclers envisioned a fantastic brave new world of border blasting: "Music of the golden Southwest, the twang of the guitar, the soft, faraway melodies of Mexico, the yodel of the cowboy, the drawl of a Southern-born announcer—this will be heard by the fur trader by his red-hot stove in the cold North, by the oil engineer in the jungles of South America, by the Englishman muttering his 'By Jove' in a tavern, and by the millions of our own fast-moving, business-loving American people, by all who have the privilege to own a radio."

The official XEPN inauguration took place a few weeks later. The mayors of Eagle Pass and Piedras Negras and other officials gave brief addresses, and Coahuila governor Naario Ortiz Garza spoke over remote control from Saltillo. C. M. Bres's daughter opened a bottle of champagne at the microphone to christen the new border blaster.

Soon the Western Hemisphere was hearing about Eagle Pass and Piedras Negras. But engineer Will Branch still had a few bugs to work out of his experimental superpower technology. During one broadcast interruption, he snapped at a local reporter, "People should not expect us to turn on such a complicated instrument the same way we turn on a washing machine. It has to be tuned and adjusted." Another time he chastised the Eagle Pass Lions Club, complaining that many in the community appeared to want his radio station discredited or closed down. He said the Gateway to Mexico had "all the possibilities of being the largest city on the Mexican border" and that XEPN could help make it so if given a chance.

Local attention may have been temporarily diverted from the border blaster by a glamorous visit from Tinseltown. Hollywood came to the border in May 1933, when a San Antonio franchise of the National Picture Company filmed *Across the Rio Grande* in Maverick County and north Coahuila. The "sonologue" picture included a scene in which the movie stars drove a herd of cattle across the Eagle Pass-Piedras Negras international bridge. Other nonshowbiz talk centered on a pair of ranchers from Alpine, Texas, held captive in Coahuila for ten days by notorious bandit leader Candelario Baeza.

During the era that XEPN broadcast—the Depression of the thirties—the American popular imagination was captivated by the romantic image of the singing cowboy. Hillbilly performers traded their bibbed overalls for embroidered shirts and Stetson hats as audiences began to expect their favorite country musicians to display a western flair. Western screen heroes such as Ken Maynard, Tex Ritter, and Leonard Slye, better known as Roy Rogers, sat by flickering Hollywood campfires and sang of the lonesome trail, the stars at night, and the wide-open spaces of adventurous opportunity. The early cowboy musicals often combined the spell of western skies with the romance of radio and other marvels of modern technology. One of Gene Autry's earliest films was *Radio Ranch*, an action adventure in which the range-riding cowboy star outwitted a society of subterranean aliens with the help of the kids in his radio fan club. Whether in the movie house or on the radio, the cowboy singers represented a vanishing breed of free-spirited, rugged individualists riding the wave of Depression-era high tech.

An endless stream of musical vaqueros rode into Eagle Pass and Piedras Negras to appear on XEPN. Often they appeared to be drifting on an informal circuit that took them to other radio stations in Acuña, Reynosa, Nuevo Laredo, Monterrey—any place a radio entrepreneur could get a permit. Some were real cowboys and some were the drugstore version, but all dressed the part in boots, bandannas, and other exotic *frontera* wear. The more-popular cowboys pitched their own songbooks on the radio. In the days before record players were household items, sheet music sales were a musician's bread and butter, and the cowboy songbooks were a direct extension of the Tin Pan Alley sheet music tradition. Many of the radio buckaroos had names to match their getups: Utah Cowboy, Lonesome Cowhand, Cowboy Max, Rio Grande Cowboys, Cowboy Sam Nichols, Cowboy Jack, Red River Dave, and Tex Ivey and His Original Ranch Boys.

Cowboy singers came to the border from everywhere. The Rambling Cowboys came from the High Plains country of Lubbock. Shelly Lee Alley's Cowboy Band rode into Eagle Pass from the bayous of Houston. And Doc Schneider and His Yodeling Texas Cowboys pulled in from Atlanta. Cowboy Troubadour Rex Kelley serenaded the hemisphere from Piedras Negras for a brief time, later enjoying some success under the name Buck Nation. "I met him in 1946," XEPN historian Dallas Turner remembered. "The man was drinkin' himself to death. . . . He was married to a girl named Texann, and she divorced him and married Merle Travis and then, I think, divorced Merle Travis and married Buck Nation again."

Another border singer whom Turner heard about was not so lucky in the land of romance. This cowboy "had a brief singing career on XEPN and got friendly with a beautiful Mexican senorita. His intentions were not honorable, and the girl's father and brothers met this old boy on the international bridge and proceeded to work him over with a tire jack. Then they took out the pocketknife and did a little operatin'. Some say they just cut him up; others say they actually succeeded in castrating that old boy."

The number one singing wrangler in Eagle Pass, however, was Cowboy Slim Rinehart. Sometimes called the King of Border Radio, Slim was born Nolan Rinehart in the ranch country near Gustine, Texas, in 1911. After broadcasting on a 250-watt station in Brady, Cowboy Slim packed up his guitar and headed for Eagle Pass. Dallas Turner, who later served a singing cowboy apprenticeship to Rinehart, recalled the story he heard of Slim's winning a job on XEPN. Don Howard, musical director of the station, told Turner that when he first auditioned Cowboy Slim Rinehart, he was not impressed with his musical style. In fact, Howard thought the gangly young cowpoke was the worst singer he'd ever heard. Then XEPN pitchman Major Kord heard a transcription of the audition. The Major said, "That is the greatest cowboy singer I've ever heard in my life. That's how a cowboy would actually sound. I'll put that boy on the air, and I'll stake a week's wages that he will pull more mail than everybody on this station put together."

During Cowboy Slim's first few broadcasts, some of the veteran musicians sat outside the studio window, making fun of the novice border songbird. "You won't be laughing a week from Monday," Major Kord warned.

And a week from Monday, as Turner recalled the story, "Cowboy Slim Rinehart pulled more commercial mail than every single act on XEPN put together." The King of Border Radio had assumed his throne in the studio on the Rio Grande. As his popularity grew, he syndicated his transcription programs on all the superpowered Mexican stations from Tijuana to Tampico.

Rinehart teamed up for several transcription sessions with singing cowgirl Patsy Montana. With her 1935 recording of "I Want to Be a Cowboy's Sweetheart," Montana achieved the first major country hit by a female artist and paved the way for many others. Her career was well under way when she traveled to Texas from the National Barn Dance in Chicago. But she was already familiar with border radio. "I used to get up real early in Chicago," she said, "and listen to border stations before I went to work. One day I heard my records being played, and they said the singer was Patsy somebody else. I had my lawyer write a letter down there and they called me Patsy Montana from then on."

At the time Patsy Montana made transcriptions, Major Kord had a studio in his garage in San Antonio. She recalled her surprise when, having left the cold Windy City, she arrived in a place where there were "roses blooming in the backyard." Although Patsy thought that Cowboy Slim could not sing harmonies very well, border radio fans across the country enjoyed their programs, which always ended with a so-long from the singing cowboy: "Well, ladies and gentlemen, the old clock on the wall says we've got to be ridin' out of the studios. Until our next period of broadcast, this is Cowboy Slim Rinehart, and I'm also speakin' for America's number one singin' cowgirl, Patsy Montana. We're sayin' so long, everybody. Good luck to you, and above all, my friends, we do wish you good health." The high-pitched voice of the singing cowgirl then chimed in, "Wait for me, Slim." "Okay, Patsy," Slim chuckled, as the duo closed their show with "Happy in the Saddle Again." Patsy did not realize how popular her partner's broadcasts were until she took Cowboy Slim on a tour of the East Coast. "I was surprised," she said, "to find out how popular he really was when we got out among the people."

Ken Maynard, the first picture-show singing cowboy, wanted to get Cowboy Slim Rinehart to appear in his western movies. "I called down in Mexico to try to get ahold of him," said Maynard, "and they told me they were just playing transcriptions of him. So I was never able to get ahold of him, but I wanted to use him in my pictures because that man, in my opinion, was the greatest cowboy singer I had ever heard in my life."

Cowboy Slim did eventually make it to Hollywood for a screen test. Dallas Turner collected one version of the story that had it that Slim got drunk and thrown in the L.A. pokey. Then he called up the film studio from the jailhouse and asked the producers to come bail him out. But the King of Border Radio told a different story. "He said they wanted him to change his style of pickin' and singin'," Turner recalled. "They wanted him to change his name because they felt there would be a war with Germany, and Rinehart was a German name. So they wanted him to take his first name, 'Nolan,' and use it as his last name. Then they didn't want him to pick and sing but wanted to put a big orchestra behind him and wanted him to become a crooner. So I guess he told them where to go, and he came back and spent the remainder of his years on the border stations."

The King of Rio Grande Radio, like many other borderland performers, was a mysterious figure. XEPN accountant Rene Gonzales, who often prayed and lit candles for the roaming cowboy singer, helped Rinehart construct secret compartments in his high-heeled cowboy boots. Dallas Turner remembered stories that Slim would even sleep in the boots, thousands of dollars safely stashed on his feet. And as happened to a number of his fellow entertainers, the colorful life on the border inspired Rinehart to hit the sauce. "Slim was very bad to drink for a number of years," Turner said. Recalling that Ernest Tubb recorded one of Rinehart's songs, "Let Me Smile My Last Smile at You," Turner added, "Back in those wild old days, poor old Slim might've given it to Ernie for a pint of whiskey, it was that bad. But let me tell you, before old Slim left this world, he whipped the bottle."

The singing cowboy reigned on the border for a number of years, making good money from the sale of his songbooks, which included songs like "The Roaming Cowboy" and "Empty Saddles" as well as pictures of Slim, "His Excellency" Major Kord, Weeping Willie Wills (the sad, sad singer of sad songs), and other notables, such as Monterrey Blanco, the canine "barker" who advertised Hamburger Bone dog food. Over the air, Slim coaxed his listeners to send in for their songbooks, even if they were short of cash. "If you don't have a dollar handy," Slim suggested, "then send a C.O.D. request that says, 'Slim, send my book C.O.D. and I'll pay the postman one dollar plus a few cents when my book arrives.'"

Though Slim knew how to sell songbooks, it soon became apparent that he didn't know much about the legal aspects of music publishing. "Slim told me," Dallas Turner said, "that they had the songbooks printed down in Del Rio. Some printer down there printed the books, and then he and the other cowboy singers would peddle their books on the radio. And he was scared to death because he almost went to prison over these songbooks. Whoever compiled the books for him, they didn't clear the songs with the publishers. And the publishers were all set to put Cowboy Slim Rinehart behind bars for copyright infringement. Rene Gonzales told me that he got on the phone and he called Bob Miller, one of the greatest publishers. Slim was always featuring Bob's songs, and Rene talked Bob out of bringing charges against Slim." Gonzales said that it wasn't Slim's fault, since other people took care of compiling and printing the books. They just asked Rinehart what his favorite songs were "and then they would go ahead and print the books up, and he would sell them on the radio. That's the way it was."

In 1948 Slim, at the age of 37, was considering entering the administrative end of the border broadcast industry. But his life was tragically cut short by an automobile accident in Detroit while he was on a rare honky-tonk foray away from the border. Some say he was on his way to cut his first commercial records, a Decca contract in his pocket. Though millions heard Rinehart on the border stations and loved his music, he never made recordings that were sold in stores.

Dallas Turner, who placed the tombstone on Slim's grave in Hobbs, New Mexico, said that Jesse Rodgers used to telephone him in the middle of the night: "He'd talk to me about the border days. This was his favorite subject too. He had gone to Philadelphia and finally achieved some success." Remembering Cowboy Slim Rinehart during one of those calls, Rodgers told Turner, "I always thought I was better than him. I always thought I was a better guitar player. I thought I was a better singer, a better yodeler, and, after all, I was Jimmie Rodgers' cousin. But you know, how would you feel if you went down to the radio station and they had two hundred orders for your songbook and Cowboy Slim Rinehart had a thousand and you watched this continue week after week and month and month? Don't you think you would finally face reality that the border stations had a king, and that king was Cowboy Slim Rinehart? I didn't know why this was for so many years, but I believe I know why now. He was just like Cousin Jimmie, just like Hank Williams. He dared to do things his own way and throw the rule book away, and that was why he was a star and why nobody else was able to achieve the success on the border stations that he did."

In November 1935, Eagle Pass greeted one of the most unusual musical phenomena that ever do-si-doed to the border. The specially painted bus of the ultimate Texas-style media-blitzing combo, W. Lee "Pappy" O'Daniel and the Hillbilly Boys, rolled into town. The celebrated musical flour-sellers from Cowtown announced that they were planning to live in the border town and play regularly over XEPN, a decision that gave a positive jolt to the station's popularity. Pappy, who moved his band back to Fort Worth after the winter broadcasting season and later became governor of the state, fondly remembered his border-blasting days. Years later, he told writer Willie Morris, "Back when we were broadcastin', we'd cross the river and go down to Piedras Negras to use that powerful station. Mexicans came in droves to hear us and listen to the music. Once we got a request from some prisoners in a penitentiary way over in Alabama, and pretty soon convicts from everywhere were writin' to get us to play songs for their girl friends."

XEPN also extolled the charms of Eagle Pass and the year-round vegetable production of the Winter Garden District. In a typical promotion for the area, XEPN's pitchman par excellence, Major Kord, addressed the Yankees he pictured shivering by their radio sets: "You people in the North who like a dish of luscious strawberries and cream, but have to be a millionaire to buy them around Christmastime, should come to the Winter Garden, where you can get all the strawberries you want and, regardless of your financial rating, will feel like a millionaire." The Major (whose real name was Don Baxter) had come to XEPN from the Brinkley organization, and he sold piano lessons by mail. "He was a pioneer," Dallas Turner said, "a guy who could stand up and fight the microphone. He'd wave his arms and go through all sorts of calisthenics."

Another popular performer on XEPN and several other border stations was Billy Truehart. This well-known Houston artist became the Fred Astaire of the Rio Grande, selling tap dancing lessons over the radio. "He'd bring a board to the studio," said Dallas Turner, "put a microphone down by his feet, and tap-dance and pitch at the same time. He sold thousands of courses that way." One visitor to XEPN, hoping to catch a glimpse of the talented toes, observed that the station had to improvise on the rare occasions when Truehart was not available in person. The visitor, peeking into the studio, saw not the famous feet but a percussionist recreating the Truehart rhythm with a pair of drumsticks.

The visitor might have checked down at the cantina. The excitement of a border radio career sent many performers chasing after the elusive pleasures of whisky and wine. Astrologer Gayle Norman, as Dallas Turner told the story, "had a very bad drinking problem that would have put Slim Rinehart's drinking problem in the Sunday school class. A lot of those old boys would drink themselves to death. Billy Truehart, according to Slim, was pretty bad to drink, and he had heard that Billy Truehart was killed in a drunken wingding out in Hollywood. He committed suicide. Well, I don't know if it's the truth, and Slim never did know either. Maybe some woman was after him, and maybe the story was false."

Golden-voiced announcer and XEPN musical director Don Howard came to the station from Nuevo Laredo, where his orchestra had been booked at the Bohemian Club. Howard decided he liked working the border stations, and his career on the river spanned four decades. Eventually rising to the executive level, Howard sometimes donned thespian robes at XEPN for the Steamboat Bill Contest. Children sent in jokes clipped from newspapers and magazines, and Howard, portraying Steamboat Bill, awarded prizes for the best jokes and read them on the air.

The Voice of the Western Hemisphere also featured mouth harp virtuoso Lonnie Glosson. Thirteen-year-old Wayne Raney, listening to XEPN in Arkansas on a battery radio set, was so inspired by Glosson's sound that he hitchhiked down to Eagle Pass to display his own harmonic finesse on the border blaster. Though Raney made only a few transcriptions and went back to Arkansas for a few more years of childhood, he and Glosson later teamed up and became famous for their ability to "make the harmonica talk."

Raney remembered that his program used to follow that of prohibition speaker Sam Morris. The Voice of Temperance, as Morris was known, usually concluded his program by saying, "I think all the beer and whiskey should be taken down and poured in the river." Raney then began his program with the hymn "Let's Gather at the River."

Rivaling the singing cowboys as mail pullers on XEPN and other border stations were the spooks. Also called radio astrologers and psychologists, these performers were vaudeville mentalists of the airwaves, players in the show business tradition from which Norman Baker had emerged. They answered listeners' questions on any subject, pitched a variety of exotic products, and predicted the futures of radio fans.

Even before the first border station raised its towers on the Rio Grande, the spooks were big mail pullers on stations in Detroit and Hollywood. Bob Nelson, who spooked under the name of Dr. Korda Ramaine, was the father of the industry. As his friend Dallas Turner remembered, "He also operated a spiritualist-medium supply house. Without a doubt, he was the greatest stage mentalist that ever lived. He personally taught many of these fellows how to do the fortune-telling pitch and the mentalist routine. All of the radio astrologers ordered supplies from Nelson Enterprises. He also invented the two-way radio that was used by fortunetellers to call people out of the audience and tell them the number of their social security cards. . . . His biggest clientele was Pentecostal preachers who posed as mystics or great prophets."

The spooks were ordered off American airwaves by the Federal Radio Commission in 1932. "They had their day and it was a prosperous one," reported a Michigan medical society newsletter. "But from now on, fortune tellers, astrologists and the whole kit and caboodle of them are barred. By this action the commission undoubtedly saves the ignorant and gullible part of the public a very considerable sum of money which they will doubtless expend in some way at least equally silly but not under radio commission control." Noting the clear reception of various medical propaganda from the Rio Grande, the newsletter pointed out, "Quacks are not the only gentry finding a radio refuge in our sister republic to the south. Lotteries flourish there. Also—quite shocking to tell—Mexican radio still tolerates fortune tellers and others of that ilk."

On the other hand, many people enjoyed the mentalists' programs. "Border radio in the old days was very entertaining," said Dallas Turner. "People made a big issue out of the spooks, but it was great entertainment. You enjoyed listening to those programs, even if you knew if you had an ounce of sense that everything was shellac."

The first radio astrologer to arrive at XEPN was a "psychist" from Fort Worth named Dr. Edward Ownen, alias Abra. Founder of the Occult Astrological Institute of America, Abra's vita listed decades of occult study in China, Africa, India, and the United States. He claimed credit for accurately predicting the death of the Lindbergh baby, the location of the first East Texas oil well, and the election of Ma Ferguson as the first female governor of Texas. With his gray hair coiffed into a pompadour, "his flashing, steely blue eyes," and his moustache and goatee, Abra "looks the part he plays," wrote the *Eagle Pass Daily Guide*. A veteran of radio stations in Fort Worth, Waco, Austin, and Wichita Falls, the astrologer said his XEPN show would "predict the outcome of important events, foretell strange happenings, and tell fortunes." Radio fans could send a question to Abra and be assured of an answer from the famous one, as he employed a staff of 25 to handle his enormous mail. The XEPN oracle liked Eagle Pass so much that he announced the establishment of a colony in the hills nearby. Hundreds of Abra followers were expected to migrate to the borderlands from his Occult Astrological Institutes in Fort Worth and Houston. But like Brinkley City, the utopia of Abraville soon vanished in the crystal ball. Abra left XEPN after his first radio season, predicting the imminent return of prosperity and heading for a carny booth at the Chicago World's Fair.

Astrologer Gayle Norman had a little more luck with the metropolis that named itself after him. Norman came to XEPN in 1933. Not long after his arrival a tiny community began to form a few miles north of

Eagle Pass. The town, which was still home to 98 persons in 1987, was christened Normandy in honor of the borderland radio mentalist. The mystic man announced plans to build a 21-room, medieval French-style castle in Normandy, but the landscape bears record of no such grandiose construction. Norman did organize a baseball team called the Spooks. One year the slugging sages won the Winter Garden softball title, defeating teams from Del Rio, Crystal City, and Carrizo Springs. They even beat their radio rivals the XEPN Whizbangers.

Other border astrologers included Dad Rango (who also took credit for discovering actor Mickey Rooney), the Reverend Ethel Duncan, Marjah, Rajah Rayboid, and Mel Roy. Hollywood's Man of Destiny, L .R. Brandon, arrived in Eagle Pass shortly after Norman joined XEPN. Brandon boasted eleven years experience as a spook on 38 different stations.

"There was another man on the radio," said Dallas Turner, "by the name of Dr. Ralph Richards. He was a doctor of psychology and a vaudeville mind reader. When they threw all of the fortune-tellers off the U.S. stations, Dr. Ralph Richards went to Eagle Pass and went on XEPN. He was the king of all the border-station astrologers. I don't think that even Rose Dawn could pull the mail that Dr. Ralph Richards could. He was a bald-headed man and traveled with his mother. I guess the two of them had played theaters and department stores and everything else. And when he came to XEPN there in Piedras Negras, he was Dr. Ralph Richards, the Friendly Voice of the Heavens. Don Howard would ask the questions, and he would answer the questions and so on, and he built up one of the biggest mail-order businesses that anybody had ever built up in the field of radio astrology."

Presenting himself as a "radio scientist," Dr. Richards, Ms.D., Ps.D., came to the Rio Grande from the Yankee Network in Boston with a staff of eight assistants. A self-professed world traveler, psychologist, and metaphysician, he claimed a wild, romantic background for his job qualifications. As the story went, his father moved the family to the Himalayas, where he went to work on a railroad project. In those exotic climes, Richards spent his time as a young boy with Hindu magicians, seers, and Yogis who taught him to perform many "difficult feats." Then, at the age of seven, the future radio star was "mysteriously kidnapped by Mohammedan religious fanatics who claimed to possess weirdly superhuman powers." After two years the boy was returned, able to "foretell of great happenings and perform many miracles. His strange powers baffled leading scientists, psychologists, and physicians."

U.S. postal inspectors, however, were not particularly baffled by Richards' "strange powers." The doctor of psychology was hit with a stack of fraud orders against several of "the most amazing deals I have ever encountered" that he offered in Kansas City, Los Angeles, San Diego, and Eagle Pass. In Texas he ran a complicated oil well investment con. Incorporated as the Rio Development Company, the scheme prospered in San Antonio from 1936 to 1938 and for another year in San Diego. Richards leased 3252 acres of Maverick County wildcat lands, rigging a deal with the driller who held the leases. Then the famous radio psychic peddled lease assignments to his mailing list of gullible speculators, gleaned from the names of those who sent in a buck to the astrologer for a horoscope reading. Richards made a whopping profit of 10,000 to 50,000 percent. When the deal turned sour in Texas, he went to the West Coast and sold the "sure thing" from San Diego. After exhausting the savings of those on his own mailing list, the Friendly Voice of the Heavens cut a deal to use Marjah's mailing list, bringing his fellow spook in for 20 percent of the take. From San Diego the persuasive mystic went to Hollywood, where he promoted Mutual Radio Enterprises, described by postal inspector J.H. Van Meter as "one of the most flagrant cases of fraud that has ever come to my attention."

"Dear Friend," the astral seer wrote to his fans. "In an impression of you today, I checked with your name in my files, and am writing you accordingly. Please don't think I am presumptuous in writing this letter to recommend one of the most amazing business deals I have ever encountered, and in which you can DOUBLE your money in less than ninety days." Richards' mailings persuaded his confidants to dig their cash out of the old mattress and send it in so that the noted spook could help them "make some really BIG money quickly." Hundreds believed Richards' assertion that "fortunes have been made in this particular field of merchandising." Many recipients of the multigraphed letters from Richards decided to invest in the budding radio network, perhaps confusing Mutual Radio Enterprises with the Mutual Broadcasting System, a well-established radio network.

Investments poured into the bogus network headquarters in Culver City, California, and Dr. Richards lived high on the hog. In a 1942 article entitled "Radio Racketeer," *Master Detective* magazine reported, "Like most of the easy-come boys, it was easy-go when it came to amusement. Richards cut quite a figure, tall, close-shaven except for a Hollywood brush on his upper lip, as he danced to numbers played especially at his request in Hollywood night spots. He was rather bald on top but it didn't seem to detract, rather singled him out as a person of distinction; a typical man-about-town, he was always accompanied by a woman—seldom the same one."

Some investors became concerned when ninety days passed and they heard nothing from their astrologist-turned-investment-counselor. Richards assured them that everything was going along as planned. Mutual Radio Enterprises had reached an agreement with an independent broadcasting station in Dunkirk to broadcast commercial programming across the English Channel, where it would reach the ears and pocketbooks of British consumers previously shielded from advertising by the non-commercial broadcasts of the BBC. The scheme was guaranteed to be successful, but the German invasion of France had caused some slight delays. Richards urged patience. Curiously, Richards' first letters soliciting funds for the broadcasting scheme were mailed on July 12, 1940, more than a month after Hitler had driven the British from the European continent.

Postal inspector Van Meter, accompanied by a deputy marshal, arrested Richards at his Hollywood hotel. Bail was set at $2500, but the suave radio star jumped bail for the wide-open badlands of South Texas radio, where he revived his horoscope racket. Shortly after the Japanese invaded Pearl Harbor, Richards was arrested again by postal inspectors in Goose Creek, Texas. The feds upped the mystic's bond to $10,000. The Friendly Voice of the Heavens charmed a friend into going his bail and promptly wandered off into the land of suckers one more time. Soon his photograph appeared on post office bulletin boards and in the Line Up section of wanted criminals in *Master Detective* magazine. Richards, wearing a wig and working under the name Dr. Raymond Vance, moved to Pittsburgh and tried to interest local residents in another radio promotion. Unfortunately for Richards, one of his prospects was an avid reader of *Master Detective* who recognized the radio racketeer and called the law. Not long after Richards was apprehended, Mexican authorities decided that they could do without knowledge of the future and outlawed seers and astrologers on all radio stations south of the border.

In the summer of 1933 the nation was gearing up for an election that eventually repealed the prohibition of alcohol. Before the vote, the Rio Grande was thick with rum smugglers looking for quick money. Though such stories were not uncommon, Maverick County residents buzzed with excitement when a young San Antonio man led the Eagle Pass police on an eleven-mile chase before 140 gallons of booze was discovered in his Pierce-Arrow. Those for and against the right to drink campaigned fervently before the election, and XEPN became the headquarters of the dry forces. A local Baptist minister arranged for a series of 26 half-hour broadcasts, purchased by organized teetotalers at a cost of $4375. Appearing on the prohibition shows were such notables as Senator Thomas B. Love and two former Texas governors, Pat Neff and Dan Moody. But the star of the series was controversial fundamentalist Rev. J. Frank Norris. When prohibition went into effect in 1920, the Texas Cyclone, as the theatrical Fort Worth preacher was often called, buried a casket of empty whiskey bottles in a public funeral for "John Barleycorn." The righteous Cyclone arrived on the border fresh from a debate in Austin with former governor James Ferguson and spoke against the devil water on both XEPN and XER. Ferguson also inquired about airtime on the Piedras Negras station. The president of the Central Committee of Texas for Anti-Prohibition alleged that Mexican breweries were financing the border radio dry campaign in an effort to fight off the competition of legal firewater in Texas saloons.

Even after the repeal of the Eighteenth Amendment, XEPN continued to blast the prohibition theme across the hemispheres. In the rodeo town of Stamford, Texas, Will Branch found an effective speaker named Rev. Sam Morris, who rode the border waves to national renown as the Voice of Temperance. Morris was on XEPN for the life of the station and appeared on other border stations as well. In one of his most famous talks, entitled "The Ravages of Rum," he asked his radio audience, "You think it will never happen to you? A mother sixty-four years of age took to drinkin'. She came in one night so drunk she started to take a bath with her clothes on. In utter disgust her husband said, 'I oughta blow yer brains out.' She snarled back at him, 'You haven't got the nerve.' He shot her dead in the bathtub and went to jail for it. Fine way to end married life." The *New York Times* once referred to him as "Carrie Nation, 1942 style." A few years later, *Collier's* magazine wrote, "Of all the voices crying in the wilderness, his is the loudest and the most potent. . . . If and when prohibition returns to this country, Brother Sam Morris will probably be more responsible for it than any other person." Morris didn't believe in moderation. Total abstinence was the only way. "Young girls try to learn their capacity for such things as whiskey or gin," he preached, "thinking they can stick to the proper quantity. And often they end up as social outcasts, unmarried mothers, gangster molls, and pistol-packin' mamas."

The Voice of Temperance's program ended with a jingle sung to the tune of "The Old Grey Mare She Ain't What She Used to Be." Morris' version went, "Alcohol is worse than it used to be, mixed with gas-o-line." The sounds of screeching brakes and crashing autos underscored the song's message.

Born in 1900, Morris broadcast over Mexican and American stations nearly every day from 1935 to 1985. After graduating from prestigious Brown University on the East Coast, he went to the small town of Stamford, Texas, to become the local minister. Morris, unlike some border personalities, did not brag about his educational background. "Degrees are just like curls in a pig's tail," he explained. "They don't put any bacon in the frying pan." In the early sixties he was about to retire to a ranch near Sisterdale, Texas. Instead he applied to the FCC for a license and opened radio station KDRY in San Antonio. The Voice of Temperance remembered his days on the border fondly. He recalled that Dr. Brinkley did a "swell, jam-up job." One time, Morris took a fellow pastor to see Doctor at his Del Rio clinic. Brinkley examined the minister and diagnosed his illness as cancer, stating frankly that there was nothing he could do.

If Morris' fellow preacher had listened to much border radio, he might have tried the Baker treatment at Laredo or Muscatine. Or, he might have gone to Dallas, where early in 1936, the year of Texas' centennial, a man named Dr. Spann set up a cancer clinic operated somewhat according to the Baker model. Choosing border blasting as the correct advertising medium for his enterprise, Spann visited Eagle Pass to contract for time on XEPN. Soon a former Muscatine associate of Baker's, Harry Hoxsey, moved in on Spann's territory and advertised his own Dallas healing mecca on Piedras Negras radio. When Hoxsey visited Eagle Pass to arrange his airtime, he told the press that he would soon deliver a "bombshell" that would shake the foundations of organized medicine.

Members of the American Medical Association gritted their teeth as they scanned the radio dial. A Pennsylvania physician, in a typical response to the border medicos, wrote to the home office in Chicago that he was "shocked two days ago on turning the radio on . . . to hear commercial advertising for a cancer hospital. Can nothing be done about this? Where are the Federal sleuths and tax-gatherers, who fine you and me or tax us on the slightest cause—how do these people get away with it, judging it from a governmental standpoint?"

The AMA, however, could not offer the physician much in the way of decisive action. "We do not definitely know," the association's Bureau of Investigation wrote back, "that there is any tie-up between the Spann Hospital at Dallas, Texas, and Norman Baker, who runs 'cancer cure' outfits in Laredo, Texas, and Muscatine, Iowa." Further confusing the different players in the faraway border industry, the bureau passed on a report that "radio station XEPN had announced a day or so previously that the Mexican Government had ruled off the air the broadcasts of the Spann Hospital at Dallas." The informant stated that "he understood station XEPN was controlled by Dr. John R. Brinkley and as the latter is a widely known quack in the 'gland cure' field, our correspondent thought Brinkley might have had an axe to grind in making the announcement, as if he were broadcasting the downfall of a competitor."

Early in 1937, shortly after the Spann Hospital disappeared from the border waves, Dr. Spann filed damage suits for 50,000 pesos in Piedras

Negras District Court against Villa Acuña station XERA and Reynosa station XEAW. Represented by former Coahuila senator Pablo Valdez, Spann asserted that slanderous statements had been made against him on the rival border blasters, presumably from the lips of Dr. Brinkley. This bit of litigious paranoia, however, was never gaveled into court.

XEPN often featured local talent from both sides of the international boundary. Even the Eagle Pass Boy Scouts got the chance to tell the Western Hemisphere about their constant state of preparedness. And other communities in the region got their messages on the station as well. Crystal City sent boosters down to the Rio Grande to solicit funds over XEPN for a town monument. They were building a statue of Popeye, the cartoon mariner, in gratitude for his popularizing the stringy green rejuvenator. Spinach could be grown in the Winter Garden District and shipped north where the ground was frozen, providing balanced diets during snowbound months.

Everything Americans heard on the radio was not so comforting. In the fall of 1937 they panicked from coast to coast in a testament to the power of the airwaves' ability to tranform reality. Orson Welles' startling narration of an invasion by warring Martians, *The War Of The Worlds*, was mistaken as a newscast of a real event and sent thousands of terror-stricken Americans scrambling through the streets, shrieking of the imminent destruction of the planet earth.

A radio war was also brewing on the border that fall, down in Eagle Pass and Piedras Negras. Disagreements arose between Will Branch and his Mexican partner, C.M. Bres. The situation got so bad in late November that the American engineer took over his station with a show of force. The *Daily Guide* reported, ARMED RAIDERS SEIZE XEPN; WIRES CUT; STATION SILENCED. Bres told the press that Branch, a number of hired assistants, and some Piedras Negras policemen had conducted a pre-dawn armed raid on the broadcasting company's property. The raiders got into the transmitter building, drove the employees out, and barricaded themselves inside. Branch then got an injunction from Piedras Negras district court to prevent his group's removal from the radio fortress until the situation was legally straightened out. They held the station for nearly three weeks. Branch thought it safe to leave and checked into the Eagle Hotel. Then, on a brisk November evening, as border-towners geared up for a Saturday night, a blast shook the desert just south of the Rio Grande. Suddenly flames engulfed the powerful transmitter of the Voice of the Western Hemisphere. The Piedras Negras police and Branch allies were held for investigation but were exonerated within the week. The wild old days at XEPN had come to an explosive end.

Branch announced a few months later, as the Winter Garden prepared for the Spring Spinach Fest, that he would rebuild the station with a more modern, streamlined transmitting plant capable of broadcasting even greater distances. Though Branch did not fulfull his promise, the Bres family built a new station in Piedras Negras—XEMU. The binational partners eventually took each other to court over control of the company they had formed together. Branch got control of another station the partners had built in Tijuana, XELO, and moved it to Juárez.

The experimental superpower technology that engineers Will Branch, James Weldon, Nestor Cuesta, and others created just south of the Rio Grande could often be dangerous and unpredictable. Cuesta recalled the story of engineer Luis Roa at station XEG in Monterrey. Working on the transmitter, Roa moved his head in the wrong direction and took an 18,000-volt sting on the top of his skull. Astonishingly, Cuesta said, the engineer lived through the experience. For years afterward Roa boasted good-naturedly about the "electric face-lift" he had gotten at XEG.

Will Branch, the man who built the muscle in border blasters from the Gulf of Mexico to Baja California, was not so lucky. In the early fifties the monster transmitter at XELO in Juárez took its creator's life as the engineer operated on its high-voltage heart. "I had always heard," said Dallas Turner, "that Mr. Branch committed suicide by turning the station on and taking the wrappings off the wires or something like that. I've heard that he committed suicide, then I've heard that it was an accident, and nobody really seems to know the truth. I guess Mr. Branch was one of the most amazing men that ever lived, from what I have heard."

Crazy, Crazy, Crazy Water Crystals

When I was a kid, I used to have a shotgun, and when that shotgun got clogged up, I used to take me a ramrod and give it a good cleaning. Now, Crazy Water does the same for you. When you get clogged up, Crazy Water is just like that ramrod.

—*Hal Collins' Crazy Water Crystals radio pitch*

When Hal Collins, president of Crazy Water Crystals, first tried out his shotgun story in a commercial from a Dallas studio, the professional entertainers found it too homespun and insisted that experienced copywriters and announcers be used to give their new sponsor a good return for his advertising investment. But the public missed the man with the ramrod story, and the switchboard at the station lit up with inquiries about "that fellow with the shotgun—he's the best thing on the whole show."

The radio merchandising of Crazy Water Crystals by Hal and his brother Carr Collins provided millions of Americans with foot-stomping hillbilly music and laxative relief. The product was a "natural combination of minerals" obtained by boiling down the fabled Crazy Water, which percolated from the Crazy Well in the small town of Mineral Wells, Texas, about 35 miles west of Fort Worth. Like Eureka Springs, Mineral Wells was "a town built on water," a healing sanctuary that billed itself as the spot Where America Drinks Its Way to Health. In the twenties and thirties more than 200,000 thirsty health seekers a year visited the "home of Crazy," and thousands more treated their sluggish systems with the "snowy-white minerals" that the Collins brothers extracted from the healing springwater.

The Crazy story began on Christmas Eve in 1877 when Judge J. A.

Lynch brought his family to the area in a covered wagon and decided to found a settlement. For a while the family hauled their water from the Brazos River, four miles west of their new home. They finally completed a well but were afraid to drink the water at first, fearing that it might be poisonous because it had an unusual taste. Motivated by either sloth or gumption, Mrs. Lynch decided to continue drinking the well water and found that her rheumatism disappeared after a couple of weeks. Soon other pioneers came to test the healing powers of the water in the valley of the Palo Pinto hills. One woman, suffering from catatonia, seemed to regain her mental powers with continued therapy at the mineral fount. Folks began to call the well the Crazy Woman Well, later shortening the name to Crazy Well, and the Lynch settlement became known as Mineral Wells, Texas.

As the town grew and the Crazy reputation spread, boardinghouses sprang up to accommodate the travelers seeking the liquid cure. In 1912 a grand hotel was erected and christened the Crazy Hotel, offering guests water from the original Crazy Well. More accommodations were added until it seemed the town boasted more hotels than homes. The Crazy motif grew increasingly popular with local merchants. Mineral Wells soon became home to the Crazy Theater, Crazy Well Drinking Pavilion, Crazy Well Bath House, Crazy Flats, Crazy Well State Bank, Crazy Laundry, and any number of other Crazy enterprises.

The health resort business boomed Crazy-style through the first half of the roaring twenties, but in 1925 the Crazy Hotel, the town's central attraction, caught fire and burned to the ground. One of the many North Texans who mourned the landmark's loss was the well-known Dallas insurance man Carr P. Collins. Collins had ventured often to Mineral Wells and had drunk deep of the healing waters of Crazy Well. He viewed the hotel's destruction as a good business opportunity. Collins motored over to Mineral Wells to purchase the charred real estate, and soon another, more magnificent Crazy Hotel graced the Mineral Wells skyline. With the slogan "Come to the Crazy Hotel and drink your way to health," the new Crazy opened for business in 1927. The seven-story hotel boasted two hundred rooms, an expansive lobby, a ballroom, a roof garden for dancing, a mineral bath department, and the Crazy Water Bar, where guests could guzzle the famous H_2O.

Mineral Wells flourished with the resurrection of its Crazy shrine. It became almost commonplace for local folks to spot such visitors as Judy Garland, Tom Mix, Jean Harlow, Marlene Dietrich, General John J. "Blackjack" Pershing, Will Rogers, D. W. Griffith, Oklahoma governor "Alfalfa Bill" Murray, and Lyndon Johnson. Even famous physicians like Charles Mayo made their way to Texas for observation of the Crazy experience. And it seems probable that Dr. Brinkley and Norman Baker checked out the bubbly phenomenon on their treks to the border from Kansas and Iowa. The Mineral Wells hierarchy resented this commercial intrusion by a Dallasite and commissioned renowned hotel contractor T. B. Baker to build a larger, more supreme traveler's palace. The huge Baker Hotel, twice as big as the Crazy and gussied up with art deco embellishments, opened in 1929, just about the time the stock market crashed.

As the economy worsened, the imaginative Collins brothers realized that Americans would have less money for travel, and they looked for a new angle to keep the Crazy Water assets liquid. The Crazy entrepreneurs thought that it would be too expensive to ship the bottled water to retailers, so they decided to boil down the mysterious mineral sauce and market the residue as Crazy Water Crystals. Packed in small green boxes displaying a picture of the Crazy Hotel, the crystals sold well in pharmacies and general stores. More and more North Texans began to "put one or two teaspoons in a glass of water and drink the mixture down," as instructed on the box. The Collins brothers recommended Crazy Water Crystals for anyone suffering from a condition "that was caused or being made worse by a sluggish system" and urged those who used Crazy Water Crystals to "drink plenty of it." Although the Collinses firmly believed in the curative power of their Crazy extract, they were less extravagant in their claims than Brinkley, Baker, and other contemporary wonderworkers. The label on the Crystals box contained the warning that "continual use of any laxative may develop a systemic dependence on same," and persistent sufferers were encouraged to consult their doctors.

Despite the local popularity of Crazy Water Crystals, the Collins brothers were not satisfied with the overall level of sales, and they held a powwow with their associates at the Crazy Hotel to brainstorm for ways to expand the market for their elixir. Hal Collins later said the solution "materialized as dramatically as the vision of an Old Testament prophet. Just then we heard a French harp down beneath us in the pavilion. It sounded real good." The Crazy guys rushed downstairs and found the music coming from an old country boy named Dick Ware.

"I had an old model A Ford," Hal remembered. "I took Dick to Dallas and paid forty-two fifty for fifteen minutes on KRLD radio. From then on, every Saturday night we'd go to Dallas. Dick would start out playing - something like 'Redwing,' and after that I'd preach. I don't mean I gave commercials. I preached. The first time we broadcast was in February of 1930. Almost before we got back to Mineral Wells, money was piled up on Carr's desk."

A popular radio show featuring hillbilly music and impassioned commercials for Crazy Water Crystals soon evolved from those early broadcasts. *The Crazy Gang Show* was at first broadcast from a Dallas studio, but later moved to the lobby of the Crazy Hotel, where hotel guests, patrons of the Crazy Water Bar, and other health seekers could watch the performers and enjoy the show. The program proved so popular that it was syndicated regionally over the Texas Quality Network and nationally over the Mutual Network, with the result that radio listeners from North Carolina to South Dakota could hear the deep, authoritative voice of Hal Collins preaching the wonders of Crazy Water in his pleasant North Texas drawl.

"Our Creator gave the world a renowned water known as Crazy Mineral Water," said Hal, "which has brought health back to many people. . . . Today millions are drinking their way to health in the simple natural way. Just drink Crazy Water." Hal recommended the Crazy treatment for a wide range of maladies: "It cures ailments brought on by constipation, high blood pressure, rheumatism, arthritis, liver and kidney troubles, autointoxication, bad complexion, excess acidity, or something else of a more serious nature." Crazy Water Crystals were always sold with "the definite, positive understanding that they must help you or your money will be refunded," a marketing technique that was an honest reflection of the faith the Collins brothers had in the curative power of the waters from the Crazy Well.

In other radio pitches, listeners learned some basic facts about biology and good health. "Water is the greatest of all cleansers," the Crazy pitchmen stated, "and this is true when it enters the body. . . . There are very few who drink enough water to supply vital organs properly and maintain thorough elimination." The announcer suggested that "as a rule, the average person should drink not less than two or three quarts of water every day" and told his audience the proper way to ingest this precious fluid. "Don't drink a large quantity of water in a few swift gulps— sip it, but sip lots of it. And that's the way to drink Crazy Water. . . . If you'll add a teaspoonful of Crazy Water Crystals to about a large glass of water, preferably warm, and drink it thirty minutes before breakfast for the next three weeks, I'm just confident that it will help you overcome any condition that was caused or being made worse by a sluggish system."

The radio audience appreciated the biological insights that the broadcasts provided: "Did you ever think how absolutely necessary water is to keep you alive? A man may live without food for forty, sixty, or even eighty days, but deprive him of water for five or six days and he'll die a horrible death. Your body itself is about four-fifths water." Many of those who heard these lectures tried the Crazy treatment for themselves and wrote to tell the remarkable results. A Louisiana woman wrote, "Have been to where I couldn't do housework and washing for some time but now I do anything. I do my housework, washing and canning. I feel proud of myself now that I've gotten on my feet again. Thanks to you for Crazy Crystals Mineral Water."

As the popularity of Crazy Crystals and the Crazy radio program grew, Hal Collins supplemented his pitches with editorials on issues of the day presented in a segment entitled *One Man's Opinion*. Different groups of performers from Dallas to Pittsburgh jumped on the Crazy bandwagon with local versions of the successful programming format. Conrad Brady emceed one show and performed in a blackface routine called *Sugarcane and February*, based on the popular radio personalities Molasses and January, while the Jack Amlung Orchestra gave the show a cosmopolitan flavor. Colonel Jack teamed up with Shorty and his Crazy Hillbillies on the East Coast. Shorty, Sue, and Rawhide played songs like "Hot Time in the Old Town Tonight" and "Pop Goes the Weasel," while Colonel Jack remarked solemnly on the plight of "every man or woman who has suffered the distress of a chronically upset stomach." He asked rhetorically, "Is there anything more pitiful than to sit at a table loaded with good things to eat and watch others regale themselves, while you drink an eggnog or eat a bowl of crackers and milk?" After quoting an unsolicited letter from a supportive physician, the colonel urged the audience to "try them. Try Crazy Water Crystals and see for yourself what nature can do. Thank you."

Other entertainers who rode the Crazy radio waves included Mary Martin of Peter Pan fame and Meredith Wilson, who later testified to the good folks of River City on the evils of pool in *The Music Man*. The Collins brothers developed several different formats for Crazy Water Crystals programs, which appeared around the country, but hillbilly music was a standard feature of each Crazy production. One of the most popular spin-off programs, the *Crazy Water Barn Dance*, was carried by fourteen stations in Georgia and the Carolinas. Performers on the *Barn Dance* included the Tennessee Ramblers, the Monroe Brothers, J.E. Mainer's Crazy Mountaineers, and Homer "Pappy" Sherrill's Crazy Hickory Nuts.

Crazy Water Crystals were often advertised on the radio through the PI, or per inquiry method, wherein the advertiser paid the radio station a certain amount for each inquiry generated by the radio ads. Other products advertised with hillbilly music on the per inquiry system included the cold remedy Peruna, which contained as much as 27 percent alcohol, the indigestion remedy Willard's Tablets, the pain reliever Hamlin's Wizard Oil, the laxative Man-O-Ree, and even several products that weathered governmental and press criticism to become modern-day standards such as Ex-Lax and Alka-Seltzer. Depression-era consumer advocate Peter Morell wrote in his book *Poisons, Potions and Profits* that most people were too intelligent to be misled by snake-oil salesmen but described what he saw as the problems of broadcast advertising. "Suppose that the pitchman is given a course in radio elocution," wrote Morell, "provided with a script turned out by an imaginative copywriter, and brought to the microphone after an eye-moistening program of Texas cowboy songs." Apparently, Morell believed that such a mesmerizing pitch required urgent government regulation. Many others agreed. In a 1935 article entitled "The Radio Nostrum Racket," the *Nation* editorialized that there existed "a crying need of action to stop the most dangerous exploitation of the public attempted in years."

Despite the press's efforts, Crazy Crystals programs became a prime outlet for the best hillbilly musicians across the country, and the Collins brothers proved to be just as successful in peddling their Crazy product as they were in promoting country music. Gross sales reached $3 million a year in the early thirties, as the aquatic gold flowed free of charge from the well on the premises of the Crazy Hotel, and the cost of packaging and promoting the snowy-white crystals was minimal. A government-sponsored exhibit at the 1933 Chicago World's Fair, however, threw a monkey wrench into the Crazy Crystals money-making machinery.

Rexford Guy Tugwell, Roosevelt's Under Secretary of Agriculture, rented a booth at the fair and set up an exhibit to promote passage of a Pure Food and Drug Act, known in Congress as the Tugwell Bill. Called the Chamber of Horrors, the exhibit displayed a number of medicinal and cosmetic products. There were bottles of the venereal disease remedy Radithor, labeled by the manufacturer as "Certified Radio-Active Water, Contains Radium and Mesothorium in Triple-Distilled Water." There were before-and-after photos of a woman who had been blinded by synthetic aniline dyes in the product Lash Lure, and pictures of a bald woman who had used the depilatory Koremlu on her legs. Sandwiched among these horrors was a Crazy Water Crystal display. The exhibit disputed the claims of Crazy Water healing power and presented an analysis of the crystals that showed that the "variety of minerals" in the product were essentially Glauber's salt, a horse medicine long out of use in treating human patients. Unfortunately for the Collins brothers, the Chamber of Horrors exhibit was seen by an exceptionally large number of fairgoers, since Tugwell had cleverly chosen a booth near that of Sally Rand, the mistress of the scandalous fan dance. Tugwell's campaign drew heated reactions from The Proprietary Association, a group of patent medicine manufacturers, who called the bill "grotesque in its terms, evil in its purposes, and vicious in its possible consequences," and fought hard to maintain the "American people's constitutional rights to self-medication." The broadcasting establishment was also firmly opposed to such a bill and lined up powerful friends in Congress to work against the impending legislation. Josiah Bailey of North Carolina became known as the Senator for Vick's Vapo-Rub and James Mead of New York became the Congressman for Doan's Kidney Pills.

Carr P. Collins strolled by the exhibit and was less than pleased with its curator's mission and tactics. He strode briskly to the nearest telephone and lodged immediate protests with the U.S. senators from Texas, Morris Sheppard and Tom Connally. His fellow Texans promptly got Crazy Water Crystals removed from the exhibit, but not until Collins agreed to advertise Crazy Water as affecting only those disorders that were attributable to "faulty elimination." Rumors later surfaced that pressure for the removal had come from as high up as Vice President John Nance Garner, and it is not inconceivable that the native of Uvalde, Texas, took a personal interest in the concerns of the Collins brothers. Other Texas legislators later spoke forcefully in Congress against federal food and drug legislation and for the rights of Carr Collins and others to sell their healing nostrums. Congressman Blanton told his colleagues in the House that he objected to Tugwell's campaign because it would "close up every country store in the United States and put out of business every country newspaper." He further asserted that Tugwell's exhibit "did a great injustice to a high-class, highly respected mineral water business in my district, at Mineral Wells, Texas, which has been curing afflicted people for nearly a hundred years."

Despite the strong support of the Texas legislators, the negative publicity created by Tugwell's Chamber of Horrors put at least a small dent in the laxative's sales. Perhaps it was this conflict with the federal authorities that caused Carr Collins' gaze to drift south to the border. He might have suspected that the Food and Drug Administration was about to pressure the FCC to pull the plug on Crazy radio stateside. Or maybe his familiarity with radio made him realize what a good investment a powerful station could be. Whatever his reason, the conservative Dallas insurance magnate decided to buy his own border radio station in the spring of 1939.

In many ways Carr P. Collins was an unlikely candidate for the eclectic fraternity of border radio moguls. Entering the insurance industry in 1913, the young man from East Texas worked hard and learned the business quickly. While Dr. Brinkley publicized goat glands as the secret to rejuvenation, Collins proved through experience the simple motto his associates heard him repeat often throughout his career: "Work is the fountain of youth." Following that dictum paid off, as Fidelity Union Life, the company Collins founded in 1927, grew to be the largest independent insurance firm in the Southwest, licensed to operate in nearly every state in the Union. The company attracted national media attention in 1943 with its innovative development of the Total Abstainer Plan, which offered preferential insurance rates for nondrinkers.

This mission to encourage insurance buyers to become teetotalers was an active manifestation of Collins' Baptist faith. Shortly after he entered the insurance field, Collins was baptized by an internationally noted preacher, the Reverend George W. Truett. Collins became a member and later a deacon of Dallas' First Baptist Church, the largest Baptist congregation in the world. In 1925 he was elected trustee of Baylor University, a bastion of the Southern Baptist faith, in Waco, Texas. Concerned about the school's financial picture, Collins helped institute the Baptist Foundation, which ultimately set Baylor on solid fiscal ground. The wealthy Dallas businessman matched his volunteer efforts with substantial personal gifts to the university, including a block of downtown Dallas real estate.

While the insurance business was his early and sustaining bread and butter, Collins felt that a variety of professional activities would keep his mind and body healthy and alert. A devotee of the cafeteria dining format, he joined a partner in 1951 to open what was then the largest cafeteria in the world. Houston's L–C Cafeteria, in the downtown San Jacinto Building, boasted that it could serve 2500 people an hour. Collins was also involved in the establishment of Dallas' Restlawn Memorial Park, a project inspired by the famous Forest Lawn Cemetery in California. The active businessman's other investments included the Vent-A-Hood Company, shopping centers, housing developments, Dr Pepper, and the Texas-New Mexico Railroad, just to name a few.

Once Collins decided to get involved in border radio, he contacted Dr. Brinkley's organization and negotiated the purchase of XEAW, Doctor's auxiliary border blaster in Reynosa, Tamaulipas. Another influential Texan familiar with the power of radio, Governor W. Lee O'Daniel, became a silent partner in the new radio venture of his good friend Carr Collins. Soon after the purchase, XEAW beamed the praises of Crazy Water Crystals out across North America at 150,000 watts.

XEAW was actually the oldest border radio station, having hit the airwaves as XED in the fall of 1930, a full year before Dr. Brinkley's mellifluous voice took flight over XER. Billed as the Voice of Two Republics, XED began broadcasting with 10,000 watts, making it the most powerful radio station on Mexican soil at that time, and the owners of the station had permission from Mexico City to boost the juice up to 50,000 watts as soon as they were ready.

The International Broadcasting Company, a Mexican corporation chartered in May 1930, owned and operated XED. Four Texans from McAllen and Hidalgo and one Mexican national were the founding partners. The Mexican Alienship Act of 1886 gave the Texans the right to be part of the Mexican corporation. Upon signing the charter, the foreigners agreed that, with regard to the broadcasting, they would legally be considered Mexicans. The American stockholders agreed not to seek protection from the U.S. government should there be a breach of contract causing them to lose "all said interest or participation in benefit of the Mexican nation."

The new company received assistance in securing the frequency concession from General Juan Alamazán. The general was Secretary of the Mexican Federal Department of Communication and had a personal financial interest in the development of Reynosa and a number of other northern Mexico cities. Will Branch, the ubiquitous border engineer, came down from Fort Worth to supervise the installation of the four tons of radio equipment it took to get XED on the air.

L. D. Martínez traveled from Monterrey to become the station's first program director. In a speech to the McAllen Rotary Club, Martínez said XED would address the growing need for rapid communication and promote friendship and greater understanding between the two nations. He pointed out that the world was growing smaller day by day, that in a few short generations communications had grown from "courier to stage, stage to steam, steam to wire, and wire to radio." The Lower Rio Grande Valley was gearing up for a bold step into the future.

Even before the transmitter was assembled, the pioneer border station caused alarm among Canadian broadcasters. They heard that a "phantom radio station" would soon start broadcasting from the Mexican border and expressed concern that it might interfere with their programming. Reporting the story, the *McAllen Monitor* noted that the United States had ninety clear channels and Canada had six. Mexico, with no clear channels of its own, had previously used some of those allotted to Canada via a gentleman's agreement.

With studios in the Hotel McAllen north of the Rio Grande and a Reynosa studio a quarter mile south of the international bridge, the Voice of Two Republics began its hundred-hour inaugural program with a crash of cymbals and addresses in English and Spanish from the respective sides of the border. Tamaulipas governor Francisco Castellanos spoke at the marathon kickoff. The Border Charros, formerly with San Antonio's Mexican Symphony Orchestra, filled "the moonlit heavens with fiery and plaintive Spanish airs," and the famous blue yodeler Jimmie Rodgers also traveled from the Alamo City to take part in the celebration. Mexico's Nightingale, Rosa Dominguez, who was later to be a regular on

XER and XERA, sang ballads, and a duo called Honeyboy and Sassa-fras provided variety entertainment, sponsored by Hicks Rubber Company of Texas.

Response to the "newly born phantom of the air of Latin America" was immediate and widespread. The first broadcasts brought thousands of telegrams from all over the country. The *McAllen Daily Press* reported that XED was received on some nights in Chicago. One would suspect that Dr. Brinkley tuned in to the Voice of Two Republics at his Milford clinic and was partially inspired to move to the border by the crackling music and shenanigans coming from the south bank of the Rio Grande.

Not long after the Reynosa station began to tell the nation about the Family Land of Golden Grapefruit, an XED editorial informed the listening audience that, although most of the country was "undergoing a severe business depression," the Rio Grande Valley was enjoying prosperity. Behind this success story were the carloads of citrus fruits and winter vegetables being shipped north. Like the Quemado Valley development, the Rio Grande Valley was a massive irrigation project designed by promoters to turn a dry stretch of borderlands into a tropical paradise.

In September 1931, while Dr. Brinkley was preparing to blast XER's mighty voice into the ether, a Houstonian named Will Horwitz purchased a controlling interest in XED. Owner of Homefolks Theaters, a Houston chain, Horwitz was described by those who knew him as a show business genius and a great humanitarian. To thousands of kids growing up in the Bayou City during the Great Depression, Horwitz was also known as Santa Claus.

Even before his purchase of XED, Horwitz displayed the flair for dramatic promotions that characterized most of the individuals involved with border radio. When movie producers threatened to cut off the supply of films to Homefolks Theaters because Horwitz refused to raise his ticket prices, the showman installed live hogs in his theater lobbies. Attached to the hogs were signs reading "Movie Hog Trust." When Democrats gathered in Houston for their 1928 convention, Horwitz dispatched his right-hand man, Fred Cannata, to the Rio Grande Valley. On the boss's instructions, Cannata gathered up a large herd of donkeys and escorted them on the train back to Houston. Horwitz then presented a donkey to each astonished delegate. The stunned conventioneers must have returned home from their visit to Texas with a vivid memory of an instance in which the state had lived up to its reputation.

The theater owner gained his St. Nicholas reputation by teaming up with the *Houston Post* in 1926 to sponsor a Christmas party for the underprivileged children of Houston. The yuletide gala was so successful that it became an annual event, and many young Houstonians learned to love

Horwitz, the man who dressed up as Santa every year and distributed gifts. Horwitz did not confine his philanthropy to the holiday season. He established free soup kitchens, called grubstake restaurants, which served up much-needed meals to more than 100,000 people, and he reached into his own pocket to open free employment bureaus that found jobs for many unemployed Houstonians.

Like most of those who followed him to the border, Horwitz crossed the Rio Grande as a seasoned American broadcaster. He established Houston's first radio station, WEAY, in the twenties. When he bought XED, Houston's St. Nicholas pumped $15,000 into improvements at the station. Rumors circulated in the City of Palms that the almighty CBS network might extend its chain to include the baby border blaster. But XED remained an independent broadcasting voice, and in October 1931, as Del Rioans fandangoed to the clarion call of XER, residents of McAllen and Reynosa paraded and do-si-doed in a Valley-wide celebration of XED's return to the air. The festivities continued for days. The City of Palms was on a roll toward ever greater prosperity: a new bank opened, commemorated by an "old-fashioned cowboy show" and a public lynching of Old Man Hard Times. Folks said that XED could now be heard as far away as the Hawaiian Islands.

For Houston's St. Nicholas, however, Old Man Hard Times still had a few tricks up his sleeve. Horwitz's troubles started when he began advertising the Tamaulipas State Lottery over XED. At first the experiment was an enormous success. As one employee remembered it, "big washtubs full of money" arrived "from all over the world" to buy chances in the radio lottery, as XED grabbed a healthy chunk of America's listening audience. But Uncle Sam's postal inspectors were also tuned in to the border wave, as they would be for decades to come. In early April 1932 they arrested the showman and his wife at the Hidalgo-McAllen airport as the two were about to step into a cabin monoplane to fly from their Valley residence to their home base, Houston.

Four XED employees were later arrested in Hidalgo and McAllen. One of those charged was the editor of *El Observador*, a Reynosa weekly. In May the group was charged in Laredo federal court with operating a lottery through the United States mail in direct violation of U.S. federal law. The trial was docketed for May 23 in Corpus Christi. Although U.S. federal law prohibited the use of the interstate mail system for promotion of lotteries, Houston's Santa Claus believed that his Mexican-based operation was completely legal. After all, the lottery was sanctioned by the Mexican government, and all orders for tickets were sent across the border to a Mexican address. And the Federal Radio Commission had recently denied a petition to ban the broadcasting of "lottery and gift programs," because such an action would, in the commission's words, "constitute an exercise of power which is not expressly or even impliedly conferred by the (Radio) Act."

The court did not agree with the border entrepreneur's interpretation of federal law, however. After proceedings taking less than a week, all those charged were found guilty. An appellate court confirmed the conviction, ruling that although the overt criminal act had occurred in Mexico, the conspiracy to commit the act was partly formed in the United States, and that action was enough to demand a conviction. Horwitz received an eighteen-month sentence, while his wife was handed a six-month suspended term. The employees caught in the radio "conspiracy" received lesser sentences.

Petitions flew and protests rang from bayou to border. When the feds put Santa Claus on a train bound for Leavenworth, Houston's Union Station was mobbed with the showman's devoted fans. Two thousand of the admirers showed up in a more jubilant mood six months later when Horwitz came home on an early release. Although President Franklin Delano Roosevelt granted Horwitz a full pardon in 1940, Santa kept well away from border radio after his arrest.

As the thirties drew to a close, Horwitz developed heart problems. He underwent a thyroid operation, hoping to alleviate the maladies. With typical showmanship, the patient arranged to film the surgical procedure so that posterity could witness the modern medical miracle that he felt sure would save his life. Unfortunately, the operation was unsuccessful. On Christmas Eve, 1941, 12,000 underprivileged youngsters attended the annual Horwitz Christmas party, and on Christmas Day, Houston's Santa Claus passed away. His final message to the thankful beneficiaries of his generosity was "The show must go on."

While XED's owner was in jail, Tamaulipas tax agents locked up an organ, pianos, and other equipment and shut the station down. But before the end of 1932, Reynosa radio was back on the air as XEAW, operated by its original owners. For the third time in as many years the Valley celebrated a gala inaugural program. Mayors, Lions Club and chamber of commerce members, and a state legislator all went before the microphones of XEAW to herald the opportunities to be found in the Rio Grande Valley. Soon letters were coming in from Vermont, Oregon, and Nova Scotia, inquiring about the magic land they had heard described as the Sanctum of Romance and History. The Voice of Two Republics was transformed into the Voice of International Service.

New performers on the rejuvenated border blaster included blues singer Viola Thompson from Pharr, Texas, and Peg Longon's Club Royale Orchestra. From XEPN came tap dancer Billy Truehart and noted astrologer-spook Gayle Norman. Yet another cancer clinic promoter blasted his propaganda on the border waves, promoting a Baker-style operation that had recently moved to McAllen.

In October 1932 Dr. Brinkley became interested in acquiring XEAW and dispatched XER managing director Bert Munal to McAllen to negotiate a possible sale. Munal traveled down the Rio Grande through the same floods that were delaying construction of XEPN. The XEAW owners signed a letter confirming their verbal agreement to sell the station, and Munal put $5000 in escrow as a show of good faith. A representative was sent to Mexico City to make certain that the frequency concession was legally secure. Munal requested that Doctor send the amplifier from Ammunition Train #1, stating that Horwitz "tore up the amplification that they did use and has a little bit of it left, but he has it in Houston." Rates for airtime were discussed, a half hour to cost $125, with discounts for repeated plays. Doctor reminded Munal that he wanted final approval of all contracts.

For a time it looked as though the sale would go through. The *Del Rio Evening News* announced that the Reynosa station had merged with the XER dynasty. Munal reported to Brinkley that the local political climate was particularly favorable for his enterprise. "We are very fortunate," he wrote, "in the election of the Presidente of Reynosa. You will remember that Rosa Dominguez was always talking about her Colonel. I met Colonel Zamora, who is a power there, and his brother is the new Presidente who will go into office the first of the year. Colonel Zamora assured me that everything possible that could be done would be done very gladly by everybody in Reynosa and the State of Tamaulipas."

The next job of XER's managing director was a trip to Austin to see the postal authorities. When Horwitz was arrested on the lottery charge, a fraud charge had been clamped on the International Broadcasting Company, preventing its receipt of mail. Obviously, such a condition would mean rapid strangulation to a border radio station. The McAllen postmaster told Munal that the order had been automatically released after Horwitz was jailed, but Munal headed for the capital of Texas, just to make sure. The radioman met with postal inspector J.W. Adamson on October 6, 1932.

"I told him who I was and what I wanted," wrote Munal to Doctor, "and he politely told me there was nothing doing but I finally convinced him that I had nothing whatever to do with Horwitz and that my intention was good and gave him a good cigar and kept pounding away on him." Adamson expressed concern about two border-station spooks, Mel Roy and Rajah Rayboid. "I had hopes of convincing them that Mel Roy was O.K.," Munal reported to the boss, "and I approached him cautiously, as to what he had against Mel Roy and he exploded. He said as long as he could prevent it, he was going to keep Mel Roy and Rajah Rayboid off of all stations. He said Mel Roy was crooked and that Rayboid was a confirmed drunkard." But Munal's insistence finally wore down the resistance of the dedicated postal worker. Inspector Adamson told Munal to write a letter detailing the situation and agreed to recommend to the Postmaster General that the fraud order in force against the station be removed.

Despite those efforts, it wasn't until 1935 that Dr. Brinkley was able to get control of the Reynosa station. Doctor ran the station in his own inimitable style and briefly operated a hospital in nearby San Juan dedicated to the treatment of colon and rectal problems. By 1939 Doctor had moved his clinics to Arkansas and had decided to consolidate his broadcasting efforts in Del Rio. When Carr Collins made an offer to purchase the controlling rights to XEAW, the Mystery Man of the Rio Grande was only too happy to accept.

Programming on XEAW under Collins' control followed the basic border blaster formula with a few modifications. Musical entertainment was predominantly western, with cowboy singers making transcriptions in Dallas and shipping them to Reynosa for airplay. During the early years of World War II, Arnaldo Ramirez, a young promoter from McAllen, purchased time on the high-powered station for his programs *La Hora de Victoria* (The Hour of Victory) and *La Hora del Soldado* (The Soldier's Hour). "That station was the most powerful thing on the Rio Grande," Ramirez explained. "I did the announcing, and everyone from Matamoros to Laredo knew my name." Ramirez delivered ads for beer distributors and restaurants in a distinctive Tex-Mex patter and featured performers from the border area, who, like their cowboy Anglo counterparts, were largely overlooked by the radio stations in the larger Mexican cities.

Advertising time on XEAW was, of course, available for mail-order products, with orders being received at a Dallas post office box. When a Tyler, Texas, nursery offered its exceptional roses over the air, sales response helped the city become known as the Rose Capital of the World. In the preacher department, normally a mainstay of the border radio repertoire, Collins allowed only one religious orator, his own minister—the Reverend George W. Truett. The first day Collins walked into the XEAW building, he carried a big stack of Truett's recordings under his arm. Veteran border radio evangelist Sam Morris, the Voice of Temperance, tried to get on XEAW but was kept from the Reynosa microphone because Collins was a strict denominationalist.

Like those who had pioneered the industry before him, the Dallas insurance man began to experience the unpredictable nature of Mexican policy. Keeping the various officials satisfied was taking more and more of his time. Younger brother Hal took up residence on the Rio Grande to keep close tabs on the situation and report back to Dallas. Carr Collins' son James, a future U.S. congressman, also worked at the station for a brief time. Despite the occasional problem with Mexican bureaucrats, XEAW returned solid profits to its Texas investors for four years. Then the station suffered almost the same fate dealt to XERA.

The demise of XEAW came in 1943, one year after *federales* seized the gland man's border blaster. "It was easy to hear the station in Dallas," Carr Collins remembered later. "One night before going to a picture show, I turned on the radio to pick up the station and it was coming in very clearly. When I returned, I turned on the radio again to check the station, and to my utter amazement, I found that a station in Monterrey, Mexico was coming in on our frequency. Within the two hour period, the Mexican authorities, acting through a squad of soldiers, had closed us down at Reynosa and had given the frequency to a station at Monterrey."

The radio *jefes* had seized his kilocycles, and Collins wisely suspected that they might try to confiscate his broadcasting equipment. He knew he had to move the hardware north of the river quickly or the outfit could end up a total loss. Permits had to be secured from Mexico City and Monterrey for such an operation. Collins began to think he might have to abandon the expensive radio equipment in the desert. Then the Mexican Army came to the rescue in the person of an elderly general. The general owned the Reynosa power company and needed a transformer for his plant. The retreating border blasters gladly accommodated him with this electronic bribe, and in return the general persuaded his nation's president to allow the rest of XEAW's equipment to leave the country unimpeded.

The Collins brothers knew they needed to act fast, before the Mexican government changed its mind. They quickly rounded up fifty to sixty trucks in the Rio Grande Valley. Both of the massive transmitters and seven directional towers had to be disassembled, a feat accomplished in less than a week. When the assortment of trucks was loaded up, the strange caravan rolled out of Reynosa. For a fee of 500 pesos the town's chief of police headed the procession, armed with a big shotgun to ensure their reaching Texas unmolested. "We looked like Barnum and Bailey's circus coming down that road," said Hal Collins, "what with that caravan of trucks and that Mexican riding lead. One truck broke down, and we pushed it across the border, because we knew it was now or never."

North of the Rio Grande the radio equipment was loaded onto railroad cars and shipped to Corpus Christi. Carr Collins offered the hardware to the Federal Communications Commission, having heard that the Office of War Information needed powerful, long-range radio equipment for use in the North Atlantic. The Washington bureaucrats eagerly accepted the offer, but then a problem surfaced: the border-blaster transmitter was one of a kind, a work of experimental technology created by engineers James Weldon and Nestor Cuesta. Weldon could not go with the equipment because he was occupied as chief engineer for the OWI in Washington, D.C., having gone there from Acuña when the *federales* seized XERA. And Cuesta could not serve the U.S. government as a communications engineer because he was then a Mexican national. So the border blaster never got the chance to do its bit for the Allied war effort.

Collins did not offer to donate the XEAW transmitter to the FCC completely out of the goodness of his heart. In return for his equipment the Dallas businessman requested permission to open a 50,000-watt clear-channel radio station in Corpus Christi. In September 1944 the FCC held a hearing on the matter in Washington to consider whether the new KWBU signal would interfere with station KLRA in Little Rock, Arkansas. The *Dallas Morning News* noted that the hearing might have "political significance to Texas." Stockholders of Century Broadcasting Company, the company applying for the Corpus Christi license, were listed as the Crazy Water Company, Fidelity Union Life Insurance Company, Pat and Mike O'Daniel (Senator W. Lee O'Daniel's sons), James Collins, and Baylor University.

Perhaps the FCC mistakenly lumped Collins' image with that of Brinkley and Baker, or maybe the officials received anti-Crazy protests from the FDA. Two of the broadcasting commissioners told the press that they wanted to examine the new station's policies. They said they had been negatively impressed by the test broadcasts from Reynosa and doubted that KWBU could be operated in the public interest. Despite their reservations, the commission eventually approved the application to operate the station on the Gulf of Mexico. Engineer Nestor Cuesta installed a 50,000-watt transmitter near Corpus Christi, and KWBU began making money for Crazy Water Crystals and the Baylor Bears. In 1956 the partners donated their interests in the station to the Baptist university nestled on the banks of the Brazos River.

Collins seemed to derive as many benefits from donating to charitable causes as he did from drinking Crazy Water. In an uncharacteristically candid article published in 1970 the *National Enquirer* reported that Carr P. Collins had given away more than $20 million to charity over his lifetime. In 1946 he revealed his fondness for regional culture by endowing the Texas Institute of Letters with funds that allow the organization to present an annual award to the author of the best Texas book of the year. In addition to his efforts on behalf of Baylor University, the former border radio operator assisted the Dallas Cancer Fund, the Salvation Army, the Dallas Inter-Racial Committee, Bishop College, Hardin-Simmons University, Scott and White Hospital, Baylor Hospital, and many other charitable organizations.

Though he sold his Mineral Wells health water business shortly after World War II, Collins continued to use the regulatory elixir right up until the day he passed away in 1980 at the age of 87. A firm believer in hard work and right living, the insurance executive had a lifestyle that differed dramatically from that of many other border operators. His unshakable belief in the curative power of Crazy Water Crystals did, however, leave Collins vulnerable to some gentle ribbing by his border compadres. Often, when gathering in a border-town cantina for some Rio Grande firewater, one radioman would turn to another and say, "You know, I'll never understand why Carr P. Collins is so against alcohol. He sure doesn't mind ruining people's stomachs with those Crazy Water Crystals."

Please Pass the Tamales, Pappy

They've come to town with their guitars,
And now they're smoking big cigars—
Them hillbillies are politicians now.
—*Campaign song written by W. Lee "Pappy" O'Daniel
for his 1938 Texas gubernatorial campaign*

As public figures with access to the most far-reaching broadcasting outlets in North America, Brinkley, Baker, and other border personalities naturally drifted into politics. Politics combined the talents necessary for proselytizing, healing, fortune-telling, and patent medicine peddling and promised a reward even greater than cash—the glittering, Faustian jewels of power. But these early border politicians were neither as gifted nor as successful at wooing the listening public as a stocky Ohio-born, Kansas-bred Irish flour salesman, known to listening audiences all over the Southwest as "Pass the Biscuits, Pappy" O'Daniel.

Born in 1890, Wilbert Lee O'Daniel grew up on a farm in Kansas under the stern eye of his hardworking mother, Alice. An active member of the Church of Christ, Alice watched as her boy helped fight the blackleg and cholera epidemics that ravaged the livestock and as he put long hours into producing the corn, wheat, hay, cider, and milk that the family needed to fill the larder. A bright boy, Wilbert worked his way through Salt City Business College in Hutchinson, Kansas, and got into the flour business, which at that time was one of the biggest industries in the area. Wilbert earned a reputation as a crack salesman and eventually bought his own mill, which prospered with the increased demand for flour brought on by World War I. In 1920 Wilbert made one of his few errors in business judgment and opened up a flour export business in New Orleans. The bottom fell out of the market, and on July 4, 1925, Wilbert accepted a job at the Burrus Mill and Elevator Company in Fort Worth, the home of Light Crust Flour.

J. Perry Burrus, the owner of Burrus Mills, also operated mills in Dallas, McKinney, and Sherman. He was an eminently successful miller, a sharp financial manager, and a good judge of character who thought highly of his new employee. O'Daniel started as the Fort Worth sales manager. He found that Texas bakers were reluctant to use Texas flour and at first sold Kansas flour to the Texans. O'Daniel began to blend Texas flour in with his order for Kansas flour, unknown to his customers. After receiving compliments on the adulterated mixture, O'Daniel revealed his secret and, with his inimitable marketing flair, promoted the use of Texas flour by pointing out its "high protein content" and its "favorable comparison with any other flour." The Texas-flour-for-Texans campaign was a success, and O'Daniel soon became general manager of Burrus Mills and, later, president of the Fort Worth mill. Always eager to stay one slice ahead of the competition, O'Daniel hired George Faltz of Kansas to create the first lab and experimental kitchen in a Texas mill.

But Wilbert O'Daniel did not bake a place for himself in history merely by creating winning recipes. O'Daniel's immortality lay in the radio, the little squawking box of songs, sermons, and serials that adorned most Texas parlors in the thirties. Among the many sounds that filled the Fort Worth airwaves was the sound of a string trio led by a fiddler and part-time barber from Turkey, Texas, named Bob Wills.

Wills and his musical partners, singer Milton Brown and guitarist Herman Arnspiger, played every Saturday over radio station KFJZ in Fort Worth. Sponsored by the Aladdin Lamp Company and known as the Aladdin Laddies, the group had some success broadcasting from the Kemble Furniture Store in downtown Fort Worth. Soon, however, Aladdin turned the lights out on the laddies, and Will's band looked for another radio sponsor.

Ed Kemble, the owner of the store, was a friend of O'Daniel's and thought that Burrus Mills might be just the sponsor for Wills and the boys. Kemble mentioned the idea to the future Texas governor. At first, O'Daniel felt that a radio show would not be worth the money, but he finally agreed to give it a try, on the condition that he pay no wages to the band members until they proved their worth.

Desperate for airtime, Wills, Brown, and Arnspiger started their 7 a.m. broadcasts in January 1931 from the KFJZ studios—described by observers as "nothing more than the back room of Meacham's store in north Fort Worth." The few hundred radios within fifteen miles of the studio heard an assortment of hillbilly tunes including "21 Years" and "The Chicken Reel." Truett Kimzey, the station engineer, performed the announcing duties, reading ads for Light Crust Flour that were written by O'Daniel. After a few days, Wills jokingly referred to the band as the Light Crust Doughboys, and the name stuck like frosting.

Response to the first broadcasts was not all that enthusiastic. O'Daniel, never one to handle labor relations delicately, fired the band and told them that he didn't like their hillbilly music. KFJZ continued the program without a sponsor for a few weeks until Wills went to talk to O'Daniel. Wills waited in the Light Crust Flour offices for two days before the wizard of pulverized wheat would grant him an audience. O'Daniel addressed Wills without looking up from his paper-strewn desk. "What do you want?" he asked.

Wills said, "I want a job. I'll drive a truck, sweep the floor, or anything, but I want a job."

O'Daniel replied gruffly, "It's out of the ordinary for musicians to want to work, isn't it?"

"Well, no, sir, not for this musician."

Sniffing a deal, O'Daniel became interested. "Well, that puts a different light on it if you're sure you want to work."

Pappy, as he was later known to his radio audience, magnanimously offered to sponsor the radio program if the band members worked a forty-hour week at the mill. The band agreed—they had no other choice. Wills drove a truck, Arnspiger sacked flour, and Brown went into sales. Each one earned $7.50 a week. After five weeks the band members had had enough. Arnspiger, who had the roughest job, put it bluntly: "I will play the broadcasts or work at the mill but not both." Luckily, the station was getting a good response to the show by that time. O'Daniel agreed to let them quit working at the mill, as long as they practiced music for eight hours a day in the mill. The band happily agreed to the new arrangement.

The popularity of the Light Crust Doughboy broadcasts picked up. Each show began with a few bars of music to the tune of "Eagle Riding Papa From Tennessee," at which point Kimzey jumped in with the announcement "The Light Crust Doughboys are on the air." The band then went into its theme song:

Oh, we never do brag, we never do boast.

We sing our song from coast to coast.

We're the Light Crust Doughboys from Burrus Mills.

The band played a variety of popular hillbilly and gospel tunes in the Wills style. With calls and yassirs, a musical trick he had learned picking cotton on the plains of North Texas, Wills provided a counterpoint to

Brown's jazzy vocals. Sales of flour picked up, and O'Daniel became a great fan of the Light Crust Doughboys and hillbilly music. He wrote all the ad copy and composed little poems and songs to spice up the broadcasts. He outfitted a bus for the band with a loudspeaker to honor the numerous requests they recieved for live appearances. On one occasion the band was booked to go on a goodwill tour with the Fort Worth Chamber of Commerce. At the last minute the regular announcer could not go, and O'Daniel decided to appear in his place. The first stop was in Weatherford, and O'Daniel's rich, soothing voice and down-home yet formal manner was well received. O'Daniel finished the tour and became the regular announcer for the Light Crust Doughboys, delivering flour-inspired song introductions and sermonettes that were to wash across the airwaves of Texas for the next fifteen years and carry the speaker to the Governor's Mansion and the U.S. Senate.

Pappy's blend of homey Christian philosophy, sentimental poetry, and rural music found an ever-increasing audience. He moved the program to Fort Worth's 10,000-watt WBAP at 12:30 p.m., a time slot that hit the largely female audience just in time for a midday respite from their household chores. In addition to the daily WBAP broadcasts, he was soon picked up by WOAI in San Antonio and KPRC in Houston. O'Daniel and the band continued to make numerous personal appearances, entertaining at memorable occasions like the Texas Bakers' Convention and a chimpanzee's birthday party at the Fort Worth Zoo. The band began to broadcast Wednesday night from Dublin, Texas, and Friday night from Waco. Leon McAulifffe, a teenager in Houston at the time who grew up to be a great western swing musician in his own right, remembered walking three blocks to the store and "never missing a word of a song. In the summer every window was open and every radio was tuned to the Light Crust Doughboys."

The great flour magnate built a special practice room for the band inside the mill, complete with a record player and a large selection of all the latest releases. He forbade the band members to make personal appearances in honky-tonks like the Crystal Springs Ballroom, a watering hole favored by Bonnie Parker, Clyde Barrow, and other notables, saying it was not good for the band's reputation. But personal appearances were extremely lucrative for the band, and the musicians began to chafe at O'Daniel's straightlaced, tightfisted control. Brown quit and quickly formed the legendary Musical Brownies. Wills had numerous run-ins with the biscuit boss. On several occasions he indulged his taste for bootleg liquor, wrecking a Light Crust vehicle and missing performances as a result. O'Daniel gave Wills's father a place to live out in the country but drove the old man to distraction by treating him like a peon. At one point Old Man Wills warned his son, "I'm gonna kill that son of a bitch W. Lee O'Daniel," and a short time later he tried, chasing the future governor off the property with a three-foot-long piece of oak from a harness.

Finally, in August 1933, Bob Wills quit the program. O'Daniel warned him that he was making the worst mistake of his life by taking the band from a money-making job to a place "where they probably won't make a dime." Wills moved his band to Waco, and they took the name "The Texas Playboys." They eventually made much more than a dime and became one of the best-known acts in the history of country music, despite the best efforts of O'Daniel. The vindictive flour salesman forced Wills out of Texas for several years by filing a lawsuit that sought to bar Wills from using the words "Formerly the Light Crust Doughboys" in his advertising. Pappy also claimed $10,000 in damages to Light Crust Flour, arising from Wills's alleged practice of "presenting promiscuous programs" at dances. While the case was found in Wills's favor in 1935, O'Daniel might have been the fellow Wills was thinking of when he coined the famous phrase, "You're a man after my own heart—with a razor."

O'Daniel need not have been so worried about losing the talented musician, as the popularity of his own talks and the now-anonymous Light Crust Doughboys continued to grow. "Please pass the biscuits, Pappy," encouraged a sweet matronly voice at the beginning of each broadcast, at which point O'Daniel spoke warmly and paternally over a musical background. While the strains of familiar hillbilly and religious music pleased audiences as much as ever, it was the silver-tongued Pappy who kept Texans glued to the radio every day at the noon hour. His deep melodic voice was modulated perfectly for the tinny radio speakers of the day, and his homages to motherhood, honesty, and good Christian living pulled at the heartstrings of his entire audience. One chronicler described his radio persona as "Eddie Guest and Will Rogers and Dale Carnegie and Bing Crosby rolled into one." O'Daniel talked "like a big brother, a pal, a guide, a friend," blending homespun religiosity with humor and good common sense. He spoke especially to homemakers, an overlooked demographic segment in those early days of electronic marketing. His persuasive voice and powdery-smooth words of affection seduced housewives into favoring his brand of flour. "Hello there, mother, you little sweetheart," he cooed during a typical broadcast. "How in the world are you, anyway, you little bunch of sweetness? This is your big boy, W. Lee O'Daniel."

One longtime acquaintance described him as "a born actor. He may not believe it, but he feels it at the time." Once, while wiping the tears from his eyes as his band played "The Old Rugged Cross," Pappy chortled under his breath, "That's what brings 'em in, boys. That's what really brings 'em in." Ever a professional, O'Daniel never forgot the dictates of his medium. While he crooned a tribute to a son's love for his mother and held his mike with one hand, with the other hand he motioned the band to stand the right distance from their microphone.

In poetry and song, much of it from his own pen, the charismatic radio star urged erring husbands to correct their ways, called for schoolchildren to be thrifty and polite, and promoted adoption and traffic safety. He designed memorial programs of all kinds. To mark the death of Jimmie Rodgers, he composed "Memories of Jimmie Rodgers." To support FDR's war against the Depression, he penned "On to Victory, Mr. Roosevelt." And to ease the torment of those suffering from a flu epidemic, O'Daniel drew up a memorable ditty with the chorus "Kachoo, kachoo, kachoo." During the Light Crust Doughboys Armistice Day Program of 1931, he recited the poem "In Flanders Fields" and dedicated a song to a wounded vet who just happened to be his flour salesman in the El Paso area. Songs of his own composition, including "Beautiful Texas," "Sons of the Alamo," and "The Lay of the Lonely Longhorn," as well as homilies and poems filled out the programs, which often ended in a prayer—and a reminder to buy Light Crust Flour.

In 1935 O'Daniel quit working for Burrus Mills and founded his own company, Hillbilly Flour. He bought flour from mills around the state and packaged it in Hillbilly Flour sacks emblazoned with the company emblem of a goat and the word "Guaranteed" in big red letters. Guaranteed of what is anybody's guess. He renamed his band the Hillbilly Boys, hired songstress Kitty Williamson (known as Texas Rose), and added his sons, Pat and Mike, with the stage names of Pattie-boy and Mickey Wickey, to play the guitar and fiddle. One of Pappy's immortal verses appeared on the sack as well: "HILLBILLY Music on the air, HILLBILLY Flour everywhere; / It tickles your feet—it tickles your tongue, / Wherever you go, Its Praises are sung."

By 1937 the biscuit baron was worth well over $500,000 and had the most popular daily show in the history of Texas radio, as thousands of ears perked up when they heard the theme song: "I like bread and biscuits, / Big white fluffy biscuits— / Hillbilly Flour makes 'em grand." Millers from all over the state approached him to market their flour. Pappy dabbled in Cowtown real estate and was elected president of the Fort Worth Chamber of Commerce. For all his homespun airs and his down-home demeanor, the radio star was one of the kingpins of Fort Worth, a tough, successful businessman who was close to some of the richest and most conservative men in the state.

Never satisfied with current sales levels, O'Daniel looked around for new ways of promoting his flour. Like so many others before him, Pappy was drawn to the mesquite-and-cedar-covered shores of the Rio Grande. He bought time for the Hillbilly Boys on XEPN in Piedras Negras and moved the band down to the border in the fall of 1937. He purchased a home in Eagle Pass, becoming one of the many radio notables that graced the border community. The salesman and his band commuted across the border in a Hudson sedan to the XEPN studios, and Pappy's voice glided out over 100,000 watts. The Hudson must have been one of the finest autos in the border town, as it was stolen one night while parked in front of the O'Daniel residence. The *Eagle Pass Daily Guide* reported that the car theft was the first to occur in many years and blamed the incident on "some drunkard, wanting some fresh air," who "took the automobile and having gone into the ditch, abandoned it."

Even the charms of Old Mexico couldn't soften the strictness of the W. Lee O'Daniel regimen, although the band members found the attractions of the cantinas overpowering at times. On one occasion several of the Hillbilly Boys retired for tequila after an afternoon broadcast, and wound up holding a belching contest in the plaza of the border town. The local constabulary did not think highly of the civil disturbance taking place directly in front of the city offices, and the band members spent the night in jail, an open courtyard guarded by rifle-toting residents who were not at all impressed by the shivering entertainers. Pappy bailed the band members out the next day just in time for a broadcast, and he made it plain that there were other aspiring musicians ready and eager to join the band.

In the spring of 1938 O'Daniel, Carr Collins, and a small group of North Texas power brokers discussed a marketing idea that was as simple as it was revolutionary—that the elder statesman of flour sales enter the 1938 Texas Democratic primary for the governorship of the Lone Star State. Pappy was intrigued by the idea but hesitant at first. He was a political novice, a Kansas-bred Republican sympathizer who had never voted in a Texas election and had not even paid the poll tax. But he was a brilliant salesman and knew instinctively that running for office would be a great way to sell flour. Neither he nor his good friend Carr Collins, who was called the Cardinal Richelieu of the O'Daniel entourage, had any way of knowing just how successful their marketing ploy would be and that soon people all over the country would recognize Texas as a leader in "whangdoodle music, flapdoodle poetry, and doodlebug statecraft."

On Palm Sunday, 1938, Pappy's fans in radio land heard the familiar greeting "How do you do, ladies and gentlemen, and hello there, boys and girls. This is W. Lee O'Daniel speaking." He spoke warmly, sooth-ingly into the microphone and told a story about one of his listeners. It seemed that a blind man had sent him a letter recently, saying that he was tired of politics as usual in the state of Texas. The man was looking for someone new to support, someone who was trustworthy, honest, and a good Christian, and the only person he could think of that would fit the description was Pappy O'Daniel. The man asked if Pappy wouldn't please run for governor, and the biscuit wizard passed his request on to his radio audience, asking if he should indeed run for the state's highest office. The audience responded with a flood of mail that dazed even the celebrated master of radio flour power: 54,499 people wrote in asking him to run for governor. Only four listeners advised against his can-didacy—they thought he was too good for the job.

On May 1, 1938, a Sunday morning, O'Daniel announced on a special radio broadcast that he would seek the Democratic nomination for gover-nor of Texas. At that time, winning the Democratic party nomination meant winning the governorship, as the powerful Democratic party ma-chinery, forged during the Reconstruction era, controlled state politics through the poll tax and primary system. While Democratic candidates were oftentimes extremely conservative, the yellow-dog Democrats, who made up most of the voting population of the states, got their nickname by maintaining that they would vote for a yellow dog before they would vote for a Republican.

Speaking to his friends in radio land, O'Daniel outlined his platform, which included the Ten Commandments, tax reform, abolition of the poll tax, and a pension program that would guarantee all Texans over 65 years of age an income of $30 per month. His campaign theme was "Pass the Biscuits, Pappy," his motto was the Golden Rule, and his campaign slogan was "Less Johnson Grass and Politicians, More Smokestacks and Businessmen." Getting right down to the really important issue in poli-tics, O'Daniel told his supporters, "The only thing that can prevent us from winning is sufficient lack of funds. . . . You had better take that old rocking chair down and mortgage it and spend the money in the manner you think best to get your pension. . . . We have not one dollar in our campaign fund."

Newspapermen and politicians took little notice at first of the O'Daniel candidacy but instead focused their attention on the two leading con-tenders, Colonel Ernest O. Thompson of Amarillo and William McCraw of Dallas. Both men were prominent conservative attorneys. Although they could get no more rise out of the electorate than a barrel of wet flour, they were seasoned political veterans and seemed the likely front-runners in what promised to be a dull campaign.

In the first week of June 1938, with only six weeks before Election Day, Pappy opened his campaign. The poetic salesman—accompanied by his wife, Merle; his daughter, Molly; his boys, Pat and Mike; and the rest of the Hillbilly Band—drove down to Jacksonville and Yoakum in the same bus that O'Daniel and the crew had used for years to promote flour sales. The candidate received a warm welcome in the towns, but the Hillbilly express didn't really get rolling until the bus pulled into Waco on June 12, Close to 25,000 people, the biggest political crowd that had ever gathered on the Brazos River, crammed into the downtown square to see the biscuit baron in person. After the Waco rally the press and political pundits sensed that a whirlwind was rising in Texas politics, one that would soon leave the Texas political machinery clogged with flour.

O'Daniel logged 20,000 miles in the next few weeks, making two or three appearances during the day and holding a major rally in the evening. He addressed a rally of 8000 people in San Angelo, the biggest thing to hit that town in fifty years, In Colorado City he talked to 3000 people who had waited more than three hours to see him after bus trouble had delayed his arrival. When the Hillbilly bus tried to pass through Wharton to attend a rally in Rosenberg, the citizens of Wharton blocked the road and forced Pappy and the boys to make an appearance. During a downpour in Fort Worth, O'Daniel instructed his band to play "I Get the Blues When It Rains," took down his umbrella, and told the wet crowd "If you folks can stand in the rain and listen to me, I sure can stand in the rain and talk to you." Twenty-two thousand Austinites heard Pappy speak in Wooldridge Park, the biggest crowd that had ever gathered in the political nexus of Texas, and 26,000 people crammed into Miller Memorial Theater in Houston, forming the biggest political gathering in the history of the Lone Star State.

Everyone in rural Texas had either heard or heard of the famous radio entertainer, and they all came out to witness his live performance, a unique blend of live music, easily digestible political rhetoric, and old-time revival. The Hillbilly Boys started each rally with a few musical selections, songs like O'Daniel's composition "My Million Dollar Smile" and the popular tune "I Want to Be a Cowboy's Sweetheart." As the crowd warmed to the music, their anticipation began to build. At just the right moment, O'Daniel's well-groomed stocky frame appeared onstage, and his round, clean-shaven face broke into a dimpled smile. "Hello, friends" he said. "This is W. Lee O'Daniel, the next governor of Texas." Before the cheers died down, Pappy led the band in singing his most popular song, "Beautiful Texas."

After the song, the chief Hillbilly began to speak, warning his audience that "if anyone came just for the music, they can leave now." Not a one left as O'Daniel's melodic voice began to croon the refrains of his campaign: get rid of the "professional politicians"; vote for W. Lee O'Daniel, the "Common Citizens Candidate"; old-age pensions for everyone, as outlined in the Ten Commandments, part of his platform. "Take the fourth commandment," he explained. "Honor thy father and thy mother. Doesn't that mean old-age pensions as plain as day?" He talked about promoting business in Texas. He told his audience that he had driven through fields of Texas tomatoes one morning and later walked into a store, only to read "Made in New York" on a bottle of ketchup. "Make your own ketchup," he cried, "and put people to work." To those who accused him of being a Yankee, he answered that he had been named after General Robert E. Lee at the request of his uncle, who, while fighting for the North, had been tenderly nursed by a Southern soldier. O'Daniel quoted liberally from the Scriptures and from his own works as well, reading selections from his poetry such as "That City for Shut-ins." The band struck up a song to emphasize the main points of the O'Daniel platform, singing "Darling Mother of Mine," for instance, when the candidate mentioned the need for pensions for aged mothers. Humor was not absent from the combination gubernatorial and flour-selling campaign. "Go ahead and try me for two years," O'Daniel teased. "You can't be any worse off than you have been." He led the band in singing a song he had written specially for the campaign, which went as follows: "They've come to town with their guitars, / And now they're smoking big cigars, / Them hillbillies are politicians now / They've chucked their boots and overalls / They've even dropped their 'howze you alls,' / Them hillbillies are politicians now." And of course, Pappy plugged Hillbilly Flour in each of his campaign stops. After all, the number one priority in the campaign was to sell flour.

The crowds, hardworking people who were just digging their way out from the depths of the Depression, loved his straightforward message. They yelled in unison, "Pour it on 'em, pour it on 'em." Women brought gifts up to the stage—a beribboned shoebox full of fried chicken, a cake made with Hillbilly Flour. Others handed Pappy lariats, rabbits' feet, and a paddle with which to spank the professional politicians. It was obvious to anyone who attended his rallies that the people of Texas loved and trusted the man they had listened to over the radio for so many years. Women were his special fans. While young mothers suckled infants in the back of the crowd, others jammed forward, swooning over the image of Pappy, and often fainting in the heat.

At the end of every gubernatorial show, O'Daniel sent his attractive daughter, Molly, out into the audience with a small wood barrel on which

*The advent of radio in the 1920s opened up new horizons for everyone within earshot of a wireless. Like millions of other Americans, this San Antonio woman (**photo no. 1**) was fascinated by the new medium that brought the wonders of the outside world into her home. The flamboyant Dr. John R. Brinkley, shown here with one of his private airplanes (**photo no. 2**), blasted hillbilly music, astrological predictions and eclectic medical information from his superpowered radio station in Villa Acuña, Mexico across the river from Del Rio, Texas from 1931 to 1941.*

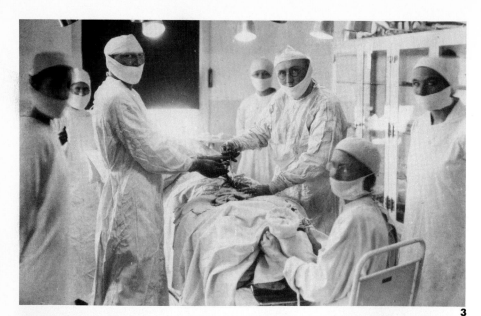

3

4

Hailed by some as the "Most Learned Doctor in America," the famous radio surgeon performed thousands of goat gonad transplants **(photo no. 3)** before the Amateur Meatcutters
Association, as he referred to the A.M.A., closed down his Kansas rejuvenation empire,
causing him to break for the border. Before leaving the Sunflower State, Brinkley tried his
hand at politics and masterminded a high-powered multi-media campaign. Even his detrac-
tors later admitted that he would have won the Kansas governorship if his supporters had all
spelled his name correctly on the write-in ballot. His campaign utilized a colorful sound-
truck **(photo no. 4)** dubbed Ammunition Train No. 1.

5

6

While Brinkley confined his medical practice to problems of reproduction and excretion, fellow media renegade Norman Baker advertised his controversial cancer treatments (photo no. 5) over his own border station, XENT, in Nuevo Laredo. He incurred the wrath of the A.M.A.'s Morris Fishbein (photo no. 6), who claimed that Baker and his associates exhibited "a quality so malevolent that it sets them apart from others of the human race."

7

DEL RIO EVENING NEWS
DEL RIO, TEXAS

XER **XER** RADIO NUMBER

VOLUME III

MEXICO PRAISED FOR AIDING XER PLANS

"THE BRINKLEY'S"

STATION XER, LOCATED AT VILLA ACUNA, COAHUILA, MEXICO,
ACROSS THE RIO GRANDE FROM DEL RIO, TEXAS.
COPYRIGHT BY LIPPE STUDIO

8

Beautiful Home of Dr. J. R. Brinkley
Del Rio, Texas
Lippe Studio

DOCTOR BRINKLEY

9

ROSWELL HOTEL, Del Rio, Texas

10

11

(Photo no. 7) *The towns of Del Rio and Villa Acuña welcomed Dr. Brinkley as a saviour from the grips of the Great Depression. Brinkley's borderland empire included a high-powered radio station (photo no. 8), a Southwestern art deco mansion just north of the Rio Grande (photo no. 9), and a hospital in the Roswell Hotel (photo no. 10). But Brinkley, Texas, a utopian community near Doctor's citrus groves between Del Rio and Eagle Pass, never advanced beyond ground-breaking ceremonies (photo no. 11).*

12

As Del Rio celebrated the opening of Dr. Brinkley's radio station, citizens of Eagle Pass and other border towns decided they needed borderblasters too. Soon, American airwaves were crowded with unusual programming from Piedras Negras (photo no. 12), Nuevo Laredo, Reynosa, Juarez, Monterrey, Tijuana and other locations in Mexico. Purple-suited Norman Baker (photo no. 13) utilized his background as a vaudeville mentalist in the operation of his high-powered station, which often featured the toots and whistles of the calliaphone, an instrument of his own invention (photo no. 14).

13

XENT STUDIO
LOOKING INTO RECEPTION ROOM
AND SHOWING CALLIAPHONE

14

15

16

*Singin' cowboys, psychics and senoritas traveled a circuit which developed along the border, pitching everything from songbooks to tap dancing lessons and laxatives. Major Kord, shown seated in a suit with the XEPN family (**photo no. 15**), was the border's greatest pitchman until he discovered Cowboy Slim Rinehart (**photo no. 16**). Although Rinehart never made a commercial recording, he was one of the most popular performers of the 1930s and 40s.*

ROSE DAWN, The Star Girl, heard over
Radio Station XERA, Del Rio, Texas.

17

*Astrologers and psychics, often called "spooks," were big mail-pullers on the border. Brinkley's personal astrologer, Rose Dawn (**photo no. 17**), divined listeners' fortunes for a dollar. With her husband and fellow spook Koran she founded the Order of Maya, which still offers esoteric wisdom from headquarters in San Antonio.*

In 1938 Fort Worth businessman W. Lee "Pappy" O'Daniel (**photo no. 18**) captured Texas' governorship with his poetry (**photo no. 19**) and charismatic radio personality (**photo no. 20**). Although a political novice, his campaign showmanship led him to a surprise victory that stunned the Texas establishment.

O'Daniel made a fortune during the Depression peddling his Hillbilly Flour (photo no. 21) over the radio. Women all over the state tuned in each day at lunchtime to hear the call, "Please pass the biscuits, Pappy."

*Stylistically akin to Brinkley and Huey Long, "Pappy" toured the state in later campaigns in a sound truck outfitted with a papier-mâché replica of the state capitol (**photo no. 22**). Shown standing next to the founder of Kraft Foods (**photo no. 23**), O'Daniel continued his radio programs with a weekly broadcast from the governor's mansion. His homey radio sermonettes continued to be popular with Texans of all ages (**photo no. 24**).*

23

24

25

26

27

*Like Brinkley, shown (**photo no. 25**) with his record-breaking 788 lb. tuna fish, Pappy considered himself a sportsman and bagged a buffalo to serve at his second inaugural barbecue (**photo no. 26**). The governor personally helped distribute (**photo no. 27**) 6000 pounds of beef, 4000 loaves of bread, 1500 pounds of onions and a boxcar load of Rio Grande grapefruit to his hungry supporters.*

HOW GOV. O'DANIEL GETS HIS MESSAGE ACROSS

Chillicothe

DALLAS

TEXAS

★ AUSTIN

Rio Grande

MEXICO

REYNOSA

GULF OF MEXICO

Texas legislators are annoyed by O'Daniel broadcasts from Mexico.

In 1941 Governor O'Daniel campaigned for the U.S. Senate over border station XEAW, which he owned with political advisor and Crazy Water Crystals magnate Carr Collins, a tactic that angered his opponents and inspired this cartoon commentary (**photo no. 28**) *in the* New York Times.

29

30

*Crazy Water Crystals (**photo no. 29**), a frequent advertiser on border stations, was a laxative that reportedly worked like a "ramrod" to clean out "sluggish systems." Mineral Wells, Texas, home of the Crazy Well located on the premises of the Crazy Hotel, erected a sign welcoming relief seekers to the "Home of Crazy" (**photo no. 30**).*

32

As hillbilly music became country and western after World War II, the rich baritone of Paul Kallinger (**photo no. 31**) boomed forth from XERF selling ballpoint pens, D-Con rat poison and "genuine simulated diamonds." Kallinger, pictured (**photo no. 32**) at the Louisiana Hayride with Elvis Presley and rockabilly great Johnny Horton, was at first hesitant to let the young King of Rock on his all-country show.

33

*Though Hank Thompson (**photo no. 33**) never found his way to the XERF studios, the young honky tonker sold thousands of his songbooks over the border stations. One of the many stars who did appear live with Kallinger from Acuña was Jim Reeves, pictured on the right with Kallinger (**in photo no. 34**) in a scene that recalls the many shootouts for control of radio stations all along the border.*

35

36

Border station studios (**photo no. 35**) *hosted performances by Mexican artists like Rosa Dominguez* (**photo no. 36**) *and Lydia Mendoza* (**photo no. 37**), *providing American airwaves an international flavor.*

38

39

Mexican citizen Nestor Cuesta (**photo no. 38**) *honed his engineering skills working at borderblasters for Brinkley, Baker and Carr Collins. He later became an American citizen and worked on U.S. military radar systems with former border radio engineering genius James Weldon at Dallas's Continental Electronics.*

Arnaldo Ramirez (**at right in photo no. 39**) *hosted XEAW's popular program* **Hora Del Soldado** *(Hour of the Soldier) during World War Two. Ramirez later succeeded in becoming the mayor of Mission, Texas and founding Falcon Records, one of the premier labels for the border's Tex-Mex sound.*

"The Voice of Temperance," Sam Morris (**photo no. 40**) *went to Eagle Pass from Stamford, Texas to preach against the ravages of rum on station XEPN in 1936. He remained on the airwaves for the next 50 years.*

41

When the Saturday Evening Post *ran this picture of J. C. Bishop* (second from left in photo no. 41) *in an unflattering article on border radio in 1948, Bishop considered suing the magazine. However, his ministry was deluged with favorable mail after the national publicity. "What they meant as a smear, I say, the good Lord turned into a blessing," he later observed. Dallas Turner* (photo no. 42) *began his long border radio career as a singin' cowboy and pitchman in the mid 40s. Performing as Nevada Slim, Cowboy Dallas Turner, or Yodeling Slim Dallas, Turner experienced a religious conversion in the late 50s and appeared on the border stations preaching as America's Cowboy Evangelist.*

42

43

Rev. Ike **(photo no. 43)** *pioneered the gospel of prosperity over border radio stations, urging his followers to "get out of the ghet-to and get into the get-mo."*

"Let God be your dentist," preached A. A. Allen **(photo no. 44)** *in the pages of his* **Miracle Magazine.** *Allen was one of the last great faith healers, who claimed that he could raise the dead until his followers began to deliver the corpses of their beloved departed to him in Miracle Valley, Arizona. Brother David Epley* **(photo no. 45)** *urged his listeners to call in and order prayer cloths, holy oil and a faith contact healing chart.*
One of the screamin'est border preachers, J. Charles Jessup **(photo no. 46)** *married a 15 year-old girl while still married to his third wife and served a year in prison for tax evasion and mail fraud.*

44

45

46

were painted the words "Flour Not Pork." As Molly passed the barrel through the crowd, Pappy urged his audience to support his campaign to get rid of the professional politicians in Austin. The arms of the country folk stretched to drop nickels, dimes, and $1 bills into the barrel, small donations to help put their good Christian friend in the Governor's Mansion. And O'Daniel, always the showman, knew just how to keep their trust. At one stop Molly returned to the stage and pulled a $20 bill out of the barrel. Pappy took the bill and addressed the crowd. "Who put this twenty-dollar bill into the barrel?" No one answered. He asked again. Finally a middle-aged man near the front sheepishly raised his hand. O'Daniel told him, "This is the campaign for the common citizen. Twenty dollars is too much—one dollar is just enough." And he promptly gave the man $19 in change, a unique occurrence in the annals of political fundraising.

Newspapermen did not give Pappy much chance of winning, but they noted similarities between his campaign and the campaigns of Huey Long in Louisiana, "Alfalfa Bill" Murray in Oklahoma, and the greatest political showman of them all, Dr. John R. Brinkley. O'Daniel's opponents began to get nervous and attacked the flour salesman. Karl Crowley, a minor opponent supported by Dr. Brinkley, called him "a fiddling carpetbagger from Ohio" and accused him of "never owning a flour mill, never having paid a poll tax, never having voted in a Texas election, and never having been a Democrat." The editor of the *El Paso Herald* wrote, "He can't even vote for himself, yet he comes before us asking to be made Governor of Texas. He has a crust all right, but it's not light crust. It's hard and tough and indigestible." An East Texas editor called him a "political hitchhiker who is trying to thumb a ride on a flour sack into office." Pappy countered the attacks of his critics with straightforward answers. When asked at a rally about his failure to pay the poll tax, O'Daniel called the band to play "I Left My Home for a Microphone" and said, "I didn't pay my poll tax because I was fed up with crooked politicians in Austin and hadn't intended to vote for anyone this year. . . . Anyway, there's only one thing I am losing, and that is one vote." Responding to other attacks, Pappy quoted Scripture: "Blessed are ye when men shall revile you and shall say all manner of evil falsely against you for My sake." When accused of being backed by big business, O'Daniel said, "How can you say I'm against the working man when I buried my daddy in overalls?" And whenever he couldn't come up with a suitable retort, he cued the Hillbilly Boys to start up a song, often calling out to the female vocalist, "Sing it, Texas Rose."

The other candidates found it impossible to attack the radio personality successfully, and they jumped on the hillbilly circus wagon as the campaign came to a close. One candidate traveled with tap dancers, while another shared his political platform with two crooners and a mind reader called the Great Solon. But it was too late. As the mother of a staunch McCraw supporter put it, "Son, I've been having breakfast with Lee O'Daniel on the radio . . . for the past eight years, and I know he's a good man."

On Election Day, Howard Hough, the Hired Hand from WBAP radio, visited the O'Daniel home, microphone in hand. Pappy spoke to his many admirers: "While I hope we get the nomination in the first primary, it would deprive me and the Hillbillies and my family of one the greatest pleasures we've ever had in our lives. It has been like floating on an ocean of joy to go out in this campaign and meet the eight hundred thousand friends who came to our little rallies. But I want you to meet the brains of this organization, the most wonderful little wife in the world." Mrs. O'Daniel then said a few words, to which her husband added, "I'm sorry we don't have television so you can see how pretty she is." The candidate then introduced his mother-in-law, Mrs. Belle Heinlein, whom he called "the best biscuit maker in the state." She told how proud she was of her son-in-law, and Pappy ended the broadcast with one of his acute observations: "This certainly shows the wonderful power of radio in our social, economic, and business life. I mustn't forget business, because I'm still selling Hillbilly Flour, you know, and I've got to get a plug in here. If I should be elected governor, and my family is privileged to live in your mansion, remember that the latch string is always out. Bring your dinners and feed for your horses and spend the day." Pappy could afford to be cocky as the votes were being counted. He was already a winner. Sales of Hillbilly Flour doubled during the campaign, and his "Flour Not Pork" fundraising scheme not only had covered the costs of the campaign but had even generated a profit. O'Daniel collected $6586 and spent $5789, donating the remainder to the Red Cross for flood relief.

Pappy won the primary with 50.7 percent of the vote and a plurality in every county of the state within close broadcasting range of stations that carried his programs. The voters had selected him to be the next governor of Texas. And victory just increased the sales of Hillbilly Flour. As Pappy put it, "A store in Beeville wants two hundred and ten barrels. They say they'll have 'em sold before they get there. . . . I can't begin to tell you how many carloads I've sold this morning. Boy, . . . is business good." O'Daniel and the family went for a vacation to Galveston, after the radio star entertained his audience with the poem "Out Where the West Begins" and described the resources of beautiful Texas. He commented particularly on the fecundity of the Texas spinach crop, saying,

"Why, we raise more spinach down here than they do anywhere else in the world," to which the band shouted, "Yeah, man, good old spinach!"

When O'Daniel returned from Galveston, he was flush with victory. He told his listening audience, "It's the first vacation I can ever remember having . . . and I like 'em. He went on to describe his luck at fishing, saying that he wished he had time to tell about the fish he caught "but the fish was too long to put on a fifteen-minute program." He turned down lucrative offers for a personal-appearance tour and a national radio show, saying that he needed the extra time to "study up on" his new job. Like other members of the Texas Democratic party machine, O'Daniel seemed honestly amazed at his political success. As he watched the Oklahoma and Texas National Guard pass for his review one afternoon, the military band broke out into the Hillbilly Flour theme song. Pappy's fleshy, round face lit up as he realized he was "commander in chief of an army," an army that marched to the beat of hillbilly music. The slightly dazed military leader prepared to move to Austin and lead Texas by the ear.

After attending a farewell dinner in Fort Worth, where Mike led the band in singing "I've Got That Old Fashioned Love in My Heart," the governor-elect set off for Austin with a twenty-car motorcade. One hundred thousand people welcomed him to the capital city, which hosted an inauguration ceremony described by the press as "the greatest fanfare and show of pomp ever witnessed in the state." Sixty thousand people crowded into the University of Texas stadium, including a busload of Confederate veterans, to hear the Texas A&M College band, the UT band, and the Hillbilly Boys. Wearing a suit made out of Texas wool and woven at Texas Technological College in Lubbock, O'Daniel took the oath of office with his hand on a 133-year-old Bible and became the thirty-third governor of the state, the first radio star to live in the Governor's Mansion. His wife, Merle, had some reservations about moving into the historic edifice. "It's beautiful, but the servant problem worries me a little bit," she confided to a reporter. "You see, they use prison help—trustees, I think they call them—and it seems the cook was a murderer. Of course, I believe in giving everybody a chance, but supposing I don't like the cooking?" Pappy himself was confident of his ability to avoid the pitfalls of the professional politicians. One reporter asked him, "You've done a good job of selling, but how are you going to deliver the goods if the machine gets after you?" O'Daniel responded, "I've got my own machine. This little microphone." And he assured another journalist, "History will record whether or not our administration is good, but surely nobody doubts it will be different. . . . You ain't seen nothin' yet."

The Common Citizen's Candidate realized that his political strength lay in the microphone. As he put it, "This administration is going to be me, God, and the people, thanks to radio." On Sunday, January 22, 1939, O'Daniel made the historic step into the ether, becoming only the second governor to broadcast from the Governor's Mansion and the first to broadcast a regular entertainment program. The Hillbilly Boys set themselves up in the high-ceilinged, gold-walled back drawing room and tuned their instruments, plucking guitars and fiddles while they waited for the broadcast time. Then, as the stately visages of Richard Coke, Michael B. Menard, and others looked on from the walls of the 86-year-old room, the prince of biscuits appeared. Smiling, he greeted the large audience with "Good morning, folks" and took his place behind the battery of microphones. At exactly 8:30 a Hillbilly Boy started playing the organ, and the strains of "Home Sweet Home" floated through the chamber and throughout the airwaves of the state over the Texas Quality Network.

Pappy raised his rich voice above the sweet music: "Good morning ladies and gentlemen, and hello there, boys and girls. This is Governor W. Lee O'Daniel speaking. . . . We are in the front room of the Governor's Mansion—and what a room—it has a ceiling so high the boys could fly a kite in it. . . . Be it ever so humble, there's no place like home." He spoke the familiar words in perfect cadence with the music, as he had for so many years in support of Hillbilly Flour, while the band played on. Pappy swung his arms back and forth, keeping time to the music, and told of his trip to Detroit, where he had met Henry Ford and outlined his plans to industrialize Texas. O'Daniel said that Ford invited him to run for the governorship of Michigan, but the naturalized Texan turned down the offer and instead invited Ford to come to Texas.

"I'm having too good a time to speak of politics," the governor continued, but he mentioned his plans for old-age pensions, which he had sent to the Legislature 24 hours earlier. He told the story of a farmhand who cussed when the cow he was milking slapped him in the face with her tail. "The Legislators who don't like this plan are the ones who were milking the state and got switched in the face," O'Daniel asserted. Then, moving from politics to religion, he led the band in rousing versions of "Bringing in the Sheaves" and "What a Friend We Have in Jesus." He mentioned that he and his family were going to church, at which time the band played "The Church Across the Way." More religious songs followed, including one of his own compositions, "When We Reach Our Happy Home Way Over There." Pappy ended the broadcast with "This is W. Lee O'Daniel of Texas speaking. Good-bye." Thus began the airborne administration of the first radio governor of Texas.

Almost immediately, it became painfully obvious that O'Daniel was as bad at running the government as he was good at selling flour. One of the first jobs the governor had to perform was to appoint important state officials to implement his programs. Pappy had more trouble with the appointment process than any other governor in Texas history did. He tried to appoint his close friend Carr Collins to the State Highway Commission. Collins and two subsequent O'Daniel appointees were turned down by the Legislature. O'Daniel's first choice for state tax commissioner was turned down, as was his appointee for the state insurance commission. The legislators did not like the newly elected governor, who continued to refer to them as "scheming professional politicians." A loner by nature, the governor became even lonelier as the session progressed.

His attempt at running the state like a business got stuck like a delivery truck in three tons of biscuit dough. As he put it, "Seems like that every time I stick my head in an office in Austin to see how they're spending your money, they slam the door in my face." At first, O'Daniel followed the custom of former governor James V. Allred and others by holding daily press conferences. After a few days, he cut the press conferences to one a week but canceled three in February. On February 27, he announced that "the regular Tuesday press conferences will be abandoned," reasoning that the news didn't always break on Tuesdays. The press surmised that the real reason was that the microphone could not ask embarrassing questions and could not talk back to him.

O'Daniel's frustration with the press and the Legislature drove him once again to the border. As governor, he did not have to commute to Eagle Press to get his message out to the people of Texas. Technicians at the University of Texas in Austin made electrical transcriptions of Pappy's Sunday morning programs and shipped them to XEAW, the 100,000-watt border blaster that O'Daniel's political protégé Carr Collins had just purchased from Dr. Brinkley. The speeches were broadcast twice on Sundays along with advertisements for Hillbilly Flour. Pappy considered a border blaster to be such a wise investment that he obtained part ownership of XEAW for himself, becoming the first and only border-blasting governor.

The forty-sixth session of the Texas Legislature was billed as the pensions-versus-taxes session, which would challenge the governor to make good on his campaign promises. The big question was how to fund the pension plan, but O'Daniel did not seem overconcerned. When asked about the pensions while attending a show in a Fort Worth nightclub, Pappy pointed to a juggler and said, "What that fellow's doing looks impossible, but he's doing it." Eventually, the radio entertainer came up with concrete plans, but they were plans that would never fly. O'Daniel proposed a 1.6 percent tax on all business transactions. The

Legislature was stunned. One state senator called the proposal "a victory for the predatory interests that for the last twenty years have been trying to put over a sales tax." The *Port Arthur News* said it was "a sales tax with its Sunday suit on." Even organized labor labeled it a "tax monstrosity."

In a radio address from the Governor's Mansion in late January 1939 the Hillbilly hero defended his tax plan, even though it meant great personal sacrifice. "I have been informed," he said judiciously, "that some merchants have said they would quit handling a certain well-known flour if the tax went through. But I am determined to fight the battle of the common people, whatever it costs me." Representatives strongly objected to the governor's "combination political speech and flour-selling campaign" and introduced a resolution to make him refrain from putting his name on any more flour and from using the radio for advertising. O'Daniel's sons had taken over the Hillbilly Flour Company prior to their father's taking office, but Pattie-boy and Mickey Wickey could not sell as well as their father, and the old flour entrepreneur could not resist the chance to boost sales. Throughout his tenure as governor, Pappy distributed copies of his broadcast poetry upon request. The copy of one poem, "I Love to Hear a Churchbell," was marked at the bottom with the unstatesmanlike slogan "USE HILLBILLY FLOUR."

By mid-April the Legislature was hopelessly deadlocked in finding a solution to the pension funding question. O'Daniel dropped the proposed transaction tax on his March 19 broadcast and asked instead for a constitutional amendment supporting a sales tax, an unpopular reversal of a campaign promise. Finding himself unable to bring the Legislature close to any kind of agreement, Pappy preferred to blame the professional politicians for his own inaction, while he continued to keep audiences enthralled with broadcasts from Texas and Mexico radio stations every Sunday morning.

The press and the Legislature expressed dissatisfaction with the governor's aerial end run of the issues. One legislator commented that there had been so many bad radiomen and so much patent medicine sold that you couldn't believe your mother's dying declaration if it came over the radio. Other legislators called O'Daniel a "Sabbath Caesar," "an Ether Egotist," and "a crooning corporal of the panoplied forces of financial marauders." Although the Legislature ended without a resolution to the pension crisis, or any other noteworthy accomplishments, Pappy remained immensely popular. As the *Dallas Morning News* noted, "The Sunday chats of Governor O'Daniel recognize the value of radio in which no one can interrupt and no one can talk back."

After the Legislature adjourned, Pappy continued his Sunday broadcasts, intoning inviolate syllables with a voice as sincere as a Methodist minister's. He explained away the failure to get funding for the pension plan: "Let me say this battle has not been lost. It has just begun. . . . It's just like waving a red flag in a mad cow's face, and they stare in green envy and turn loose all the volleys of poison and corruption at their disposal. His Thanksgiving address mentioned the bounty of Texas," where we can raise the finest oranges, grapefruit, apples, peaches . . . the biggest yams, finest potatoes, reddest tomatoes, greenest spinach, hottest onions, and bestest other varieties of garden truck." He told his radio audience how happy they made him feel. One Sunday he began by saying, "It surely is refreshing to get in front of this friendly old microphone. . . . It makes me feel that I am seated in your own front room, with two children playing around on the floor and the old folks rocking in the old rocking chair. . . . Yes, sir, be it only a microphone, it's home sweet home to me." At Christmastime, Pappy announced that families were going to the Waco State Home and the Corsicana State Home to take an orphan home for the holidays. A few days later O'Daniel said that "the mail was just loaded with requests from people in all walks of life asking for particulars as to how they could get a little boy or girl or both to spend Christmas week in their home."

Though still popular with rural Texans and conservative businessmen like Carr Collins, the governor was extremely unpopular with the members of the Texas media establishment. One of the oldest stations in the state, WBAP in Fort Worth, decided that O'Daniel was using his airtime to further his political career, not just to inform the citizens of Texas about the goings-on in the state capital. In order to ensure the nonpolitical nature of the broadcasts, the station management decided to review his scripts before they were broadcast. They requested an advance copy of O'Daniel's October 22, 1939, script, but Pappy was outraged and refused. The station management was equally adamant and pulled the governor off the air.

O'Daniel's large listening audience was shocked by his disappearance from WBAP. "I was disappointed to tears Sunday morning when you didn't come on at 8:30 o'clock," wrote one woman from Mexia. "I have such a few relatives that I have adopted you and your family somehow hoping that I may really know all of you someday." A Dallas resident commented, "What a rude awakening I had Sunday morning! If I had been transplanted to Germany, I would not have felt the shock more keenly." Others less surprised by the disappearance supported the governor nonetheless in his refusal to submit his scripts for examination. One gentleman wrote, "Congratulations! More power to you! We are proud that you refused to submit a transcript of your broadcast to be blue penciled by the controllers of the radio."

O'Daniel himself was equally outspoken and addressed the issue in his October 29 radio address. "Now they have set up this censorship of your governor," he began, "and refused to carry my program because I did not let them censor what I had to say. You will remember several months ago that I told you on the radio that I had been informed there was a movement on foot by the professional politicians to have me cut off the air." Some stations followed WBAP's lead and canceled O'Daniel's programs, but most small stations could not afford to lose as popular a program as the Governor Pappy show and overlooked the matter entirely. In any event, O'Daniel's voice continued to blast out from XEAW, twice a day on Sundays. After all, he was part owner of the station.

In early 1940 the wheels of Texas political machinery began to turn in preparation for the upcoming gubernatorial elections. The governor continued to hammer at the professional politicians over the radio, comparing the biannual elections to the plowing up of crops for pay by the federal government. "In Texas we plow under every other year with political plowwow," he said. "We might call that the PPP—Professional Politician Plunderers." His opponents were not as naive as they had been in the 1938 campaign. They knew Pappy was the man to beat, and they knew the only way to beat him was to silence his microphone.

O'DANIEL IRKS FOES ON MEXICAN RADIO, read a *New York Times* headline on March 3, 1940, and the paper reported, "Over the border facilities are held vital to candidates evading local restrictions." In late February state senator George Moffett of Chillicothe led the protest against the use of Mexican radio stations by Texas politicians. The senator complained that broadcasting from Mexico enabled O'Daniel and other candidates for Texas office to make statements "no Texas station would have dared permit to go out." While the Chillicothe native's protests never resulted in actual legislation barring candidates from the border, the "powerful and politically controlled" press enjoyed hounding the governor even into Mexico.

In late March, O'Daniel, who continued to turn down lucrative offers to be a full-time radio personality, aired a special broadcast from XEAW. He lambasted the broadcasting outlets that censored his words and urged his listeners to patronize the firms advertising on the radio stations that still carried his programs. After blasting the press for their "deception, propaganda, and unreliable dissemination of news," Pappy announced the arrival of a new, less biased publication entitled the *W. Lee O'Daniel News*, and he told his listeners, "I will be back each night at this same time with more news about the *W. Lee O'Daniel News*."

The announcement of the paper coincided almost exactly with his announcement to run again for governor. In an hour-long broadcast on

April 3, 1940, O'Daniel defended his record of the past two years, reviled the uncooperative Legislature, and said he would run once again with the Ten Commandments as his platform. He began a series of daily live broadcasts from the Governor's Mansion over the thirteen stations of the Texas State Network to advertise his newspaper, assuring his audience that the broadcasts would be nonpolitical, and he continued to broadcast daily by transcription over XEAW. He cooed into the microphone, "Send in your subscription now. Send one little quarter—twenty-five cents . . . the biggest bargain in a newspaper that was ever offered."

Designed to "keep the masses of citizens of Texas properly and reliably informed," the *W. Lee O'Daniel News* was published without advertising by Mrs. O'Daniel, Pat, and Mike. Despite the dramatic buildup, the paper itself made for fairly light reading. Pappy wrote "The Governor's Own Column" and occasionally printed the text of his radio messages. He explained that "my preferred and accustomed way to communicate with you is by radio, but when the professional politicians and their henchmen deprive me of free speech on the radio stations in this Land of the Free and the Home of the Brave, then I am going to use the next best means." Molly O'Daniel, at that time a student at the University of Texas, wrote a column for young people entitled "Molly and Her Pals." She began her first column with the almost audible shriek, "Oh, boy! Oh, boy! Oh, boy! Oh, boy! I still haven't gotten over the thrill. Daddy's going to run again for governor!" She signed her columns, "Your Pen Pal, Molly O."

The rest of the paper read like a rural *National Enquirer.* Headlines screamed, MOTHER CAT ADOPTING BABY RABBITS, FLOYDADA WOMEN MARCH TO WAR ON DIRT WITH MUSIC, HONEY BUSINESS IN MAGIC VALLEY, and, for a political diatribe about professional politicians, HEEL FLIES, TOP WATERS AND SLIME DISTRIBUTORS. In every issue, O'Daniel advertised his daily and Sunday radio broadcasts, giving times and stations and urging readers to "keep your dials set to the kilocycles of your favorite station to get your state government news truthfully and direct from headquarters."

The *O'Daniel News* printed letters from fans as far away as Boston. One week, readers were treated to a reprint from the editorial page of the *Monroe Journal* of Monroeville, Alabama. The editorial was entitled "Something New in Politics" and applauded one particularly moving O'Daniel speech, "Mortality and Religion in Politics." The editor of the paper praised O'Daniel's high Christian morals and invited "the good people of Monroe County to listen in" on the governor's next broadcast.

Pappy's radio broadcasts continued to cover the entire spectrum of human endeavor, from religion to politics and good old-fashioned fun. He sang the praises of church, reading a touching letter from a recently electrocuted convict who had managed to write a note to the governor before his demise. While O'Daniel read the words "I am going to the electric chair because of my parents' failure to take me to Sunday school and church," the Hillbilly Boys played the religious favorite "Whispering Hope." On Easter Sunday, Pappy informed the large crowd at the Governor's Mansion that his college-age children—Pat, Mike, and Molly—had "started chasing bunnies all over the mansion grounds before the company arrived and found just oodles and oodles of brightly colored Easter eggs."

O'Daniel's political opponents were quick to attack his publishing and broadcasting efforts. Harry Hines of Houston scorned the *O'Daniel News* and other "subservient newspapers that only praise . . . conduct in office and never dare print even constructive criticism." State senator Jerry Sadler warned that O'Daniel would "make a one-man government, like Communistic Russia, transforming Texas into a dictatorship." Sadler also struck out against O'Daniel's daily blasts from the border, saying that the governor evidently believed that Texas was still a part of Mexico "since he is doing his campaigning from there over a radio station in the state of Tamaulipas." Sadler went so far as to suggest that O'Daniel change his famous slogan from "Pass the Biscuits, Pappy" to "Pass the Tamales, Pappy."

The campaign of 1940 began with a rush of remarkable candidates. Cyclone Davis, Jr., entered the race as a pro-pension candidate, backed by the Social Security League of Texas. In his campaign appearances he dressed as Uncle Sam, wearing a long beard, striped trousers, a starspangled vest, a long coat, and a top hat and vowed to "eat earthworms, drink branch water, and sleep on Johnson grass hay to frighten this granddaddy taxation spider away." Ernest O. Thompson again sought the governor's office, promoting "A Nickel for Grandma," a five-cent tax on each barrel of oil to pay for pensions. Jerry Sadler also entered the race. A successful East Texas oilman, Sadler was known as an expert barbecue chef who liked to dip snuff, drink buttermilk, and eat cornbread. He campaigned with a band called Sadler's Cowboy Stringsters and an all-American football star, John Kimbrough. Ma Ferguson, the wife of former governor James Ferguson and herself elected governor in 1924 on an anti-Ku Klux Klan ticket and again in 1934, also threw her bonnet into the ring.

There was speculation as to whether O'Daniel would campaign again with the Hillbilly Boys, until a sharp-eyed reporter learned that the state's chief executive had placed a rush order for seventeen uniforms bearing the lettering "Vote for W. Lee O'Daniel." Pappy did indeed declare that he was going to hit the road—but not on a statewide swing. He told his radio audience that he was going to "attempt to boil the whole thirty-day campaign down to one speech—and when I say *boil* it down, you can expect it to be *hot*. So *hot*, in fact, that it will not be broadcast. . . . Meet me in Waco next Tuesday night, July second, eight p.m."

While O'Daniel made preparations to attend the Waco rally, he knew that the Hillbilly Boys would be appearing without two of their most popular members: Leon Huff, the leader of the band, and steel guitarist Kermit "Horace the Love Bird" Whalin. Many people, especially musicians, found the cost-conscious, straightlaced O'Daniel difficult to work for. One Fort Worth entertainer referred to Governor Pappy as "a horse's ass of the first water." Huff did not go that far, saying that he had quit for economic reasons. "I quit," Huff said, "because my conscience would not let me work for a man who broke his pledge and had no consideration for anyone but himself. I worked for Mr. O'Daniel for eight years, and he promised me a raise. He never gave it to me, and I began to feel that I might be the next one on the list to get the ax. I have a wife and two fine children, and it is necessary for me to provide for them as well as for myself." Huff and Whalin went to work for the Sadler campaign and left O'Daniel, who maintained that "the gang of professional politicians" had "caught the boys in their snare" and induced them to quit, even though "they had each just recently been given increased remuneration without their demanding it."

Even without Huff and Horace the Love Bird, O'Daniel appeared in Waco to a large but less enthusiastic crowd than had greeted him in 1938. The governor did not contain himself to the one promised appearance but covered the state, making five or six appearances a day in the last two weeks of the campaign. The tone of his speeches grew increasingly bitter. O'Daniel referred to the *Dallas News* as "the great grandcadoodle of the corporation press" and defended his record vociferously. He said that his transaction-tax recommendation was a practical plan, that it was "such a shock to the professional politicians and their henchmen that their gang of loudmouthed watchdogs in the legislature, the brain trustees in the sanctum sanctorum of secret hotel rooms in Austin, the poison pen editors of the big newspapers, the lesser lights of cartoonists, 'stinking out loud' columnists and 'give-me-an-offer' story writers, all started throwing poison gas in every direction."

Those who opposed his plan for funding pensions in the Legislature were "a little bunch of pin-headed legislators so pig-headed as to keep the sovereign voters from voting on anything." Critics pointed out that his expensive new sound truck, topped with a papier-mâché replica of the Capitol dome, had been donated to the campaign by the Hillbilly Flour

Company in direct conflict with the penal code of Texas, which forbade campaign gifts from corporations. O'Daniel responded by saying, "This sound truck that has shocked the sensibilities of these influence-peddling lawyers at Austin and these make-me-an-offer columnists for the corporation press . . . is just an ordinary truck bought by our family flour company. . . . Pattie-boy signed a note for it, for $500. . . . Thank you son." He ended his campaign in Abilene, leading the band in a song of his creation, "There Ain't Gonna Be No Runoff," and urging the crowd to give a "good old cowboy yell" for the benefit of the radio audience.

The other candidates spent a good deal of their energies in attacking O'Daniel, saying he was an "ignoramus," "a medicine show candidate," "a Kansas Republican," and "a crooner." A supporter of Ma Ferguson compared O'Daniel to Nero, accusing the governor of "fiddling around" while "the political house of Texas is on fire," and addressed a rally by saying, "We have the spectacle of government by remote control and transcription from a Mexican radio station." Ma Ferguson's husband mocked O'Daniel's style in a radio broadcast speech from Lufkin: "Hello, ladies and gentlemen. Hello, boys and girls, and all you folks out in radio land. Thank the Lord this is not O'Daniel speaking. . . . Six flags have reigned over the domain of Texas. Descending from the sublime to the ridiculous, we now witness the spectacle of our grand old state being ruled by a flour sack as an emblem of our proud history." E. O. Thompson complained of trying for weeks "to get the governor to come out from behind his microphones and discuss his record with the people man-fashion." Harry Hines pulled a coup by requesting the prime radio time of the Carr Collins Crazy Water Crystals show on WBAP. Collins wished to relinquish the time to O'Daniel but could not, as Hines had made his request first, and the WBAP management refused to budge. Collins pulled his band off the air and bought a fifteen-minute slot directly after Hines to make observations of his own on the political situation.

Despite the attacks by O'Daniel's opponents, Pappy's popularity had been steadily on the rise since the close of the legislative session in 1939. Pollsters attributed the phenomenon to "the paucity of political activity that might have engendered opposition." O'Daniel was much better at attending functions and issuing proclamations for Yam Week, Bottled Soft Drink Week, and Black-eyed Pea Day than he was at fighting the hard battles of the Legislature. On Election Day he retained the support of the rural population and the older people who still believed that he was "a good Christian man." As one supporter put it, "He's a good man. It ain't his fault he didn't do nothing." O'Daniel got more than 54 percent of the votes cast for governor, and Texas was headed for another term of flour-coated politics with Wilbert and Merle.

Pappy invited everybody in the state to come to a free inauguration barbecue on the grounds of the Governor's Mansion. Supporters donated cattle, sheep, goats, pigs, chickens, and turkeys for the occasion. The king of biscuits himself helped stock the larder. As he told his radio audience, he "shouldered the old musket" and "went out west to the beautiful country around Kerrville and there found a fine herd of buffalo on the Schreiner ranch." With daring and skill and half a dozen farmhands to corral the beasts, O'Daniel succeeded "in picking out the finest buffalo in the herd and causing him to bite the dust." He then invited everyone to come to Austin and "taste some of this deliciously barbecued buffalo, brought in by the skilled hands and steady nerve of your governor in possibly the last great wild buffalo hunt of this century."

Twenty thousand people took the governor up on his offer and consumed 6000 pounds of beef, 4000 loaves of bread, 1000 pounds of potato chips, 1500 pounds of onions, and a boxcarload of Rio Grande grapefruit, as well as the 900-pound buffalo. While citizens danced in the street behind the Capitol after the barbecue, the City of Austin dealt with the refuse from 20,000 dinners, and O'Daniel began to deal with the refuse of his stalled plans for running the state.

The main issue in the forty-seventh Legislature, as it had been in the forty-sixth, was how to pay for pensions. O'Daniel still supported a transaction tax but could get nowhere in the Legislature with his proposal, continuing to lay the blame for his failure on the professional politicians. Like Pontius Pilate, O'Daniel essentially washed his hands of legislative action and focused his efforts instead on winning the war.

Just a few months earlier, Pappy had preached total isolationism to his radio audiences, but he changed his tune in the spring of 1940 and began to talk of the importance of supporting the war effort. His exhortations had a distinct O'Daniel flavor, however. He warned his radio audience that "disease germs are the greatest sabotage agents loose in Texas today" and urged his fellow Texans to "keep our bodies clean and strong and our minds pure and healthy." In addition to his stand against destructive microorganisms, he began a campaign against evil macroorganisms, those scheming fifth columnists who participated in un-American activities. He wired President Roosevelt with the news that he had confidential information concerning the activities of fifth columnists in Texas and was sending officials of the Texas National Guard and the Texas Public Safety Department to Washington to confer with federal officials. Although nothing more was ever heard of this conference, O'Daniel asked his listening audience to inform his office of any un-American activity they might observe.

The listening audience quickly responded to the governor's appeal for patriotic snooping. The editor of the *Slaton Slatonite* confided, "I am afraid of the treasonable rats that work by cunning subterfuge to undermine the security of our country and strive to destroy utterly all the rights they invoke whenever their acts are questioned." Another correspondence was from an avowed "park bench warmer" who on several occasions "overheard conversations and two or three times personally contacted individuals whose talk was all together un-American." An Austin woman reported a mysterious Mr. Faulkenstein who had a radio station in Mexico and one in Taylor, Texas. The informant warned that Mr. Faulkenstein "has been in contact with different Germans on the Rio Grande River, Big Bend country and other German sections." Even the head of the Texas Junior Chamber of Commerce wired O'Daniel, pledging to report to the governor in writing "any breach of Americanism" that he or any of the members of the local units observed.

While O'Daniel was busy ferreting out fifth columnists, the Texas Legislature managed to pass a tax bill to pay for pensions. The governor at first described the bill as "stinking" but eventually supported it and even took credit for it, saying that his work for old-age pensions was completed with its passage. That happened just in time, as events in the spring of 1941 once again forced him to take to the campaign trail.

On April 9, 1941, the 65-year-old dean of Congress, U.S. senator Morris Sheppard, died. The next day O'Daniel conferred with his advisers Carr P. Collins, Maco Stewart, and James M. West. On April 19 O'Daniel announced that a special election would be held for the vacated Senate seat on June 28.

On San Jacinto Day, 1941, Pappy astonished the Texas political establishment with yet another stroke of political peculiarity. Standing in front of the San Jacinto Monument and speaking over a statewide radio hookup, O'Daniel recalled the victory of the Texas independence fighters over the Mexican forces of Santa Anna and extolled the virtues of the victorious commander in that campaign, General Sam Houston. Then, 105 years after the historic battle, O'Daniel announced his appointment for interim senator, 87-year-old General Andrew Jackson Houston, the only surviving son of the great leader. The crowd was completely baffled. Never an outstanding politician, the Republican general had been politically inactive for twenty years and was in extremely poor health. O'Daniel was genuinely pleased with his unique appointment and described for his radio audience the moment at which he informed the elderly Houston of his appointment to the Senate: "The sun suddenly shot through the dark rain clouds in such a fashion that it appeared dazzling. I said, 'General, do you know what caused that sun to suddenly burst through those dark and heavy clouds? It appears to me as if our great and good loving God has just spread the clouds apart so the spirit of your illustrious father could smile down upon his son on this particular scene and see the big smile on your face.'"

The grinning octogenarian was approved to take his powerful new position by a rather stunned Legislature. He took the oath of office in Washington on June 2, 1941, and appeared three more times in the Senate chamber before being taken to Johns Hopkins Hospital on June 20. He died six days later of stomach ailments. O'Daniel sent Houston's relatives a telegram of condolences in which he confused the Battle of the Alamo with the Battle of San Jacinto. Although Governor Pappy was fuzzy on Texas history, he soon proved once again to be as sharp as a razor in getting Texas votes.

The bidding for General Houston's Senate seat quickly turned into a salute to political zaniness, Texas-style. It was the first statewide special election for the purpose of selecting only one man for office. Anyone who filed his name on time and paid the $1 filing fee could enter the race, and a great number of aspiring politicians did. *Life* magazine ran the headline 27 CANDIDATES SEEK SENATE SEAT IN SCREWY TEXAS RACE and printed photos of several of the more theatrical candidates, including bearded Cyclone Davis, Jr., who told the press he didn't have to campaign because "Providence will place me in the Senate" and tax opponent E. A. Calvin, who campaigned attired in a wooden barrel. Others in the race included Congressman Martin Dies, who was the founder of the House Committee for Investigation of Un-American Activities and who, according to *Time* magazine, "eats two Communists for breakfast every morning"; Homer Brooks, the leader of the Communist party in Texas; the Reverend Sam Morris, known on the border stations as the Voice of Temperance; Hal Collins, Crazy Water Crystals announcer and XEAW personality; O. F. Heath, Sr., whose platform was "Keep cool. Deport all aliens. Stop all immigration"; W. W. King, who favored the annexation of Canada; and Dr. John R. Brinkley of Del Rio.

The two strongest candidates were attorney general Gerald Mann, a former SMU football star known as "Little Red Arrow" and a Harvard law school graduate, and Congressman Lyndon Baines Johnson, whose picture was sandwiched between photos of Dr. Brinkley and Commodore Basil Muse Hatfield in *Time*. Johnson's campaign was the best-funded, as the former head of the National Youth Administration used political patronage to gain the support of large contributors. Running with the campaign motto "Roosevelt and Unity" and standing on a platform of "Roosevelt, Roosevelt, Roosevelt," Johnson had the firm support of his good friend the president, who noted that the election of Dies or O'Daniel would be "too frightful for contemplation." While Mann was the initial front-runner and drove hundreds of miles each day to address small crowds in county squares, the well-oiled Johnson machine appeared to be bound for victory as the campaign progressed.

The governor at first assured Johnson and others that he did not have any ambitions to move to Washington. The dome of the nation's Capitol proved alluring, however, especially after a group of state legislators passed a resolution asking Pappy to serve as senator. Although the legislators had passed the resolution in an effort to rid the state of the ineffectual governor, the great flour salesman took their support to heart and on May 15, 1941, announced that he would run for the Senate. He took to the airwaves, telling his audience about his "old, old friend the president" and his trusted campaign companions "the Ten Commandments, the Golden Rule, an inbred and inerasable common touch with the common man, and, I hope, your unceasing prayers." Immediately after the announcement, LBJ fell sick for two weeks, smitten with the indigestible realization that he was up against the greatest vote getter in Texas history.

O'Daniel was confident that he would win the campaign handily, but he had not counted on the snail's pace of the forty-seventh Legislature. He planned to open his campaign in Waco on June 2 but had to cancel his appearance there, as well as two subsequent appearances, because legislative duties kept him tied to Austin. Pappy began to lose some of the heartwarming poise that had made him so appealing on radio for so many years. He compared the federal politicians to "stinkweed," saying that Roosevelt had surrounded himself with "a group of pussyfooting, pusillanimous politicians who were not fit to run a peanut stand." O'Daniel shouted that the "professional politicians, big monied interests and their mouthpieces, the big political newspapers," had tried to ruin him. Appealing to his radio audience in a slightly frenzied tone, Pappy called for "a hundred thousand minutemen and women" to volunteer for his campaign and write a penny postcard declaring their intention to work "for the Common Citizen's Candidate for U.S. Senate." The governor promised that he would send a "complete outfit" to anyone who wrote in, including window stickers and literature. But O'Daniel's call for "minutemen to help preserve democracy" did not receive the rush of support the biscuit wizard had come to expect. He started up the *W. Lee O'Daniel News* once again and sent Pat, Mike, and Molly out on the campaign trail with recordings of his voice. At one rally the recording got stuck, and the crowd guffawed as they listened to the tired governor saying, "I want to go to Washington to work for the old folks, the old folks, the old folks. . . ." A Texas editor called it "The Old Refrain."

While O'Daniel was stuck in Austin, Johnson came back from his illness rip-roaring and designed a Pappy-style campaign. His wife, Lady Bird, later recalled the campaign as one of the most enjoyable she had ever experienced. It was certainly one of the most entertaining. Her home movies of the '41 campaign show LBJ as the star of an "All-out Patriotic Revue," which featured a six-piece swing band called the Patriots, dressed in red, white and blue; 285-pound Sophie Parker, the Kate Smith of the South; and an immaculately dressed master of ceremonies who stood before a backdrop painting of FDR and LBJ shaking hands above the slogan "Roosevelt and Unity—Elect Lyndon Johnson United States Senator." After the emcee lauded the masterful leadership of Roosevelt, he introduced "that dynamic young native Texan, six foot three, that high-riding Texan from the hills of Blanco County . . . Lyndon B. Johnson."

Johnson jumped onto the stage and delivered his address, stressing the necessity of preparing for war and his unfailing support of Roosevelt: "We must beat Hitler. We must keep aggressors from American shores. If not, we shall writhe under the dictator's heels as more than a dozen formerly free European nations now are writhing." He continued by saying, "All proponents of every ism except Americanism must be wiped out," a refrain similar in tone to that of the Red-eating Dies and the fifth columnist-fighting O'Daniel.

Audiences did not respond enthusiastically to Johnson's oratory, but they did hang around until the end of the Patriotic revue to see who won the $25 or more in defense stamps that the Johnson organizers gave away at the end of every rally. An even more effective Johnson campaign strategy was to send field-workers throughout the state pushing the idea that the old folks needed Pappy more in Texas than in Washington to defend their interests. The technique was extremely effective among the old-timers who genuinely loved O'Daniel, and a great deal of mail urging Pappy to stay in Austin reached the Governor's Mansion.

Worried over Johnson's successes and finally freed from his legislative duties, O'Daniel renewed his campaign on June 18, just ten days before the election. He traveled with the same Capitol-dome sound truck he had used in the 1940 gubernatorial campaign, and he relied on his Hillbilly band to entertain the crowds with their old favorites. O'Daniel's speeches began to sound a little shrill. He coined the phrase "Communistic labor leader racketeers" and used it to attack the press, his opponents, his enemies in the Legislature, and almost everyone else besides his postman. He attacked Johnson and Dies, saying, "If I couldn't do more for the president before breakfast than both of them have done all the time they have been in Washington, I would give up." Each day O'Daniel's statements got stranger and stranger. He suggested that Texas form its own army and navy to protect the southern borders. He swore that he would purge Congress if it did not pass a bill to outlaw strikes. He vowed to eliminate the federal debt and force Congress to provide $100 million per year for a national pension plan. He accused the Texas newspapers of being politically controlled "instruments of the devil," provoking one editor to write that the governor had "spoken with such looseness, committed such contradictions, posed with such grossness as to invite the shafts immemorially attracted by bombast, buncombe and pretense." Pappy filled the airwaves, broadcasting his diatribes over his border blaster XEAW and a dozen Texas stations, while Johnson's machine put its man on the air all over Texas five times a day. The race for the U.S. Senate in 1941 was one of the first all-out media blitz campaigns in the annals of American political history, a great event for the broadcasters of Texas who could take each and every campaign speech directly to the bank.

As Election Day drew near, it was a toss up as to whether the Johnson or the O'Daniel stage act would win the popularity contest. Sometimes, however, a politician's enemies are more important than his friends, and in this case the biscuit king's enemies were anxious to get him safely out of the state. Political columnist Drew Pearson broadcast over the NBC radio network that fifteen influential Texas politicians had met with representatives of liquor and brewery interests and had decided that O'Daniel must be elected to the Senate at all costs. Their desire to further the governor's career came from the fact that O'Daniel was a fervent dry who was convinced that liquor was a tool of the devil. He favored banning alcohol for ten miles around military bases and had recently backed a prohibitionist as chairman of the three-member state Liquor Control Board, the regulatory body that granted liquor licenses. The liquor lobby wanted Pappy out of the Governor's Mansion, and it delivered a substantial number of votes to the O'Daniel-for-Washington camp. In the end, O'Daniel won the election by a mere 1311 votes over Congressman Johnson.

O'Daniel addressed the Senate for the first time on the second day of his membership, breaking Huey Long's record for senatorial impatience. In his first speech he spoke more of aesthetics than politics. "I do like hillbilly music," he confessed to his fellow senators. "I also like popular music, church songs, and grand opera, but unfortunately I do not play or sing any kind of music. Since I have pleaded guilty to liking music, I presume I had as well plead guilty to using the radio. . . . I want to say frankly that I intend to continue to like hillbilly music and to use the radio to talk to the people of this nation."

In a very brief time Pappy managed to make enemies of most of his colleagues in the Senate and the members of the press corps. He constantly abused professional politicians and insisted on introducing quirky bits of unpassable legislation, such as an antistrike bill that was read twice and killed in committee and a bill to eliminate overtime pay for labor, which got nowhere. He was defeated in his attempt to institute prohibition in Army camps, and he failed to defeat an extension of the Selective Service Act. Pappy's legislative ineptitude was described as "so overwhelming as to be embarrassing." While O'Daniel continued to speak to Texas from Washington via transcriptions that were still broadcast on border radio, he began to lose touch with the people of Texas, and his political batter lost much of its rise.

Senator O'Daniel announced early in 1942 that he would run for the full term beginning in 1943. In his fourth political campaign, the radio star faced two former governors, Dan Moody and Judge James V. Allred. O'Daniel opened his campaign in Waco, but it was obvious that times had changed for the super flour salesman. Instead of 20,000 people waiting to greet him on the banks of the Brazos River, there was a quiet crowd of 2000. Sharing the platform with Carr P. Collins and musicians from the Crazy Water organization, Pappy seemed distinctly out of touch with the realities of the times. He declared that gasoline rationing was "the prizewinner of all crackpot ideas that ever originated in Washington," and he announced, "There ain't gonna be no gasoline rationing in Texas, we ain't gonna lose the war, and there ain't gonna be no runoff."

Both Moody and Allred successfully attacked O'Daniel's worn-out campaign methods. Allred took along recordings of Pappy's voice, played them for his audiences, and responded to various segments, fighting microphone with microphone. One of the segments that got the most laughs was taken from a February 1939 speech in which the senator told his audience, "I don't think we are near war. We hear a lot of howling in Europe, but they aren't going to do us any harm over here." Allred attacked O'Daniel's tenure in the Senate, saying that it was "mortifying to the state" and had "boiled generally with obstructionist tactics, isolationism, appeasement, labor baiting, and arraying class against class." Moody told his supporters, "O'Daniel is as lost in the U.S. Senate as I would be on a circus trapeze." Noted Texas historian J. Frank Dobie became involved in the campaign and spoke about Pappy: "No man claiming to represent a people ever stood more isolated from them than W. Lee O'Daniel stands today among Texans." Newspapers throughout the state were almost solid in their opposition to O'Daniel's candidacy. The *Abilene News* wrote, "He failed us in our time of crisis," and the *Gladewater Times Tribune* called O'Daniel "one of the most dangerous isolationists."

O'Daniel for his part asserted, "We do not need to discuss the war effort in this Senate campaign," and he dwelt increasingly on the threat of the "Communistic labor leader racketeers" who supposedly had a "slush fund of one billion dollars" for political campaigns and had allocated from $1 million to $5 million to defeat him. "Money is being spent like water to prevent my reelection," Pappy maintained. "The Communistic labor leader racketeers are trying under cover of the war to steal our American form of government, and the politically controlled *Dallas News* and *Fort Worth Star Telegram* are in on the steal." He called his opponents "the Gold Dust Twins" and said they were acceptable to and financed by the Communistic labor leader racketeers. He made a thinly veiled accusation that labor leaders had offered Allred $200,000 to enter the race and an additional $200,000 if he won. "Of course, I'm not going to say positively that they made such a deal," Pappy said. "They didn't call me in on their meeting. But I'll let you form your own conclusions." The senator did not spare the radio stations. He said that no one could get the truth from the radio, because the broadcasting stations had their "high-powered lawyers" edit the script two days in advance and left only what suited them.

In a complete turnaround from the previous voting patterns, the antipopulist, anti-Roosevelt conservatives of Texas swung to support O'Daniel and delivered 48.3 percent of the vote to him, a plurality that forced him into a runoff with Allred. Pappy, who believed that Allred was insulting him by entering the runoff election, appeared to be more frightened of defeat than at any prior time in his political career. Although O'Daniel described his campaign as a "little appreciation tour" to "thank the people of Texas for the 475,000 votes" he had received, one writer commented that it was "the most frantic appreciation tour on record." Pappy appeared on radio twice a day, four times a day during the last week of the campaign, offering free subscriptions to the new edition of the *W. Lee O'Daniel News*. O'Daniel described Allred and his accomplices as "skunks, buzzards, wolves, thugs, termites, pirates, outlaws, racketeers, and hatchet brigades," and he regaled the press, saying that their publications were "slanderous, yellow sheet, dirty newspapers . . . all bought off by filthy gold" and were supplied by "Communistic labor leader racketeers by the hundreds." His personal attacks on Allred grew in intensity, with Pappy referring to him repeatedly as "my little yes man." Allred read to his audiences an old message to him from O'Daniel, which the senator had inscribed with the words "To my good friend Jimmy and his wonderful family. I predict even greater success and wish you continued happiness and prosperity." Allred commented, "I am sorry than any former governor of Texas would call another a little squirt. . . . I am particularly sorry in this case because these harsh and intemperate statements and the ugly insinuation upon my honor and integrity come from the lips of a man who repeatedly professed to be my friend."

In the end, Pappy won the bitter campaign with 51 percent of the vote. A staff writer for the *Dallas Morning News* wrote, "These voters won't believe that O'Daniel is at heart anti-new deal or an isolationist or anything else charged against him. They were satisfied in their belief that he's 'a good man,' and didn't care much about anything else. Many Texans were just as convinced by Pappy's political promises in 1942 as they had been by his flour advertisements a decade earlier.

The bitterness and acrimony that marked the 1942 senatorial campaign accompanied O'Daniel for the rest of his political career. In 1944 he was booed and pelted with eggs by a crowd shouting, "We want Roosevelt" as he gave a speech in support of the conservative Texas Regulars group over a statewide radio hookup. He fought with fellow Texas senator Tom Connally and drew the ire of his party by voting with Republicans more than 80 percent of the time. His voice disappeared from Texas radio as he feuded openly with his old friend and supporter Carr P. Collins. In the 1948 campaign for the Senate, Collins supported O'Daniel's opponent and accused the senator of taking $50,000 in campaign contributions from conservative millionaires H .R. Cullen and Oklahoma Republican senator Ed Moore to fight the New Deal. O'Daniel accused Collins of supporting his opponent simply to gain appointment to the State Highway Commission, but the ideological split between the two Texas businessmen ran much deeper. While Collins became a strong supporter of civil rights and the improvement of educational opportunities for blacks, O'Daniel labeled any move toward integration a communist conspiracy. In a 1948 speech before the Senate, he charged that the report of President Truman's Civil Rights Committee contained a "communistic philosophy" that "originated in Moscow." Later in the speech, Pappy attempted to show how "the orders of Joe Stalin trickled down through his stooges right into our White House." Even O'Daniel's down-home radio poetry took on an unsavory tone: "Yes, friends, way down south in the land of cotton, when the New Deal's gone but not forgotten, we'll still be segregating, and we'll still be voting straight. Whites and blacks respect each other, but they don't intend to mate. This is your U.S. Senator, W. Lee O'Daniel, speaking from your nation's capital, Washington, D.C., and wishing you, one and all, a pleasant good day."

By the late forties O'Daniel's song was out of tune with the rest of the state as polls showed O'Daniel running far behind Governor Coke Stevenson and other candidates. Pappy chose not to run for reelection to the Senate and returned to Fort Worth, where he opened the W. Lee O'Daniel Life Insurance Company. He later reentered politics and ran unsuccessfully for governor on a strong segregation platform in 1956, campaigning with a white fire truck, a bus, and a new bunch of hillbilly musicians who were too young to remember the words to "Beautiful Texas." In 1958 the former flour salesman made another run at the governorship, declaring himself 100 percent for segregation and calling incumbent governor Price Daniel a "would-be little dictator." He told his radio audience, "Tomorrow you can vote for and elect W. Lee O'Daniel as governor of Texas or you can vote for my opponent and have integration, intermarriage, and ultimately a mongrelized race of people in Texas." Although he used a helicopter in his campaign, Pappy's border radio-style politics were out of place in the era of Elvis, sputniks, and television, and he ran far behind the winner, Price Daniel. On May 12, 1969, Wilbert Lee O'Daniel, the first and only border radio governor, the man who had passed so many biscuits and gladdened so many hearts with his hillbilly music and down-home poetry, died.

Radio Waves Pay No Attention to
Lines on a Map

All the world is there, Singing in that little box; . . .
You hear high-horn Columbia's languid *bambuco,*
Or the United States' waggish dialogue;
And from Mexico you hear
The impassioned *jarabe*
—Expressing the joy and sorrow of the race—
A song, deep from the Indian's heart.
—*From "Las Voces del Radio," by Rogelio Sotela,*
translated by Philip Barbour, 1940

From the earliest days of broadcasting, American *federales* disapproved of what they heard about Mexican radio. At the outbreak of World War I, German U-boats scored a rapid series of victories against American ships operating in the Pacific. The Federal Bureau of Investigation suspected that the Germans were using wireless technology in a remote broadcasting lookout, probably in Mexico, to send out information about United States shipping.

Although Mexico was officially neutral, American officials decided that this kind of activity could not be tolerated, and they sent Al Scharff into the desert country of Sonora to dispose of the offending station. Scharff, a miner, rustler, counterfeiter, and former soldier in the Mexican Army, chose a Pima Indian Army guide named Red Slippers and four Yaqui Indians to accompany him on his covert operation. Telling inquisitive locals that he was on a fishing trip, the intrepid agent and his crew motored across the border about eighty miles west of Nogales in two Ford sedans. Scharff and his compadres wound their way through the washes and rocky barrancas of northern Sonora's Altar district, known as *las garras del infierno* ("the jaws of hell"). After spending several days searching for the Kaiser's station and living on jerky, *pan de huevo,* canned pineapple juice, and mescal, they came across a well-used trail leading up to the mountainous Gulf of California coastline near Cabo Lobos ("Cape of Wolves"). Indians in the area told the adventurers that many trucks had brought equipment up the trail a few months earlier, and one of the Yaqui guides spotted a tall antenna rising from the mountains. Scharff knew they had located the target, and he prepared to strike.

In the predawn light of the following day, the radio raiders crawled toward the German hideout, carefully avoiding the ocotillo, prickly pear, ironweed, and catclaw on their way up the mountain. They came within fifty yards of the covert broadcasting operation before they were fired upon. Scharff was hit, wounded slightly in the forehead. Red Slippers squeezed off a shot and blew open the head of a German broadcaster. A few moments later, Scharff's Yaqui compañeros located another German in a nearby tent and tore him apart with well-placed rounds from their American-made .30–30's. When the smoke cleared, Scharff found the offending transmitter in a nearby cave. A telegraph key lay on a table in the cave next to an open logbook listing detailed information on American shipping routes and schedules. The commando crew wasted no time. They buried the bodies under a pile of stones and placed dynamite charges at the mouth of the cave and at the base of the spies' radio tower, which was on the top of a nearby mountain. With an echoing *kerblam*, the adventurers sent one of the first Mexican broadcasting stations tumbling into the sparkling blue waters of the Sea of Cortés.

For several years after Scharff's radio raid, the United States government took almost no notice of broadcasting developments south of the border. Federal officials in Washington were too busy dealing with the stampede into their own electromagnetic spectrum to worry about international developments. Americans cheered when Secretary of Commerce Herbert Hoover finally decided to bring a halt to the chaotic radio free-for-all and began allocating the available broadcasting frequencies to Americans in an orderly manner. Broadcasters in Canada were not so pleased with Hoover's initiative, as his plans left no room in the electromagnetic spectrum for Canadian stations.

When American officials at the Department of Commerce learned of the Canadians' concern, they agreed to meet with their northern neighbors. The two negotiating teams worked out an informal agreement in October 1924 that gave Canada the right to broadcast exclusively on 6 of the 106 frequencies available between 550 and 1500 kilocycles, as well as the right to share exclusive broadcasting time with the United States on several other frequencies. The informal agreement remained in effect with only slight alteration until the booming sounds of the border blasters invaded American and Canadian airspace.

"Sprung from the head of Zeus, so to speak, in full armor, the Athena of radio in Mexico knew no childhood." Thus wrote one classically in-spired NBC employee in the forties. Actually, the radio industry in Mex-ico did not develop as quickly as it did in the United States and Canada, largely because most of the Mexican people did not have as much dis-posable income as their neighbors to the north did. Those Mexicans who could afford radios quickly became enthusiasts, however, and created a demand for regular broadcasting stations. On September 16, 1923, Mexican independence day, a leading cigarette manufacturer named El Buen Tono announced the opening of an "estación central transmisora de radiotelefonía" in Mexico City and even introduced a brand of cigarettes called El Radio. Later given the call letters XEB, El Buen Tono facility was one of the first commercial stations in Mexico, and it broadcast re-cordings and live performances of everything from police and military bands to jazz orchestras. Those who had radio receivers in the ancient Mayan capital city enjoyed tuning in to the latest opera recordings beamed from the station every Sunday morning.

Radio listening did not achieve wide popularity south of the border until 1926, when Mexican merchants began importing radio sets in quantity from the United States. By the end of the twenties, Mexico had become enthralled with the magic of radio, and more than 100,000 Mexican citizens owned their own receivers. Even the poorest Mexican had the opportunity to listen to the radio, thanks to the efforts of the Mexican government and Mexican breweries, which distributed hun-dreds of sets to schools, workmen's centers, and cantinas throughout the country.

More than thirty privately owned commercial stations, as well as ten government-owned educational stations, served the ever-growing Mexi-can listening audience. Equipped for the most part with American-made broadcasting gear, the commercial stations varied in power from 30 to 10,000 watts and supported their operations with a barrage of adver-tising. Centro Mercantil pushed its special bargains on ladies' hats. Smooth-talking announcers declared the El Buen Tono and Aguila ciga-rettes were as good as any imported brands. The Mexico Music Company sponsored an hour of recorded music to promote phonograph sales. American advertisers were quick to jump into the Mexican airwaves as well. Ads for Coca-Cola, Kolynos toothpaste, and Gillette razors filled the airwaves from Vera Cruz to Guadalajara. One U.S. advertiser even trumpeted the benefits of an American-made insecticide as the house-maker's best friend and a roach's worst enemy. By the early thirties, radio was an important part of the Mexican educational, political, and enter-tainment system.

One of the rising stars of the Mexican radio industry was a former shoe

salesman who came to be known as Don Emilio. Emilio Azcárraga Via-
durreta was born in 1893, the son of a minor government official in the
northern Mexico town of Monterrey. A strong, powerfully built man whom
Time magazine described as combining "John L. Lewis's burliness and the
late Wendell L. Willkie's charm," Azcárraga attended St. Edward's University in Austin, Texas, a small liberal arts college run by German priests
of the Holy Cross order. He was a star on the 1912 football team but left
college because of a combination of bad grades and a desire to get into
business quickly. And get into business he did.

Like so many Texans, Don Emilio headed for the oil fields, where
money flowed as swiftly as petroleum. He began selling shoes to workers
in fields around Tampico, on the Gulf Coast of Mexico. He was so successful that he traveled to Boston and acquired the rights to sell a fashionable
line of footwear all over Mexico. He journeyed from the jungles of the
Yucatán to the deserts of Chihuahua, selling shoes and learning the tastes
and styles of his fellow countrymen. Don Emilio proved to be a super-
salesman and extended his product line to higher-dollar items. He imported several carloads of Fords from Texas and sold them like tamales in
Mexico City. He marketed record players for the Victor Talking Machine
Company and served as a talent agent for the Victor technical unit that
toured the country twice a year to make recordings. When Victor merged
with RCA, Don Emilio began to sell radios as well and established strong
ties with NBC, the premier broadcasting company in the United States.
Soon afterward, Don Emilio started building his own empire of the
airwaves.

Azcárraga actually began his broadcasting career in 1921 when he and
his four brothers opened a small station in Mexico City. According to Don
Emilio, the station was "just one of those things you operate for fun," and it
closed in 1924. Five years later, when Don Emilio was on one of his
frequent sales trips, a customer complained, "I buy your radio, but I hear
nothing but gringo music." Don Emilio realized that the time was right for
an intensive Mexican broadcasting push, and he opened up station XET in
Monterrey, on March 19, 1930. Called La "T" de Monterrey, the station
achieved notable success, and nine months later Don Emilio set up a
5000-watt transmitter in Mexico City and began broadcasts from radio
station XEW. Known as La Voz de la América Latina desde México ("The
Voice of Latin America From Mexico"), XEW eventually became the most
powerful and most popular station in the country.

By the early thirties Don Emilio and other Mexican broadcasters were
ready to expand their radio markets and increase the power of their stations, but the Mexican radio operators were restricted in their ambitions.
They found that there was no room for them in the electromagnetic spec-

trum, as the Americans and Canadians had filled all of the available frequencies years before. Seven Mexican stations were already broadcasting on channels assigned to stations in the United States, including WMC in Memphis and KTM in Los Angeles, and two Mexican stations were beaming their signals on frequencies reserved for Canadian stations in Toronto and Winnipeg. Some of the 50,000-watt stations in the United States interfered with Mexican signals as well, increasing the aggravation of the Mexican broadcasters. In addition, American officials seemed to take little or no interest in the problems of the Mexican radio operators—that is, until the arrival of the border blasters.

DR. BRINKLEY FINDS MEXICO LAND OF MANY DELIGHTS, read the headline of the *Wichita Beacon* magazine section on February 22, 1931. In the accompanying article Doctor told of his travels to Mexico City with Mrs. Brinkley and Johnnie Boy. "The American people have the idea that it is difficult to meet Mexican officials or do business in Mexico," he reported. "I found it quite the contrary." On his sojourn Brinkley met with General Juan Alamazán, who controlled the republic's radio, telegraph, telephone, railroads, steamships, and roadwork. Brinkley described the general as "kind, sympathetic and fearless, anxious to assist anyone that wishes to help Mexico." Brinkley found that the official worked "from 8 o'clock in the morning until long past midnight" and that he was involved with efforts to build a tourist highway from the Atlantic to the Pacific. While the hardworking Mexican official ate a banana and drank a glass of milk, Dr. Brinkley proposed constructing a high-powered radio station on the northern border. General Alamazán strongly supported the idea, according to Brinkley, who reported that "it is the wish of the officials of the Mexican government to have a powerful broadcasting station located . . . at some point near the Rio Grande, over which may be broadcast the ideals of the Mexican people." The persecuted surgeon felt a kindred spirit in the Mexican government. "The Government of Mexico realizes all the injustice that has been done to them through misleading press reports," Brinkley said, "just as a great injustice has been done to me." Brinkley returned to Kansas with the approval to build a high-powered station anywhere he wished in northern Mexico.

Brinkley was not the first to broadcast to the States from the Rio Bravo. The International Broadcasting Company had previously opened XED in Reynosa, Tamaulipas, across the Rio Grande from McAllen, Texas. At 10,000 watts, XED was the most powerful station in Mexico at the time and caused some concern among American broadcasters. But it was the shadow of Dr. Brinkley on the Rio Grande that made bureaucrats in both Washington and Mexico leap into administrative action.

An Associated Press dispatch from Mexico City in September 1931 reported that U.S. ambassador J. Reuben Clark, Jr., had formally asked the Mexican government to refuse a medical permit for Dr. Brinkley. The Mexican newspaper *El Nacional* added to the report, informing the Mexican public that Dr. Brinkley had lost both his medical and his broadcasting licenses in the United States and that the Mexican health department had requested that Brinkley be denied entrance into the country.

Doctor was outraged. He asked his good friend and fellow Kansan Vice President Charles Curtis to look into the matter. The U.S. State Department informed the vice president that the AP report was incorrect. Doctor responded with a lengthy telegram to Curtis. Although Brinkley threatened an investigation to "expose the whole sordid mess," he was still denied a visa and had to resort to remote broadcasting to get his medical messages out to the people of North America.

El Nacional kept the political pressure on Brinkley, reporting that "he could offer no proof of medical studies which would justify his practice" and suggesting "that our authorities put a check on Brinkley's quack crusade." A week later another Mexican newspaper, *La Prensa*, reported that radio fans in Coahuila, the state in which station XER was located, lodged a formal protest to the governor, Naario Ortiz Garza, about the tolerance shown to XER. The fans complained that the owners and all the station employees were Americans and that almost all of *las transmisiones* were in English. According to *La Prensa*, "The protesting patriots protest before the Government of Coahuila against the tolerance shown this propaganda of Yankee imperialism."

Doctor, "famous for the methods he uses in the application of monkey glands," according to *El Nacional*, had more friends than enemies south of the border. Officials in the Mexican government welcomed the opportunity to tweak the American broadcasting establishment and the Yankee imperialists who had established hegemony over the North American airwaves. In addition, *la frontera* was a sparsely populated area, far from Mexico City. And if the programming was in English, at least the Spanish speakers south of the border would not be misled into purchasing dubious products or medical treatments. Soon after Brinkley opened his station, the Mexican authorities granted him permission to boost the power of his station to 150,000 watts, making it one of the most powerful broadcasting outlets in the world.

Reports on the radio renegades flowed back and forth among Washington, Mexico City, and the U.S. consul in Piedras Negras. American officials fully understood the danger of letting Brinkley loose behind the controls of the most powerful station in North America. They realized that they could not stop the determined surgeon simply by denying him entrance to Old Mexico, and they were concerned that Norman Baker was also eyeing the border. *Broadcasting* magazine warned of "Mexican-Cuban wave grabs" and noted that a congressional move was under way to halt the station-building activity in Mexico, which seriously endangered the operation of stations in the United States and Cuba.

A congressional move was indeed under way, spearheaded by Senator Clarence C. Dill of Washington, the powerful chairman of the Senate Interstate Commerce Committee. "Mexico is taking stations she would not take under ordinary arrangements," Dill declared. "American capital is going into Mexico and building stations out of line and operating them without any control from this government, simply because they cannot get on the air in this country." Dill proposed a series of resolutions to the State Department that would protect American frequencies from the onslaughts of the border blasters. Norman Baker led his United Farm Federation of America in a vociferous campaign against the senator's resolutions. Baker maintained that the Dill bill "would work hardships on American citizens who are driven from the U.S. into Mexico seeking freedom of air." He called the complaints about interference "nothing but propaganda of the FRC, of the trusts of America, who have taken the freedom of the air away from the American people," and he cited the complicity of the American Medical Association, whose members "don't even know a positive cure for a common, ordinary cold."

While legislative battles raged on the domestic front, American diplomats were busy preparing for the International Radio Conference scheduled to take place in Madrid in the summer of 1932. Prior to the opening of that conference, American officials attempted to establish a diplomatic beachhead by meeting with influential Mexican politicians. To this end, the U.S. ambassador to Mexico, Reuben Clark, paid a visit to General Plutarco Elías Calles, a former president of the republic and a powerful public figure. Ambassador Clark spoke about the high-powered radio stations at Eagle Pass and Villa Acuña and pointed out that they were, for all intents and purposes, American stations. He told former president Calles that the stations were broadcasting in English and had been established to reach American audiences. He asked the general what might happen if disgruntled Mexican nationals erected similar stations in the United States. This final point seemed to have an impact on Calles, who assured the American ambassador that he would take the matter up immediately with the Minister of Communications.

At first it seemed as if the American groundwork would pay off. Josephus Daniels, who succeeded Clark as ambassador to Mexico, had served as Secretary of the Navy in World War I and for the war years was the U.S. administrator in charge of broadcasting. In a letter to FDR,

Daniels confided, "Inasmuch as when we were in the Navy, all wireless was under our control, I know everything connected with its expansion and improvement . . . is personally interesting to you." Daniels believed that the negotiators would achieve great results in Madrid "if they can escape the hoodoo that seems to haunt all international conferences."

Unfortunately, the hoodoo hovered over the delegates in Madrid. The conference, held in September 1932, failed to pull the plug on the border operators. No agreement was reached between the United States and Mexico regarding frequency allocations. Mexican newspaper reports praised the delegation, headed by the Mexican ambassador to Spain, Genaro Estrada, for not signing the resolutions adopted at the conference table, which "had been supported by certain countries . . . interested in obtaining the control of space in the matter of radio communication." *El Universal* denounced what it perceived as an attempt by the United States to gain complete control of the airwaves: "The United States desires to have a great majority of the radio frequencies so that no one can molest it in its advertising broadcasts. . . . Europe and its colonies in other continents are ready to fight to protect themselves against the imperialistic aerial designs of the United States." The paper surmised that American attempts to persuade the Mexican government to prohibit the building of high-powered stations on the border "have a direct relation to the aspirations of imperialism of the air which that neighboring country seeks to obtain in this important branch of human progress." While acknowledging that some of Dr. Brinkley's "curative methods" might be "prejudicial to the public health," the Mexican press maintained that the basic desire of the United States was to remove the "wall of noise" that "prevents the waves of many broadcasting stations in the southern part of the United States from reaching our country."

Several powerful American lobbying groups inadvertently joined forces with the Mexican delegation to ensure the survival of the border radio. As a former Federal Radio Commissioner commented, "From such an international conference, the U.S. has only to lose and nothing to gain." American broadcasting executives were more intent on preserving the radio status quo than in supporting any massive international redistribution of the electromagnetic spectrum. They had their own methods of dealing with the interference problems from south of the border. At one point, CBS reportedly sent a man to meet with an official in Mexico City with $50,000 in *mordida* ("bribes," literally, "the bite") to make sure that a particularly bothersome Mexican station changed its frequency.

The wire communications companies such as Western Union also worked hard to make the conference a failure, as the radio conference was held concurrently with the International Telegraph Conference, and wireless officialdom did not wish to be bound by any international treaties covering all communications media. Thanks to the combined efforts of these unlikely allies, the border radio "wall of noise" withstood the battering ram of the Madrid conference.

The *Journal of the American Medical Association* responded to the failure of the negotiations by publishing a ferocious diatribe against the border stations. "The purpose of these stations on the Mexican border is to invalidate the attempts of the FRC to keep clean the material coming through radio channels into this country," the periodical reported. "Apparently, the Mexican government is more concerned with the possible income that may be derived from the licensing of outlawed American stations than with the detriment to American health and sanity that ensues therefrom."

Even the sedate *New York Times* ran the headline STATIONS FEAR TROUBLE FROM MEXICAN BROADCASTERS. The paper went on to explain that the Mexican government had authorized Brinkley to crank the power of XER up to 500,000 watts, making it the most powerful radio station in the world. At that power, Doctor's messages could effectively cover most of the United States, blotting out any stations that came within fifty kilocycles of its frequency path. Stations threatened by the Brinkley power surge included WSM in Nashville, WGN in Chicago, WJR in Detroit, WSB in Atlanta, and WEAF in New York City, the flagship station of the NBC network. The Mexican government also authorized the building of two more 500,000-watt superblasters, one in Matamoros and one in Monterrey. And Norman Baker, curer of cancer and inventor of the calliaphone, began building his own border station in Nuevo Laredo, the 150,000-watt XENT.

Despite a strong show of support for the border stations in Madrid, Mexican authorities were not altogether comfortable with their broadcast babble. They met with American radio negotiators shortly after the conference and agreed to host a North and Central American Regional Radio Conference in Mexico City in July 1933. The American press once again leapt on the anti-border radio bandwagon. Drew Pearson headlined his column with the announcement, "U.S. will demand Mexico drive exiled charlatans out of broadcasting field—Delegates to radio parley hope to squelch such renegades as goat gland faker and cancer quack." He further reported, "The Roosevelt administration is determined to put a stop to international wave pirating. The American delegation goes to Mexico City with secret instructions to sign no agreement that does not eliminate such stations as Brinkley's and Baker's."

As opposing sides took their positions, the upcoming fight for frequencies promised to be a heated one. Norman Baker's biographer recorded

Baker's determination to win "the fight the privileged class interests have waged against him." Baker thought that the "blatant jingoistic" press reports of the upcoming conference were "written from a biased and prejudiced viewpoint" that took no account of the "serious interference with Mexican stations of the high-powered American stations, particularly of the chain station groups." Baker had long been a supporter of Mexican interests in the United States. In 1926 he had invited Colonel M. O. Ruiz, the consul of Mexico, to speak over KTNT and present a talk entitled "The Religious Controversy in Mexico."

Baker's criticism of the American government bordered on the hysterical. His biographer and publicist, Clement Wood, wrote that the U.S. government "hadn't the faintest right in the world to let out one yap or yelp about what Baker was going to do." Wood observed "Al Capone would have had a higher standard of morals than this," and he ended his diatribe with the comment, "Just a bit premature, old zanies."

Baker's persecution complex had at least some basis in fact. On October 14, 1932, Under Secretary of State William R. Castle wrote a letter to Reuben Clark, the U.S. ambassador to Mexico, expressing concern about the opening of XENT. Castle feared that negative broadcasts by Baker over the superpowered outlet would hurt Herbert Hoover's chances in the upcoming presidential election, pointing out to the ambassador that "cranks of this kind always have a large following in our great country." Castle told Clark that if he could "bring about delay in the opening of the station for a month, it would be a real help." He encouraged the diplomat to "persuade the Mexicans to wind a bit of red tape" around Baker's project, using his mind, which was "fertile in intrigue." Later in November, a member of the consular staff did indeed interview Baker about his broadcasting plans, but no amount of red tape could stop the calliaphone virtuoso from opening his border station.

Dr. Brinkley joined Baker in the battle over the international airwaves. Doctor urged his radio audience to fight against U.S. government interference in Mexico and organized a forceful squad of lobbyists. He hired his good friend former U.S. vice president Charlie Curtis to lead the diplomatic assault team. Before he left for Mexico, Curtis visited the State Department to inquire about diplomatic efforts to influence the Mexican government against Dr. Brinkley's operations. The State Department told the loyal former vice president that although there was no official word on the matter, the situation would be examined.

Curtis set out for Mexico City with a team of lawyers to support Brinkley's position. When Ambassador Josephus Daniels learned of the imminent arrival of the pro-Brinkley lobbyist, he jokingly wired his good friend Will Rogers, asking him to come immediately to Mexico City.

"Unless a Democratic Indian is here to protect me," the ambassador cabled, "I may be scalped by the Republican Indian." Rogers promptly wired back: "Making movie. Can't come now. Tell old friend Curtis hello. Don't let em vote static out of radio. That's the best thing in it." The telegram was signed, "Guiermo Rodrigues alias Will Rogers."

Curtis arrived in the capital city of the republic just prior to the opening of the July conference and met with the ambassador. "You know," Curtis told Daniels, "my friend and client Doctor Brinkley has a claim on you. He was born in North Carolina." The fellow Tarheel was not particularly impressed by this connection with the "disreputable individual," as he referred to Brinkley. Curtis told the ambassador that he thought Brinkley had stumbled on a real remedial secret. He opined that if "Sen. Sterling of South Dakota and two or three others in the seats of the almighty had gone to Dr. Brinkley's hospital for treatment . . . they would now be alive." Curtis confided that if he was affected by prostate trouble, he would rather be treated by Dr. Brinkley than by any surgeon in America. Daniels later commented on Curtis' defense of his fellow Kansan, saying that "state pride is a powerful factor." The ambassador listened attentively to Curtis' entreaties but politely declined to assure the former vice president that Brinkley's station would not be closed by the Mexican government.

Not yet satisfied, Curtis arranged to meet with the president of Mexico and the Minister of Communications. The American embassy made the appointments with the high-ranking government officials as a courtesy to the former vice president but warned the Mexican officials that any representations made by Curtis were in no way indicative of the official U.S. position. Although the meeting with the Mexican head of state never occurred, Curtis and the Brinkley brigade succeeded in raising questions in the minds of many delegates and giving some legitimacy to the position of the outlaw broadcasters.

Judge Eugene Octavius Sykes, chairman of the Federal Radio Commission, led the U.S. delegation to the conference. Stopping in San Antonio on his way south, Judge Sykes addressed a local civic club and described the chaos in Mexican radio affairs. With Judge Sykes were a number of diplomatic officials, including Roy T. Davis, American minister to Panama, whose job it was to handle the delegations from the Central American countries. The veteran Washington negotiators were confident of their ability to impose order on the American airwaves.

It seemed as if the American negotiators would have few problems in achieving their goals. At the start of the negotiations, papers in the United States reported that a "Mexican edict dooms border radio stations." In a surprise announcement the Mexican government issued a series of regulations that did indeed appear to be "designed automatically to wipe out all stations along the border by so-called renegade American broadcasters." The new regulations forbade foreign ownership of Mexican stations, prohibited foreign studios from rebroadcasting in Mexico, and outlawed all non-Spanish and medical programming unless it had special permission from the Mexican government. The American delegates were elated. They demanded that Brinkley be put off the air immediately and that Mexico should operate no broadcasting stations on the border that could carry messages into the United States. Despite the recent legislation, the Mexicans resented the American attempt to dictate what they should do with stations in their country. They demanded twelve frequencies with absolute clearance across the United States and insisted on letting border stations operate on five of those frequencies for the stated purpose of promoting tourist travel. The Mexican delegates did not appreciate the high-handed attitude of the United States and contended, in the words of one Mexican commentator, that "America has too many and too trashy stations."

Border operators gained support for their position from unexpected allies. The National Committee on Education by Radio, an industry watchdog group, distributed literature at the conference that strongly condemned the American commercial broadcasting system. The organization objected to radio advertising and urged an increase in educational programming on the airwaves, making the point that the United States already had more stations and more frequencies than it could use effectively. As in Madrid, the private broadcasting industry was not officially represented in Mexico. Many members of the American broadcasting establishment were hostile to the idea of a new agreement on frequency allocations. They feared that any agreement would upset the U.S. radio applecart, forcing broadcasters to fight once again for hard-won frequency allocations. *Broadcasting* magazine reported that the industry "cannot stand another reallocation at this time" and that any reallocation would "inevitably mean disaster to dozens of independent stations" that could not afford to pay the high price for litigation over broadcasting assignments.

MEXICO'S DEMANDS BREAK UP WAVE PARLEY, proclaimed *Broadcasting* on August 15, 1933. American diplomats gnashed their teeth. A memo from the Treaty Division of the State Department told the sad tale: "The American delegation to the Mexico City conference tried hard, but unsuccessfully, to get an agreement on principles which would have put an end to the whole border menace, including the Brinkley station." American radio station owners and their representatives heaved a collective sigh of relief, heralding the failure of the conference as a "complete blessing" from the broadcasters' standpoint, although a "legal and engineering calamity." Baker's supporters viewed the unexpected turn of events with glee. "The attempt at persecution, by our government," wrote Clement Wood, "of one American citizen, Norman Baker, had failed. Shame to everyone connected with that illegal and outrageous attempt." The author went on to praise the spirit of Mexico in standing up to the United States, "whose past history has been stained often enough with bloody and unfair attacks on its southern neighbor."

While some broadcasters cheered, others shuddered at the prospect of more border blasters. The *Washington, D.C., Sunday Star* warned of impending problems in a story headlined RADIO WAVE WAR WITH MEXICO SEEN. *Tower Radio* magazine ran a story with the headline MEXICO MENACES AMERICAN RADIO. Speculation on the border grew, and by early 1934 nine superpowered stations along the Rio Grande were either operating or authorized to begin construction. The aggregate power of these nine stations was a whopping 2,432,000 watts, an astounding figure, considering that the combined wattage of all U.S. stations at that time was a meager 1,700,000 watts. American broadcasters huddled in terror as they anticipated the crushing power of a broadcasting tidal wave from the Rio Grande.

The list of aggrieved American station operators grew longer. Former senator John S. Cohen of the *Atlanta Journal*, owner of WSB in Atlanta, complained of interference from XER. XEPN in Eagle Pass piled up on WOW in Omaha, KMJ in Fresno, California, WOBU in Charleston, West Virginia, and WIBW in Topeka, Kansas. XEAW interfered with channels in Canada, Chicago, and Seattle, while XENT put a "heterodyne whistle" on stations in Virginia and Texas, and XEBC in Baja California smacked into WCCO in Minneapolis. The president of the Minnesota station was Henry A. Bellows, who also happened to be a vice president of CBS. International agreement or no international agreement, angry broadcasters demanded congressional action to stop the border menace.

Washington bureaucrats manned their battle stations. When a radio-monitoring station in Grand Island, Nebraska, reported the beginning of broadcasting over XENT, Federal Radio Commission chairman E.O. Sykes complained to the State Department. "The establishment of this station is a direct violation of the spirit of the conversations recently concluded in Mexico City," he said. One day after Sykes filed his complaint, Senator Dill, the tough legislative opponent of border radio, introduced a Senate bill amending the Radio Act of 1927 to answer the threat of the invading stations, a move that Baker described as "rank discrimination against Mexico." The amendment stated in part that "no person, firm, company or corporation shall be permitted to locate, use or maintain a radio broadcast studio or other place of apparatus from which or whereby sound waves are converted into electrical energy or mechanical or physical reproduction of sound waves produced" and sent to a radio station in a foreign country for the purpose of being broadcast in such a way "that its emissions may be received consistently in the United States."

A similarly convoluted piece of legislation was introduced into the House Committee on Merchant Marine, Radio and Fisheries, whose responsibilities for radio dated back to the early days when transmitters were used mainly for ship-to-shore communication. A lively hearing was held before the committee, a group of legislators perhaps more familiar with problems faced by the whaling industry than the technicalities of radio broadcasting. Judge Sykes told the committee about "the menace of border broadcasting stations . . . camouflaged American stations operating in Mexico." Dr. Charles B. Joliffe testified that "all these stations are financed by United States capital and carry programs of a character which would not be tolerated in this country." Congressman George W. Edmonds of Pennsylvania said, "I got Dr. Brinkley even in Philadelphia." "I had the damnedest time keeping from getting him," chimed in Congressman Albert C. Wilford of Iowa. Congressman R. Ewing Thomason of Texas read to the committee a telegram from the citizens of Del Rio: "Del Rio is 100% behind Doctor Brinkley because he brings us prosperity." Above the shout of laughter that greeted the reading of the telegram, one congressional wag asked, "Does Brinkley use Texas goats in his gland operations?" The unflustered Thomason answered, "We have the finest in the world. Even Congressmen might be interested in the treatment."

While the Brinkley Clause became the law of the land, it did little to stop the border blasters. Dr. Joliffe pointed out that the remedy to the border situation was "in the hands of the American public." He explained that "the American public supports these stations and sends them lots of money and then complains because the Federal Government doesn't do something about it." Spokesmen in Mexico were even more blunt: "The programs come from the United States. If you don't want them, why don't you keep them from originating in your country?"

Many Americans enjoyed the programming from south of the border. Irving R. Potts, president of the Newark Radio Club, wrote to the management of XEW in Mexico City, expressing a desire to hear more Mexican concerts. The station manager wrote back and suggested to Potts that XEW should have a clear channel in the United States and Canada "so you may be able to enjoy this beautiful Mexican music and learn more about our interesting country." Cordel Hull spoke approvingly of Mexican radio programs, saying they "present to other nations the story of their national achievements and attractions." Another radiophile asked the Federal Radio Commission to cut off the American stations so that stations could be heard more clearly, because "the music of the Mexican stations is often quite different from that of our own stations." Congressman Harold McGugin of Kansas received letters from constituents who complained of American interference with Brinkley's Mexican operation. The congressman warned the State Department that Brinkley had a great deal of support in his district. Even the *Forum* magazine praised Brinkley's independence by writing, "The worthy Doctor promptly showed true American spunk by removing across the border to a country with more enlightened policies against restricting individual radio enterprise."

In 1934 a change of governments in Mexico prompted a crackdown on the border operators. Lázaro Cárdenas, the new president of Mexico, realized the importance of maintaining firm control over the media and moved to enforce the existing Mexican broadcasting legislation. The Federal Department of Communications charged Brinkley with breaking Mexican regulations governing medical advertisements and the practice of medicine by foreigners. Mexican officials ordered the suspension of broadcasts from XER for thirty days, with the possibility that the station's broadcast license might be revoked. The governor of Coahuila also found XER to be in violation of the regulations and ordered the station silenced. In February 1934, federal troops marched into Villa Acuña to enforce the government's ruling. Brinkley closed down his operation to "avoid a war," in his words, between the *federales* and the local constabulary, which supported him. A cloud had passed over the Sunshine Station Between the Nations.

Other border broadcasters, however, were untouched by the government crackdown. Baker took great pains to observe all Mexican broadcasting regulations and worked hard to cooperate with regulatory officials. When he started XENT, he gave the Mexican authorities one hour a day to broadcast educational material, and he set aside other blocks of time for entertainment programs in Spanish. The former vaudevillian offered to advertise tourism in Mexico and told Mexican authorities about his plans to build a lake and an amusement park next to the XENT studios in Nuevo Laredo. Baker contended that he always submitted his medical scripts to government censors for approval before his broadcasts and experienced few of the troubles that erupted upriver in Villa Acuña.

Despite the governmental wrist slap, Brinkley's graphic lectures concerning "that troublesome cocklebur," the prostate, reappeared on the airwaves with his purchase of XEAW in Reynosa. At five in the afternoon on December 1, 1935, Doctor commenced broadcasting from Villa Acuña once again, thanks to a favorable ruling by the Mexican federal district court in Peidras Negras that nullified the confiscation of his property. No one can doubt that Doctor savored the courtroom triumph, one of the few he would ever experience in his most litigious life.

The rest of the thirties were glory days for border broadcasters and the people in the small towns on the south side of the Rio Bravo. Field-workers referred to radio as the mockingbird and enjoyed both the Spanish and the English musical entertainment. Border musician Juan Raul Rodriguez grew up in the shadow of XERA's tall radio towers and described the station as "something amazing." According to Rodriguez, "We played near the station, we slept near the station, we never left it. Always there were big cars and people coming and going. And at night you heard the beautiful music everywhere, and you saw flashing lights dancing along the wires, just like the angels in heaven."

The high-rolling radio renegades ingratiated themselves to the Mexican people who lived near their broadcast facilities. Dr. Brinkley purchased uniforms for the Villa Acuña police, distributed Christmas packages to Mexican children, and engaged in spur-of-the-moment philanthropy with a distinct Brinkley style. "We used to play baseball outside the station," Rodriguez explained. "We had a piece of wood we used for a bat. One day Dr. Brinkley drove up to us. He got out of the car, and we were all afraid of what he was going to do to us. He walked up to us and picked our piece of wood up off the ground. He looked at it and shook his head. Then he went back to the car. The next day we were playing baseball again. A man came out from the station and gave us a brand-new bat and ball. Dr. Brinkley was always generous with us."

The border stations brought tourists, technicians, and entertainers to the towns along the Rio Grande, providing high-powered charges to the local economies. While most of their programming was in English, the stations provided an important outlet for some excellent Mexican musicians as well. A mariachi group brought their distinctive sound to XEPN from the plains of Jalisco, and Lydia Mendoza of San Antonio, the Lark of the Border, regularly performed "Mal Hombre," "Cold-Hearted Man," and other popular Spanish ballads on the border blasters. After one performance, a fan asked Lydia how she could play a concert in one town and be on the radio in Del Rio at the same time. Lydia later found out that a different woman had taken her name and was performing her songs over the air. The Lark of the Border quickly put a stop to the unauthorized impersonator.

In addition to performance opportunities, the border stations provided a training ground and operating model for Mexican broadcasters who wished to establish their own stations. Mexican-owned stations started up in Nuevo Laredo, Juárez, Tijuana, and other towns along the border.

Quick-witted Mexican entrepreneurs found that they could make good money leasing large blocks of time from the high-powered border stations. Arnaldo Ramirez, a McAllen native, formed an ad agency at the start of World War II with his boss at a local furniture store and hosted a daily program on XEAW. Ramirez began each program by saying, *"Esta es la hora commercial de la victoria en el año de la victoria"* ("This is the victory channel in the year of victory"). He sold so much Spanish-language advertising that he soon expanded his program to four hours a day. With his humorous, informal radio style, he introduced musicians who had a distinctive *norteña* sound, a sound that featured the button-type accordion and blended German polkas with traditional Mexican ballads. This *conjunto* sound was the equivalent of the hillbilly music featured in the English programming on the border stations, a rougher country sound than was played on stations based in Mexico City.

In Mexico City, Emilio Azcárraga, had become the most powerful figure in Mexican broadcasting. Don Emilio successfully fought off internal labor struggles, competition from other broadcasters, and even terrorist attacks to control the biggest chain radio network in the nation. The flagship of this network was XEW, the 50,000-watt Voice of Latin America From Mexico.

Don Emilio used the contacts he had made with the Victor recording team to attract Mexico's top composers, writers, and entertainers to the XEW studios. Augustín Lara, one of Mexico's most famous composers, hosted *La Hora Azul* ("The Blue Hour"). *Ranchera* singers, the Mexican equivalent of singing cowboys, became tremendously popular on XEW. Some of them, like Jorge Negrete, went on to star in hit films based on their most popular songs. Pepe Guizar, El Mariachi Vargas, and *orquesta típica* leader Tata Nacho, alias Ignacio Fernández Esperón, added their audience-pleasing talents to the XEW musical roster.

Don Emilio described his operation to a *Newsweek* reporter as "the most colossal music organization. . . . We are a real menace to your Tin Pan Alley." Most of the performers had no written agreement to work for XEW, but they found that they were treated well by Don Emilio, who demanded only that they work exclusively for his organization. One writer described the sumptuous XEW studios as "banked with flowers, hung with arrow-pierced hearts, and bathed in subdued lighting." Don Emilio supported the composers and musicians in their work and let his talent use the XEW facilities for jam sessions. The informal gatherings produced some of the biggest Mexican hits of the era, songs like "Amor," "Bésame Mucho," and "Maria Elena." XEW produced a lavish musical sound that proved extremely popular for decades.

Don Emilio, however, preferred hillbilly music. One of his favorite tunes was "Pistol Packin' Mama," a song that he described as "something both Americans and Mexicans understand." Mexico's radio mogul had ample opportunity to enjoy this and other American songs, since he copied the programming of Brinkley and Baker on his own personal border blaster, XET in Monterrey. "These old songs are just about the best, aren't they?" surmised Brother Bill Guild, announcer for the Carter Family. "And speaking of old things, this city of Monterrey is noted for its ancient landmarks, buildings, and backgrounds." Brother Bill's sidekick, Denny, went on to describe the *Good Neighbor Get-together Program*, "four hours packed solid with fun and music from six o'clock until ten o'clock every evening over this station. *La estación* XET, Monterrey, Nuevo León." Brother Bill translated, "That's station XET, Monterrey, down Mexico way. Now, if you're ready, Cowboy Slim Rinehart, come on in and introduce Doc and Carl to the folks."

A great deal of the programming on Don Emilio's network was musical variety entertainment. Comedy was not as popular on Mexican radio as it was in the United States. As the assistant manager of XEW explained to a reporter from the *New York Times*, "The Mexican mood is not so gay. You Americans laugh at anything. The Mexican people must have something very, very funny to make them laugh." While Mexican audiences may not have been interested in laughs, they were definitely interested in love.

"In America," Azcárraga explained, "the soap operas emphasize plain talk. We, perhaps, are a little more . . . amorous." Some of the most popular of the Mexican radio soap operas included *La Intrusa* ("The Gossiping Woman"), *Extasis* ("Ecstasy"), and *Lo que Solo el Hombre Puedo Sufrir* ("What Only a Man Can Suffer"), which was subtitled "Secrets of the Masculine Heart from Real Life." The characters in these shows followed strict rules of Mexican etiquette. In one episode a ghost visited a dying man to taunt him about his misdeeds. The ghoul was polite enough to ask about the well-being of his victim's relatives before beginning to terrorize him. These *dramas en serio* were very popular, but the biggest hit created by superpowered XEW was *Colegio de Amor* ("School of Love").

Each Thursday night, beginning in the mid-forties, three men and three women recited love letters in front of the four-hundred-person studio audience. Each letter had to begin discreetly, with just the initials of the reciter's beloved, after which the honeyed love tones were allowed to gush forth. On one occasion two heartbroken lovers proposed to the same woman, who made her choice on the following program. The losing lover was so despondent that the popular woman switched her choice on the next broadcast. One woman went on the air to attract a lost love.

"Doubt," she said, "is beginning to gnaw at my heart. You said when you left that you were merely going around the corner to buy a package of cigarettes. Now I learn that you have married and have three children. Time is passing, and my heart grows suspicious. But I am only a weak woman, and I forgive you." Studio applause determined the winner, who took home a prize of 50 pesos, or about $7. But money was not the highest reward for a prizewinning performance on the program. The goal that contestants strove for was love. XEW had files full of letters from happy couples who had realized their dreams through *Colegio,* altough the sponsor accepted no responsibility for the marriages forged on the air.

Although Don Emilio avoided political controversy over the airwaves, saying, "Politics are very touch-me-not," he was a powerful behind-the-scenes political operative. He expanded his broadcasting operations throughout the thirties, joined the NBC network for a time, and provided programming to some 43 stations throughout Mexico by the end of the decade. By 1937 Don Emilio was ready to increase the power of his stations and clear the North American airwaves to receive his radio messages. He decided that it was time to confront the one group that stood in the way of his plans for aerial expansion. That group was Brinkley, Baker, and the rest of the border blasters.

The confrontation occurred at the First Inter-American Radio Conference held in Havana, Cuba, in the winter of 1937. Delegates from Canada, Cuba, the Dominican Republic, Haiti, Mexico, and the United States held a preliminary conference in Havana early in 1937. Those who attended the diplomatic warm-up established the agenda for the full conference and called for the "reallocation of broadcast frequencies to eliminate interferences from border stations" as one of the unofficial objectives of the regional meeting. Lieutenant Commander T.M. Craven, head of the Federal Communications Commission, traveled to Mexico City at the close of the preliminary meeting and met with Señor Gomez Morentin, director general of the Mexican Postal and Telegraphic Service. Despite the lukewarm support of American broadcasters, who still mistrusted any international frequency reallocations, the two men hammered out the parameters for an agreement, no doubt with strong guidance from Don Emilio.

The advance work paid off, and after seven years of trying, the United States finally persuaded Mexico to agree to a reallocation of radio frequencies in North America. The North American Regional Broadcasting Agreement (NARBA) was signed at Havana on December 13, 1937. Complete success eluded those who wished to solve the Mexico-America radio controversy, however. By August 1938 only the United States had ratified the agreement, thanks to political pressure from the border broadcasters and bureaucratic sloth on the part of the other governments involved. Moreover, many who supported the NARBA had initially thought that the agreement was not specific enough to ensure that the border blasters would disappear from the air. In addition, Mexican negotiators believed that the NARBA provided inadequate protection for Mexican high-powered clear-channel stations, an important ingredient for both Azcárraga and government officials. It was decided that a further gentleman's agreement was needed between the United States and Mexico to eliminate, in the words of the American ambassador's office in Mexico City, "interference from Mexican broadcasting stations along the Mexican border at Villa Acuña, Nuevo Laredo, and Reynosa."

That agreement was hammered out in Mexico City and Washington and was signed by Mexican president Cárdenas on April 14, 1939. Again, however, a solution to the problem eluded the grasp of the legislators. The gentleman's agreement could not go into effect until the NARBA was ratified by Mexico. *Broadcasting* magazine reported that "operators of border stations had been instrumental in prevailing upon influential members of the Senate to oppose formal ratification" of the agreement. In addition, Mexican officials had stepped on the toes of the one person who might have been able to push the broadcasting agreements through quickly. Don Emilio was upset.

With more than eighty stations serving the entire nation, Mexican broadcasting was a mature industry by the end of the thirties. By that time the Cárdenas regime believed even more strongly that the propaganda power, as well as the revenue-generating power, of radio should be kept under strict government control. According to *Variety*, American tourist dollars were beginning to pour into Mexico, and politicians in Mexico City realized that "Mexican radio, old style, impeded rather than aided the country in its wish to attract American and Canadian tourists." Planning was under way in Mexico City for a huge world's fair, and the Mexican government wished to close the border stations and other high-powered stations and replace them with five high-powered radio outlets owned and operated by the government. In addition to running commercial broadcasts, these stations would run spots "for the upcoming World's Fair, for Tampico, for Mexico City, the Popocatepetl, Floating City, and tamales." *Variety* reported that Mexican politicians thought that "if the border radio stations can sell the Americans penny-a-day insurance, rupture cures, perfume packages and similar items, they can also sell Americans Mexico as the continent's playground."

In the spring of 1937 the government took a direct hand in the Mexican broadcasting business with the inauguration of a radio program entitled *La Hora Nacional* ("The National Hour"). The program was produced by the Departamento Autónomo de Prensa y Publicidad, the government's publicity agency located in Mexico City. *La Hora Nacional* became an unavoidable feature of Sunday night radio south of the border, as every station in the republic was required to rebroadcast it. In a further effort to increase the central government's control over radio, a new law became effective in 1937 entitled Regulations for Commercial, Cultural, Scientific, Experimental, and Amateur Radio Stations. The new regulations required that every radio program "must contain at least 25 per cent of typically Mexican music" and outlawed commercial breaks that lasted longer than two minutes.

Mexican broadcasters had seen similar regulations in the past and were not very concerned until the government proposed a much stronger piece of legislation in early 1938. As part of the new law, a supercommission would have "absolute power over radio broadcasting." Characterizing the bill as the work of "fanatic politicians," Don Emilio cried, "Radio belongs to relaxation, not to education."

As World War II threatened to engulf North America, the border blasters, Don Emilio, and the "fanatic politicians" struggled for control of the Mexican airwaves. Don Emilio became head of the Mexican Broadcasting Association and visited the National Association of Broadcasters convention in San Francisco in 1940 to ingratiate himself with American commercial broadcasters and convince them that his positions on frequency allocations were the most appropriate. In the end, Don Emilio prevailed. The Mexican government's plans to nationalize the radio industry evaporated. A new administration came into office, and President Ávila Camacho pushed the Mexican legislature into ratifying the NARBA, along with the gentleman's agreement, on March 29, 1941. In return for a commitment to close down the border stations, Mexico was given six class 1-A clear-channel frequencies, at 730, 800, 900, 1050, 1220, and 1570 kilocycles. Except for local American stations assigned to 1050 and 1220 kilocycles, the United States agreed to limit its stations on the six channels to daytime operation only with a maximum of 1 kilowatt of power.

XERA disappeared from the air. XENT went silent. Arnaldo Ramirez drove across into Reynosa one day for his four-hour program, only to find that XEAW no longer existed. Meanwhile, Don Emilio broke ground for Radiopolis, a broadcasting center in Mexico City designed to rival New York's Radio City. His flagship station XEW broadcast with a thundering 200,000 watts. Azcárraga announced plans to boost the power to 250,000 watts after the war, and he pushed for a hemispheric wave band for one strong station in each country. "When we can listen to one another every night without jamming," Don Emilio confidently maintained, "we'll really get to know each other at last."

Congressmen, American Medical Association officials, and U.S. broadcasting executives were all pleased with the new hard-line attitude exhibited by the Mexican government toward the border stations. Even the FBI had good reason to be thankful for the change. In 1942 the Mexican federal police heard rumors of a clandestine radio station run by Axis undercover agents near the United States border at Chihuahua City. This time, unlike the German radio espionage incident in World War I, the United States government did not have to send special forces into Mexico to shut down the operation. The *federales* moved in on their own, destroyed the station, arrested thirteen Japanese operatives, and tracked down three others who had fled to a nearby mining town. By the beginning of World War II, it seemed as if Mexican authorities had learned from their American counterparts that the border airwaves should be kept clean for freedom, democracy, and tasteful commercial messages.

Coast to Coast, Border
to Border . . . Your Good
Neighbor Along the Way

They feed you chili and tamales hot—
Everything is yours that they have got
in Del Rio, down Texas way.
Look out Del Rio, I'm comin' back to stay.
—*From "Del Rio Boogie," by the Delmore Brothers and Wayne Raney, 1949*

Shortly after Hank Thompson got out of the Navy in 1946, the up-and-coming country singer was thinking about border radio. The Waco native had just cut his first record, "Whoa, Sailor," and was looking for some airplay.

Thompson had grown up listening to old-time hillbilly music on the powerful radio stations located down Mexico way. He recalled the broadcast combat of Brinkley and Baker, comparing the put-downs exchanged by the superwatt mavericks to a "slugfest like Jack Benny and Fred Allen."

So it was only natural that the future King of Western Swing headed for the Rio Grande and the fabled radio frontier that covered the landscape with the music he was raised on. Remembering that Brinkley had once owned a station in Reynosa, Thompson went to McAllen and crossed the river in search of the border blaster. He spoke very little Spanish but managed to find a station and present his 78 rpm disc to an employee. The somewhat bewildered radioman explained in broken English that the station was not a high-powered border blaster but only a 250-watter that programmed exclusively in Spanish. Thompson left the station, his record in hand, disappointed to find that the border blasters of his youth had vanished.

Or had they?

"Coast to coast, border to border, wherever you are, wherever you may be, when you think of entertainment, think of XERF, in Ciudad Acuña, Coahuila, Mexico." A rich, impassioned baritone rose from the banks of the Rio Grande like a defiant Comanche war cry: "This is Paul Kallinger, Your Good Neighbor Along the Way from down alongside the silvery Rio Grande, where the sunshine spends the winter."

Like a broadcasting phoenix, rising from the regulatory ashes, border radio once again took flight in the postwar years. Villa Acuña was again the hub of border activity, as two of Dr. Brinkley's former associates, Don Howard and Walter Wilson, decided to get back into the border radio business. They set up an advertising agency with offices in the Roswell Hotel, formerly the site of Brinkley's clinic, and retained the Del Rio attorney Arturo C. González to help recapture a radio license and frequency from the Mexican government. González, a self-taught lawyer described by Wolfman Jack as "the godfather of that southern portion of Texas," had previously assisted Brinkley with XERA's legal matters in Mexico. With dual U.S. and Mexican citizenship, González was an especially effective negotiator, and his list of clients eventually included many Texas luminaries, one of whom was President Lyndon B. Johnson.

The Del Rio entrepreneurs were successful in their negotiations, and in 1947 Dr. Brinkley's old station was back on the air, this time with the call letters XERF. The station sported a brand-new 50,000-watt RCA transmitter that replaced the old XERA transmitter, which had been dismantled and carted off for use by station XEX in Mexico City. Three notes from the trumpet of Juan Raul Rodriguez began the first song played on the revived station, "Incertidumbre" ("Uncertainty"), which was followed by the first program, *Hillbilly Roundup Time*. Border radio was back in business, and Paul Kallinger was one of its most eloquent spokesmen.

"Folks, if you're overweight, do you realize that you're shortening your life?" intoned the authoritative announcer. "Now, there's a lot of you out there that are carrying thirty, forty, fifty, sixty, seventy pounds of excess fat around. It's like carrying a sack of flour or a sack of potatoes around all day long. You couldn't take the motor of an automobile and put it in a diesel truck and have that truck perform properly, could you? . . . Now, if you'd like to lose as much as a pound a day, then listen to what I have to say. Pounds Off is available, guaranteed to help you lose as much as a pound a day, thirty pounds in thirty days, or double your money back. . . . Just send your name and address to Pounds Off, XERF, Del Rio, Texas."

Ever since he was a boy growing up on the midwestern plains, Paul

Kallinger had a love for the spoken word. "I would always go to the auctions in Nebraska and watch the auctioneers," he said. "They inspired me, and I thought, 'Boy, I'd like to be an auctioneer. I'd love to be an auctioneer.'" Radio proved to be even more fascinating for the youth than the incantation of cattle prices. "I remember when my dad bought our first radio. It was an old Crosley radio . . . We could pick up KFAB and WOW out of Omaha." Like a youngster swinging a stick in imitation of a World Series homer, Kallinger fantasized that it was actually his voice traveling for miles through thin air and emerging miraculously from the radio speakers: "I'd get behind the radio speakers and imitate all the announcers, mainly the commercials. The commercials were what I really liked."

Kallinger served in the Navy in World War II and moved to Los Angeles with his family after his time in the service. He worked in an air conditioning and refrigeration factory, until a magazine advertisement caught his eye. "The ad said, 'If you are a G.I., I will train you, and the government will pay for your education to become a radio personality.'" Kallinger enrolled in a two-year course at the Frederick H. Sphere Radio Announcing School on Sunset Boulevard, appearing weekly on KXLA radio as part of the Frederick H. Sphere's Career Theater of the Air. After graduation, he barnstormed across the Southwest, applying at every radio station from Los Angeles to El Paso. He finally landed a job at KDLK, a 250-watt station in Del Rio, but moved on after a short time to KPLC, a 5000-watt radio outlet in Lake Charles, Louisiana.

Kallinger's ambition could not be contained by KPLC's 5000 watts, and he sent an audition tape to Arturo González at XERF. "He called me back in about three days and said, 'Come on down. You got a job,'" Kallinger recalled. "And I thought, 'Boy, this is great. Here I am going to go on this big powerful radio station. The whole world will hear me now.'"

XERF's clear-channel signal, located at 1570 near the top of the dial, gave the station tremendous nighttime range. Its isolated location, its 50,000 watts of power, and the small number of competing stations ensured that the whole world could indeed hear Paul Kallinger. In the early fifties Your Good Neighbor Along the Way decided to take an informal poll to see just how wide the station's coverage really was. "One night I asked the listeners to call in," Kallinger explained. "Would you believe it? I got eighty calls that night from forty-five different states. And at that time we only had forty-eight states." Kallinger was not completely satisfied with the results. "I didn't get any calls from Arizona," the DJ confided. "So I said, 'What's wrong with the people in Arizona? Isn't there anyone who lives there?' 'Oh, I know,' I said. 'That's why they have a town called Tombstone. Everybody's dead.' Right after that I got ten to fifteen calls from Arizona." On cold, clear winter nights, when the atmospheric conditions were particularly favorable, XERF's coverage was truly global. "We heard from Canada, Japan, Germany, England, Greenland, South America, Australia—all over. And everybody said they received the signal very well."

During the Korean War, the mighty X in Coahuila provided a link to home for American military personnel. Kallinger recalled the letters of the servicemen. "We were out on ship," one letter read, "and we heard you and it made us very lonesome, 'cause we're from Texas and we heard the good ole USA." Even the Soviet Union's KGB was listening in. The Russian intelligence specialists would tune into the super-powered Tex-Mex station to learn the English language. One can picture a group of earnest Soviet agent trainees, sitting in a drafty office near Red Square, carefully repeating the words of Paul Kallinger, "From down alongside the silvery Rio Grande River, where the sunshine spends the winter."

From the outset, Kallinger specialized in programming hillbilly and gospel music, which was becoming known at that time as country and western. The border stations had a tradition of programming that type of music, which was aimed at the ears and feet of rural listeners and recent immigrants to the city. In the thirties Dr. Brinkley introduced Roy Faulkner, the Singing Cowboy, to the border, and Pappy O'Daniel brought his Hillbilly Boys to Eagle Pass for the winter broadcasting season. As radio entrepreneurs across the country learned about the tremendous sales power of the border stations, they started purchasing time to promote their own entertainers and products.

The Consolidated Royal Chemical Corporation of Chicago was one of the first to take advantage of the marketing muscle of the border stations. In 1937 Harry O'Neil, the company's advertising agent, decided to send one of its most popular hillbilly acts, the Pickard Family, down to Del Rio. "He said, 'How would you like to go down and play at Dr. Brinkley's station in Villa Acuña, Coahuila, Mexico?'" explained Ruth Pickard, a member of the group. "He said, 'That's near Del Rio, Texas.' We, of course, were thrilled to death. We were all young kids then. We were delighted with the idea of going to Mexico. So we went down and sang at that station that belonged to Dr. J.R. Brinkley. He was a Texas billionaire who was developing pink grapefruit."

Ruth Pickard and her family became one of the most popular acts on the border. At eight o'clock every evening, their show began over XERA. "My, my, my," began the warm voice of Ruth's father, Obed. "How is everybody out there? Mammy and pappy and grand mammy and grand pappy and everybody, come on in and sit right down. This is one place that you sure are welcome. The family's just gettin' along fine away down here in Del Rio, Texas." The family launched in to an old favorite like "How Many Biscuits Can You Eat This Morning?" followed by Obed's fiddle on "The Arkansas Traveler." To slow it down, Obed introduced "Sleep, Kentucky Babe," a quiet ballad. "Sing it sweet, now, chillen," Obed directed. "Don't make no sour notes." Ruth later observed, "One of the reasons for our popularity was that we always ended with an old-fashioned hymn, and people in those days were a lot more religious than they are now." The Pickards ended their broadcasts with a rendition of "I'm Gonna Walk the Streets of Glory," "Work, For the Night Is Coming," or some other popular hymn, followed by Obed's invitation to "listen in again tomorrow night."

Harry O'Neil and the Consolidated Royal Chemical Corporation were more interested in selling products than in providing spiritual sustenance. Broadcasts over the border stations did much to boost the popularity of their cold remedy Peruna (pronounced "Pee-roo-na"). "Now, friends," a male voice said, beginning the Peruna pitch, "if you're one of those folks who's always bothered with bad colds during the winter months . . . why don't you do as thousands of others in the same boat have done? . . . Take the new Peruna to help build up your cold-fighting, cold-chasing ability. . . . If you'll just mail your name and address to Peruna, P-E-R-U-N-A, Peruna, care of the Pickard Family, Del Rio, Texas, you're gonna receive without any cost a liberal test bottle of the famous Peruna Tonic. . . . And remember this too, if you want to try Peruna right away, all drugstores have it, and you get it under the maker's guarantee—you must be satisfied or your money back for the asking. Is that fair enough?"

The Pickards also offered a solution to a problem even more serious than the scourge of colds—gray hair: "How many of you have gray hair? Well, you just listen to this announcement please. Don't let gray hair cheat you out of your job and cause you a lot of worry. No, sirree, that isn't necessary anymore. Not when it's so easy to get rid of gray-hair worries and handicaps. And here is all you have to do. Get a bottle of Kolorbak from your nearest drug or department store." According to the earnest pitch of the Pickard boys, Kolorbak "scientifically imparts color and charm to gray hair" and was sold "under the maker's positive guarantee it must remove every trace of grayness and make you look five to ten years younger and far more attractive or your money back." Listeners were urged to send in a carton flap from their next purchase of Kolorbak for a "big special gift offer," a free box of Q-Bak shampoo.

The Chicago-based drug manufacturer received as many as 20,000 responses a week to the Pickard Family broadcasts, a marketing gold mine for manufacturer and performer alike. "All my dad's old friends from the Grand Old Opry on WSM in Nashville and WLW in Cincinnati wanted to know if there were any openings down there," remembered Ruth Pickard. "Those other stations weren't paying much money in those days. My dad was making a thousand dollars a week, which was a lot of money in those days, back when the Depression was on. The rest of us got about a hundred a week."

Harry O'Neil sent other performers down to the border, including the Carter Family, who were regular performers on the border stations from 1938 to 1942. "This Good Neighbor Get-together Program lasts for four hours," announced Brother Bill Guild, "and here's that well-known Carter Family to carry on—A.P., Sarah, and Maybelle, Jeanette, Helen, June, and Anita. And, of course, they'll have to sing that good old theme song for you, 'Keep on the Sunny Side.'"

Soon after they arrived on the border, the Carter Family began to supplement their live performances with electrical transcriptions. Dr. Brinkley had pioneered the use of transcriptions to avoid broadcasting regulations, and subsequent federal litigation against Norman Baker had legitimized the use of the recordings for international broadcasting. Major Kord, alias Don Baxter, and his wife, Dode, set up a transcription studio in their garage in San Antonio. The Carter Family used their facility, often sharing it with other performers like Patsy Montana. "At that time, A.P. and Sarah were separated," Patsy recollected. "Whenever A.P. wanted to say something to Sarah, he'd call me over, and I'd have to relay his message. It sure was awkward."

The use of transcriptions became increasingly popular as performers realized they could distribute them to a number of stations while maintaining a live-in-the-studio feel. Advertisers also took advantage of electrical transcriptions and distributed recordings of commercials for a variety of products, including one pitch aimed at indoor gardeners. "Thank you for the many letters telling us about the remarkable success you are having with the indoor garden," the announcer said. "I knew you'd be amazed to see how fast vegetables and flowers grow without any dirt whatever. . . . Here's what I'm going to send each one of you who mails his request tonight . . . a large package of Miracle Grow, which will make four gallons of water culture solution . . . two quarts of horticultural peat to be used as per directions to anchor the young plants . . . five gen-u-ine imported Holland bulbs . . . eleven choice American bulbs . . . two cuttings of the beautiful white cedar . . . four fine little shrubs and vine cuttings . . . two hundred lovely flower seeds . . . and fifteen seeds for the new everbearing strawberry plants, the runnerless strawberries recently brought here from Europe." All of that cost only $1 plus postage.

Another resonant male voice plugged family security between the songs of hillbilly performers: "It's the Guarantee Reserve Life Insurance Company dollar-a-month two-way family group life insurance policy. Every member of your family insured against death, from any cause, under one policy, for one low cost of one dollar a month. This is the most amazing family life insurance offer ever made." Poultry was the bargain of another amazing offer: "Right now, friends, the famous Allied Hatchery is offering you listeners one hundred of the regular five-ninety-five baby chicks for only four dollars and ninety-five cents per hundred." The rich, impassioned voice of border radio announcer Randy Blake continued, "Now, at this low price we, of course, don't guarantee color, breed, or sex, but we do guarantee healthy day-old broiler-type chicks, which are sent to you on a one-hundred-percent guarantee of satisfaction or your money back. . . . If any of these chicks that you receive in this offer die in the first two weeks, we will replace them at one-half price. Think of that . . . Address your card to Baby Chicks—that's Baby Chicks, Laredo, L-A-R-E-D-O, Laredo, Texas." The chick pitch ended with a rendition of "The Cacklin' Hen," a hillbilly favorite. "Sounds like some of those Allied chicks grew up," commented Blake after the performance. "That takes care of the chicken business for tonight."

While the use of transcriptions remained popular, radio station managers on the border and elsewhere discovered that there was something compelling about a live announcer's voice. Paul Kallinger at XERF, Nelson King at WCKY in Cincinnati, Eddie Hill at WSM in Nashville, Squawkin' Deacon at KXLA, and Hi Pockets Duncan on KDAV in Lubbock were all part of a new breed of radio entertainer born in the postwar boom years—the disc jockey. The disc jockey became a dominant force on the airwaves after World War II partly because of a court ruling that allowed radio stations in the United States to play purchased phonograph records over the air, a move that had been fought by performers' organizations since the beginning of radio. The postwar years also saw the first glimmerings of television, which threatened to dominate the broadcasting media. Radio operators across the country scrambled for ways to trim costs with the impending video invasion, and the platter-spinning disc jockey was the obvious solution.

But the disc jockey soon developed into much more than a pair of hands to change records. A good disc jockey had the ability to create a personality, a friendly persona that established a direct relationship with the listener, and Paul Kallinger was one of the best. His smooth voice and personable delivery launched out from the border late every night at a time when reception for long-range broadcasting was at its best, and audience susceptibility to a "good neighbor along the way" was at its highest.

The postwar disc jockey era brought a great boom in the commercial marketability and popularity of hillbilly music, and Paul Kallinger was at the right place at the right time to be part of this explosion of a uniquely American popular music genre. As record sales began to take off, country-and-western performers flocked to the border to promote themselves over one of the most powerful radio stations in North America, and Paul Kallinger was the man they came to meet. According to the popular deejay, Hank Snow, Ernest Tubb, Lefty Frizell, Hank Williams, Jimmie Davis, Pee Wee King—most everybody who was anybody on the fifties country-and-western scene—paid a visit to Villa Acuña to spin some discs and tell some tales. In 1979 Kallinger was rewarded for his service to country music by induction into the Country Music Disc Jockey Hall of Fame in Nashville. Kallinger became especially good friends with Webb Pierce, Jim Reeves, and Johnny Horton. The Good Neighbor often hosted celebrity fishing trips on the Rio Grande as well as numerous fiestas at Ma Crosby's or one of the other well-known cantinas across the river from Del Rio.

Kallinger helped make hits out of songs like Pierce's "Wondering" and "There Stands the Glass," Reeves's "He'll Have to Go," and Snow's "I'm Movin' On." But even Kallinger missed a hit every once in a while. One night the XERF disc jockey received a phone call from an aspiring musician. "Mr. Kallinger?" an anxious voice politely inquired. "I'm Elvis Presley. I heard Johnny Cash on your show last night, and I wonder if I could be a guest on your show?"

"I'm sorry, Elvis," said the Good Neighbor, "but I don't allow rock and roll on my show."

"Well, thank you anyway," replied the King. "I was just passing through Del Rio, and I thought perhaps you'd put me on your program."

A few months later, Kallinger got a call from Hank Snow and Ernest Tubb. The Singing Ranger and the Texas Troubadour invited him to go on the Louisiana Hayride in Shreveport to appear as Special Disc Jockey of the Year for 1957. They said Elvis was making his last appearance of the season on the popular show, and they wanted to combine the King's music with Kallinger's platter patter. Kallinger said that he'd love to go, but he didn't think Elvis would want to see him after the XERF rejection.

Arriving in Shreveport, Hank Snow's manager took Kallinger to Presley's hotel. The border DJ squeezed past the crowd of girls hyperventilating in the hall as he entered the inner sanctum of the King. Although the infamous Colonel Parker was there, Kallinger was relieved to find out that neither Parker nor the royal rocker held a grudge against him.

By the mid-fifties, American radio fans had a plethora of border radio stations from which to choose. There was XEFW in Tampico, on the Gulf Coast of Mexico, which blasted out programming in English until it was destroyed by a hurricane. XEXO took the place of Norman Baker's XENT in Nuevo Laredo, blasting out at 50,000 watts, and the voice of Uncle Jim Christy powered up through the Midwest on 150,000-watt XEG in Monterrey. On the West Coast there were XEAC, XERB, and XEMO serving the Los Angeles area with border-style entertainment from Baja California Norte. And across the Rio Grande from El Paso in Júarez was XELO, which received its mail in the tiny town of Clint, Texas. "That's C, as in corn, L-I-N-T, Texas," as singing cowboy Slim Hawkins told the folks.

Companies such as the American Radio Program Sellers in Dallas distributed transcriptions of programs by country artists who couldn't travel to the border stations for one reason or another. Hank Thompson never returned to the Rio Grande to perform live, but he did become a regular on XERF and other stations, appearing on programs like the *Good Neighbor Barn Dance*, transcribed in Dallas. Introduced as "one of your favorites . . . tall, lank, and leany Hank Thompson," the Brazos Valley performer told the listening audience that appearing on the border radio program was "an opportunity that I have been waiting for, for a long, long time." The announcer ensured Hank's return to the airwaves with an "invitation to come back to the *Good Neighbor Barn Dance* just any time you want to. Make it tomorrow night or the night after. We'll be lookin' for you."

Like most country artists, Thompson sang songs to boost his record sales and sold his songbooks over the air. He asked listeners to send $1 per songbook to the station's post office box and paid the station 45 cents for each order received. Even paying this large commission, the songbook offer proved to be quite lucrative for the country performer, as thousands of listeners wrote in for Thompson's collection of tunes.

Many other performers offered songbooks over XERF, for country-music fans seemed to enjoy singing their favorite tunes with or without radio accompaniment. Red River Dave McEnery, "America's new singing favorite . . . your favorite Texas Farmboy," advertised "the most sensational songbook offer of all time": "How would you like to have in your home to keep and to own a complete library of cowboy, hillbilly, and sacred songbooks? Six books, all printed in different colors, all with pictures, words, and music to your favorite new and old-time songs. Wouldn't that be a wonderful gift to have in your home? Well, you can own this matched set, yes, this new songbook library, for less than seventeen cents a book. . . . This complete songbook library for only one dollar." Red River Dave concluded his pitch with a soulful rendition of his song "The Blind Boy's Dog," which went, "Now that you're sending heroes home, I just can't understand. / Why don't you send my dog home, Uncle Sam?"

Regular American radio was slow to catch on to the popularity of country-and-western music, while the border stations played gospel and country almost exclusively. Doc Hopkins and his Country Boys played "The College Hornpipe" as Doc cried, "Cornstalk fiddle and a hickory bow, / Take your honey and around you go." The Maddox Brothers and Rose, led by the guitar-playing "Frenly Henry, the working girl's friend," jammed through their foot-stomping version of "Boogie Woogie on a Friday Night." One of the Maddox boys shouted, "Stop it! I can't stand it! It's drivin' me insane!" Pete Malaney and the Riders of the Rio Grande launched into "Whoa, Mule, Whoa," the Wilburn Family sang "Radio Station S-A-V-E-D," and Asher Sizemore and Little Jimmie sang "a tune we wrote especially for all the little boys and girls in the audience." At the end of the program, Asher spoke to his radio pals: "Don't forget to write in, boys and girls, and let Jimmie know the songs that you want him to sing for you. . . . We'll close with an old-fashioned hymn, 'Turn Your Radio On.'"

The Delmore Brothers, Alton and Rabon, spent several months in Del Rio in 1949, cutting transcriptions for the border stations. The popular duo was often joined by harmonica player Wayne Raney. The three even composed a song about their days on the border, "Del Rio Boogie." Raney remembered that the song was written after a fierce hailstorm. "The sleet and hail knocked me down. / But I got right up from the muddy ground," the trio sang in the hillbilly boogie style. The storm had been so severe that the musicians lost a brand-new Pontiac to nature's temper tantrum. The song also praised the women of Del Rio: "The girls down there, they love the best. / So don't forget to stop and rest / In Del Rio, down Texas way," lyrics that could almost have been used as advertising for the Brinkley Hospital a decade earlier. The Delmores soon found that the border rainbow held no pot of gold for them, and they moved on to a radio station in Houston, seeking greater financial reward and a climate less arid. Wayne Raney, however, struck a mother lode on Mexican radio, selling a million harmonicas a year for five years straight. "Border radio did more for getting my name known than anything else," remembered the man who made a mouth harp talk.

In the forties another popular brother duo, Bill and Joe Callahan, broadcast from the border via transcriptions they cut at Sellers' Studio in Dallas. "We ended up receiving one hundred sixty million pieces of mail during our career," remembered Bill Callahan. "We were sponsored by things like Crazy Water Crystals, Black Draught, Dr Pepper, Wichita Overalls, and Wichita Feed." Reminiscing in 1986, Bill said radio had "too much crapola on it now. Country music seems like it's not country music anymore." Like many radio fans he longed for the way it used to be, when border stations filled the air: "We'd listen to 'em at night when we'd be driving, going to personal appearances. You could get 'em all over America."

Other border performers included a pickup group called the Studio Frolics. "I was born a rover on the rhy-th-mic range, / A rootin' tootin' terror, and I never will change," sang the Frolics. Carl Shrum and his Rhythm Rangers sang the soulful ballad "Meet Me in Dallas, Sweetheart." Molly O'Day and Her Cumberland Mountain Folks performed a musical version of Matthew 24, and Uncle Henry and His Original Kentucky Mountaineers sang "The Trail to Mexico." T. Texas Tyler (the man with a Million Friends), Hawkshaw Hawkins, the Herrington Sisters, the Shelton Brothers, and countless other country performers relied heavily on border radio to get their music out to the American people. Hank Thompson said that border stations "were about the only ones where you could hear country-and-western music all the time." Webb Pierce agreed. "Border radio did a lot for country music," said the popular singer, noted for his guitar-shaped swimming pool. "If it hadn't been for border radio, I don't know if country music would have survived."

The full-bodied voice of America's Good Neighbor Along the Way, Paul Kallinger, rode the airwaves from down along the silvery Rio Grande to ever-increasing renown. In 1953 *Billboard* magazine rated him one of the five most popular country DJs in the United States, a distinction he would maintain for eight consecutive years. Some thought that Kallinger would have been rated number one had it not been for the lingering prejudice of the American media establishment against the border stations. "They might have been jealous of our border-to-border coverage," Kallinger surmised.

Despite his tremendous popularity, Kallinger never forgot the code of the border blasters—pull mail or perish. "You had to practically sell ice to Eskimos to keep your job on XERF!" he exclaimed. Many big-time radio gabbers came down to the Mexican superpowered stations from New York, Los Angeles, and Chicago but weren't able to sell à la Rio Grande. "Lots of them were good announcers," Kallinger explained, but they just couldn't sell border-style." Kallinger's secret lay in his mind's eye. "You had to visualize your audience," he said. "You had to respond to the way your audience felt. I would talk slow, be dramatic, and repeat myself for the older audience. Lots of times I'd turn up the volume, because I knew a lot of my listeners were hard of hearing." Hotshot copywriters sent fast-paced, crisp commercials to Kallinger to push certain products. Many times he had to throw them away. "I'd tell them, 'The copy is excellent, but not for XERF.' 'The people aren't gonna buy it,' I'd say. 'Break your words down a little.'"

Kallinger was the quintessential border radio announcer, a man who could sell anything from black-eyed peas to knotholes. His honeyed baritone pitched weight-loss pills, weight-gain pills, fishing lures, laxatives, burial monuments, prosperity billfolds, patchwork quilt pieces, and plastic bronco ponies, and it introduced listeners to the popular rat killer D-Con. Kallinger advertised discreet borrowing from the Dial Finance Company, back in the days when debt was a source of embarrassment. He calmly told those who were in financial difficulty, "Send your name and address and the amount you need to the Dial Finance Company. We will answer your request in a plain sealed envelope. Not even the postman will know you are getting a loan."

The border station merchandise moved like Carta Blanca beer at Ma Crosby's. On good days the XERF mail count ran up to 14,000 letters. During one Christmas season, cardboard toys offered over XERF were all the rage. "We sold around ten thousand orders in one day," Kallinger said. "Now, that's a lot of toys. . . . And nobody ever returned them, to my knowledge." He drew the line at some products, though. "Some people have heard that I was the one that sold autographed pictures of Jesus Christ, but I've never done that, not Your Good Neighbor Along the Way. However, we did sell the picture of the Lord's Last Supper on a tablecloth. It was in vinyl. It was a big seller—vinyl was very popular in those days—and we sold a lot of them for two ninety-eight."

Diamonds were almost as popular as vinyl on border radio. For several years, Hawley Pettit, former owner of a local bus line, was known to XERF listeners as the Diamond Man. Pettit and his brother-in-law, Phil Foster, ordered thousands of artificial diamonds from a jewelry company and sold "diamond" rings over the air for $3.95 apiece. Often when traveling out of town, Pettit was surprised by his fame. "Gee, the only person I know in Del Rio is the Diamond Man" was a common refrain. Pettit and Foster combined on one other successful border promotion that was destined to revolutionize communication in America. They were the first to advertise the ballpoint pen. "The Reynolds Company came out with the first one, but it was expensive and didn't work very well," Pettit explained. "Ours worked pretty well, and we sold a lot of them."

A bizarre barrage of commercial messages bombarded American households from the border throughout the fifties. A sweet female voice sang the following jingle to the tune of "Rock-a-Bye, Baby": "If you are nervous, wakeful all night, / You should try Restall, then rest all right, / Rest well with Restall. Here's how you spell / R-E-S-T-A-double L."

Then a deep male voice continued, "Hello. This is Del Sharbis speaking. In this age of atomic weapons, worry, and stress, scientific research has produced a substance to help calm and soothe worried and nervous people. Such a substance is in the sleep aid Restall. . . . During this special introductory offer, you may obtain a package containing forty capsules for just two dollars and twenty-nine cents—that's less than six cents per capsule. . . . Insist on the genuine, the only Restall. Manufactured exclusively for the Globe Pharmaceutical Corporation, the trademark that is a symbol of quality and scientific formula."

Federal Home Products offered a fountain pen "so revolutionary in style and performance . . . you'll want one for every member of the family. . . . This amazing fountain pen never seems to need filling because it writes almost fifty miles of words without a refill. You could actually write your name on a piece of paper stretching from Baltimore to Washington, D.C. . . . These sensational pens are guaranteed for life. Drop them, step on them, throw them against the wall, yes, even if you lose them, if at any time this amazing pen fails to write as smoothly, as evenly as it should, anytime you lose it, we'll send you a brand-new one absolutely free."

Shutterbugs, as well as authors, learned of fantastic opportunities, courtesy of border radio: "The famous Hollywood Film Studios has an amazing offer for you. Listen to this. If you mail your favorite snapshot, photograph, or negative to the Hollywood Film Studios, care of this station, you'll receive a handsome silk-finished five-by-seven enlargement mounted in a rich gold tooled frame, with glass in front and standing easel back. . . . As a special get-acquainted offer, the price is just nineteen cents each for the picture and frame plus the cost of mailing. . . . This is a truly sensational offer you can't afford to miss. . . . Address your envelope to the Hollywood Film Studios at Laredo, Texas."

After a spirited number by Bob Nolan and the Sons of the Pioneers, the voice of Randy Blake announced, "Right now I have an amazing free gift offer to tell you about. Our friend the Blade Man is making this truly sensational offer for a limited time only. One hundred of his finest-quality, extra-sharp double-edged razor blades for only one dollar. . . . Each blade is first ground in oil, then honed, then stropped to superkeen sharpness. Each blade is rigidly inspected, individually wrapped, and rewrapped to keep that factory-keen sharpness. . . . For each order of one hundred blades, while this special offer lasts, you'll receive this slim, streamlined, modernistic pocketknife, free. . . . You'll marvel at its spring-action push button, which instantly slides a tough specially treated steel blade into cutting position. Then another touch of the finger and presto—the blade disappears like magic into its shiny metal case. . . . Send no money, just your name and address to the Blade Man at Laredo, Texas."

For enterprising business people, border radio offered a surefire route to financial independence: "Friends, here's an easy way to earn extra spending money, enough to really help the family income. . . . Just send your name and address. We will send you twenty-four eleven-by-seven-inch motto cards to sell to your friends and neighbors for just twenty-five cents each, with satisfaction guaranteed. When you've sold all twenty-four motto cards . . . you keep two dollars and send the balance to us. . . . These mottoes sparkle like diamonds in the daylight, and they glow like stars in the dark. . . . Send your name and address to the Motto Company. I'll spell that. M-O-T-T-O, the Motto Company, Fort Worth, Texas."

Fort Worth 11, Texas, was another address familiar to border radio listeners, the address of station XEG in Monterrey, Nuevo León. From 1950 to 1980 Harold Schwartz controlled the advertising on station XEG and became one of the most influential mail-order merchants on the border. A Chicago-based marketer, Schwartz's varied interests included advertising and promotion for *Moose Magazine*, management of a photographic company called Mansfield Industries, and ownership of the Illinois Merchandise Mart and Alamen tablets, a medicine for relief from gaseous indigestion. Schwartz eventually contracted for all the aevertising time on station XERB near Tijuana as well as XEG, and he operated both stations until he gave up his border interests to acquire ownership of radio stations in the United States and run successful land development projects in Florida and Texas. According to another border-radio hand, cowboy evangelist Dallas Turner, "Harold did eventually become a millionaire, and it couldn't have happened to a more wonderful person."

Turner himself had a long and memorable career on the border stations as a singing cowboy, a pitchman, an advertising rep, and an evangelist. "When I was a little boy," he remembered, "I always dreamed of being on the powerful Mexican border stations. I heard my favorite singers on there. Cowboy Slim Rinehart—he was always my idol. Other people wanted to go to the Grand Old Opry and the National Barn Dance. I only had the desire to broadcast from Mexico. That was always my dream."

Shortly after his birth in 1927, Turner's parents gave him to a woman named Lizzie Brown and entrusted her with raising their baby. "Lizzie Brown was a religious fanatic," Turner said. "She was a combination of Pentecostal and Seventh-Day Adventist rolled into one. She met my foster parents on the street in Elko, Nevada. As my daddy always said, 'It was colder than Billy Hell.' Those were his exact words."

Lizzie Brown approached Jim and Liz Turner looking for help in supporting her charge. The middle-aged couple hired the woman to cook on their ranch, the Quarter Circle Nine outfit outside Elko. Lizzie Brown almost immediately ran into trouble. "Being an Adventist, she refused to fry bacon and she made pies with tallow. The cowboys couldn't eat her cookin', so she was fired and threw me on the floor," Dallas said. The Turners picked up the infant and adopted him. "I'm very proud to bear the name 'Turner,'" said Dallas, "because the only man that I've ever known as a daddy was that old bronc-stompin' cowboy Jim Turner."

The young Turner got his start on border radio in the mid-forties, following in the footsteps of Cowboy Slim Rinehart. "Slim was to me what Elvis Presley was to the kids of the fifties," Turner explained. "I tried to sound exactly like him. I tried to pick the guitar like him, tried to sing like him, and I tried to talk like him." After duplicating the style to his own satisfaction, Turner traveled to the border to audition for the popular singing cowboy. "Slim listened to me and then he looked at me with that eye. He had this eye, and when he got mad, that eye would start rollin' like a set of loaded dice. He said, 'Will you answer a question for me?' And I said, 'Yes.' He said, 'Now, look, I'm glad you admire me and all that, but you're a thief!' I felt like I was about two feet high. So he says, 'You take this Martin guitar, you go into that room, and you don't come out of that room until you pick and sing like yourself, and when you do, I'll help you get on these Mexican border stations.' He kept his promise, so I guess I owe all the success that I have to Cowboy Slim Rinehart."

Like Paul Kallinger, Turner quickly learned what it took to be a success on the border. "When I got to my first border station," Turner said, "I learned very fast that they didn't hire you to sing. They hired you to sell, sell, sell. I was a pitchman. A pitchman's success depended entirely on his ability to pull mail. The greatest announcers in the country would come to the border, and they wouldn't last overnight. The best radio pitchmen came off the carnival circuit or the vaudeville halls. "Often the techniques were passed from master to apprentice in the tradition of most arcane knowledge. "Major Kord was probably the greatest border station pitchman who ever lived," Turner said. And one day he put his arm around Cowboy Slim Rinehart and said, 'I'm gonna make you the greatest pitchman that border radio ever had.' And many years later, Slim put his arm around me and he said, 'I'm gonna say the same thing to you that the old major said to me.' And I believe that he succeeded in doing exactly what he set out to do. Major Kord made Slim Rinehart the greatest pitchman that border radio ever had. And I believe Slim probably made me second, exceeded only by him."

Every day, Turner entered the recording studio with a jug of cough syrup, and cut electrical transcriptions of his singing show. He used different names for each station that ran his program, names like Nevada Slim the Yodelin' Cowboy, Cowboy Dallas Turner, and Yodelin' Slim Dallas. He pitched songbooks and guitars in addition to a wide variety of other products. "I pitched Sterling Insurance, Banker's Casualty and Life Cross Plan, and many of the patent medicines." He was the Blade Man, offering listeners one hundred of the "finest-quality, extra-sharp double-edged razor blades for only one dollar."

Turner split the money from the mail orders he drew with the station management, and he did quite well for himself, so well in fact that he had the opportunity to perform on high-powered radio stations in the United States. "I was on one radio station in Portland, Oregon, that changed hands while I was there," Turner related. "I never will forget the words of the man who bought the station. On the day he took it over, he had a meeting, and he stood up before everybody in that radio station, and he said, 'I'm gonna tell you people one thing. No goddam border station singin' cowboy is gonna make more money on this radio station than the manager. That day is over with.' That's when I said good-bye to American radio and went back to the border forever."

The singing buckaroo did change his mind in the fifties and performed for a brief time on American radio stations. "My programs on WCKY and WWVA in the late fifties were very successful, but I feel that I was probably swindled terribly on the deal, because they never did send me the money they were supposed to, and they never did give me the mailing list. My heart has never been in it on an American station since. The only place I've ever really enjoyed broadcasting in my life is down on the Mexican border stations. That's where I prefer to broadcast, because I feel that those have always been the most legitimate stations in operation."

By the mid-fifties Turner was selling time on the stations as well as singing and pitching products. He signed infamous anti-Semite Gerald L. K. Smith, flanked by two bodyguards, to a $25,000 contract, with the understanding that Smith was not to speak out against the Jews. But Smith could not resist the temptation of the high-powered border blaster. Even the permissive management was insulted and yanked the anti-Semite off the air, giving him back most of his money.

Turner was involved in a tremendous variety of deals in the gullible fifties. "When I had my advertising agency," he said, "I was approached by the con men of con men. I was approached by every type of ridiculous promoter you have ever seen. People had the idea that all you had to do was put together something worthless and put it on the border stations and sit back and get rich and laugh at the suckers." The border ad executive gave several illustrations: "One black gentleman purchased time on XEXO in Nuevo Laredo to sell his product to make black people turn white. You couldn't give his product away. . . . A doctor bought - time to sell his Happy Grow Relief Toenail Adjuster. . . . Another man bought time to sell his pole holder, a forked stick you were to drive in the ground and attach your fishing pole to with a rubber band. Then you could snooze on the river and catch your limit."

One of Turner's high-rolling clients proposed selling a funeral home elevator over the air with this pitch: "No C.O.D. orders, friends. No C.O.D. will be accepted. No personal checks. Send only three thousand eight hundred fifty dollars in cash to Elevator in care of radio station XEFW, Brownsville, Texas." Turner maintained, "I told him he would never get a response, but he insisted. After he ran the ad, he blamed me for his not selling any elevators." Another Turner client had an $8000 pump he wanted to sell over the air. "He said, 'I'm gonna give you two percent on this deal. You'll become a multimillionaire.'. . . He believed that there would be poor people out there who would be suckers enough to buy something like that."

Other products that Turner was familiar with sold only too well. "One of the greatest border station individuals was a friend of mine named Loren J. Rowell," Turner said. "Here is a pitch that made him over a hundred thousand dollars per year for four consecutive years: 'Do you ever suffer with a backache? Do you have to get up frequently during the night? Does rheumatic stiffness hamper you? Do you ever notice puffiness under your eyes? . . . Don't make the terrible mistake of neglecting your body. You have about fifteen miles of kidney tubes and filters in your body. And they were placed there to do the all-important job of carrying off excess poisonous waste matter from your blood. . . . What are you going to do to help your kidneys carry off these venemous poisons? . . . I don't need to tell you about the great strides forward by modern medical science during and after the last war. In keeping with those strides comes a new scientifically compounded formula that we shall call LR. Now please don't look for my amazing scientifically compounded formula in any drugstore in the world. Only I can bring this product to you direct from my laboratories."

Rowell offered a bottle of 112 LR tablets for $3.98, which left a healthy profit margin, considering the product only cost 12 cents to manufacture. The former adman for J. Walter Thompson opened a pharmaceutical company in San Antonio called R&F and expanded his product line to include Lorinal (a Geritol-like tonic named after himself) and LRO, a salve for piles. Rowell's products were among the hottest sellers on the border until a terrible packaging mistake put an end to the adman's bonanza.

"The girls in the shipping department got the labels mixed up," Dallas Turner explained. "They put the labels for the kidney pills on the pile salve and the pile salve labels on the kidney medicine." Anxious recipients of the medications were somewhat baffled by the directions but willing to try anything. "People with kidney problems were trying to eat the salve, and people with piles were using the kidney pills as suppositories." According to Turner, Rowell's business "just gave up the ghost after the complications. His lawyers had to go to Washington and argue with the postal inspectors to keep him from going to jail."

Another successful border pitch was the lonely hearts club. Cowboy evangelist Turner described it: "The original lonely hearts club was the Golden West Club, started out in California in around 1936. In about three to four years it was the biggest lonely hearts club operation in the world, and it was on the border stations." One of Turner's female acquaintances in his border days was good friends with a couple who ran an equally popular West Coast-based lonely hearts club, the Hollywood Four Hundred. Turner remembered the broadcasts well: "This gal would come on with sexy music playing behind her pitch, and she would say, 'Fellas, I'm a lonesome girl. I need and want the love of a good man. Maybe one of you big, strong, handsome men would want to meet me and love me and maybe spend the rest of your days with me? I'm just one of thousands of beautiful, warm, affectionate women who are members of the Hollywood Four Hundred Club. We're all looking for the right man. Some of us are young and anxious to know more about life. Perhaps you could teach me more about life? Others of us are at the interesting thirty to forty years of age. And some of us are a little older. We're outdoor sports and indoor playmates.'" This radio personals service was a tremendous success, according to Turner. "Boy, oh, boy, I'm telling you, this pitch would drive men crazy. They would get out of bed at three o'clock in the morning to write to the Hollywood Four Hundred Club." For the women a male voice offered himself, with "The Sweet Mystery of Life" playing behind him. Lonely hearts clubs were so successful that they were a standard feature of border radio programming for decades.

In the view of former ad executive Dallas Turner, border radio was unjustly accused of "a lot of so-called rackets." There was the story of the guaranteed bedbug killer, for instance, a package supposedly sold on border radio that included two blocks of wood and a piece of paper. The paper directed the purchaser to "lay the bedbug on one block of wood and hit it with the other." Turner emphasized, "Most of these stories you can take with a grain of salt because no stations that have ever been on the air have been under greater scrutiny than the Mexican border stations." Through the years, mail-order marketers probably lost much more money than they made on surefire border radio schemes. "In reality," Turner maintained, "only three things will sell on the border: health, sex, and religion."

Larry King, author of *The Best Little Whorehouse in Texas*, passed up a chance to get into the health, sex, and religion business about 25 years before his musical celebrated the history of a small-town Texas brothel called the Chicken Ranch. "In 1951 I was doing local news and spinning country records for Station KCRS in Midland," King told writer Billie Lee Brammer, "all for the grand sum of $70 a week. One day this thin fella with a prominent adam's apple and sporty two-tone shoes walked in and introduced himself. Looked something like a 1930s road drummer come on good times: big sparkly rings and gaudy string ties and big car and hard essence of ambition. Said he had heard me on his car radio, just passing through, and I had the kind of palaver and down-home delivery that would make me a fortune if I would let it—and him—just do it. I said for money I would just about do anything, and he explained how he was connected with that Del Rio/Villa Acuña station. Described himself as an independent time contractor, which meant he bought up time in blocks of sixty minutes from the station and used it as he wished. He then sub-contracted to guys like me who could impersonate some evangelist, say, preach a little, sing a little, then give a spiel for etchings of the Last Supper or prayer cloths to be placed anywhere you happen to hurt. He said they even once tried selling bottled Holy Water from the Rio Grande.

"Or I might come on as Uncle Buddy or Cowboy Jim or whatever, so long as people liked me enough to buy tonics or hymnals or unsexed baby chicks or genuine simulated diamond rings. The deal was he would pay me $125 weekly to start, and more if I was good at it, plus a percentage of whatever came in from the good folks out there in Radio Land. If I liked it, and proved to have the talent he thought he saw in me, then he would sell me some of his own time and I could invent my own programs and characters and keep all I made—and conceivably become a high-time independent contractor like himself." For some reason, though, King could not get excited about the prospect of a glamorous border career and kept spinning honky-tonk sounds at the lower-powered West Texas station.

Even though they had been in operation for more than twenty years by the end of the fifties, the border stations still caught in the craw of federal authorities who continued to look for ways to turn off their high-powered transmitters. Lloyd Richardson worked as an announcer on XERF in the late fifties and early sixties. "I would do different characters, you know, the cowboy type, the religious type," he remembered, laughing. "We sold everything. Sex pills, how to quit smoking, medicine, Bibles, songbooks, preacher's manuals—oh, man, you name it. Hadicol was one of the things we sold. It was a tonic. It came from Louisiana. I remember they said, 'We Hadicol it something.' We pulled a lot of shenanigans back then." One day Richardson's shenanigans caught up with him. He was broadcasting from Del Rio by telephone line across the international boundary to the XERF transmitter in Acuña. The FCC monitored the broadcast, came down to Del Rio, and arrested the unsuspecting disc jockey for violating Section 325(b) of the Federal Communications Act, the infamous Brinkley Clause.

"They was gonna hang me," Richardson explained. "They made me post a fifteen-thousand-dollar bail." Luckily for the offending radio personality, his boss was also one of the most respected lawyers in Del Rio, Arturo González. "Arturo posted the bail for me, and we went to court. The judge said, 'Are you guilty?' and I said, 'Yes, sir.' The judge said, 'You didn't intend to do it?' and I said, 'No, sir. I didn't know it was wrong.' He said, 'Ignorance of the law is no excuse. That'll be a hundred dollars when you can pay it.'" Richardson was amazed at the court's leniency. "He said, 'When you can pay it,' and it didn't even go on my record."

While the border station managers could successfully circle the wagons against outside attacks from federal bureaucrats, they had a more difficult time avoiding internecine struggles among themselves. Don Howard first came to the border in 1933 as a tenor banjo player with a dance band booked at the Bohemia Club in Nuevo Laredo. The band made good money in the busy cantinas along the border and began to perform on border radio stations as well. By the late forties Howard had formed an advertising company with Walter Wilson, a close friend of Dr. Brinkley's who had inherited the advertising rights to XERA from the noted rejuvenation specialist. Howard and Wilson reopened XERA as XERF with the help of Arturo González, who had done some legal work for Doctor. Howard eventually managed to get control of the advertising rights to a number of smaller border stations, including XEMU at Piedras Negras, owned by the Bres family (the former owners of XEPN), XELO in Juárez, and XEDM and XEFW in Tampico. His hold on the border ad dollar seemed unshakable.

Howard, however, did not reckon with the skill and daring of Arturo González. According to Dick Reavis, Sr., former editor of the *Del Rio News-Herald*, González decided to cut his gringo partners out of the XERF mail-order bonanza. González and a former gardener at the station took control of the station in the late forties. The gardener ran the station awhile but found out that he didn't have the clout to get the

American advertising, so he turned the station over to Arturo González. By the mid-fifties, González was in firm control of the station.

Wilson passed away, but Howard was determined to regain control of the station and get even with González. Sparks flew whenever the two ran into each other in the small town. Howard supposedly punched out González when he saw him in the stands at a Del Rio high school football game. Dick Reavis once spoke to Howard about González. "Why didn't you just kill him?" the newspaperman asked jokingly. The radioman answered in deadly earnest, "You don't know how many nights I thought about that."

In the late fifties Howard made another attempt to take over the border blaster, according to Reavis. At that time González purchased a 250,000-watt transmitter for XERF and moved the operation to a new station building. A dispute arose between González and Mexican authorities over customs fees. After a battle in the Mexican courts, Don Howard wound up with a court order to claim management of the station. In the early sixties, Howard sent a representative to take control of XERF. The border grapevine soon crackled with news that a lower echelon XERF employee killed the Howard rep in a moment of passion, seized by an overzealous desire to protect his boss's property. "They put the killer in jail in Acuña, where he himself was killed," said Reavis. "It was common knowledge in Del Rio. Everyone heard about it. But the publisher said the story was too hot to put in the paper."

González managed to fight off Howard's claim to the station but had to contend with another group of radio spoilers, the Sindicato Nacional, a Mexican union organization. According to González, "We had some labor disputes in the early sixties. Two, three, maybe four, people were killed." Other people who were associated with XERF at that time remembered the shoot-out in more detail, although an absolutely reliable account of the bloody confrontation will probably never be known.

Lloyd Richardson was an announcer on the border blaster at that time. "We had some trouble with the union, you know," he explained, "because U.S. citizens were not supposed to be on the air. . . . And the guy who paid the Mexicans who worked at the station, well, sometimes he would get drunk, he would cash their check, and he wouldn't pay them, you know. . . . They had the army there to protect us and all that stuff. Sometimes right behind you there was a guy sitting there with a machine gun. You'd say over the air, 'If you don't write tonight, I won't be on the air tomorrow,' and the guy would cock the hammer." Richardson laughed. "Oh, it wasn't all that bad, but they were armed you know."

In early 1963 the Sindicato gave the station an ultimatum—pay so much money by a certain date or else. The date passed. The Sindicato decided to move on XERF. A group of armed *banditos* attacked the station. "They started shooting these guys all around me," Richardson recollected excitedly. "I hollered through the door to my friend who was doing the shooting. I said, 'Hey, I'm in here!' And he says, 'Ah, Lloyd, I thought it was your day off!' He gave me just two minutes to get my Jeep started. It was an old Jeep, you know, and it didn't normally start, but it had that morning." Richardson pushed his Jeep toward the road to the Rio Grande, hoping and praying that the old Willis would turn over. "It started, and I took off. I stayed off the road. I went down canyons. Then I saw soldiers coming with machine guns, and I hid in the brush. Finally I made it to the international bridge. The Border Patrol said, 'Well, by God, we had you written off. We were listening and heard the gunshots over the radio.' They asked me, 'You going back?' 'No, sir,' I said. 'I'm heading for Oklahoma,' and I got out of there as fast as I could go."

This time the *Del Rio News-Herald* covered the flare-up of the border radio range war in a story headlined ARMED MEN SEIZE CONTROL OF XERF. "Station manager Lorenzo Blanco and operator Hilario Aguilar were beaten as they and seven other employees were chased from the property by two carloads of men armed with a machine gun and pistols," the paper reported. The raiders succeeded in taking over the station and holding it until the wee hours of the following morning. Then, according to the paper, "half a dozen state police from Sabinas arrived with orders from a federal quasi-judicial commission in Mexico City" and put a union steward in charge. The following day manager Blanco went to Piedras Negras to report the attack to the federal district official.

The Good Neighbor Along the Way, Paul Kallinger, was caught up in the middle of the fighting. "I was doing a live show at the time," Kallinger nervously recalled, "when a gunman poked a gun in my back as I was sitting there pitching a commercial. He told me to get up and leave, in Spanish. Then he said, 'I'm gonna kill you, gringo.' I walked out of there with my hands up and that forty-five in my back. As we got out of the station, he said, 'Turn around.' And I said to myself, 'Here we go.' As I turned around, there was another man covering the guy with a Thompson submachine gun." Kallinger had momentary thoughts of escape. "I said to myself that I could knock that gun away, but that machine gun would just mow me down like a rat." He stood with his arms raised, tense, waiting to see what the gunman's verdict would be. "He looked at me and said, 'Turn around.' I turned around, and he said, 'Run, gringo, run, run.' The more he said, 'Run,' the slower I walked, but after I got out of range, I did run."

Kallinger took off running down the road to Del Rio. When he heard machine gun fire from the direction of the station, the radio announcer left the road and made his way through seven miles of prickly pear cactus and greasewood back to the safety of Del Rio. Although the union trouble subsided and González eventually retained control of the station, Paul Kallinger, one of America's most popular disc jockeys, never again crossed the Rio Grande to address his millions of fans from beneath the starry skies of Old Mexico. "I haven't done a live show since then," Kallinger explained, "because I want to stay alive."

Howlin' on a Quarter
Million Watts

I'm here day and night for you folks all over the United States, Canada, Mexico. . . . God bless you. . . . Keep your ears clean. . . . BYE!
—Wolfman Jack on XERB, Rosarita Beach, Baja California

The Japanese know him as the Emperor of Pleasing Graciousness. The Germans know him as the Laughing Chancellor of Comedy. Here in the States, the man with the late-night howls, fang-toothed wit, and heart-pounding party music is known simply as the Wolfman, a national institution of radio naughtiness. For more than a quarter of a century, the gravel-on-black-velvet voice of Wolfman Jack has filled the late-night American airwaves with raunchy dance music, racy telephone patter, and a right-on blend of rock-and-roll philosophy that has made him one of the greatest renegade radio performers of all time. "I wouldn't be real if I didn't say I'm an egomaniac," purred the Wolfman. "I think I've accomplished something."

No one can deny that Wolfman Jack has accomplished something. Born Robert W. Smith in 1939, Wolfman grew up poor. "You see, I was left out in the breeze," he explained, "born in Brooklyn amongst the garbage cans and roaches and poor Italians and poor blacks. . . . Why, I was so poor that I used to put grease on my face when I'd go over to other kids' houses so they'd think I'd just had steak and wouldn't ask me to eat with them." Moved around among his relatives, Wolfman quickly became a street-smart hustler. "I belonged to a street gang, the whole thing. There were gang wars, and you had to learn to protect yourself.

When you saw an opportunity, you didn't run away from it. You jumped right into it with both feet."

A member of the gang known as the Taggers Club, with a reputation as a good man with a zip gun, Wolfman was fascinated by radio. "I had so much misery around me, I escaped into the fantasy world of the jocks. I studied their style. Man, I dug those jocks." The Wolfman's fantasy world was inhabited by characters like George "Hound Dog" Lorenz out of Buffalo, Danny "Cat Man" Stiles from Newark, "John R." Richbourg from Nashville, Tommy Smalls (better known as Dr. Jive) out of New York City, Doug Jocko Henderson, host of *Jocko's Rocket Ship* out of Philadelphia, and Moondog, alias Allen Freed, who was the top-rated rock-and-roll DJ in the Big Apple until a payola scandal torched his career. These wild men of the airwaves played the best in rhythm and blues—music by the Drifters, Faye Adams, T-Bone Walker, and La Vern Baker and introduced radio audiences to a new musical phenomenon called rock and roll. Though these kings of the turntables were often white, they all copped a hip black sound, a sound like that of early black DJs Professor Bob in Shreveport, Louisiana, Jocky Jack in Atlanta, and Sugar Daddy in Birmingham, Alabama. Wolfman felt at home with the music and the sound. "We all emulated the black culture," he explained. "There wasn't any other."

Wolfman's family moved to Newark, and he entered high school. He worked at a car wash, where his abilities as a hustler immediately paid off. "You could make pretty good money," he said. "Not the wages—the crap game in back. I remember one game, I had the owner's papers on the floor." Wolfman never lost his love of the airwaves, however, and he practiced the mysterious art of the disc jockey in his basement, designing a studio with two beat-up turntables and a tape recorder. A friend finally got him out of the auto-detailing industry by landing him a job at WNJR, a local radio station. Wolfman began sweeping the floors of the station but managed to hustle his way onto the air, occasionally spinning a few discs and pitching ads for dog food and raffle tickets. The ambitious cub from Brooklyn soon became frustrated with his slow rise to fame, and he lit out from New Jersey when he was sixteen, driving an aged Oldsmobile.

The teen Wolf's quest for his true identity led him to odd jobs and short stints at radio stations in Trenton, Richmond, and Washington, D.C. As Wolfman later described it, "I got into a lot of situations. Basically I was a hustler." The hustler hit on a good thing in Newport News, Virginia, landing a job as an announcer and salesman at a local radio station. He landed a wife as well. Lou, then Lucy Lamb, met her future mate in a dancing school. She was looking for a job; he was looking for advertisers. She described their first meeting: "He was wearing a funny hat with lots of colors. Boy, was he a hustler. He said, 'I'm gonna marry you.' I thought he was crazy."

Little did the future Wolfwoman know the full range of craziness that awaited her. In Newport News, Wolfman was Big Smith With the Records. He spun hot rock and rhythm and blues and refined his on-the-air persona. When the station switched from rock and roll to an easy-listening format, the rockin' Big Smith became the mellow-sounding Roger Gordon, but the transformation didn't take, and within a few months the Wolfman was on the move once again.

He wound up in Shreveport. As Big Smith, the young man from Brooklyn spun records, sold advertising, and began to concoct a new radio persona, one that combined the characteristics of his favorite DJs into a new, hair-raising radio presence. The quiet Piney Woods community of Shreveport could not satisfy the Wolfman's ambition, and he sniffed around for something bigger. Like Dr. Brinkley, Norman Baker, Pappy O'Daniel, and others before him, Smith was inexorably drawn to the border, the land of high-powered radio dreams.

"I began to listen to XERF as a little kid in New York. That station was so strong in those days, man, that it used to come into New York like a local," Wolfman explained. "The thing that fascinated me was that it was the most powerful commercial radio station in the world. Birds used to fly around the tower and drop dead. Y'know, they'd come around and go *pssssshhhhh!*" Despite the station's deadly effect on wildlife, the Wolfman dug the preachers and pitchmen that broadcast on XERF. "I followed the station over the years and knew it was like a bandit operation. They had all these jockey preachers who operated out of their back pockets. Don't get me wrong. I loved those guys," confided Wolfman, who indeed had an amazing capacity for love of all kinds. "They were great, great radio entertainers, you understand. Nowadays they've become so clean. . . . They don't have that raunchiness or the fervor they used to have. You know what I mean?" Smith further developed his radio character, combining the gritty black sound of artists like Howlin' Wolf with fast-paced humor and outrageous suggestions. He never used any profanity, but each heavy, throaty word he spoke oozed the possibility of hidden nastiness. Smith remembered a line from the New York disc jockey Dr. Jive, who asked his listeners, "What's up, Jack?" He decided to adopt a lupine persona, one that would howl on the air after midnight. By early 1960 Wolfman was ready to prowl the border.

Determined to get on the magic powerful XERF somehow, Wolfman drove down to Del Rio with his partner, Lawrence Brandon. They arrived in Del Rio and made an appointment with Arturo González, the power behind the station, for the next day. Unable to restrain themselves, the duo set out that evening to see the superpowered border blaster. Thus began the Wolfman Jack Border Radio Shoot-out Saga, a semiapocryphal tradition the true origins of which are forever lost in the hard, baked sands of the Coahuilan desert.

"I paid some Mexican taxicab driver to take me over the border, man, over to the station. It was real scary 'cause there was no roads goin' out to the station. Had to go over sand dunes an' everything to get out there. I thought the guy was takin' me for a ride, you know. I didn't know whether I was gonna get back or not." Wolfman finally made it to the station, arriving in the middle of a management crisis.

"The station was in receivership," Wolfman recalled, explaining that González was embroiled in continuing disputes with the Mexican government over XERF taxes, bills and policies regarding the sale of air time to preachers. The Del Rio lawyer found himself facing the same type of arrangement that border radio businessmen endured three decades earlier. "There was a small clause in the contract that said if the government took the station over, you know, they lost their money and he was not responsible. And that's what happened.

"The Mexican government came and put the station under a government receiver called an *interventor*. But this guy was crooked. I mean he was a real gangster. Another guy there, Mario, spoke perfect English. So I explained to him who I was. I played the Wolfman tapes for him and he got the idea, and then proceeded to tell me what they were tryin' to do. They wanted to get the crooked receiver out and get one of their own guys in, so they would be paid more and so the taxes would be paid to the government.

"They didn't know what to do. They all had real big families to support," Wolfman lamented. "So I offered to send this guy to Mexico City to appoint their own receiver from the union that ran the radio station. And I laid about fifteen hundred dollars on him for the trip. Right away I was their friend, right? At the same time, they appointed me the representative from the U.S., and we booted the not-nice man out. Well, we started the process, and the old receiver, the not-nice man, got a little angry and started takin' shots at me in the middle of the night. So Brandon and myself went to San Antonio and spent the last dime we had on barbed wire, sandbags, lights, and guns. We even got an old thirty-caliber machine gun, an old fossil, man. We built the station up like a fort."

Wolfman also informed the preacher clientele that from then on they were to pay him in advance for their shows by sending cash to a Shreveport address. The preachers didn't believe the threats of the border newcomer, but two nights later their programs were replaced by the granitein-satin voice of the Wolfman, howling at a quarter million watts or at least something close to it. The preachers got the message and began sending their money to the new border radio jefe.

At first, all was fine with the station. "I showered the workers with gifts," Wolfman said, "and we started payin' the government their taxes. All the workers were livin' at the station, so I had fifty, sixty people— whole families—to take care of. I even had a doctor out there to take care of their ills. One time I threw a five-thousand-dollar party that they will never forget. And they loved me—plus I was on the air with this Wolfman Jack crazy stuff, so they figured I was a real man, you know?"

González did not bother the operation, since Wolfman had the *federales* and the station workers on his side. "I used to look like Viva Zapata! I had a forty-five strapped to one hip and a Smith and Wesson strapped to the other and—what do you call them?—*bandoleras* strung across my chest. I had bodyguards. We used to roast a goat right outside the station and eat it. You know, man, I got ambushed goin' through the pass one night. I know what it feels like to have bullets goin' by my head."

Despite this radio terrorism, Wolfman was able to leave his barbecued cabrito after a couple of weeks and took up residence in a suite at the Roswell Hotel in Del Rio, the same hotel that had housed the Brinkley Hospital twenty years before. Wolfman never needed the Brinkley treatment, however, and it was while he was getting naked that Montez struck.

"So my old lady comes down, and we were gettin' it on one night. Now, I'm not sayin' this 'cause I'm a man, I'm a man, I'm a man—I mean we were actually gettin' it on. I listened to the station constantly, and I was listenin' even then. And all of a sudden, in the middle of a sermon from Brother J. Charles Jessup, some little Mexican kid comes in on the mike and says, '*Pistoleros, pistoleros,*' and I hear *pnnnyyyooowww, pnnnyyyooowww.* So I jumped in my Starfire Oldsmobile convertible and boogied across the border, spreadin' hundred-dollar bills all over the place. I got the sheriff and guys in garbage trucks and ridin' scooters and on horseback, maybe about forty people, to go out to the station to save those boys out there that was protectin' it. Just as we started comin' over the hill, the sun was comin' up and these guys were circlin' the station like Indians would circle a wagon train fortress or somethin'. You could see the dust around the station from horses ridin' around. So we come over the hill, over the horizon, whoopin' and hollerin', and they saw us comin' and took off. Luckily, there was no one got seriously hurt on our side. There was one person got killed on their side, shot right between the eyes. But they attacked us, you know, so nobody went to jail. It costs me about five hundred dollars to have it forgotten about. Anyway, Montez never came back, and I was in control of XERF."

Whether or not Wolfman actually fought his way onto the XERF frequency, his molasses-coated jackhammer voice shattered the border skies every evening until 4 a.m. "Ah you wit me out deah? Ah you readeh? 'Cause we gonna try to do it faw ya, honey! We gonna blow your mahn, babe-eh! OOOOOOWWWWOOOOO, *do it!* Ad needja soul, Ah needja soul." Between the white-hot rhythm and blues of James Brown and Johnny Otis and the jazz of Count Basie, the Wolfman grunted, groaned, and howled an endless stream of exotic exhortations, such as "I've got these little—what do you call them? gonads?—on my vocal cord," he explained. "It makes my voice richer."

"Wherever ya are, and whatever ya doin', I wancha ta lay ya hands on da raydeeooo, lay back wid me, and squeeeze ma knobs. We gonna feeel it ta-nite. . . . OOOOOOWWWWWWOOOOooooooooooo. . . . This is Wolfman Jack down here with the donkeys. Gonna get you some soul, man, OOOOOOWWWWOOOOO. "Get Naked," "Blow the evil weed," "Kiss your teachers"—Wolfman was a PG-rated Lenny Bruce, a badass Dr. Joyce Brothers, a blastin' combination of Howlin' Wolf and a used car salesman. Listeners from Amarillo to Reykjavík tuned in every night to be scandalized by the wizard of the turntables. Men believed him when he said, "Wolfman plays de best records in the business an' then he eat 'em!" Women flushed when he growled, "If you don't like this next song, I'll kiss your face, darlin's." The Russians flinched when he said nasty things about Nikita Khrushchev, and they proceeded to jam his broadcasts, which rode the sky wave around the globe. And everybody rushed to buy whatever it was Wolfman had for sale.

"I sold more-weight pills and less-weight pills, all kinda stuff. I sold baby chicks, a hundred for three dollars and ninety-five cents. They were chicken rejects from a farm outta Nashville, and they would actually send them a hundred baby chicks in the mail, C.O.D. I'd say, 'Now, just imagine all the fun you're gonna have with these baby chicks. You lead 'em around on little leashes, you give 'em little names, and then when they grow up—you gonna eat 'em.' Man, we'd do sixty, seventy, eighty orders a day for those baby chicks."

Some of Wolfman's most popular products were rhythm-and-blues record packages. "In those days, a lot of the records were hard to find in white record stores. I sold two different types of record packages from Ernie's Record Bar in Nashville and Stan's Record Shop in Shreveport, Louisiana. They had all the great rhythm and blues forty-fives. Back in those days we sold five or six hundred packages a day of those dollar ninety-five three-record sets. On the albums, you usually had forty songs, a two-record album package, and you'd call it *The Lucky Forty* for just four ninety-five—cash, check, or money order. And if you order right now, we're gonna send you free of charge a life-size picture of me that glows in the dark. Now, just think of all the fun you're gonna have watchin' me glow in the dark. Just send your cash, check, or money order to the Lucky Forty, XERF, Del Rio, Texas."

In addition to rosebushes, songbooks, and dog food ("Da Wolfman eat it alla time"), one of Wolfman's products in particular seemed to fit the great tradition of Dr. Brinkley. "I put this thing called Florex together with a guy in Mexico City and pitched it every night. It went like this: 'Let me talk to the older people in the audience right now. If you find that in your forties, fifties, and sixties that your marital situation isn't what it used to be, you find your wife nagging and you just don't feel happy at home anymore, there is a little pill here called Florex that will make you feel like a young man again. In fact, your wife should take them too. They will make her feel like a young woman.' This stuff hit like dynamite. The day after it went on the air we got like four thousand orders. We cleaned up until the FTC made us take it off the air because all they were was little sugar pills with some aspirin. It did so well that four years after we took it off the air, we were getting reorders."

In addition to making a 50 percent commission on the products he sold, Wolfman sold time on the border blaster to others. "We didn't turn the station on till about six in the evening," he said, "because even with the superpower, daytime signals high on the dial don't go as far as signals low on the dial, and with two hundred fifty thousand watts you're burning up a lot of electricity just to get to San Antonio. I would go on as Big Smith With the Records and play down-home country stuff for an hour and a half, and then we had a Spanish hour. We had to have a Spanish hour because it was part of the Mexican FCC government thing, and I had some Mexican guy come in and do that. The preachers came on about seven-thirty, eight o'clock, fifteen- to thirty-minute spots, and if they had the money, they could buy spots through twelve-thirty at night. . . . It was a lot of fun. I was on with J. Charles Jessup and Reverend A. A. Allen and all them cats, and they was sellin' Jesus all day and I was sellin' sin at night." The Wolfman upped the preachers' rates and still managed to stay on good terms with the numerous radio proselytizers. "I got to know the preachers all real good. They were the greatest pitchmen I heard in my whole life, and I'm sure a lot of it rubbed off on me, you know. It wasn't that they were doing anything wrong. They weren't ripping anybody off. They were giving the public what they wanted. All these guys were extreme professionals. They really knew what they were doing. We had the cream of the crop, the real hustlers, guys who had a tremendous following."

Wolfman himself began to develop a certain lupine radio perspective: "I'm a radio performer, you understand. I just want people to get it on.

I'll do all I can to try to turn people around, to try to steer 'em in the right direction. That's the whole trip in life, you know. . . . I must save four or five people each night. . . . I'm givin' what I got as long as there's folks out there that wants to take it. . . . I'm just like a 'hallelujah, Jesus' screamin' preacher. I want people to clap their hands and stomp their feet on the floor, only I don't use the name of God." Like other border operators, Wolfman had a basic philosophy of empathetic libertarianism. "I would suggest to everybody to do your thing," Wolfman told a reporter in 1970. "Don't worry whether this cat's got more than you or that cat. . . . If you enjoy what you're doin', you're gonna get right up with that otha cat. . . . So what does it come to? Love, right? Love your brother, right?"

Wolfmen and wolfwomen across the globe were fascinated by the midnight howling from the border. Was Wolfman black? Was he Mexican? Was he white? Where did he live? What did he eat? What did he wear? Requests for personal appearances flooded Wolfman, who turned them all down at first. "I was a businessman at that point," he explained. "I wasn't into an entertainment thing." He told his eager fans, "The Wolfman don't move for less than fifteen thousand dollars per hour." A group of college students in Kansas eventually met his price. Wolfman, somewhat amazed, told the students that they'd have to deliver the money to him in advance in $20 bills. Quicker than a wolf howl, a Brinks truck showed up in Del Rio with a load of brown paper bags filled with $20 bills.

Wolfman decided to start his stage career and hired some midgets and a makeup artist to help create a living legend. The Brooklyn native donned a flowing black cape, huge sunglasses, a red Afro fright wig, foot-long fingernails, and multicolored face paint and burst onto the stage to the delighted squeals of his devoted Kansas cubs. "I looked real Neanderthal, you know? I could have been Mexican, I could have been black, I could have been anything. But I still didn't know what the hell to do onstage, so I stood there and growled and talked a little bit and threw around some profanities and left. Dey loved it."

Under the guiding paw of the Wolfman, XERF was making a profit of some $150,000 a month, and Wolfman, like Brinkley, knew what it took to keep the money flowing: "I was like the Robin Hood of Del Rio, givin' money to who needed it. . . . Must have been fifty Mexican families that participated in all that good money, including the *federales*, the political people, folks in Mexico City. . . . A little *mordida* here, a little *mordida* there, a slap on the back over here, and the same for there." Things weren't all tostadas and hot sauce for the border wolf. In addition to performing, spreading around *mordida*, and holding cookouts for the *federales*, the new station manager was under considerable pressure from Arturo González, the man who had formerly controlled the station. "I think I got a lawsuit from him everyday," Wolfman recalled. "That's how I got to know him. He's a very wise, crafty old man, a sharp operator, a very brilliant guy, a self-taught international lawyer. An amazing man, no question about it. . . . We got along real well. As a matter of fact, it developed into almost like a father-son type of relationship." González, who smiled when asked about the Big X shoot-out, spoke highly of Wolfman Jack as well: "Wolfman Jack is a hard worker and a good businessman. When I first met him, he told me he had an offer I couldn't refuse. He said he would work for free and just take a commission. I couldn't refuse, and I hired him. He went to work and earned a lot of money. He is a great salesman."

XERF's huge earnings were enough to pay the back taxes in two and a half years, but the pressure on the radio executive proved to be too much. "I was tired of getting shot at every day," Wolfman said. "I lived in a fortress, you know, and had a truckload of Mexicans follow me everywhere." Wolfman handed control of the station back to Arturo González, made an arrangement to broadcast a taped show on XERF, and moved north with Wolfwoman and their two children, Joy and Todd. The former border recluse acquired part ownership of station KUXL in Minneapolis, but the cold climate and slim paychecks did not suit his outlaw temperament. By 1967 the Wolfman was once again howling from the border.

"You're listening to the Big X, XERB, mighty ten-ninety, fifty thousand watts of soul power over L.A." With the most powerful radio pulpit on the West Coast at his disposal, Wolfman became the undisputed master of the California airwaves, the preacher of soul with a congregation of thousands who met every night at midnight in fourteen western states. Wolfman came to XERB after making a deal with Harold Schwartz, a well-known border radio salesman who controlled the U.S. rights to time sales over XERB and to XEG in Monterrey. Wolfman briefly shared the disc jockey responsibilities with the Magnificent Montague, who left the border just as his catchphrase "Burn, baby, burn" became a sixties anthem. "We got into L.A. in the daytime real good as well as the nighttime," Wolfman said. "I had offices down on Sixth Street and built studios and everything. I'd tape the programs a day ahead of time and ship them down across the border, and they'd run the tapes. XERB was the thing that really made it for me." With his voice blasting out from XERB, XERF, XEG, and XELO, Wolfman was the undisputed king of the border.

"Dis heah's de Wolfman comin' atcha AAWWWRRIIGHT, Baaayyyybeee . . . Aaaawooooohhh. I mean this next record gonna knock you right on da flo-wa, bayyayyyybeee. I hafta change my clothes every time

I hear it, ya know, it git me so excited. . . . OOOOOO, AAAAHHH. Fo da next three minutes ya can all make love, but when de record's ovah, ya gotta stop. Can ya dig it? Have moicy." Wolfman sold record packages and an updated version of the potency drug Florex called Mr. Satisfy. His growing popularity enabled him to branch out into other items as well. He hocked Wolfman T-shirts, his own compilation albums, and even Wolfman roach clips. "Now, bayybeee, you get dese little roach clips heah and ya can catch de little roaches by deah hin' legs and throw dem right out de winda, AAAA, OOOOHHHHH."

In addition to collecting his percentage from the sale of merchandise on his own program, Wolfman sold time to the preachers he had met at XERF. "I ran all the stuff that the other stations didn't want to run—fortune-tellers and all that kind of stuff." He even tried to make an advertising deal with the major U.S. tobacco companies when cigarette ads were banned from the U.S. airwaves. "I told them that I'd hire the best jocks in the country and blast out cigarette ads from the border," said Wolfman, "and they almost went for it. . . . But all those companies are into foods and stuff as well as cigarettes, and at the last minute they decided they couldn't afford to piss off the FTC, you know what I mean?" Even without the cigarette advertising bonanza, XERB brought in a lot of money, and much of it made its way to the lair of the wiley Wolfman.

At the stroke of midnight the radios of every hip hot-rodder in California tuned in to the Wolfman's rock-and-roll mantras. "We gotta whole lotta soul comin' at ya. . . . Rock and roll with da Wolfman. Lay yo hands onna radio right now an' feeeel mmmeeee." Incoming calls jammed the Wolfman telephone. "Who is dis onna Wolfman Telephone? . . . Speak up. You gotta mind tumor? . . . How sweet are your little peaches? . . . Stand on ya head and howwwwllll. . . . BYE." The Wolfman was making anywhere from $15,000 to $30,000 a month on the radio and doing 75 to 100 live performances a year. He was developing a record label of his own and building a recording studio in Pasadena. He hobnobbed with John Lennon, Johnny Rivers, and other L.A. notables and moved his family into a Beverly Hills den. Wolfman was a fat cat, but not for long.

"Somebody got to somebody," he explained. "I was giving this Mexican company a lease for the station, you know? I was payin' them thirty thousand a month, and the station was making eighty, ninety, a hundred thousand a month. They figured they could throw me out and make all the money themselves, you know. They did it politically. They went down to the Mexican government and complained about the Pentecostal preachers on the air. Now, Mexico is a very Catholic country, you know, and the government knew about the preachers but kinda looked the other way until the owners decided to make noises. So for a while there, the government made all the stations cancel those prayer-cloth preachers. That more or less put me out of business 'cause that was like sixty percent of my revenue. So I couldn't operate anymore, and I turned the station back over to them. About a month later, the government canceled the ruling, and they went back and put the preachers on the air. But they've never made the money they made with me. They really cut off their nose to spite their face, you know what I'm sayin'?" Although Wolfman owned the U.S. rights to the XERB call letters, they did him no good without a frequency to howl over. Even worse, the Brooklyn broadcaster found that no U.S. station manager would hire him because of his reputation for unpredictable border craziness. Wolfman found himself out of work and $500,000 in debt.

Bob Wilson at KDAY in L.A. finally gave Wolfman a shot at the legitimate U.S. broacasting scene by hiring him as a DJ for his experimental progressive-rock format. Wolfman's salary was $18,000 a year. "Man, every day Wolfwoman would pack my lunch, and I'd boogie down to KDAY. I was livin' in Beverly Hills but packin' a lunch. Everyone still thought I was a millionaire." For a year or so, Wolfman drove past the homes of neighbors Mary Pickford and Sammy Davis, Jr., on his way to the KDAY studio, until a young filmmaker named George Lucas asked the radio announcer if he wanted to play a part in the movie *American Graffiti*. After reading the script, Wolfman decided it was time to step from the shadowy caverns of the broadcasting booth and enter the bright lights of the cinema. "*American Graffiti* was like a documentary for Wolfman Jack. . . . I felt like asking them how much they were going to charge me to do it," Wolfman said.

Wolfman played himself in the first Lucas smash hit, which was as much an ode to the mystery of border radio as it was a classic American coming-of-age story. Gary Kutz, the producer of the film, explained how the Wolfman had influenced the youthful Lucas: "When he was a high school kid in Modesto, they used to cruise the streets, just like the kids in the film. They all listened to the Wolfman on XERB in Tijuana, and the signal would come and go so ethereally, it sounded like a godlike voice from someplace." Wolfman acted for three days at $1000 a day and put some of his own money into promoting the film. "Some people said my acting was a cross between Euell Gibbons, Rodney Allen Rippy, and Sheena, Queen of the Jungle." The Wolfman of *American Graffiti* was a quiet, understanding fellow, a lonely, wise man who had plenty of friendly advice and Popsicles to share with anyone who dropped by. "That's the life of a disc jockey," Wolfman later philosophized. "You spend your life talking to a microphone, and when a real person comes along, you're hungry for him."

As it became clear that the picture was going to be a hit, Wolfman was able to share in the glory—and the more than $40 million the picture made in its first year. "When it began to look like they had something big, they turned around and gave me a piece of it," he said. "I mean I didn't expect it. I'm a grown man, and I cried. . . . It's the only thing I ever lucked out on. Everything else I had to work my tail off for." Wolfman earned more than $500,000 from the picture, enough to get him back on his financial paws. Even more important, the Wolfman character portrayed in the film polished the image of the grisly border blaster to a standard of cleanliness acceptable to the media establishment. "Clap for the Wolfman" became a pop hit in 1972. Soon after, Wolfman scored a $300,000 DJ job with WNBC in New York City and spent a year in a tough ratings battle with WABC's Bruce "Cousin Brucie" Morrow. In addition, Wolfman became host of the variety show *The Midnight Special* and made numerous appearances on other television shows, including *The Odd Couple* and *The Sonny and Cher Comedy Hour*. The ruthless routine of plane flights, hotel rooms, and manic performances took its toll on the poor kid from Brooklyn, who began to lose his identity. "Bob Smith don't exist no more, man," the Wolfman said. "I been talkin' like dis so long I don't remember nothin' else, you dig?" Lou, the supportive Wolfwoman, sighed and admitted, "It was the closest we ever came to getting a divorce." Even Wolfman found he wasn't enjoying it anymore. "I was becoming like the regular plastic merchandise you see every day, you know?"

Wolfman dropped his New York gig and moved back to the coast. He eased off the tube and began to syndicate a rock-and-roll show that aired on KRLA, one of the biggest rock stations in L.A., and on other stations across the country. "It's the first time a major market station has run a nightly syndicated show like this, man," Wolfman reported. "It's exciting. We're on stations all over the place. And I'm on the Armed Forces Radio Service all over the world." Wolfman even returned to the border airwaves, recreating the magical era of the superpowered X stations with an afternoon rock and roll show on the last of the AM borderblasters, XETRA in Tijuana. Although thankful for the exposure that his film, television shows, and live appearances had given him, the Wolfman was glad to focus his efforts once again on his favorite medium, the radio. "Radio's the greatest because it's all in here," he said, tapping the side of his head. "It's theater of the mind." OOOOOOWWWWWWOOOOooooooooo.

Blasting From Baja

I wish I was in Tijuana . . .
I'm on a Mexican radio, woh-oh.
—*From "Mexican Radio," by Wall of Voodoo, 1982*

Wolfman was undoubtedly the best-known West Coast border radio personality, but he was only one in a long tradition of performers who invaded the radio airwaves of the Golden State from the sandy hills of Baja California. Soon after Texas broadcasters found gold along the Rio Grande, radio forty-niners in California struck out for the Mexican border. But the geography of the region did not lend itself as well to superpowered broadcasting. While XED, XER, and the other early border blasters had had a straight shot across the well-populated farming communities of the Great Plains clear up into Canada, border stations on the West Coast had to boom their signal out over the sparsely populated Rocky Mountain states. There was one population plum, however, that attracted broadcasters to the dry hillsides of Baja California: Los Angeles. Radio operators quickly realized that a powerful border station in Southern California would carry into Los Angeles with a signal as clear as moonlight over the Pacific Ocean.

In the 1920s Baja California was one of the playgrounds of the Hollywood elite. In the days of prohibition the major industry in the otherwise sparsely populated area was gringo entertainment, and nightclubs, restaurants, and resorts attracted partying Yankees from all over Southern California. One of the most popular resorts was Agua Caliente, a complex about two miles from central Tijuana that offered horse racing, golf, drinking, gambling with gold coins in the Salón de Oro, and bathing at the Agua Caliente Spa, built of the finest Italian marble. The owners of the resort realized the advertising potential of radio early on, and in 1931 they made inquiries about the possibility of establishing a station as part of the resort. They asked their attorney to inquire about the legalities of broadcasting race results and running a sweepstakes from their station. They planned to take orders for the sweepstakes by telegraph and announce the winners over the air. Their legal experts believed that the United States had "no jurisdiction over aerial activities in Mexico," and the happy health-spa owners forged ahead with their plans for a regulation-free radio station.

The Agua Caliente Company built XEBC and began broadcasting everything from race results to interviews with the lesser lights of Hollywood. Large lounging rooms were open near the studios day and night so that patrons of the resort could marvel at the wonder of an operating radio station. A special 24-hour broadcast, "believed to be the longest broadcast ever originated by a station for a special occasion," according to the *San Diego Union,* marked the first anniversary of XEBC. The paper reported that "the engineers of the station have scooped the networks on a real radio innovation" during the broadcast by using one of the first portable transmitters ever constructed. Verne Routh, station manager and creator of the portable transmitter, looked on proudly as one of his fellow engineers followed announcer Art Johnson up the campanile that marked the entrance to the border resort and "gave listeners a word picture of the midnight scene" as the chimes tolled the hour. The transmitter sent short wave signals to the main studio, where they were amplified and rebroadcast. Throughout the evening, Johnson and his transmitter-laden engineer strolled through the grounds of the elegant resort, interviewing personalities like "prominent Hollywood director" David Butler and describing couples as they glided past on the ballroom dance floor to the music of Terry La Franconi, Beatrice Ynez, and Benito Serrano's orchestra. The next day, the Riders of the Purple Sage, under the direction of Jack Dalton, performed hillbilly selections for listeners who later thrilled to on-location descriptions of Agua Caliente's airport, casino, and dining room, broadcast by Bob Morrell over the unique portable transmission equipment. The entire remote broadcast went without a hitch, according to the newspaper, which applauded the achievement and pointed out that "the major radio networks are not always responsible for innovations in broadcasting technique."

While Anglo broadcasters in Agua Caliente danced until dawn with the blessing of local Mexican authorities, Mexican broadcasters north of the border had a lot tougher going. In 1934 Pedro J. Gonzalez was a respected figure in the Los Angeles Chicano community. During the Mexican Revolution he had worked as a telegrapher in northern Mexico and was arrested for spying by troops serving under Pancho Villa. The terrified teenager was brought to the commander of the revolutionary army. "Son," said Villa, "you have two choices: either I execute you, or you can go with me." Gonzalez made the obvious choice and served as Villa's telegrapher from 1913 to 1917. He saw action at the battles of Torreón, Lerdo, and Gómez Palacio and was mustered out at the end of the hostilities.

In search of good wages and steady employment, Gonzalez moved to Los Angeles. He worked as a longshoreman and entertained his coworkers with songs from their homeland. He auditioned for the Mauricio Calderon Music House in 1924, cut a few recordings, and quickly became one of the most popular Spanish entertainers in Southern California. He wrote ads for Folger's and other American companies that were just beginning to market their products to Spanish speakers. He formed an advertising company, the Spanish American Broadcasting Agency, and became a regular on Los Angeles stations KNBC and KELW. He formed a group called Los Madrugadores ("the Early Risers"), which performed live from four to six every morning from the Teatro Hidalgo in east Los Angeles. Women worshiped him. "Dedicate a song for me," one fan wrote. "I adore you." Another fan called his home and told Gonzalez's wife, "I am waiting for him now in the plaza. Please tell him to hurry." Gonzalez and his group recorded more than a hundred songs for various record labels, including Columbia, Okeh, and Victor. He created a unique L.A. musical sound and rode through the booming twenties as the king of Spanish radio north of the border.

When the Depression hit, a good deal of the anger and frustration of the Southern California Anglo community focused itself on the Mexican American population. More than half a million people of Mexican heritage, including many U.S. citizens, were deported. Pedro Gonzalez, the former Villista, fought the injustices to his community over the air. He composed a *corrido*, or ballad, protesting the plight of Juan Reyna, a Mexican American unjustly convicted of killing a policeman. Gonzalez often used his airtime to tell his people about possible employment opportunities. One day he announced that workers were needed to clear land at a particular site near Los Angeles. Hundreds of his listeners arrived at the scene with picks and shovels. The local police did not understand what was going on. They saw the shovels, feared a riot, and started making arrests. Pedro Gonzalez began to acquire the reputation of an influential troublemaker.

Byron Fitts, Los Angeles district attorney at the time, was infamous for his attitude toward *los mojados*, ("the wets"), as undocumented Mexican workers were called. He tried to have Gonzalez arrested several times in 1933. Each time, the outspoken singer was freed for lack of evidence. Fitts then tried to get the federal authorities to cancel Gonzalez's broadcasting license but failed in that as well. Finally, in March 1934 Fitts had Gonzalez arrested for the rape of Dora Versus, a dancer Gonzalez had worked with at one time.

Gonzalez's trial took place in a packed courtroom. The popular entertainer smugly looked on during the proceedings, smoking a cigar and confident of his innocence. "I tried to signal him to take the cigar out," his wife said with a sigh. "He seemed to be . . . ridiculing the law." After the confusing testimony, during which the prosecution's main witness contradicted herself several times, the all-white jury found Gonzalez guilty as charged and sentenced him to fifty years in San Quentin. The trial judge offered Gonzalez probation. Gonzalez said, "I won't plead guilty for something I didn't do. I won't stain the name of my wife and five children."

A few months later, Dora Versus admitted that she had perjured herself. She said that Gonzalez was innocent, that she had testified under pressure from Fitts to save herself from jail. But the judge on the appeals court failed to admit the new evidence, citing a technical flaw in the motion filed by the defense. Pedro Gonzalez was taken to San Quentin, where he served six years in the state penitentiary for making trouble in Spanish over an L.A. radio station. When Gonzalez was paroled in 1940, he was immediately deported to Mexico. His loyal fans gave him a hero's welcome at Union Station in Los Angeles when his train stopped there on its way to the border. Settling in Tijuana, Gonzalez continued to entertain and inspire his supporters for many years over XERU and was finally allowed to return to the United States in 1971 to be near his children, all American citizens.

While Pedro Gonzalez was being sentenced to San Quentin, a number of English-language radio stations were springing up in the vicinity of Tijuana. Fred and Alberto Ferreira built XEMO in 1934 and broadcast music and advertising aimed at the Los Angeles market. One of the station employees, John Griggs, was walking to work on a stormy day in February 1936 when he heard a loud crack and looked up to see two-hundred-foot radio tower wobble and begin to fall. Griggs huddled in a corner of the station building as the tower came crashing down around him. Oscar W. Erickson, a co-worker at XEMO, took refuge in a car parked nearby and watched as timbers jammed through the roof of the station, shattering six-inch concrete walls and destroying the 5000-watt transmitter. Although the house next door was totally destroyed, no one was seriously hurt, and Griggs, buried in the rubble, suffered only a cut wrist. The owners, in the spirit of true radio pioneers, looked over their $10,000 loss and started to rebuild—this time with a 10,000-watt transmitter.

XERB, like XEBC, was a resort-based border blaster located on the Pacific Coast. In 1928 Manuel Barbachano and his brother built a hotel on a deserted beach called Rosarita. The spot was a favorite place for sportsmen hunting quail, duck, rabbit, deer, and mountain lion, and it soon became a popular retreat for Californians simply hunting a good time. The brothers expanded the hotel, building elaborate ballrooms and dining rooms, and graced the entrance with an arched portal on which the following words were written in white tile: *Por esta puerta pasan las mujeres mas hermosas del mundo* ("Through this door pass the most beautiful women in the world.") The sentiment was not far from the truth, as Hollywood's most glamorous came to vacation at the resort. Orson Welles and Gregory Peck vacationed on the sands of Rosarita Beach, and Burgess Meredith and Paulette Goddard were married and honeymooned at the resort hot spot. A small town inhabited by cooks, bartenders, and janitors grew up around the hotel. The Barbachano brothers did everything they could to facilitate tourist traffic, paving the highway from Tijuana to Ensenada, as well as constructing the first power company and the first telephone company in Baja California. The brothers did not overlook radio, and they became partners in the International Broadcasting Corporation to build a powerful border blaster on the ground of the newly established Rosarita Beach Country Club.

Representatives of the company attended the Pan-American radio conference held in Mexico City in 1937. While border broadcasters along the Rio Grande suffered at the hands of the conferees, the West Coast contingent, backed by former Mexican president Abelardo Rodríguez, came away with a license to open a 100,000-watt clear-channel station. J.A. "Foghorn" Murphy, Roger Arnebergh, former San Diego city attorney C.L. Byers, and the other major players in the company began to purchase the equipment necessary to set up the biggest border blaster on the West Coast.

The promise of a border radio fortune caused a rift between the entrepreneurs. Foghorn Murphy, who believed he had been frozen out of the deal, tried to halt construction by challenging his partners' ownership of transmission equipment destined for Rosarita Beach. Foghorn's partners were too fast for him and managed to move the equipment south of the border before Foghorn could get effective court action. The bitter would-be radio operator sued his partners for $450,000 but was frustrated again, because the federal district attorney refused to take any action, saying there was no evidence of illegal activity. While Foghorn gnashed his teeth, the Barbachano brothers and their partners covered eleven western states with a powerful blend of music and advertising from the transmitter of XERB in Rosarita Beach.

Just as the border stations strung along the Rio Grande constituted a circuit for performers and personalities, the stations in Baja California drew from and fed into the same itinerant talent pool. E. R. Rood, one of Norman Baker's codefendants in the 1937 sound waves case, shuttled back and forth between the Texas and California borders, as did many others. In March 1934 the *San Diego Union* reported, "E. R. Rood, who as 'astrologer of the air' broadcast for a time from a Tijuana station, yesterday won probation on a charge of violating the state corporation securities act." As a condition of the probation, Rood was required to pay back "approximately $20,000 he had received from various local concerns in connection with promotion of the Tijuana station and his recording devices." Restitution was not considered to be much of a problem, as "Rood testified that his income from his astrological reading and his radio broadcasting frequently runs to $1000 a day." As a sign of his good intentions, Rood posted $1000, the money "advanced by a radio station at Eagle Pass, Texas, with which Rood has a contract." The story also noted that, at the time of his arrest, Rood was on probation for violating the California Medical Practice Act, specifically by using the prefix "Dr." without having the credentials to prove it.

Dallas Turner encountered Rood when Turner was handling advertising accounts for a Baja border station. "I never did meet him," Turner remembered. "He wrote to me at XERB. I think this was in 1949 or 1950. He was a radio astrologer, and he'd gone into the patent medicine business. He had a rheumatism remedy that he called Rood's Linguets. Boy, what a name for a product. Anyway, I couldn't get the product on the air, so I had no further correspondence with the man, but he told me that he had worked with Norman Baker. Then several years later, I guess Rood had passed away, because another man contacted me and told me that he had learned astrology from Rood and that Rood had predicted the very date of his own death and had died on that date, and this man wanted to get on the radio. But I had no further correspondence with this individual. He did go to Mrs. Jimmie Rodgers in San Antonio, Texas, the widow of the Blue Yodeler, and I think he swindled her out of a thousand dollars to get enough money to get on the border stations, and he went on XEXO and his program flopped. And that was the last I ever heard of the man—I can't even remember his name."

As the years passed, numerous other Texas border radio personalities migrated to the golden west in search of broadcasting fortunes. Will Branch moved station XELO from Piedras Negras to Tijuana after a quarrel with his partner, C.M. Bres, only to move it a few years later to Juárez. Branch's son-in-law, Jack McVeigh, operated the Juarez station for many years from a ramshackle transmission building, playing Spanish programming at night, gospel preaching in the evening, and occasionally performing with his wife and son on a peculiar talk show in which the three pretended to be talking animals. Border personality Rupert "Slim Hawkins" Dougharty began his border career as a singing cowboy on XERA in 1940 and eventually took over as manager of XERB, a job he held for more than 25 years. "I worked for every border station there was," Slim recalled after his retirement from XERB. "I sold plastic statues of Jesus that shine in the dark, hymnals, horoscopes, and good-luck charms. I'm the last of the border-radio outlaws."

Other outlaw broadcasters made their way to XERB, including Harry M. Hoxsey, the cancer specialist who had at one time stood beside Norman Baker in the KTNT studios as they fought off gunmen. After his falling-out with the calliaphone inventor, Hoxsey achieved notable success in promoting the cancer treatment developed by his great-grandfather. By the mid-fifties, he was based in Dallas and ran the largest private cancer treatment operation in the world, with clinics in seventeen states serving more than 10,000 patients at any one time. The herbal cancer specialist was under constant attack from the government, however, particularly the Pure Food and Drug Administration, who received more than two hundred complaints a day about Hoxsey and posted warnings about the controversial treatment in post offices across the country emblazoned with the red and black headline PUBLIC BEWARE!

Hoxsey threatened to fight the regulators to the bitter end, and vowed to "beat their brains out." He enlisted the help of Dr. Gerald F. Winrod, a notorious racist and anti-Semitic fundamentalist preacher who was charged with sedition for supporting the Nazis during World War II. By the thirties Winrod had transformed himself into a Bible-thumping Red baiter, leader of the Defenders of Christian Faith, publisher of *Defender Magazine*, and host of *The Defender Hour*. Actually only fifteen minutes long, *The Defender Hour* achieved tremedous coverage, as it was broadcast over border stations XERB, XEDM, XEG, and XELO every evening.

Winrod became one of Hoxsey's strongest supporters, using his radio show and publication to "bring a wave of enlightenment" to the American people regarding "the greatest controversy of this century." FDA investigator Frank McKinlay made recordings of Winrod's broadcasts over XERB as an "extracurricular surveillance" activity and sent the recordings to the California State Department of Public Health, which kept a close watch on the Hoxsey-Winrod media blitz. According to McKinlay's records, Winrod attacked the medical establishment in fine border style. "I do not know any pathologist anywhere who can tell the difference between a malignant and a benign cell," he told his radio audience, quoting a letter from an anonymous but prominent doctor in the South. "The medical fraternity is bleeding the public commercially in the treatment of cancer." Winrod characterized the powerful propaganda of vested interests. "The public must be given no hint of hope for cancer," he said. "The victim must be cut and bled and burned and drugged and buried after paying heavily for the privilege of being taken through the torture of a burning hell of surgery and radiation." He preached further, "And so I say to you that Dr. Harry M. Hoxsey and his staff of doctors, nurses, and technicians are offering an incomparable service to suffering humanity." Winrod compared Hoxsey with "Harvey, Pasteur, and others, persecuted while they were alive, praised after they died." He told XERB listeners to visit the Fremont Christian Clinic in Los Angeles or the Defender Health Research Foundation in Monrovia, California, and learn more about the Hoxsey method. In Winrod's estimation, no miraculous healing was beyond Hoxsey's reach, and he told of a "steady stream of letters . . . testifying to cures of cancer by the Hoxsey method of treatment after cutting and burning had proved fatal."

While he alleged that his brother had been healed by the Hoxsey method and assured his listeners that "our interest is religious, rather than medical," Winrod's real interest in promoting the cancer specialist was pecuniary: Hoxsey paid Winrod a large sum of money for publicizing his cancer treatment. After Winrod's death in late 1957, Hoxsey took complete control of *The Defender Hour,* using the border radio show to talk about his cancer cure while inspector McKinlay kept his tape machine rolling. Don Howard, former associate of Dr. Brinkley and onetime owner of XERF in Villa Acuña, introduced each Hoxsey broadcast with the echoing words "Know the truth." Hoxsey then spoke to his audiences in a gruff voice, "If you have got cancer, wake up," he said. "Don't let 'em burn you, cut you, mutilate you, barbecue you. Investigate the Hoxsey method of chemotherapy." Quoting an article in the *Police Gazette* entitled "New Cancer Menace in Foods—Suppressed Government Report," Hoxsey described the dangers of maraschino cherries and launched into a tirade against the Food and Drug Administration. He said he would jump off the Empire State Building and quit broadcasting if the FDA could show a cure for even one case of cancer. He accused the FDA of spending hundreds of thousands of dollars to attack him, throwing away taxpayers' money "like drunken sailors, happy drunk sailors at a carnival." He asked, "Why don't they protect your foods?"

Hoxsey often went on to describe some of his own eccentric dietary theories. He estimated that 65 percent of all human diseases were caused by the transplantation of viruses from chickens via eggs. To stamp out this scourge, Hoxsey raised six thousand virus-free chickens at the Hoxsey farm in North Carolina. He treated them with his internal cancer medication and sold "Bonded Eggs" that were certain to be free from any viral infection. The cancer specialist noted with pride that Dr. Samuel C. Schmittel, former director of the Poultry Division of the University of Georgia was now director of Virus Research of Bonded Eggs. Hoxsey saw many similarities between the treatment of humans and barnyard fowl. "You must treat a patient just like I treat these chickens over in North Carolina," Hoxsey said. "You must start them on the medicine . . . and get rid of the toxemias and viruses of that body and eliminate that cancer through the lymphatic system." At the close of his broadcasts, Hoxsey asked that his listeners "say a prayer for those poor victims who are doomed to die after being burned up, cut up, mutilated with radium, x-ray, and surgery. This is Dr. Harry M. Hoxsey. Good night, good-bye, and God bless you."

After Hoxsey's sign off, Don Howard offered listeners the "Truth Package . . . a package of valuable literature containing information that will astound you" and Hoxsey's book *You Don't Have to Die*. Howard warned, "Cancer may strike any fireside anytime. You need to be fortified with the information this amazing book contains."

Inspector McKinlay and his associates at the FDA were indeed amazed by the information Hoxsey distributed. In 1960, FDA officials padlocked all Hoxsey clinics around the country and closed down Hoxsey's Dallas operation by pressuring the Texas Legislature to outlaw naturopathic medicine. Hoxsey's chief nurse, Mildred Nelson, moved the clinic to Tijuana, where it continued to operate for many years. Hoxsey, herbalist, oilman, and poultry specialist, died in Dallas in 1974. Reportedly he was a victim of the disease he claimed to have cured, cancer.

Many people who received treatment at the Hoxsey clinic, however, believed that his methods were successful, at least in slowing the spread of the disease. *The Quack Who Cured Cancer*, a 1987 film documentary, presented surprisingly compelling pro-Hoxsey testimony from patients, their families, and a wide range of credible experts.

While Hoxsey was describing cancerous chickens over the air, other luminaries of the radio industry had decided to get a piece of the radio action on the border. Gordon McLendon was a Texas native who took over station XEAK in Tijuana in 1961. By that time, McLendon was already a legendary figure in broadcasting. A skilled linguist, McLendon learned Choctaw as a child growing up close to an Indian reservation in

Oklahoma, and majored in oriental languages at Yale. After graduating in 1943, he served in the Army intelligence unit, translating Japanese documents, interrogating prisoners, and working for the Armed Forces Radio Service, using the name Lowell Gram Kaltenheatter. Returning home after the war, McLendon pursued his interest in radio. Backed by his father, who owned a large chain of movie theaters, McLendon acquired a license to build a station in the Oak Cliff area of South Dallas in 1947. The station, appropriately designated KLIF, was to become one of the broadcasting powerhouses of the Southwest, a trailblazer in the techniques of modern radio formatting and promotion.

McLendon compared his first years at KLIF to "a great giant fish leaping out of the water, catching the rays of sunshine for a fleeting moment before disappearing into the depths of the sea—never to be heard of again." He did most of the announcing work for KLIF, assisted by a well-trained parrot that shrieked "Klif, Klif" on cue. McLendon had done play-by-play coverage of baseball and basketball games for the radio station at Yale, and he wanted to cover baseball games on his Dallas station. Although Texas did not have a major league ball club at that time, it had a successful minor league, known as the Texas League, and the baseball hierarchy prohibited the broadcasting of major league contests within fifty miles of a minor league game.

McLendon figured out a brilliant way to get around the broadcasting restrictions. Instead of broadcasting games live, he re-created them in his Oak Cliff studio. Relying on wire copy of the action sent to him directly from ballparks across the nation, McLendon added commentary, humor, and a background of sound effects that made his versions of games even more interesting than live broadcasts. The 27-year-old McLendon took the identity of the Old Scotchman, a crochety commentator in the catbird seat, and began each broadcast with "Hello, evvabody, evvawhere. This is the Old Scotchman, Gordon McLendon." He played recordings of the "Star-Spangled Banner" as it was heard in each different ballpark. Wes Wise, a future mayor of Dallas, sat next to him, shouting out vendor's calls in appropriate accents. When the game got dull or the Teletype stopped working, McLendon graphically described fictional fights in the stands, stray dogs on the field, and on one occasion credited a batter with a time-consuming 58 foul balls in a row. Sometimes McLendon would let his partners take over the commentary while he provided a running translation in Japanese, presumably for overseas audiences. "Well, I'll be a suck-egg *mule!*" he exclaimed after particularly important home runs.

The broadcasts came to be known as the *Game of the Day* and were joined on KLIF by McLendon re-creations of football games—actually the first regular broadcasts of pro football—and re-creations of historic sporting events, called *Great Days in Sports*. McLendon syndicated his programs, and by 1951 he had created the second-largest radio network in the United States, the Liberty Broadcasting System, with more than 450 affiliates. "We originated the various things the network didn't do," McLendon explained. In 1952, major league baseball brought suit against McLendon and shut down his operations, forcing him into bankruptcy. But McLendon eventually won a $13 million suit for restraint of trade and turned his attention to the lifeblood of modern radio: station promotion.

McLendon was one of the first to program his stations with a Top 40 format, which restricted playlists to a small number of popular songs. Todd Storz pioneered the format at KOWH in Omaha after realizing that people liked familiarity with the music they listened to. McLendon brought the concept to KLIF in 1952, boosting the station's ratings to a staggering 45 percent of the market. McLendon refined the format, adding fast-talking DJs and lively newscasts supplemented with localized reports from a roving radio car. But the one thing that separated McLendon from all other radio operators in the industry was his tremendous use of promotions.

According to an old protégé, McLendon was "the king of broadcast promotion for the time. Some people in the industry thought he brought a carnival to radio, but the public loved him." As McLendon himself put it, "Our objective at KLIF was to create a station of such sparkle and immediacy that you couldn't turn away." McLendon was the first to use a promotional jingle, the singsong repetition of the KLIF call letters. To introduce morning DJ Johnny Rabbit, McLendon lined up overturned autos on the freeways surrounding Dallas and had the words "I just flipped for Johnny Rabbit" painted on the bottom of the cars. He created the Mystery Millionaire, a well-groomed person who attracted citywide media attention by handing out dollar bills, and a few tens and twenties, in downtown Dallas. When interviewed live on television, the mystery man revealed that he was the new morning DJ on KLIF. Ten thousand people gathered on the corner of Elm and Akard streets in downtown Dallas on Good Friday, 1954, snarling traffic throughout the city, while a KLIF employee released hundreds of money-stuffed balloons from a window in the Adolphus Hotel. Several months later, hundreds of people were injured scrambling for money dropped from a helicopter over P. C. Cobb Stadium. McLendon gave away "radio's biggest prize," a mountain on an acre of land in the Texas Hill Country, and treasure hunters went berserk when he buried $50,000 in a Coke bottle somewhere in downtown Dallas. A former KLIF employee explained, "The town got tore up. We had to stop because people started diggin' up public as well as private property." A much more soothing promotion was hiring a beautiful blonde in a shocking-pink bikini to wave to commuters from an enormous KLIF billboard on the Central Expressway.

McLendon built on his success, eventually owning radio stations in Oakland, Buffalo, Detroit, and Chicago, and he even opened pirate radio stations off the coasts of Ireland and Sweden. To signal the format change at any new U.S. station, a disc jockey working for McLendon would burst into the control room and announce that he had taken over the station and would play nothing but his favorite song. The lucky listeners in one market heard "Purple People Eater" for eighteen hours straight. To meet the letter of Mexican law, McLendon, like so many border broadcasters before him, put the stock for the company that owned the Mexican station in the name of an *hombre de paja* ("straw man"), a Mexican national who agreed to be titular head of the company but signed over the stock as bearer certificates to his American backer. McLendon also branched out into motion pictures and produced three B-grade horror films: *The Giant Gila Monster, My Dog Buddy,* and *The Killer Shrews.* When a newspaper critic decimated one of his films, McLendon responded valiantly. "I resent your allegations that *The Killer Shrews* was one of the worst movies of all time," he wrote in a letter to the editor. "I made two other movies that were worse than that."

It was probably inevitable that such a radio innovator would be drawn to the border with its tradition of laissez-faire broadcasting. Sure enough, in 1961 McLendon took control of XEAK, a 50,000-watt Tijuana station with a strong signal going into the Los Angeles market. After acquiring XEAK, McLendon surveyed the L.A. radio dial with an eye for a format opening. "It's always been my belief," McLendon once surmised, "that a radio station, to be successful in any market, must do things that others aren't doing or aren't doing very well." McLendon decided that radio news was not being done very well in the City of Angels and launched an all-news radio station. He changed the call letters of the station to XETRA, as in "X-tra, X-tra, read all about it." On May 6 the station began broadcasting news 24 hours a day. At first, XETRA began a new newscast every seven and a half minutes, but McLendon soon lengthened the program to fifteen minutes and finally a half hour when he learned that people usually spent longer than thirty minutes commuting to work by car. Unlike his other operations, which relied heavily on local news, XETRA was exclusively a rip-and-read station. Twelve announcers pulled stories off the Associated Press and United Press International wires and supplemented them with material from national and Los Angeles-based clipping services. News teams alternated newscasts to give each program a fresh sound, and the Mexican identity of the station was hidden as much as possible. XETRA was "six ninety on your Los Angeles radio dial." The station promoted itself as "the world's first and only news radio station—in the air everywhere over Los Angeles." At the top of each hour, a soft female voice gave the obligatory station identification over a bed of Mexican music, which was followed by an English description of tourist sites in Mexico. Most listeners believed the station was in Los Angeles and ran ads promoting tourism south of the border.

XETRA made money during its second year in operation, becoming the first successful all-news station. Soon thereafter McLendon was seized by an affliction common to border radio operators—politics. He entered the 1964 race for the U.S. Senate in Texas, trying to wrest the Democratic nomination from the liberal incumbent, Ralph Yarborough. In a campaign that the newspapers described as "the most colorful Texas election campaign since W. Lee O'Daniel was elected governor in 1938," McLendon crisscrossed the state. In Dallas the conservative candidate shared a stage with John Wayne, who asserted that he was "a damn good Republican . . . not a politician" in Texas to help an old friend. Robert Cummings piloted McLendon's campaign plane for several days, adding celebrity sparkle to every landing and takeoff. The campaign had moments of high drama, as when a woman attempted to assassinate the radio candidate by shooting at an unsuspecting passenger in the Dallas airport with a .32-caliber pistol sprinkled with holy water. Even with the Hollywood backing, McLendon lost the primary, although his staunch conservativism drew a surprising number of votes.

XETRA had its share of border difficulties as well. Broadcasters in Los Angeles complained vigorously to the Federal Communications Commission about McLendon's activities, contending that he had camouflaged the identity of the border blaster and warning that if others did the same thing, advertising dollars would be drawn away from U.S. businessmen. The FCC ignored the complaints. In 1966, however, the station ran afoul of Mexican authorities. Police in Tijuana accused the staff announcers at XETRA of not having work permits and deported them all, slapping the general manager with a fine of several thousand pesos for good measure. For a few weeks the station played newscasts taped by announcers on the American side of the border and carried into Tijuana, but finally the fugitive newscasters got their Mexican working papers and returned to rewrite and read the news from the XETRA studios in Old Mexico.

An even worse calamity befell the McLendon border blaster in the late sixties, when the wiley American's straw man turned out to be a strongman. McLendon liked the Mexican national he had chosen to lead the company that owned XETRA, and the two were in the habit of frequenting popular San Diego watering holes whenever McLendon came to town. On one occasion McLendon's partner asked if he could borrow the XETRA bearer certificates, explaining that he was so proud of working with McLendon that he wanted to show them off to his family in Tijuana. In a burst of generosity, McLendon took his compadre to the bank vault where he kept the stock certificates and magnanimously handed them over. His partner took the certificates back to Tijuana, claimed ownership of the station for himself, and switched the format to Top 40.

McLendon was furious, and his father was even angrier. They tried to regain ownership of the lucrative station, but since the bearer certificates were made out in the name of the Mexican partner, there was nothing the Texas broadcasters could do except curse their bad judgment. McLendon turned away from the border, eventually selling all his broadcasting outlets. In his later years he spent most of his energy speculating heavily in gold and silver investments. The Old Scotchman apparently found the commodities market much less risky than the unpredictable world of border radio.

Radio Station S-A-V-E-D

Oh, this station's owned and operated by the soul of Jesus.
Won't you listen in to station S-A-V-E-D?
—*Roy Acuff and Odell McLeod, 1944*

"**O**nly believe, dear friends. All things are possible if you will only believe that Jesus is here," urged Brother Abernathy on his regular program over XERF. "So turn up your radios real loud and listen here to the word of God." For fifty years millions of devoted listeners across the globe have followed the advice of preachers like Brother Abernathy and have listened to the word of God blaring from the superpowered transmitters across the border. Fading in and out eerily with the atmospheric conditions, the prayers, exhortations, entreaties, and ravings of border radio preachers have helped countless listeners come to terms with their own personal tragedies and ailments and have provided a valuable means of financial support for scores of fundamentalist holy men. Many of these preachers stepped from the sawdust of revival tent meetings onto the airwaves, developing highly successful and complex church organizations founded not on the rock of Peter but on the fleeting electromagnetic impulses of the X stations.

Bible-thumping, hellfire-and-brimstone fundamentalist preachers never had a place in the world of the radio networks. Early on, network executives learned that selling time to preachers meant trouble. In 1931 and 1932 Father Charles Coughlin of the Little Flower Church in Royal Oak, Michigan, purchased weekly airtime on the CBS network to preach his fiery brand of populist politics. He attacked the gold standard, prohibition, monopolistic "concentration of wealth in the hands of the few," and "machine competition," which he described as "modern industrial slavery." When CBS officials urged Coughlin to tone down his rhetoric, he broadcast a blast against radio censorship. Burned by the priest's tongue, the network quietly let Coughlin's contract expire in April 1932 and created a new network policy against selling airtime to religious groups. The NBC radio network adopted a similar policy, unwritten but strictly enforced. Preachers could buy no airtime on the networks. They could be given airtime on certain stations but were strictly forbidden from asking for donations on the air.

Network policies did not deter preachers from finding a way to spread the gospel over the airwaves. After all, God's work was above and beyond the laws of the Federal Radio Commission. As the thirties progressed, the operators of the border stations became convinced of the importance of allowing access to the ether to prophets and apostles, both to spread the word of God and to widen their profit margins. The border operators knew that the hillbilly and gospel music they programmed attracted a huge audience of rural listeners, just the sort of audience that fundamentalist preachers would pay a handsome price to reach. Mexican law specifically forbade the broadcasting of "public occasions of a religious character," but the ever resourceful media moguls of *la frontera* found that Mexican government officials were inclined to grant special permission for religious broadcasting in English if the proper application, license, filing, and inspection fees were paid to the proper authorities and their associates. During the late thirties and early forties, border operators began to draw fundamentalist preachers out from their tents and clapboard country tabernacles to the seemingly omnipotent airwaves. Like Moses crossing the Red Sea to escape from the Pharaoh, preachers soon swarmed to the banks of the Rio Grande, crossing its waters to escape the yoke of government and network interference.

One of the first preachers to break for the border was the Reverend J. Harold Smith. Born in 1910 in Woodruff, South Carolina, Smith was a country boy whose great-grandfather, Captain Morgan, refused to surrender to the Yankees at the end of the Civil War and retreated to the Glassy and Hogback mountains of the Blue Ridge Range, where he was buried in his Confederate uniform. Brother Smith graduated from college and was headed for medical school when on Sunday, September 4, 1932, at 6:30 p.m. he met Jesus and trusted Him as his "precious Lord and Savior." Brother Smith started preaching, drawing large audiences in the South Carolina countryside. The faithful brought him chickens, eggs, vegetables, and canned goods, a gospel aid program referred to as "pounding the preacher." In addition to barter, Brother Smith attracted enough financial support to allow him to take to the airwaves.

He inaugurated the *Radio Bible Hour* over a Greenville, South Carolina, station in 1935. His strict adherence to the gospel was too hot for the timid management of the station, which soon refused to sell Brother Smith airtime and instead established a policy whereby a local council of ministers allocated free time to preachers in the area. The same thing happened to the would-be radio preacher in Spartanburg, South Carolina. Like King David leading his people toward the promised radio frequency, Brother Smith moved his church to Knoxville, Tennessee, and broadcast over the 10,000-watt voice of WNOX radio. During the war years Knoxville was a boomtown, one of the main construction sites for the first atomic bomb. Although the mountain folks, farmers, and newly arrived nuclear physicists welcomed Smith into their community, the radio station managers were not so supportive and once again forced him off the air by barring all paid religious broadcasts.

Smith realized that there was more to his persecution than the whim of a few station operators. He sensed a well-organized move by the Federal Council of Churches of Christ in America to ban nondenominational fundamentalist preachers from the air. He preached against the organization, calling it "this mad dog from hell, this green-eyed monster, this hydra-headed Frankenstein, this destroyer of the faith, this red front for the principles of communism, socialism, and fascism, the best friend the devil has in America today."

Brother Smith led his followers in a massive demonstration against WNOX in Knoxville. The *Greenville Observer* reported that "20,000 people from East Tennessee, Kentucky, and Virginia participated in a protest march against radio station WNOX. . . . The multitude, ranging from babes in arms to old men who limped along shouting, singing and waving the American flag, was led by J. Harold Smith, a young Radio Evangelist with a dynamic personality and a physique like that of an all-American halfback." The assembled multitude was as mannerly as it was enthusiastic in its support of the radio preacher, and the Knoxville city police later commended Smith and his thousands of supporters for their orderly conduct.

Inspired by the immense support shown in the rally, the evangelist managed to build his own religious broadcasting station in Knoxville, WBIK. It went on the air on August 11, 1947, but was free from controversy for only a few short weeks. On September 1 an examiner of the Federal Communications Commission visited Brother Smith in Knoxville and informed him that the commission was holding a hearing about his ownership of the station. The government maintained that Smith owned one third of the infamous border blaster XERF and was therefore prohibited from owning a station in the United States. After a six-year legal battle, Brother Smith lost WBIK, and XERF became the backbone of his evangelistic radio operations.

"I never owned any part of XERF," explained Brother Smith. "I was introduced to 'border broadcasting,' or the use of the Mexican stations, while I was in Knoxville. I went on XERF February 15, 1947, with one full hour of broadcasting each day, six to six-thirty a.m. and eight to eight-thirty p.m., seven days a week. This time was arranged with the owners of the station while they were building same. By making a pre-purchase of time, I was able to help the owners of the station build the station. . . . The night that we went on the station, we had paid one hundred thousand dollars for this time slot. That time was to continue through the life of the concession, or as long as that station used the call letters XERF." As the station increased in power, Brother Smith increase his payments to management. Eventually the "final base down payment" for time on the border station reached $540,000, a price Smith thought was fair, considering the number of souls he was able to reach.

According to his calculations, Brother Smith preached more than 61,000 sermons during his fifty-plus years in the ministry. *Radio Bible Hour* is the "oldest seven-day religious program in the world," he said. His style was that of a straightforward fundamentalist, a Baptist preacher of the old school who remembered sleeping in his grandfather's special "prophet's chamber." Some of his most popular sermons, available on cassette from the *Radio Bible Hour*, were entitled, "Let Me See Your Tongue," "Get Mad," "Gourd Soup," "Earthquakes," and "Is America Doomed?" In a sermon on Hebrews 12:3 entitled "Are You About to Faint?" Brother Smith began with a warning: "May I remind you at the outset of our message that the word of God is very extreme, very dogmatic, that it makes no relative statements but only those that are absolute and final. Nowhere in the word of God can you find that God is kidding with you or joking with you. . . . The word of God is absolute. It is pure, true, holy, undefiled, and, my friends, inerrant."

Brother Smith stuck to the Bible and put up with none of the extraneous showbiz puffery that marked the performances of other preachers. To make the point, he told the story of a woman in his congregation who suddenly stood up and began speaking in an unknown tongue. When she had finished, the preacher asked the woman, "Ma'am, do you know what you said?"

The woman replied, "I do not. I was speaking in a heavenly tongue."

Brother Smith then announced that he was able to interpret what she had just spoken. He asked, "Ma'am, are you married?"

The woman answered, "I am."

"Then you have just stated that you have been stepping out on your husband and that if none of us will go out and tell it, you will donate $500 to the building fund." The woman was furious and threatened to sue, but nothing ever came of her threats. After that incident few people dared to speak in tongues in the presence of border radio preacher J. Harold Smith.

Exactly four years after the conversion of J. Harold Smith, another of the great border preachers, Reverend George W. Cooper, came into the fold. At the time of his conversion, Cooper was running moonshine in Wilkes County, North Carolina, alongside his notorious partner, Hog Head Bolen. With 27 arrests for bootlegging and four hitches in prison, including four years on a chain gang, Cooper hardly seemed the type to go into evangelism, but he began listening to preachers on the radio and slowly got interested in God's word. At one point a drinking buddy of his named Ernest Spoon was lying on his bed, dying of moonshine. Spoon, who looked as white as "a gutted snowbird," asked Cooper to pray for him. Cooper obliged. "Lord, we're here tonight with poor Ernest Spoon, our brother. Lord, Ernest is badly in need of help. Ernest is mighty drunk, Lord, and . . ."

"Wait," Ernest said, clutching at Cooper with a trembling, pale hand. "Don't tell him I'm drunk, George. Tell him I'm just sick."

Cooper's real conversion did not come until three of his old gambling friends cornered him and forced him to go to a prayer meeting. Cooper agreed only after realizing that he couldn't fight his way out of it. The Lord descended to the prayer meeting and took him up, however, and Cooper began his career as a preacher. He eventually became "one of the most listened-to hellfire-and-brimstone radio preachers in the United States," in the words of Sam Kindrick, writer of the "Offbeat" column for the *San Antonio Morning Express* and author of *The Amazing Biography of Evangelist George W. Cooper.* Kindrick told of Cooper's early days in the ministry, when the evangelist's reputation was such that people from all over the county came to hear the reformed moonshiner preach the gospel. Cooper bought a tent and started a traveling spiritual tent show called the Cooper Evangelistic Party. He bought time on a local radio station in High Point, North Carolina—$18 a week for a daily fifteen-minute program. He spoke out against "grasshopper Christians," those who "hop on their faith when it behooves them and then hop off when it is to their advantage." He railed at those "religious nincompoops with their vulcanized spare-tire religion who go bumping through life, annoying other people." And he warned of the dangers of life in this glitzy world of fleeting pleasures. "I submit," he preached, "that all movies are bad, and there is no Christian who has any right to attend them, whether they are educational or not."

It seemed only natural that a man with such outspoken opinions would wind up on the border, and so it happened. In 1946 Reverend Cooper was holding a revival in Knoxville when a preacher by the name of J. Bozzel Mull approached him. J. Bozzel told George about a powerful radio station in Juárez, Mexico, that would sell time to preachers—fifteen minutes five nights a week for $800 per week. "To tell you the truth, George," J. Bozzel confided, "I just don't feel I can tackle anything this big."

George responded with the courage of a former midnight moonshiner. "I figured that all a mule can do is try," he said later. Cooper contacted Jack McVeigh, whose father-in-law, Will Branch, had built XELO and several other border stations. The terms seemed reasonable, and Cooper "packed up his tent and moved to El Paso." Within a year the *Cooper Old-fashioned Gospel Hour* was booming out from XERF, XEG, and XERB in addition to XELO.

Brother Cooper's success enabled him to build a studio in San Antonio to record his programs, and he continued preaching his noncompromising stand on the sins of the flesh. Dancing, miniskirts, lipstick, and the liberization of most denominational groups affronted Cooper and his hammer-and-tongs approach to the devil: "When some hear me say, 'You old beer-guzzling, liquor-soaked, wine-sipping, woman-chasing, bleary-eyed, peanut-brained, red-nosed, whitewashed, galvanized, petrified, dried-in-the-kiln, hypocritical deacon,' they remark, 'Oh, George, you shouldn't talk about the church that way.' Well, brother, if that's your church, it's in bad shape. The billy goat needs dehorning!'" Cooper's messages were "as simple and common as pig tracks" and stirred up deep emotions, even among those who could not fully appreciate his oratorical ability. "I am a deaf mute and cannot hear," wrote one fan, enclosing a $12 donation. "I am doing this for the Lord so others, who can hear you on the radio, may come to know Jesus. This is my prayer." Another listener did not take so kindly to Cooper's strict interpretation of the Scriptures and threatened to kill the preacher. Cooper announced the death threat over XEG and "D-double-dog-hog-tie"-dared the person to carry out the threat. For the most part, those who listened to Brother Cooper approved of him, and he received as many as 2500 pieces of mail a day in response to his broadcasts.

Cooper financed his ministry by offering listeners calendars, ballpoint pens, a Bible encyclopedia for $5, eight-by-ten color pictures of Brother and Mrs. Cooper for an offering of $3, thirteen multicolored Bible pictures, gospel albums, Scripture cards for every occasion, an automatic needle threader, a "large-print red-letter Bible approximately one-inch thick," and "a big surprise package of closeout items" for $5, among other things. Brother Cooper's wife, Verda Grace, sang gospel songs on the program and carried on the ministry after her husband passed away in 1974. Even after his death, some listeners could not forget Brother Cooper's powerful exhortations. As a woman from Arkansas wrote to Mrs. Cooper in 1975, "Some nites I almost think I hear Brother Cooper as yet. I cannot get used to him not being on the radio. His voice just thrilled me through and through."

Cowboy evangelist Dallas Turner came into the fold after a long border-radio career as a singing cowboy, pitchman, and ad rep. In the early fifties a tragic fire took the life of his young son, and the singer turned to the bottle. "I was bad to drink for seven years," he recalled. "I drank whiskey, Old Grand Dad, and Wild Turkey. I guess one of the fears I had when I was a drinking man was the fear of having to go to wine. Boy, I tell you, I wouldn't want to go to wine." Wine or no wine, high rolling and fast times finally caught up with the Nevada cowboy. Unhappy with his life, sitting in a run-down Kansas City motel, Turner took out a gun and was about to pull the trigger when he heard the strains of the old gospel favorite, "God Put a Rainbow in the Cloud," coming from his bedside radio. Heartened by the sound, Turner put down his gun and picked up Gideon's Bible, which he held fast to ever after.

Brother Turner got encouragement and spiritual guidance from many of his former radio associates and clients, including the Reverend Sam Morris and Brother Bill Guild, the announcer for the Carter Family. "Brother Bill prayed for me so many times," Turner later said. "He played a big part in my own conversion." But the early career of the young evangelist was a real struggle.

"I almost starved to death at the very beginning of my ministry," he remembered. "I went to one church one time where the offering was over a hundred dollars. The preacher stole all of the money, and I didn't get anything. Another time I got into a church where the snake handlers came in with a box of rattlesnakes. They played with the snakes while everybody fled for cover. Boy, I got out of there as soon as the show was over. Another time I booked a church and didn't know it was a love cult church. When I got in, they locked the gates, and while I preached, they had some beautiful gal that was fanning me. I didn't see anything indecent, except that some of the wives were sitting on the laps of other women's husbands. Well, I suddenly developed a very bad headache and got out of there very, very quickly at the end of the service."

The young preacher became known as the Cowboy Evangelist and published the story of his conversion in a booklet entitled "From Cocktails to Christ." He worked for the General Finance Company by day and developed a unique approach to the spiritual realm, combining Catholic beliefs in the communion of saints with a thorough understanding of metaphysics, which he studied from a mail-order course offered by his boss at the finance company through the Neotarian Fellowship. Turner delved into other areas of research as well. "I studied spiritualism from *A* to *Z*. I bet I have attended over five hundred seances in my lifetime. While ninety-five percent of the seances I attended were a complete fraud, I did see enough to convince me that it is possible to communicate with the other world. I have had visitations from Cowboy Slim Rinehart many times. My father, my mother, the priest I knew as a boy, and many, many others have appeared to me and communicated with me from the other side."

The blossoming evangelist eventually collected enough offerings to form his own organization, the International Church of Spiritual Vision. Incorporated under the laws of Nevada, Turner's church was one of America's few for-profit evangelical institutions. "I don't believe in nonprofit religious organizations," Turner said. "No place in the Bible can we find anyplace where Jesus Christ ever told anybody to open up a nonprofit organization. If so, I want to see the verse! Nonprofit religious organizations are set up for one reason, to get a junk-mailing permit."

Turner's long experience on the border left him wary of many of his fellow radio ministers, and numerous other evangelists felt the same way. "You know," said Turner, "my old buddy T. Texas Tyler, who was a great country singer, we used to be drinkin' buddies together before we got religion. He got religion before I did. And I remember what he told me after we both became evangelists. We were talking one time, and he said, 'You know, when I was a hillbilly singer out there, those gals, they would throw it in my face. But when I became an evangelist I found that those Holy Ghost sisters would rub it all over me.' And that is just exactly the way it is. You wonder why things down on the border turned out like they did. Well, I think a lot of it was because of the loose lives that some of those preachers have led and some of the gimmicks that they have used and the hatred that some of them saw fit to get on the air and attack the Catholics and the black people and the Jewish people and so on. I've always felt that if there is a heaven, and I know there is, and if there is a hell, and I know there is, that Yahweh, Infinite Intelligence, Almighty God, has a place worse than hell prepared for some of those individuals. Yes, I've always felt that some of them are sanctified and some of them are cranktified. They're the ones who completely destroyed border radio because they would keep coming up with their hate and the gimmicks, and Mexico just wouldn't tolerate it anymore. That's where it all started, and they destroyed border radio forever. By the sixties it was all over but the shouting."

Turner saw no incongruity in his border career changes from yodeling cowboy to pitchman to evangelist. "The border stations, in my opinion, have always been the most honest stations on the air," he asserted. "Everything advertised has always carried an ironclad money-back guarantee. And the border stations reached the audience that I wanted to reach. When I was a singing cowboy, I reached the people who still loved the old-time songs—the people out there in the small towns all over the world." Those same small-town dwellers responded well to Turner's preaching of the Bible and have made Turner's many years in radio evangelism "very, very satisfying."

Another of the most popular border preachers, the Reverend J. C. Bishop, followed a career path similar to Turner's. Born in Ozona, Texas, a small town about 110 miles from Del Rio, Bishop grew up on a ranch in the thirties. "I learned to play the guitar and sing," Bishop remembered. "When they asked me to go on that superpowered Brinkley station, XERA, I'd have to say it scared the daylights out of me." Bishop overcame his fear, and at the age of seventeen appeared regularly on XERA, singing cowboy yodeling songs in the style of Jimmie Rodgers. By the time he was nineteen, Bishop was a wild West Texas teenager, living a fast life and driving even faster: "I was racing in a car with another young fella, and we went end over end about six times, going about seventy miles per hour. And I came out of the accident with a broken back and spent two years in a wheelchair. Then I heard about some people in San Antonio, Texas, that claimed that you could be healed. So, you know, a drowned man will grasp for anything." Bishop went to San Antonio and listened to the faith healers. He was skeptical and looked for loopholes in their faith and in their religion. Despite his wariness, he was eventually converted and was "up and going" soon thereafter, even though the best medical doctors had given him no chance of ever leaving his wheelchair. "That's what got me into this kind of work," he confessed.

Bishop moved to Dallas and established "an old-fashioned sawdust-floor, Billy Sunday-type tabernacle" there. For a few years he preached in the sawdust, until he was invited in the mid-forties by the management of XEG in Monterrey, Mexico, to put a show on the air. "I took this morning broadcast on XEG, just, I guess you'd have to say, by faith. Had never done it before in my life, for a religious broadcast. It finally caught on, and I stayed on XEG for over twenty years, at six a.m. every morning, seven days a week." About six months later, the managers of XERF invited Bishop to appear on their station once again, this time as a preacher. Bishop agreed and became one of the most popular border preachers in the following decades.

The format of Bishop's program was simple and sincere: "I'd say,

'Hello, everyone. This is Brother J.C. Bishop speaking to you direct from our radio studios here in the city of Dallas, Texas.' We'd organize a little prayer group who would consecrate themselves at the meeting every night and pray for people that needed help. I went on the air and asked people, if you were in trouble, marital trouble, sick, or afflicted, broken home, broken heart, financial troubles, that the good Lord said He'd supply all of our needs. I said, 'Call on us to pray for you because the Bible does say send your requests to God.' So people began to write me and tell me their troubles and ask us to pray for them. As simple as that. We met every night, and we would take these requests and lay them out, and we would pray for these people."

In addition to praying over the letters, Brother Bishop played gospel music on his fifteen-minute programs, selections from the Speer Family, the Happy Goodmans, the Musical Hearts, or the Chuckwagon Gang, whom Brother Bishop rated as "the best gospel singers in the country." The response to Brother Bishop's simple message was strongly supportive. "I guess I have over ten thousand letters," Bishop said, "authentic letters from people declaring that their prayers were answered. Some of them are hard to believe. They are absolutely miraculous. That's what kept me in it. People seemingly were getting help. It's as simple as that."

Letters came from as far away as England, Poland, and the Hawaiian Islands, sometimes as many as a thousand letters a day. "On the radio I would ask people, 'If you feel like you've really gotten help, well, send us a little offering of some kind so we can tell others about it.' So they would do that. . . . They would send offerings, mostly one, two, five, and ten dollars. They would send it because they felt like they'd received help and they wanted to help someone else." Radio listeners trusted Brother Bishop, and he did his best not to betray that trust. "A rancher from Oklahoma sent me a check one time for two hundred seventy-five dollars and wrote, 'I just sold some prize bulls here. You take out seventy-five dollars and return the two hundred dollars back to me.' So I did."

Brother Bishop remembered getting burned by negative coverage of his evangelistic work in the press: "When we first opened these daily broadcasts, the *Saturday Evening Post* sent representatives to my office and said, 'We just want to ask questions about your work. We're impressed with it.' And I said, 'Well, on one condition. We're sincere in what we're doing, and we don't want to be burlesqued. We don't want to be smeared.' 'Oh, no,' they said. 'The Post doesn't do anything like that.' So I allowed them to take two or three pictures, and, boy, they came out with the biggest smear they could. But the funniest thing happened. Right after this big smear went across the nation, my mail jumped nearly a hundred letters a day. People would say, 'Oh, I read the most wonderful article about you in the *Saturday Evening Post*. Here. I want you to pray for me.' What they meant as a smear, I say the good Lord turned into a blessing."

Brother Bishop was well aware that not all of the border preachers were as honorable in their activities as he was. "We're sincere in what we're doing," he said. "And we don't go at all for the fanatical things that people do, claiming all this kind of power." Brother Bishop worked hard for his "type audience," as he put it. "The working people, the house-wives, the homemaker, the rancher, the farmer—that's the kind of people we thought like we could reach the best. In fact, that was the bulk of our listening audience. . . . And it's miraculous how we kept it going."

Born in Ridgeland, South Carolina, in 1935, the Reverend Frederick Eikerenkoetter II, Th.B., Ph.D., D.Sc.L., commonly known as Reverend Ike, was the son of a preacher man and described himself as follows: "I am unreal. I am incredible. I am unbelievable to those who think only on the limited consciousness level of mind." The Reverend began his amazing Bible-thumping career as the fourteen-year-old faith-healing associate pastor of the Bible Way Baptist Church in Ridgeland. "I have saved a lot of souls," remarked Rev Ike in later days. "It must have been me who saved them, too, 'cause most of them have backslidden already. . . . I'd knock people down and pray over them and grease them with oil and give them prayer cloths. I used to break up canes and yank people out of wheelchairs. I'd either heal them or kill them." After graduating from high school, attending several fundamentalist Bible colleges, and serving two years as a chaplain in the Air Force, Reverend Ike made his way to the border.

"I started Reverend Ike on XERF, back in '61 or '62," remembered Wolfman Jack, another personality not known for his low self-esteem. "He was a young man at the time and wanted to go into broadcasting. He came down with a bagful of money and wanted to buy three time slots. I talked him out of that and only gave him two. He paid in advance for the whole year."

The broadcasting deal struck at that historic meeting between the Wolfman and the self-proclaimed Divine Sweetheart of the Universe led to one of the most dramatic evangelistic-broadcasting careers of the twentieth century. Reverend Ike soon founded the Miracle Temple in Boston and then moved to New York City. After two years of preaching out of a dilapidated movie theater on 125th Street in the heart of Harlem, Reverend Ike underwent a metamorphosis in his approach to preaching. He was quoted in 1969 as saying, "I am fed up with it. I've had it with all these ideas and this tradition and I can't preach it anymore." He warned his listeners and followers, "My presentation is going to change. Right now I sound just like another Holy Roller, but when I get my philosophy together, I will change my method of presentation." Addressing his fellow preachers with a warning about his impending change of style, Reverend Ike said, "With all due respect, there are different strokes for different folks."

And change he did. Telling his followers, "You can't lose with the stuff I use," Reverend Ike styled himself "the first chocolate minister to preach positive self-image psychology and positive motivation in the evangelistic context." The *Amsterdam News*, Harlem's leading newspaper, called him "the first and only non-white to operate on a sophisticated mass media level." Under the new umbrella organization, the United Christian Evangelistic Association, Reverend Ike abandoned all pretense of being a fundamentalist and became a supercharged black Norman Vincent Peale, a rapping philosopher of prosperity consciousness who sought the betterment of his followers through mind power. "We are not interested in pie in the sky bye and bye," preached Reverend Ike from XEG, XERF, and more than 1500 other stations in the early seventies. "We want our pie now, with ice cream on it and a cherry on top."

Rev Ike was a guru of immediate gratification: "Stick around. Don't be a clown. Pick up on what I'm puttin' down." Mind power could be used most effectively in overcoming what Reverend Ike perceived as the major evil in the ghetto and the major stumbling block to the advancement of the black community—poverty. He preached that "the lack of money is the root of all evil." He urged his followers, "Don't be a hypocrite about money. Admit it openly and inwardly that you like money. Say, 'I like money. I need money. I want money. I love money in its right place. Money is not sinful. Money is good.'" He talked to his parishioners who were tired of "short stakes and bad breaks," telling them to "get out of the ghetto and get into the get mo'.'" He reminded his radio friends that "right ideas make millionaires" and used Henry Ford and Thomas Edison as examples of men who had used mind power to make their ideas succeed, "for mind power is God power, mind power is money-getting power. It takes mind power to get green power." Quoting Ecclesiastes 10:19 as saying, "Money answers all things," Reverend Ike preached that "the best thing you can do for the poor is not to be one of them. . . . If you give a man a fish, you can feed him for a day; teach him how to fish and you'll feed him forever." Reverend Ike continued, "Welfare has its place, but don't make it a resting place."

The mind-power campaign that Reverend Ike broadcast over the border blasters became tremendously popular. In the seventies he used a Boston mailing address and was New England's biggest post office customer. His mailing list contained more than two million names. Reverend Ike admitted that he did not read all the letters but understood their meaning through "subconscious correlation" and "vibratory affinity." He even proclaimed the effectiveness of "graphotherapeutics," or the act of being healed by just writing a letter. His periodical *Action!* blared headlines describing the good things that came from Reverend Ike's blessing plan: THIS LADY BLESSED WITH A NEW CADILLAC, SECRET HAIR GROWTH FORMULA REVEALED, SISTER RAG MUFFIN NOW WEARS MINK TO CHURCH, BLESSED WITH NEW BUICK IN 45 MINUTES. After one woman followed Reverend Ike's Visualization Prayer Treatment, a headline screamed, HER VISUALIZATION TURNED INTO A FABULOUS CARIBBEAN CRUISE. Reverend Ike relied on a tried-and-true border technique to get responses to his broadcasts—the prayer cloth.

Reverend Ike urged his followers to write him for their own special prayer cloth, a three-by-five-inch piece of soft, bright red synthetic fabric with serrated edges. He quoted Acts 19:11-12, as scriptural support for the healing power of his fabric: "From his body were brought unto the sick handerkerchiefs or aprons, and the diseases departed from them and the evil spirits went out of them." He promised to "tell you how to use it for healing and blessing, for deliverance of those with habits like drinking, narcotics, tobacco, for breaking evil power, witchcraft, and many other things." Many listeners told Reverend Ike about the power of the prayer cloth. One woman said that she tried to get a fighting couple to make up by cutting her cloth in two and putting the pieces under the twin beds of the dueling twosome. The trick worked, and Reverend Ike approved. "You did that?" he cried over the air. "You rascal, you! Let's all give God a great big hand."

In addition to offering prayer cloths and methods of immediate wish fulfillment, Reverend Ike was not at all shy about asking for monetary donations. Wearing expensive suits and heavy gold and silver jewelry and proclaiming, "I come to you lookin' good, feelin' good, and smellin' good," Reverend Ike quoted Revelation 22:12: "I will pay every man according to his works," with the emphasis on the word "pay." His literature was covered with headlines like THE QUICKER THE GIVING, THE QUICKER THE PAYOFF! THE MORE THE GIVING, THE MORE THE PAYOFF! and he exhorted his followers, "If necessary, borrow some money to give." The man who sipped water from a silver chalice while preaching warned his followers, "Don't be too lazy to write or too stingy to give" and reminded them, "When you stop giving, you stop your blessing." The money did pour in to Reverend Ike, making him one of the most financially successful border preachers of all time. By the mid-seventies, Reverend Ike was so successful that he took out ads in the *Wall Street Journal*, inviting the financial community to stop "living bear" and being "bullied by the lack of money."

Through the years dozens of preachers with a bewildering myriad of beliefs and practices rode the airwaves of the border blasters into the late-night consciousnesses of listeners around the world. Preachers were the economic mainstay of the border blasters. "Without the preachers, you couldn't make any real money," confessed Wolfman Jack. The preachers were so important to the managers of XEG that they were enshrined in the station's theme. "From early evening, till late at night, the gospel voice to help you think right. Stayed tuned to ten-fifty on your dial to ease the burden of life's many trials. XEG, ten-fifty."

Each border preacher carved out a special niche among the listening audience. Dr. Gerald Winrod promoted Harry Hoxsey's cancer cure and mixed quotations from Scripture with attacks on the "godless communists," telling hair-raising stories of FBI agents who had infiltrated communist organizations in the United States. He urged his listeners to subscribe to his periodical, *The Defender,* and to order one of his many books, including the classic *Atomic Power in Prophecy.* Billy James Hargis, who was to run afoul of the FCC in the famous Red Lion case, addressed his radio audience with a soft-spoken Arkansas drawl. He told of the erosion of American morals, at one time citing a Supreme Court ruling that it was legal to wear the American flag on the seat of one's pants. Hargis contended that the ruling had done more to harm the country than anything the Supreme Court could have done. He commented further, "How can the Supreme Court justify such disrespect? A person wearing the American flag on the seat of his pants has only one message—that is contempt for this country. . . . He cannot impress us with his disrespect . . . for it is indeed sick." Hargis offered his listeners the opportunity to travel with him to the Holy Land, touring Bethlehem and Golgotha in "new Mercedes buses, air-conditioned when they're needed." He told his audience that "the reason so many folks go with Billy James Hargis to the Holy Land" is because "our prices are so much more economical"—$749 for all expenses paid, and no extra charge for visiting the popular site of Petra.

Brother A. B. McReynolds warned his audience with a heated croaking of "the yellow traveler . . . the so-called liberal," whom Brother McReynolds described as "a thousand times more deadly and dangerous than the communists." Brother McReynolds moaned, "Liberalism is the oldest and most deadly disease, worse than leprosy and cancer. It has destroyed nations, just as cancer and leprosy destroys the individual. . . . Oh, I tell ya, we need to *prrrraaaayyyyyy* for America." For many years Paul Kallinger was the announcer for the *Lifeline* program, underwritten by oil tycoon and food faddist H. L. Hunt. *Lifeline* warned listeners of the many dangers of modern life, including communism and the evils of marijuana. The program also advertised spinach, "a leafy green plant that everyone likes," as well as other food products marketed under the billionaire's own HLH label.

"I found the answer—I learned to pray." These stirring words introduced *The Bible Institute of the Air,* hosted by Dr. C. W. Burpo (that's "Bur-*po*," with the emphasis on the last syllable). Dr. Burpo spent a good deal of his broadcasting time secluded in "the throne room" and his "secret closet of prayer," places where he could be alone with God. As he left his private chambers, he asked his listeners, "Will you lay everything on the altar and come outside where I am? . . . I think we'd better shut the door and leave all our troubles with God." *Clunk*—the sound effect of a door closing assured the audience of the reverend's sincerity.

When Dr. Burpo was not in his secret closet of prayer, much of his preaching dealt with politics. "If you feel you are too busy to take an interest in your government," Dr. Burpo warned, "teach your children to count in rubles—that is Russian money." Confusing photographic and defense technologies in one overzealous moment, Dr. Burpo wrote in his *Bible Institute News* of "widespread public indifference concerning the threat of world communism. . . . There are Polaroid submarines with atomic power pointed at every major city in the U.S." Dr. Burpo saw terrifying tendencies in the American education system as well: "The enemies of our country creep insidiously into our schools and churches. They use . . . phrases like 'human rights, above property rights, and security above all,' which in reality are snares that lead our country toward autocratic government by mob rule." Dr. Burpo supported his ministry by offering record albums, including the first, second, and third albums of songs by Dr. Burpo, and books like *Throne Room Rights* and *Dr. Burpo Goes to Washington*. He gave his mailing address in Mesa (M-E-S-A), Arizona, many times during each broadcast, in the hopes that his listeners would "write a man that seems as peculiar as I am."

Brother Lester Roloff preferred to stay out of politics and concerned himself instead with religious education. He began broadcasting the *Family Altar Program* on May 4, 1944, and used his radio time "to trumpet the truth that sets people free." He told people to avoid the Revised Standard Version of the Bible, referring to it as "the rotten Sinful Version," and preached on the evils of alcohol: "Statistics show ten thousand people killed by liquor annually, while only one is killed by a mad dog. Yet we shoot the mad dog and license the liquor. That's strange, isn't it?" Brother Roloff found other things about the world strange as well. He included a story about "a little poodle dog" in one sermon.

"Somebody snipped a little skin at a pet spa," he said, "and the owners said he'd been mentally retarded and traumatized. The court gave nine thousand dollars for a little poodle dog. Oh, get mad at me if you want to, dear friends, but I tell you, I wish we could get interested in people again." Brother Roloff's interest in people led him to run the Rebekah Home for Girls outside Corpus Christi. When the Texas welfare agency ordered his home closed in 1973 for not having a state license, Brother Roloff began a seven-year campaign against the Lone Star State, eventually winning his case with the support of Governor William P. Clements. Brother Roloff financed his legal campaign in part with the sale of "bacteriostatic water treatment units," which came in various models—sink mount, wall mount, or hose adapter for RV units, priced from $76 to $130 each. The purchase of the units helped Brother Roloff carry on his ministry and pay his legal fees while allowing listeners to "enjoy the full flavor of fruits and vegetables."

While politics absorbed the energies of many radio preachers, the vast majority addressed themselves to helping with the spiritual and physical troubles of their flock. The Reverend E. E. Duncan, "a man that walks and talks with God," claimed to have personally visited his "holy and elder brother" Jesus Christ. "When I went into the Holy City," Brother Duncan breathed over the airwaves in a low, throaty voice, "Jesus placed on me a golden crown and a golden girdle. I talked with Jesus for some time then in heaven in my own body just like I am now. . . . Of course, with me talking to God face-to-face as Moses had, I'm one of the most sought-after men in the world today." Brother Duncan also claimed great blessings for those who were able to attend his prayer services: "Many totally blind received their sight in one service. Stretcher cases got up and walked—all of them. The wheelchairs was all emptied. Deaf and dumb could both hear and speak after prayer." For those who could not attend the prayer meetings, Brother Duncan offered "a prayer cloth that laid in God's footsteps of compassion," as well as a free little Bible. He urged recipients to "place this prayer cloth in your billfold, shoe, clothes, or wherever the Lord leads you. Take it with you when you transact your business."

Brother Mack Watson was also fortunate enough to be a direct witness to God's supernatural power. "I felt the angel of God touch me on the shoulder in my radio room," confessed Brother Watson. Immediately after the visitation, Brother Watson "got a whole bunch of miracle packages" out of his prayer tower and proceeded to bless them. He encouraged those who were "sick or tired or whatever" to write for the packages, which included anointing oil, a prayer cloth, and a scarlet thread. Brother Spencer distributed special prayer cloths, "red for devils and demons, white for healing the body, or gold for financial blessing." Not satisfied with a prayer cloth, Thea F. Jones of the Evangelistic Association, Inc., urged his audience, "Write me, and I will send you the hem of His garment, and send you instructions what to do to receive your miracle. Don't pass it up. Don't miss your blessing, for God told me to do this."

Brother David Epley, pastor of the Baptist Church of the Good Shepherd, was probably the most sophisticated marketer among the radio preachers. In addition to providing listeners with the "unusual rose prayer cloth" that, according to testimonials, healed a stroke, cured cancer, removed paralysis, and brought in $22,000, Brother Epley offered a choice of various holy oils: oil of gladness, oil of joy, oil of healing, or oil of prosperity. Along with the oil, Pastor Epley distributed "Your Contact Healing Chart," a Visible Man rendition of the human body with lines, boxes, and names drawn to specific body parts. Pastor Epley recommended, "PLEASE CHECK THE BOX NEXT TO BODY ORGAN YOU NEED PRAYER FOR. NOW ANOINT WITH OIL THE PLACE ON THE CHART YOU NEED A HEALING TOUCH." Brother Epley also instructed his correspondents in the Miracle "Bread Braking" (sic) Service. "Remember the 7th Slice," he advised, giving a hint to the power of a ritual that might appropriately be described as the best thing to happen to the spiritual community since sliced bread.

Other border preachers used their broadcasting time to prophesy the end of the world, sometimes in horrifying detail. Brother James Bishop Carr of Palmdale, California, warned that the "curse of the bad figs" was on all nations and exhorted his listeners to "be freed from the slavery of the Pope Gregory calendar" so as to avoid the "punishment for all that follow after false Gregorian calendar dates." He held out the welcome invitation to be "free from the burden of the spirit of Christmas," emphasizing that the apostles "never heard of or celebrated Christmas, the Roman New Year of January 1, or Easter, Palm Sunday, or any other Saturday or Sunday." Brother Carr worked out his own calendar, disclosed to him by the Lord. By Brother Carr's reckoning, Jesus was born in October, not December, and was going to return again on his birthday. Although Brother Carr wasn't sure of the exact year of the Second Coming, he was sure of the total blackout and the great earthquake that was to follow, and he offered to send information concerning the dates when a "wise and holy angel" would come, bringing salvation to the city of each of his radio listeners.

Evangelist Bill Beeny refused to tell his zip code over the air, since he regarded the numerical postal sorting system as a plot to confuse the nation. Brother Beeny foretold a violent end for the present world and offered his listeners the opportunity to receive for a contribution of $25 a Riot Pack containing a stove, five fuel cans, a rescue gun, a radio, and the marvelous Defender, a weapon that discouraged attackers by covering them with a blue dye. Or for the not-so-well-heeled listener, a $10 donation brought a blue steel, pearl-handled, tear-gas pistol plus the inspirational Truth-Pac #4. Those with concrete plans for Judgment Day heeded closely the words of Brother Beeny.

Brother David Terrell was the most extreme prophet of doom to appear on the border stations. Brother Terrell's broadcasts were outbursts of incredible energy, usually taped live at prayer meetings. Shouting at peak volume for as long as twenty minutes at a time, Brother Terrell delivered discontinuous tirades with warnings, pronouncements of doom, and feisty assertions of his own preeminence as an apostle of the Lord. "I shall smite ye with insanity. I shall smite ye with violence. I shall smite ye in your knees. I shall smite ye in your elbows. I shall smite ye in your shoulders. I shall smite ye in your bones. . . . and man shall see diseases that medical science has not been able to diagnose. For the earth is fixin' to be cursed with a curse. They that robbed me in America is fixin' to be cursed. I'm fixin' to make the rich be eaten. I'm fixin' to eat the rich. . . . There's fixin' to be a frog epidemic in Florida, like in the time of Moses," Brother Terrell prophesied. "Two toads can produce twenty-five thousand frogs a year so that there can be millions in a square mile. Right now there's a plague has hit this nation. Minnesota is being eaten up by caterpillars, and Canada is five inches deep in caterpillars. Beetles are coming across Mexico and headed this way. In Georgia, hail is eight inches thick. Automobiles have been beat to a total loss." Brother Terrell urged his listeners to deny the flesh and to fast often. "Moan, my people. Moan until your bowels feel like they are going to burst in you. Moan until your voices are hoarse. Moan until you hurt in your chest. . . . Cry until you weep. Fast until you weep. . . . Let me hear the cry, the cry for renewal, or I'll rip you apart." He warned of sartorial dangers in the land: "The print designs on the cloth and men wearing things that do not appertain to he-men! And everyone that wears this strange apparel is going to receive punishment from God." Oftentimes the power of the Spirit became too much for Brother Terrell, and he spoke only in tongues. "Rapha, nissi, handa bahayah, lamaricosayahilatarisaya honodabbabayaya bokokori." As one observer noted, Brother Terrell "doesn't have gears meshed in with the business world or the church world. He just lives in a little world of his own."

As strange as the border preachers might seem to those Americans whose religiosity leads them to the more established and less vociferous churches, the evangelists on the whole provided a great deal of help to their listeners. The majority of them provided psychological mechanisms to assist their listeners with a myriad of spiritual, physical, and financial problems. Some preachers, like Brother Terrell, were more outlandish than others, but most seemed to believe sincerely that they had a mission in life, and they sought funds from their listeners for the primary purpose of carrying on that mission. As with any group of individuals, however, there were several border preachers who were not so well intentioned or who at least seemed to be involved with the dark side of the spiritual universe.

In the late forties, regular listeners to XERF could hear the voice of the Reverend J. Charles Jessup leading his five brothers in song and pleading for money to "keep this little boy from the clay hills of Alabama on the air. I'm your brother. I'm doing the best I can. Won't you, friend, send me your offering today?" For more than a decade Brother Jessup was a regular feature on the border stations, delivering what *Time* magazine called "high-pitched nasal prayers for whatever his listeners suggest." Fast-paced western swing music introduced his broadcast, *The Old-fashioned Gospel Program*. With high-speed rhythmic speech punctuated by quick breathing, Brother Jessup filled the airwaves with sermons he recorded at revival meetings. "My friend, you may not conceive of it, modernists may not accept it, church members may not conceive of it, and some of you may be so stupid that you won't acknowledge it, but let me say this—he that is born of God cannot sin." Brother Jessup ended every broadcast with a prayer. "Friends in radio land, there's somebody that loves you tonight, and that somebody is Jesus. I'm praying every night that God'll let these messages *burn* within the heart of every listener. Man, why don't you give up that life of sin and straighten up your life? . . . Jesus, with those nail-scarred hands, is passing your way tonight." Brother Jessup told his listeners of his amazing healing power. "Now, I've prayed for people that have been healed of blindness, of deafness, total paralysis, and many other such like disease, even leprosy. And I want to say God gave me the gift of healing." He assured his listeners that he would include their letters in all-night prayer vigils and would appreciate any and all "free-will offerings."

The federal postal service, however, did not appreciate Brother Jessup's use of the mail. In 1964 the reverend was arrested and charged with fraudulent solicitation of funds. Although Brother Jessup maintained that the charges "are so completely ridiculous that it is difficult to believe they are seriously and honestly made," the court did not agree.

"Instead of praying for the people, you preyed on them," said U.S. judge Dan M. Russell, Jr., of New Orleans, who found Jessup, his ex-wife, Rose Oden Jessup, and their partner, Murphy M. Maddux, guilty of tax evasion and mail fraud. "I have no sympathy for you," the judge continued. "You have larceny in your heart." The court found that Jessup and his organization, the Fellowship Revival Association, had collected more than $10 million for charity work in Mexico but had spent it instead on real estate, cars, boats, seaplanes, and cockfighting. Funds that Jessup collected for a faith hospital allegedly went into his own pocket, while the hospital remained a vacant hotel building in Gulfport, Mississippi. The indictment further charged that Jessup represented himself as "a holy and devout man whose life was devoted to God's work, a man who had talked with God," and yet he had concealed that he had been married four times, the last time to a fifteen-year-old girl while he was still married to his third wife.

Jessup paid a few thousand dollars in fines, served a year in prison, and was on probation for five years, during which time he was forbidden to engage in self-promotion activities. With the indomitable spirit of a border blaster, however, Brother Jessup returned to the airwaves after his probation and preached the gospel regularly over XERF and other border stations to a small but faithful audience.

"Thousands of people from all church denominations who are tired and disgusted with cold, dead religious form and tradition and who are hungry for the reality of God's blessing are coming into these great crusades and are finding salvation for the soul, healing for their bodies, deliverance from demon powers, nicotine, alcohol, dope, witchcraft, spirits, and the curse of poverty." Thus ended each border radio broadcast of Brother Asa Alonso, or A. A. Allen, "the fiery evangelist of whom *Look* magazine says, 'He feels, he heals, he turns you on with God.'" Brother Allen was one of the most popular of the border preachers, an old-style Bible-thumper and faith healer who was as at home on the sawdust floor of his Miracle Restoration Revival tent as he was in a recording studio.

A. A. Allen began his life in 1911, in Sulphur Rock, Arkansas, far from the side of the Lord. His father was a confirmed alcoholic, and A. A. himself was smoking at age six, was having sex at age twelve, and was married to a common-law wife by age eighteen. "If my family had a coat of arms," he preached, "it would have been a beer bucket with a gin bottle emblazoned on it." He converted to the Lord in the mid-thirties, becoming a minister with the Assemblies of God, and made his living playing a $12 Montgomery Ward guitar and singing religious songs "in one key." By 1947 he was pastor of a church in Corpus Christi, and was a devoted follower of Oral Roberts' healing ministry. In 1951 he bought a tent and started holding the powerfully moving revival meetings for which he was to become famous. In 1953 he made his first purchases of time on the radio, and the Allen Revival Hour was on the air.

Allen's broadcasts consisted of tapes of actual services, during which Allen performed miraculous faith healings through prayer. The pages of his *Miracle Magazine* described some of the healings. IN THREE DAYS HYDROCEPHALUS DISAPPEARS! LEG INSTANTLY GROWS 1 1/2 INCHES, WIFE RETURNS, BREAST REMOVED BY SURGERY RESTORED were some of the headlines. Brother Allen asserted that his revivals were the "sure cure for cancer." DELIVERED FROM 11-POUND TUMOR screamed a headline of one testimonial. I TOOK MY CANCER TO CHURCH IN A JAR, proclaimed another.

At the height of his popularity in the sixties, Brother Allen published more than 55 million pieces of literature a year, and *Miracle Magazine* had a monthly circulation of 350,000. With a staff of 185 persons and a multimillion-dollar organization, Brother Allen created an entire community at Miracle Valley, consisting of 2500 acres of purchased and donated land near Bisbee, Arizona. He founded the Miracle Valley Bible College, built an airstrip, founded a record company that produced dozens of gospel albums, and started the Miracle Valley Estates subdivision. He built a "pool of Bethesda" with healing waters in the development, and a twelve-sided wood and cut-stone mansion for himself with a swimming pool covered by a simulated stained glass canopy.

Throughout his career Brother Allen stayed in close touch with the fears and sufferings of his followers. He challenged the racial barriers in the late fifties, stating that "souls are all one color," and he preached that "black helps white and white helps black to find God" to mixed groups of white and black believers. In 1960, during the Cuban Missile Crisis, he asked his followers, "What can be done when the A-bomb falls? Once again, God has the answer!" and then he announced "God's cure for radiation poisoning." He warned his readers of the terror to come after the bomb falls: "Present plans of the military and civil defense call for removing survivors from a bombed area as promptly as possible to a decontamination center. There the victims will be sorted out, like grading potatoes. . . . The incurables can only be hauled away to pens where they will be left to await death. . . . Yes, God can and will heal even radiation poisoning." Allen even used the A-bomb theme in marketing homes near Miracle Valley, advertising the "lowest atomic fallout in the world."

Brother Allen's broadcasts were taped live at his healing services "under the greatest gospel tent in the world." The redheaded Allen, who fancied green and lavender suits, whipped his audiences into a healing frenzy. Sometimes he had to work hard to achieve the proper fever pitch. "Some of you won't shout," he accused. "Well, why don't you go to hell? I don't like to preach like this, but I got to." While believers, lost in the

Spirit, moaned and shouted in tongues in the background, Brother Allen went about his healing. "Look at this little baby girl," he said. "She has a hole in her heart. . . . Now we're gonna ask the Great Surgeon, the greatest the world has ever known. He's a lung specialist. He's an eye, ear, nose, and throat specialist. He's a bone specialist. He's a brain specialist. But best of all, he's a heart specialist. He said, 'Behold, I will give you a new heart and put a new spirit within you.'" The preacher addressed his prayers to the believers in "death row," a lineup of those suffering from exceptionally serious maladies. "I saw the spirit of God come upon that woman and knocked her down into the shavings. . . . Is that Bible? Remember John said, 'I fell at his feet as one dead.'" Brother Allen replaced kneecaps, lifted old men from wheelchairs, and cured arthritis with the words "Be healed." He replaced fillings and urged his followers, "Let God be your dentist." A crowd in Fresno, California, thrilled to the testimony of a former hermaphrodite who "was slain under the power of God" at an Allen revival and was reborn "a real man." Another believer lived 21 years as a woman before Brother Allen's healing touch turned him into a man. His wife declared, "He's all man now," to which Brother Allen responded, "Surely his wife should know?" Brother Allen was always careful to give the actual miracle worker his due. "I never healed anybody," he explained. "God heals them. I just pray. I encourage people to come worship God. Healing's just a bonus. It "occasionally involves driving out some demon." A disclaimer in *Miracle Magazine* stated that "A. A. Allen Revivals Inc. and 'Miracle Magazine' assume no legal responsibility for the veracity of any report nor do they accept responsibility as to the degree of permanency of reported healings" and cited John 5:14 as saying, "For those who do not continue to live for God, even worse things may come."

To support his work, Brother Allen asked for gifts from his listeners, warning them to give in order to keep God happy, "because it is a fearful thing to fall into the hands of an angry God." In addition, he offered his radio listeners a wide range of Miracle items to be sent upon request. Listeners were encouraged to ask for Miracle Sawdust, gathered from the floor of the tent, or Miracle Beans (Buried for centuries with the dead, so old and dry even color was indistinguishable, Miracle Beans have a message for you!). Some particularly powerful items were available only to those who were lucky enough to see the reverend in person. At one revival in Chicago Brother Allen "became inspired under the anointing of God to take his shirttail out and tear his shirttail and sleeves into shreds." According to *Miracle Magazine,* "Multitudes surged to the platform to obtain a bit of cloth from the torn shirt." Donation pitches were handled more directly at the meetings themselves. "The Scriptures say you got to vow and pay, vow and pay, vow and pay," chanted Brother Don, one of Allen's assistant preachers. "You got to promise God, and you got to keep your promise. If you want him to lift your pain, to make you whole, to bring you joy, you got to have faith. Faith. And faith is to vow and pay."

With success came challenges to Allen's ministry, as preachers, reporters, and government officials tried to tear down the walls of Miracle Valley with accusations of fraud. Brother Allen fought against them, shouting over the airwaves about the "racketeering preachers" who questioned his healings and sought to undermine his message to the faithful. In Knoxville, Tennessee, Allen's followers slugged a newspaper reporter suspected of attempting to mislead the public and warned him not to return. Using a more subtle approach, Brother Allen had his own photographers take pictures of a *Sacramento Bee* reporter. Allen later displayed the pictures and pointed out the three demons clearly visible above the reporter's head, demons that bore a strong resemblance to other demons that Brother Allen periodically displayed in formaldehyde-filled jars during his revivals.

Even those who found themselves in conflict with Brother Allen admitted he had a special gift. In 1959 the Internal Revenue Service challenged the nonprofit standing of Allen's organization. The IRS ruled that Allen's function as a faith healer was similar to a doctor's function and taxable as such, and they demanded $247,000 in back taxes from the reverend. Brother Allen countersued in the Fort Worth federal tax court and won in 1963, with the court ruling that healing was a basic tenet of Allen's religious work.

Although Brother Allen was able to defeat the devilish press and the even more demonic IRS, there was one demon that he could not overcome—demon rum. Allen was arrested for drunk driving in Knoxville in 1955 and forfeited his bail rather than stand trial. He later contended that he had been kidnapped and knocked unconscious and that his enemies had poured liquor down his throat. Despite his disclaimer, he was dismissed by the Assemblies of God and became a nondenominational preacher. In later years charges of drunkenness haunted Allen in Cleveland, Las Vegas, and Laguna Beach, California, each incident decried as press persecution by a sobered-up Brother Allen.

In the mid-sixties, Allen claimed to have received a special power from the Lord, the power to raise the dead. Unlike his mentor Oral Roberts, who once made such a claim only to retract it later, Brother Allen firmly believed in his power over the Grim Reaper. Allen told his followers that he had raised two small children from the dead and announced on the radio that all who came to his next revival should "come expecting the dead to be raised." Pictures in *Miracle Magazine* showed large groups of people "taking the 'Raise the Dead' step with Reverend Allen," walking up a ramp "on which was placed a prayer rug made for the old Miracle Tent." Brother Allen's necromantic abilities caused an uproar among his followers, some of whom reportedly sent the bodies of their dearly beloved to the deserts of southern Arizona. Response to Allen's newfound ability was so great that he was forced to issue a "STATEMENT CONCERNING RAISING THE DEAD!" in *Miracle Magazine*. In the statement Allen reminded his followers, "The law today forbids the holding of the dead beyond a reasonable period of time. The law also forbids individuals from moving the dead. . . . We do not knowingly encourage any person to do anything that is unlawful or unscriptural." Brother Allen noted that in each case "where the dead were raised, the minister was either on the scene or went to the scene. In no case was the dead body transported to another place for prayer. It is against the law." The statement ended on a more hopeful note: "Medical science is having great success in developing new ways to bring the dead back to life. They feel that sudden death is a needless waste and that a large percentage of those that die suddenly can be resuscitated."

One of those influenced by Allen's raise-the-dead theology was evangelical TV personality Tammy Faye Bakker, who with her husband, Jim, starred on the glitzy *PTL Club* show. As a child, Tammy sang at Allen's tent revival meetings. "I was so small Mr. Allen would pick me up and put me on a chair in front of the microphone," she remembered. Years later, when her pet Chihuahua named Chi Chi died, Jim handed the dog's body to a realtor showing their home and asked the puzzled salesman to dispose of the pet.

Recalling the ministrations of A. A. Allen, Tammy pleaded, "Jim, have them keep Chi Chi for a couple of days. Please, don't let them bury him right away because I know God can raise things from the dead. Please, don't let them bury Chi Chi."

She prayed for Christ to raise Chi Chi from the dead but finally adopted a more pragmatic approach to the issue of canine resurrection. "The fact was," Tammy wrote in her autobiography, *I Gotta Be Me*, "that Chi Chi was a naughty little dog. I loved him so much, but several times I had wanted to give him away because he wet on our drapes, especially when he'd get mad at us. He'd chew on everything. We never knew what he would tear up next. But you see, God knew how to take care of Chi Chi for me."

Brother Allen's venture into the world beyond the living shadowed him in the years to follow, as did his devotion to alcohol. In 1970, just a few months after both *Time* and *Look* magazines published articles proclaiming his healing powers, rumors of Brother Allen's death began to spread among the faithful. One day, border radio listeners heard the following: "Here is Brother Allen interrupting this program with a very important bulletin." Then came the concerned voice of Brother Allen. "This is Brother Allen personally. . . . People as well as some preachers from pulpits are announcing that I am dead. Do I sound like a dead man? My friends, I am not even sick. Only a moment ago I made reservations to fly to our current tent campaign, where I'll see you there and make the devil a liar."

While border stations blasted his denial-of-death message across North America, Rev. A. A. Allen died in a room at the Jack Tar Hotel in San Francisco. It wasn't until a few days later that Allen's advertising company succeeded in pulling the "very important message" from the airwaves. At first, newspapers reported that Allen died of an apparent heart attack. Twelve days later the city coroner announced the real cause of death. Dr. Henry W. Turkel wrote, "Asa A. Allen died of acute alcoholism and fatty infiltration of the liver." Demon rum had finally conquered the healing preacher. Weeks after his passing, as Allen's associate Brother Bob took to the airwaves to advertise "the complete and heartwarming biography of Dr. Allen's life and teaching, which was completed only days before his death," a new rumor spread among the faithful. Many believed that Rev. A. A. Allen had risen from the dead.

The liberal border-station programming policies for religious broadcasts even allowed for some satire. In 1972 Red Wassinich and Paul Spragens, a pair of pranksters in Austin, Texas, purchased time on XEG to border-blast *The Brother Human Hour.* "The Church of the Coincidental Metaphor was our denomination," recalled Wassinich. "Spragens was a big fan of border radio, and he made some inquiries to see how much airtime cost, and it turned out to be amazingly cheap. The most expensive was twenty-two dollars and fifty cents for fifteen minutes. We sent the checks and the tapes to Harold Schwartz in Chicago, and two weeks later it would show up on Mexican radio."

"Humble natives!" began a typical Brother Human sermonette on XEG. "I come here tonight as a messenger of your great white friend Brother Human, who has commissioned me to indoctrinate you, here in this last stronghold of ignorance, in the principles of humility and servitude, which enable great men such as himself to lead you in prayerful obedience."

After Brother Human became a veteran of radio evangelism, Spragens and Wassinich (both sons of preachers) began to suffer from the satirist's curse—that fiction can never be stranger than truth. "It was hard to parody them because they did pretty extravagant things themselves. I would often listen to the station, waiting for our show to come on, and I would just shake my head and say that they had a lot more imagination than we do. They're really doing much weirder things than we are. My favorites were Mack Watson from Hot Springs, Arkansas, and Brother E. E. Duncan. Reverend Ike, of course, is an all-time favorite of everyone."

Not only did Brother Human fail to win souls for absurdism, but he also failed to bring home the border-radio bacon. "Part of the joke was we made constant money appeals," said Wassinich, "half a dozen a show, because it seemed a major part of the parody was to be constantly asking for money, and no one ever sent us a single penny."

In the winter of 1986 the government of Mexico put pressure on border broadcasters to suspend all religious programming in English. Not even Arturo González, the skilled attorney who had managed to keep preachers on XERF for more than forty years, could fight the pressure, and the preachers disappeared from the Mexican airwaves. In a recent letter to his flock, Rev. J. Harold Smith bemoaned the loss of XERF as a broadcasting outlet, saying that the loss had seriously damaged the financial structure of his radio ministry. "One day He will defeat the enemies of the cross in Mexico," Brother Smith assured his followers and went on to point out that the Mexicans "have had nothing but trouble ever since this diabolical ruling. The price of their oil has dropped from $30 to $12 per barrel, and may drop lower. They have had two major earthquakes in their capital city, Mexico City, and their unemployment has risen so high until many are risking their lives by coming across the border. Their money is almost valueless. Their tourist traffic has come to a halt. God has lifted His hand against Mexico and the present administration." Who is to say that bringing the preachers back to the border won't help the Mexican economy? After all, stranger miracles than financial security have come about with the prayers of the border-radio preachers.

That Outlaw X

I'm talkin' 'bout that outlaw X
It's cuttin' through the air . . .
I heard it, I heard it, I heard it on the X.
—*From "Heard it on the X," by Gibbons, Hill,*
and Beard, and recorded by ZZ Top

For more than five decades, border radio operators have maintained their fierce independence, walking a fine line between the FCC and the Mexican *federales* to deliver a unique form of radio service that has been highly profitable, highly controversial, and highly entertaining. The eccentric stars of the border universe pioneered many areas of radio technology and programming and inadvertently helped to shape international agreements and regulations that control broadcasting today. The border radio legacy is a broad one, reaching from the halls of Congress to the dashboard of almost every American car. For wherever there's a radio, that outlaw X has left its mark.

The superpowered border stations were broadcasting laboratories where some of the most talented engineers in North America, including Nestor Cuesta and the eccentric Will Branch, experimented with high-powered, long-range broadcasts. Jim Weldon was perhaps the most brilliant of the border engineers. His experience on the border made him an expert in the field of superpowered broadcasting and added much to the knowledge of radio-wave propagation and characteristics. Weldon went on to form Dallas-based Continental Electronics, one of the premier broadcast engineering firms in the United States, and he designed the original Voice of America transmitters, as well as powerful transmitters for several generations of U.S. radar. The crowning glory of Weldon's superpowered career came in 1973, when he built the most powerful radio transmitter in the world, a 2,000,000-watter blasting from the deserts of Saudi Arabia. The expertise that Weldon acquired in building transmitters for miracle healers on the border now serves the needs of Allah, as the faithful round the globe can now tune in to the muezzin's call to prayer, direct from the Prophet's homeland.

FCC regulations forced Dr. John Brinkley and the border broadcasters to make extensive use of another broadcasting innovation, the electrical transcription. Barred from entering Mexico by Mexican officials and prevented from using phone lines by the United States government, Brinkley had to rely on electrical transcriptions to get his message across the border. A proud announcer's voice heralded the broadcasting of those recordings with "This program comes to you by electrical transcription." Independent broadcasters around the country followed Brinkley's example and came to rely on electrical transcriptions as a source of inexpensive and convenient programming. Advertisers also came to depend on electrical transcriptions, as they gave clients the ability to pitch a product with the same program on several stations at the same time. Electrical transcriptions were a mainstay of the broadcasting industry until after World War II, when they began to be replaced by tape recording. While the extravagant live productions of the radio networks, who shunned the use of electrical transcriptions and other prerecorded material, have gone the way of the dinosaurs, most radio stations today use a highly automated system that relies heavily on prerecorded music, commercials, and syndicated programming—a direct evolution from the Brinkley method of broadcasting.

The border stations were programming innovators, from before the first broadcast of Norman Baker's whistling calliaphone until after Dr. Burpo's invitation to come into the throne room in the seventies. Hillbilly, western, and gospel music, as appealing to the people of the Midwest as it was foreign to radio executives in New York, was the lifeblood of border operators. Through the years, country music found some of its most important outlets on the border. According to historian Bill Malone, the superpowered border blasters "popularized hillbilly music throughout the United States and laid the basis for country music's great popularity in the late forties and early fifties." In the thirties, the days of "potted palm" network music, the sounds of the Carter Family, Mainer's Mountaineers, the Pickard Family, Cowboy Slim Rinehart, and others wafted up from the studios along the Rio Grande, bringing audiences a fresh and invigorating brand of unprecedented all-American entertainment.

In the late forties and early fifties the border continued to be a programming testing ground. Network programming in 1950 was quite similar to the 1930 sound, as more than a hundred network programs had been on the air for more than a decade, some for more than two decades. Programmers on the border could not afford to be so conservative. They were among the first to experiment with the programming creation that was to save radio in the television age—the disc jockey. The smooth-voiced entrée of Paul Kallinger, Your Good Neighbor Along the Way, introduced Webb Pierce, Johnny Horton, Lefty Frizell, Johnny Cash, and dozens of other country performers to national audiences in the fifties and early sixties. Wolfman Jack and Dr. Jazmo brought the sound of rhythm and blues to the border, keeping addled baby boomers glued to the late-night radio dial and anticipating the mainstream radio sound by many years.

Although most of their programming was directed toward American audiences, border stations were among the first advertising outlets to serve the Hispanic market. Lydia Mendoza and Pedro Gonzalez, as well as other popular Spanish-speaking performers, appeared regularly on the border stations, sponsored by Carta Blanca beer and other advertisers aiming at a Hispanic audience. Emilio Azcárraga, the David Sarnoff and William Paley of Mexican broadcasting, founded his empire on radio station XET, a high-powered outlet based in Monterrey and aimed at the lucrative U.S. and Spanish market to the north. In later years, Don Emilio became one of the major producers of motion pictures in Mexico and formed a television network called Televisa, which today has almost a monopoly on the Mexican television market as well as a strong influence on Spanish-language television programming in the United States. Arnaldo Ramirez, who hosted widely heard programs on XEAW, went on to become one of the most successful Tejano music promoters and record producers. His Falcon Records spotlighted the talents of many border artists, including Los Alegres de Terán and Baldemar Huerta, who was first known as the Bebop Kid and later achieved national success under the name Freddie Fender. Ramirez and other Spanish-speaking border disc jockeys such as Willie Lopez did much to popularize the *conjunto* sound—gritty button accordion-based polka and waltz rhythms that blared out of cantinas and honky-tonks from Dallas to Monterrey. Today the *conjunto* format is one of the hot marketing targets for U.S.-based advertisers. Whether the stations call themselves Radio Éxcitos, La Rancherita, or Radio Cañon, Spanish-language radio stations on *la frontera* owe a tip of the sombrero to the border blasters.

Border radio stations were among the first to add a good dose of spice to the otherwise G-rated world of network radio programming. The U.S. broadcasting establishment forbade any mention of sexual matters on the air for many years. In the early twenties, entertainer Olga Petrova was banned from the air after she tried to discuss the issue of birth control by reciting an adapted nursery rhyme: "There was an old woman who lived in a shoe. She had so many children because she didn't know what to do." In 1937 a storm of protest howled around the FCC when Mae West appeared on Edgar Bergen's show and performed a sketch about Adam and Eve with Bergen's wooden sidekick, the dummy Charlie McCarthy. Editorials across the country decried the "indecent burlesque of Eve on the radio," and some members of Congress called for an investigation into the "foul, sensuous, indecent, and blasphemous radio program" that had had invaded the homes of America, the "last bulwark against the modern emphasis on sensuality."

The Boys Towns, or red-light districts, of Nuevo Laredo, Juárez, Tijuana, and other border communities have always been strong lures for American dollars and have been the focus of American sexual fantasies for more than 150 years. In keeping with the border's spicy tradition, broadcasters in the region did not blink at addressing explicit details of a sexual nature. "All energy is sex energy," declared Dr. Brinkley before describing treatments guaranteed to make any man "the ram what am with every lamb." Wolfman took a more direct approach, urging his audience to "git nekked" and growling his female listeners into squeaking masses of excited giggles. The ears of radio listeners perked right up at the words of the border personalities who provided some of the most open explication of sexual matters in broadcasting's Victorian era.

While the FCC took exception to Brinkley's frankness and censured him for broadcasting obscene material, Doctor's prescriptions of friendly advice were tame in comparison with the diagnosis of later media physicians. Dr. Ruth Westheimer discusses the penis, masturbation, and sexual intercourse in the same matter-of-fact manner that Brinkley once used to describe that troublesome old cocklebur, the prostate. Today some cable television services air explicit sexual material for discriminating audiences, and infamous radio personality Howard Stern, who sometimes gives graphic descriptions of fans coupling in the broadcasting booth, has become the loudmouthed master of a trend known as blue radio. Director Russ Meyer celebrated the racy heritage of border radio in his film *Beneath the Valley of the Ultra-Vixens*, a bosomy tribute to the sexual mores of Small Town, U.S.A., and its radio station, Radio Rio Dio. Norman Baker's reputed flagrante delicto broadcasts anticipated the plot of Russ Meyer's film by decades. The whines, grunts, and howls that puzzled audiences tuned to XENT may in fact have been the first X-rated broadcast programming. Once again, border radio was ahead of its time.

While it is true that Doctor's surgical techniques were undisciplined and sometimes even dangerous, his operations did have a tremendous curative impact on many forlorn individuals. Like tribal initiates who undertake a pilgrimage to partake in ritualistic ceremonies, the old-timers who traveled to Del Rio got a tremendous pyschological boost from their journey, from the stories they swapped with fellow patients, and from the unorthodox surgery that awarded them a distinctive scarification. In recent years the idea of transplantation has lost its shock value, as organ transplants between humans are almost routine, and surgeons have even transplanted a baboon heart to a human.

Sexual specials of the eighties offer other types of surgical operations that make the goat gland proposition seem timid. For $6000 men who are unsure of their ability to perform can have a semirigid rod implanted in the penis. A hydraulic type of penile prosthesis is also available, in which two spongy cylinders are inserted along the failing body part. The simple push of a button in the abdominal area releases bodily fluids into the cylinders, and the patient is ready for action. Doctors in Mexico offer ewe extract to increase potency, a treatment closely related to Doctor's belief in the curative power of the Toggenburg. Despite the advancements of medical science, some aging Americans still have faith in Brinkley's technique. Every few months the Del Rio Chamber of Commerce fields a call from a randy old-timer asking, "Is Doc Brinkley's clinic still around?"

Border radio operators were innovators in the use of the mass media for political purposes and as such helped define the fairness doctrine, which discourages broadcast editorializing and supports the evenhanded treatment of political issues by journalists and station operators. In the late twenties Norman Baker assisted local politicians in their fight against corruption in state government by giving them free airtime on his Muscatine station, KTNT—Know the Naked Truth. Poor penmanship was the only thing that kept Dr. Brinkley from the Kansas governor's mansion after his trailblazing campaign, the first to depend heavily on a down-home combination of heavy radio play and touring hillbilly bands. Huey Long, the powerful Louisiana demagogue, learned many a public relations trick from Brinkley that he put to use in his gubernatorial and senatorial campaigns. While Franklin Roosevelt and other conventional candidates began to make use of the radio networks in the thirties, Brinkley, Baker, and other more idiosyncratic politicians moved to the border to maintain their freedom of speech. Pappy O'Daniel was the first Texas governor to realize that his strongest political weapon was the mass media. His constituency knew him as a radio personality, and he kept their support through two gubernatorial and two senatorial contests by speaking to them continually over the radio. O'Daniel sent transcriptions to the border to avoid censorship of his material, a problem that Upton Sinclair, another independent political voice, also experienced in his campaign for the governorship of California. "One trying feature of the campaign," Sinclair explained, "was that I was forced to submit copy in advance. And having to read a speech takes all the life out of it for me. But the big stations asserted that federal regulations required this."

Actually, in both O'Daniel's and Sinclair's cases, federal and industry regulations required just the opposite. Section 315 of the amended Communications Act of 1934 states that a radio station licensee "shall have no power of censorship over the material broadcast" by "a legally qualified candidate for any public office." At the same time that some stations were attempting to censor legally qualified political candidates, other stations were promoting suspect ideological beliefs with little or no official condemnation. George A. Richards purchased three 50,000-watt stations in the thirties that he used to disseminate his overt anti-Semitic beliefs. In his desire to get Jews out of government, Richards ordered his station personnel to use specific expletives in their news coverage, expletives such as "pig boy" or "tumbleweed" for Henry Wallace and "pipsqueak" for Harry Truman. Far from being condemned, as O'Daniel, Brinkley and other border politicians were, Richards was praised as a broadcaster, and one of his stations received the 1945 Dupon Public Service Award.

While the federal officials who closed down the radio stations of Brinkley and Baker held that "a truly free radio cannot be used to advertise the causes of the licensee" and that "the broadcaster cannot be an advocate," the current FCC trend is to downplay the so-called fairness doctrine, treat broadcasting outlets more like newspapers, allowing for a certain amount of editorializing. Once again, the border blasters were ahead of their time. Today's political candidates seem to be taking a lesson from the border politicians, using radio and television for flamboyant displays worthy of Brinkley and Pappy O'Daniel.

President Reagan, one of the most popular presidents in modern times, built up a great deal of his popularity through the Pappy O'Daniel scheme—that is, by distributing daily radio broadcasts free of charge to stations throughout the country. His presidential photo opportunities, carefully choreographed in ghettos, palaces, and barnyards, are visual representations of what was once created by the words of the border candidates. In 1930 a *New York Times* reporter noted that "a movement has gained considerable headway which . . . might easily point the way for the future selection of public servants without the aid of political organizations." Some present-day political pundits agree with this analysis and see the imminent breakdown of the political party system in campaigns that focus almost exclusively on radio and television appearances. Border operators, among the first who learned to catch the public's ear with political messages, paved the way for the great media blitz of the modern political era.

Border stations have always attracted people seeking freedom of expression, whether for political, sexual, or religious messages. Like Miles Standish and other pilgrims of the Plymouth Bay colony, the preachers who colonized the airwaves south of the border sought freedom of religious expression—freedom to spread their vision of righteousness over the far reaches of the electromagnetic spectrum. Preachers with somewhat radical views discovered early on that their descriptions of the road to paradise were not always welcomed by the American broadcasting establishment. Father Charles Coughlin, one of the great radio preachers of the thirties, was eased off the air by the CBS network after diluting the wine of his religious broadcasts with the poisonous water of anti-Semitic politics. Flapper evangelist Aimee Semple McPherson regularly broadcast her controversial vaudeville sermons from stations KFSG (Foursquare Gospel), a radio outlet located within her $1.5 million Angelus Temple in Los Angeles. In May 1926 the attractive blond preacher swam out into the Pacific Ocean and vanished for 32 days, reappearing in the Mexican border town of Agua Prieta and claiming that she had been kidnapped. While local officials were concerned about rumors of a liaison between the divorced McPherson and a married protégé of hers, federal officials were more concerned with her annoying habit of changing the frequency of her radio station whenever God told her to do so. When finally ordered to shut down her station, the Queen of the Heavens wired President Herbert Hoover, beseeching him to "please order your minions of Satan to leave my station alone."

When the broadcasting establishment moved to restrict religious groups from access to the airwaves, preachers migrated to the border and established a tradition of religious broadcasting that continues to this day. J. Harold Smith, who began his border preaching career in the mid-forties, still broadcasts his *Radio Bible Hour* from Newport, Tennessee, and advertises that it costs only $44 "to win one soul for Christ." The Reverend Sam Morris, the Voice of Temperance who began preaching on XEPN in Eagle Pass in 1936, eventually founded his own station in San Antonio with the appropriate call letters KDRY. One of the shows featured on KDRY is *The Family Altar,* from the Roloff Evangelical Association, which features taped messages of Brother Lester Roloff, a border preacher for many years, now departed. Oral Roberts, R.W. Shambaugh, and many of the leaders of the modern-day electronic church got their radio baptism on the banks of the Rio Grande.

A tremendous revival of Christian broadcasting has once again shown the prescience of the border broadcasters. In 1974 there were 118 radio stations with a religious format in the U.S. By 1979 there were more than 1100. High-powered American stations that broadcast over the Bible Belt, such as WOAI in San Antonio and WWL in New Orleans, schedule large blocks of religious programming in the late-night hours, finding that it is both popular and lucrative. A recent survey of the radio dial revealed *The Amazing Facts Broadcast*, as well as messages from a woman calling herself the Missionary Jewess from East St. Louis, and the English accent of Ray Masters, who told one listener, "I am God. You are nothing. Like it or lump it."

Television too has proven to be fertile ground for religious programming, as the all-religious cable networks clearly testify. The love gifts that pour into programs like *The 700 Club, The Roger Program, The PTL Club,* and others come from the same type of viewers that once gave to A. A. Allen, Brother David Epley, and the Reverend E. E. Duncan. For many years it was the border stations alone that ministered to the spiritual needs of the fundamentalist listening audience who tuned their radios to the gospel voices of the X stations.

In the early thirties, radio listeners were just as interested in astrology as they were in theology. Koran, Rose Dawn, Ralph Richards, and others were border radio favorites, ethereal personalities with insight into universal secrets available for a small fee. While the spooks disappeared from the networks, they remained on the border. Up until recently, faith healer Sister White asked her listeners, "Losing hair? Have an unhappy marriage? Write to Sister White." Rose Dawn, Dr. Brinkley's personal astrologer, eventually moved from the border to San Antonio, where she continued her radio career by advertising a not-so-secret society she founded, the Sacred Order of Maya. Although Rose Dawn passed away, mailings from the Mayan headquarters in San Antonio continued to bear her signature. With the deregulation of the broadcasting industry today, there has been a resurgence of spooks on the radio. Talk shows regularly feature psychics who answer questions from inquisitive listeners wanting to locate lost rings or lost husbands. Handwriting experts and personality specialists all appear on fully accredited American broadcasting outlets, though it takes tremendous skill to analyze handwriting over the phone.

The broadcasters who moved to the border frontier helped to define the American broadcasting industry by proving the effectiveness of broadcasting advertising. While network officials decried the hucksterism on border radio and took public actions to promote broadcast standards, they realized what the border radio operators knew all along—

that nothing makes money like a hard sell. In 1935 CBS won praise for proposing a ban on products "which describe graphically or repellantly any internal bodily functions, symptomatic results of internal disturbances or matters which are generally not considered acceptable topics in social groups." The ban was to go into effect as soon as "present commitments" expired, but CBS allowed companies that had been advertising to continue broadcasting their messages as long as they wished. CBS got a great deal of praise, lost not a dime in advertising, and continued to run ads for questionable products.

The border blasters were only slightly more outrageous in their advertisements than other broadcasters of the era. In the thirties, 671 American stations filled the nation's homes with pitches for Marmola, a fat reducer made of delirium causing thyroid extract and bladder wrack, and Koremlu, a depilatory made from the rat poison thallium acetate. Some reputable broadcasters touted Lysol as an effective and safe douche and the networks ran hundreds of commercials advertising Lucky Strike cigarettes as "slenderizers" and "throat balms." No major radio network ever received more than a raised eyebrow for questionable advertising. Dr. Brinkley and the other border radio operators were outside the establishment, though, and as outsiders, they were convenient scapegoats. Brinkley, Norman Baker, the Collins brothers, Pappy O'Daniel, and the myriad of spooks, diamond merchants, and faith healers who lived on the border wave were closely tied to the products they sold over the air, whether it was baking flour or a cancer cure. They had direct responsibility for what they sold, which made them different from network executives and station managers. As mere time brokers, these pillars of the American radio establishment were able to make millions from advertising questionable products while remaining fairly well insulated from consumer and regulatory repercussions. The border broadcasters, however, as fighters for individual freedom, stood directly behind what they advertised, pocketed all the profits from the products, and fell when the products they pitched were yanked from the market.

As with the case of program content, advertising content has come full circle. Today network broadcasting stations advertise products that would have been considered indecent and obscene in the golden era of the border broadcaster. Condoms are promoted to combat AIDS. Thankfully, ads for the douche R-Bella, ZPG-1 pills and other more questionable AIDS remedies have yet to hit the airwaves. Girls leap around in spotless white leotards to advertise the freedom of absorbent panty liners. Tampons and douches receive heavy airplay and other items such as herpes medication, early pregnancy tests, and home detection tests for colon-cancer are all finding their way into American homes and automobiles. Dexatrim, Fiber Trim, and European body wraps promise media consumers the opportunity to "lose up to fifty pounds without dieting" or enjoy "all the figure toning of 3000 sit-ups without moving an inch." According to the *Wall Street Journal*, CBS executives describe the 9 p.m. to 11 p.m. time period as a "personal product ghetto" and are allowing personal product ads to move into time periods when children are likely to be watching. The slogan "Constipation is Disaster" for Dulcolax laxative is worthy of the pen of Doctor Brinkley, and the country musician who sings of Doxadan, a laxative "as sure as the sun rises," would fit right in with Colonel Jack and Shorty's Hillbillies, extolling the wonders of Crazy Water Crystals.

Border stations were the most audacious practitioners of the per-inquiry advertising system, which reimbursed the station according to how much business a particular advertisement generated. Per-inquiry, or PI advertising, became popular in the mid-thirties, when the Depression cut down on available advertising dollars and forced broadcasters to go into the retail business. The border stations, with their powerful range and mysterious aura, continued to be successful with PI advertising long after it went out of fashion on most radio outlets. PI advertising is now a common broadcasting arrangement and is responsible for the enormous television sales of Moulis, Vego-matics, cap snafflers, Boxcar Willie compilation albums, and mechanical beds. In fact, one of the hottest new areas of broadcasting is the continuous per-inquiry advertising format, pioneered by Home Shopping Network, which operates fourteen broadcast television stations devoted to the per-inquiry sales of diamond rings, boom boxes, and grandfather clocks.

In recent times a new breed of media salesmen has surfaced on cable television with schemes as grand as those proposed by Dr. Ralph Richards and other noted border operators. Mark Hughes, the founder and chief executive officer of Herbalife International, has enlisted more than 700,000 television viewers to repeat his mantra "Lose weight now—ask me how" and racked up millions of dollars in health products sales. While Herbalife boasts an extensive research lab staffed by a battery of Ph.D.'s, its main additive expert got his health degree from a correspondence school. Ed Beckley, the force behind the TV program *The Millionaire Maker*, sold more than $35 million worth of home-study materials in 1985, and his media buyer contends, "We do as well as Johnny Carson does in some markets."

The border blasters, always on the broadcasting frontier, provided test cases around which the American system of broadcasting regulation developed. Broadcasters defended themselves against the intrusion of the federal government into radio broadcasting. General Electric was one of the first companies to file suit against the Federal Radio Commission to test the legality of the regulatory body. Norman Baker, head of the American Broadcasters Association, started a campaign against the FRC, saying that the law was designed to eliminate the little guy in favor of the radio trust. Baker held that the FRC was trust-appointed, and he demanded an industry investigation, which caused some midwestern politicians to oppose the act that created the commission.

In some ways Baker was correct. It was easier for the FRC to test the teeth of the federal radio legislation by taking on small businessmen rather than RCA and the large radio networks. In 1928, FRC order number 32 asked 164 stations why they should not be abolished. At that time Brinkley's station KFKB did well, but two years later the commission went on the attack. While the Federal Radio Act specifically forbade the commission to exercise any censorship over programs, the FRC began to use the method of regulation by raised eyebrow. The commission warned stations that if they did not operate in the public interest, their license might not be renewed. Federal officials further maintained that a broadcaster's past performance could be used as evidence in judging his suitability to own a broadcasting license. Members of the commission realized they had a censorship dilemma. Harry Bellows, who was an FCC commissioner at one point and later a vice president of CBS, spoke to the League of Women Voters about the issue. "The law tells us that we shall have no right of censorship over radio programs," he said, "but the physical facts of radio transmission compel what is in effect a censorship of the most extraordinary kind." He went on to comment that judging programming previous to license renewal is "a flagrant violation of the very law we were appointed to administer."

Brinkley's and Baker's stations were among the first to come under the federal regulatory guillotine. When Brinkley appealed the FRC ruling in 1931 to try to regain his lost station, the court decision read in part as follows: "Appellant contends that the attitude of the commission amounts to censorship of the station. . . . This contention is without merit . . . since the commission has merely exercised its undoubted right to take note of appellant's past conduct, which is not censorship. . . . Obviously, there is no room in the broadcast band for every business or school of thought." As if to give a divine stamp of approval to its action, the court cited Scripture in its decision: "By their fruits ye shall know them." The Brinkley and Baker decisions became regulatory landmarks that helped to define how the federal government could control broadcasters who were considered to be acting outside of "the public interest, convenience and necessity."

Critics of the broadcasting establishment were quick to question the decision to close down the small-time operators while allowing the large networks to continue advertising questionable products with little more than a hand slap. Ruth Brindze wrote in her 1936 book, *Not to Be Broadcast*, "The question might logically be raised how it is any more reprehensible for a purveyor of patent medicines to use his own stations to advertise his wares than it is for competitors to buy time from commercial stations." The FRC and the FCC could always play ball with the networks, applying pressure to remove the most objectionable programming while never really threatening the removal of a station license. The small businessman, the single-station owner, and the broadcasting frontiersman were much more vulnerable to attacks from the commission and have been the culprits the FCC has used to strengthen broadcasting regulations through the courts.

On the international front, border operators provided Mexico with a valuable bargaining chip in the competition for broadcasting frequencies. Mexican authorities cared little more for the border stations than did their American counterparts in the FCC, but as long as license and inspection fees were paid, the *federales* were willing to look the other way and even use the X stations to fight the aerial imperialism of the Americans. Mexico ratified the first North American Radio Broadcasting Agreement in 1941, after eight years of negotiating with the United States. Unfortunately for the negotiators involved, the agreement was binding only for a period of five years.

For the last forty years high-ranking government officials have spent thousands of hours attempting to settle once and for all the problems of international frequency allocations precipitated by the border operators. A new agreement was signed in 1957 and ratified in 1961, with one U.S. negotiator warning the Senate Committee on Foreign Relations that without such an agreement, "chaotic interference would be bound to result as a radio wave does not respect international boundaries," a restatement of Dr. Brinkley's own sentiments. President Richard Nixon supported the ratification of a further agreement in 1969, assuring the wary Senate that the agreement was "generally satisfactory to broadcasting interests in the U.S." The agreement was ratified in 1970 and was in force until the eighties.

The many agreements signed prior to the eighties were more or less similar to the first agreement hammered out in 1937. They maintained the right of the signatories to broadcast over certain frequencies that were kept free of other broadcasters, frequencies known as clear channels. In 1986, however, a North American Regional Broadcasting Agreement was forged that dramatically altered the clear-channel allocations and dealt a crippling blow to the power of the border blasters. The agreement allowed both Mexican and American broadcasters to use the other country's clear-channel frequencies for low-powered stations in the evening. That meant that the signals of the border stations would be drowned out in many communities by local broadcasts, effectively putting an end to the era of high-powered, far-ranging radio. Border station operators were furious about the agreement. Arturo González, the man who defended the rights of XERA and XERF for more than forty years, commented that "the new agreement has ruined has ruined everything. Our station can no longer have the power it once had. We do not have as big an audience, and this will hurt our business. Your clear-channel stations will be angry too, once they realize what was happened." Like fences on the open range, which ended the era of the great American cattle drives, the newest international agreements effectively cut off the range of the border radio operators, the broadcasters who once drove their signals all the way from Mexico to Canada to take their products to faraway markets.

Recent Mexican broadcasting regulations pose another threat to the operation of the X stations. These licensing agreements, called concessions, were promulgated by the federal government early in 1986 and give dramatic power over radio to the Mexican Secretary of Communication and Transportation. According to the concessions, station operators are allowed to operate their stations for a period of only ten years, at the end of which time the government has the option of purchasing the stations for the depreciated value of the assets, a figure roughly equivalent to zero pesos. "The government will be the owner of every radio station in Mexico!" cried Eduardo Villarreal, whose family has owned and operated radio station XED in Nuevo Laredo since 1936 (not to be confused with the former XED at Reynosa). "According to the new regulations, you cannot build a new rest room for your employees if you don't have a permit, and the radio station must run programs that contribute to the 'equitable distribution of income.' Do we live in socialism or communism?" Arturo González, the canny international broadcasting attorney, also shook his head at the thought of the new regulations. "It's absolutely crazy," he said. "The government needs dollars, and we bring dollars in by accepting American advertising." González, who tried to interest his son in taking over the station's legal work, said, "He was not interested. It is too much work, too much dealing with the politicians in Mexico City. And they care only about one thing—money in their pockets."

While it is not clear whether the Mexican government will indeed enforce the concession agreements and nationalize Mexican radio, the *federales* have cracked down on the border operators. Government inspectors recently demanded that the border stations ban all religious programming, although preachers were the lifeblood of stations like

XEMO in Tijuana, XELO in Juárez, XEG in Monterrey, and XERF, the station Dr. Brinkley founded in Villa Acuña. There are still some radio renegades on the border who program in English. XETRA in Tijuana, the first all-news station started by Gordon McLendon, entertains its Los Angeles audience with an all-hits rock-and-roll format called 69 Extra Gold. An FM station in Tijuana, XHRM, plays contemporary black dance music, pausing to reveal its location at midnight with the Mexican national anthem.

For the most part, though, Spanish has replaced English as the language of choice for border operators. Wolfman's XERB in Tijuana is now XEPRS (Radio Express), an all-Spanish station serving Southern California. XELO, founded by engineer Will Branch, is now Radio Cañon, broadcasting Spanish programming out of Juárez. In late 1986 a controversial Juárez attorney began using XROK's 150,000 watts to sell books telling illegal immigrants how to manipulate the new INS amnesty program. XEG, once the Gospel Voice at 1050 and the flagship of Harold Schwartz's border empire, now broadcasts in Spanish as Radio Melodía. Since the early seventies, XERF had been operating at a lowly 50,000-watts until electronics whiz Mike Venditti revived the station's experimental RCA 250,000-watt transmitter in 1983 and cranked it up to full power. Venditti, who had listened to the station while growing up in Philadelphia, moved to Del Rio and began a program of contemporary Christian music called *Love 16*. At the same time, XERF scored a coup by hiring popular country-and-western DJ Bill Mack from Fort Worth's WBAP. The rejuvenation of the station was short-lived, however, and by 1968 XERF had devolved to the bargain-basement programming of screaming preachers and items like *The Elvis Show*, which featured thirty-second fragments of Presley recordings followed by fifteen-minute commercials for King of Rock memorabilia and objets d'Elvis. Finally, Arturo González, the broadcasting coyote who kept Brinkley's station on the air for decades and brought Paul Kallinger and Wolfman Jack to the border, decided to throw in the towel and turned XERF over to the government in February 1986. When asked how he felt after giving up control of the renegade station that had intrigued Americans for more than half a century, González said, "I feel relieved. That station was nothing but a headache."

The gain of the Spanish-speaking radio audience is a loss for English speakers, who will miss the mysterious, static-filled screeching of the border stations. Gone now are the superpowered blasters that merged the showmanship of the nineteenth-century medicine tent with the technological marvels of the twentieth century and filled the late-night ether with hope, humor, and amazement. Border radio was raw, scandalous, and sometimes downright illegal, but it never suffered from the curse of the modern radio dial—automated monotony. When the outlaw X boomed out from the border, audiences around the world never knew quite what to expect. Anything was possible on border radio.

One can take consolation that somewhere some creatures may still be listening to the broadcasts of Brinkley and Baker, hearing the praises of Crazy Water Crystals and Hillbilly Flour, and tapping their feet to Paul Kallinger's favorite Hank Thompson hit and the Wolfman's hottest rock track. The broadcasts sent out from the high-powered transmitters south of the Rio Grande are today making their way to the farthest reaches of the universe and are perhaps at this minute being monitored by radio fans in another galaxy. Those beings, hunched over their sophisticated receiving equipment, could be forming a picture of the earth from words that the FCC and the Mexican broadcasting authorities banned from the North American airwaves. We can only hope that when they come to visit "The Sunshine Station Between the Nations" by the silvery Rio Grande, they will heed the good Doctor's advice to "clean up, clean out, and keep clean."

Selected Bibliography

BOOKS

Baker, Norman. *Cancer Is Curable*. Laredo, Tex.: Baker Hospital, 1934.

_____ . *Where Sick Folks Get Well*. Eureka Springs, Ark.: Baker Hospital, 1938.

Bakker, Tammy. *I Gotta Be Me*. Harrison, Ark.: New Leaf Press, 1978.

Barnouw, Eric. *The Golden Web—The History of Broadcasting, Part II*. New York: Oxford University Press, 1968.

_____ . *A Tower in Babel—The History of Broadcasting, Part I*. New York: Oxford University Press, 1966.

Bowers, Q. David. *Encyclopedia of Automatic Musical Instruments*. Vestal, N.Y.: Vestal Publishers, 1978.

Brindze, Ruth. *Not to Be Broadcast—The Truth About Radio*. New York: Vanguard Press, n.d.

Brinkley, J. R. *Doctor Brinkley's Doctor Book*. Del Rio, Tex.: Brinkley Hospital, 1936.

_____ . *Doctor Brinkley's Doctor Book*. Little Rock, Ark.: Brinkley Hospital, 1938.

_____ . *Roads Courageous*. Asheville, N.C.: Pelley Publishers, 1938.

Caro, Robert A. *The Path to Power*. New York: Alfred A. Knopf, 1982.

Carson, Gerald. *The Roguish World of Doctor Brinkley*. New York: Holt, Rinehart, and Winston, 1960.

Chase, Francis, Jr. *Sound and Fury.* New York: Harper and Bros., 1942.

Clugston, W. G. *Rascals in Democracy.* New York: Richard R. Smith, 1940.

Cramp, Arthur J., M.D. *Nostrums and Quackery.* Chicago: American Medical Association, 1936.

Delmore, Alton. *Truth Is Stranger Than Publicity.* Edited with introduction, commentary, and discography by Charles K. Wolfe. Nashville: Country Music Foundation Press, 1977.

Douglas, C. L., and Francis Miller. *The Life Story of W. Lee O'Daniel.* Dallas: Regional Press, 1938.

Eureka Springs Carnegie Public Library Association. *Eureka Springs— A Pictorial History.* Eureka Springs: Eureka Springs Carnegie Public Library Association, 1975.

Fornatale, Peter, and Joshua Mills. *Radio in the Television Age.* New York: Overlook Press, 1980.

Geijerstam, Claes. *Popular Music in Mexico.* Albuquerque, N. Mex.: University of New Mexico Press, 1976.

Gutierrez, A E. *A History of San Felipe.* Del Rio, Tex.: Whitehead Museum, 1978.

Hadden, Jeffrey K., and Charles E. Swann. *Prime Time Preachers.* Reading, Mass.: Addison-Wesley Publishing Co., 1981.

Harrell, David Edwin, Jr. *All Things Are Possible—The Healing and Charismatic Revivals in Modern America.* Bloomington, Ind.: Indiana University Press, 1975.

Hoxsey, Harry M. *You Don't Have to Die.* New York: Milestone Books, 1956.

Jones, Rosemary Whitehead, ed. *La Hacienda.* Del Rio, Tex.: Whitehead Museum, 1976.

Kahn, Frank J. *Documents of American Broadcasting.* New York: Meredith Corp., 1968.

Lamb, Ruth deForest. *American Chamber of Horrors.* New York: Grosset and Dunlap, 1936.

Landry, Robert J. *This Fascinating Radio Business.* Indianapolis: Bobbs-Merrill, 1946.

Lowenthal, Leo, and Norbert Guterman. *Prophets of Deceit.* New York: Harper and Bros., 1949.

Malone, Bill C. *Country Music U.S.A.* Austin, Tex.: University of Texas Press, 1985.

Matthews, Wilbur L. *San Antonio Lawyer.* San Antonio, Tex.: [Corona Press] 1983.

McKay, Seth Shepard. *W. Lee O'Daniel and Texas Politics, 1938–1942.* Lubbock, Tex.: Texas Tech Press, 1944.

Midgley, Ned. *The Advertising and Business Side of Radio*. New York: Prentice-Hall, 1948.

Miller, Tom. *On the Border*. New York: Harper and Row, 1981.

Morell, Peter. *Poisons, Potions and Profits—The Antidote to Radio Advertising*. New York: Knight Publishers, 1937.

Morris, Willie. North Toward Home. Boston: Houghton Mifflin, 1967.

Moser, J. G., and Richard Lavine. *Radio and the Law*. Los Angeles: Parker and Co., 1947.

Musial, Matthew. *Doctor Brinkley—A Man and His Calling*. Del Rio, Tex.: 1983.

National Association of Broadcasters. *The ABC of Radio*. Washington, D.C.: National Association of Broadcasters, 1938.

———. *Standards of Practice for Radio Broadcasters of the United States of America*. Washington, D.C.: National Association of Broadcasters, 1937, 1955.

National Opinion Research Center, University of Chicago. *Radio Listening in America*. Analyzed and interpreted by Paul F. Lazarsfeld and Patricia L. Kendall. New York: Prentice-Hall, 1948.

Neville, Dorothy. *Carr P. Collins—Man on the Move*. Dallas: Park Press, 1973.

Pingenot, Ben E. *Historical Highlights of Eagle Pass and Maverick County*. Eagle Pass, Tex.: Eagle Pass Chamber of Commerce, n.d.

Powe, Lucas, Jr. *American Broadcasting and the First Amendment*. Berkeley and Los Angeles: University of California Press, 1987.

Prieto, Jorge Mejia. *Historia de la Radio y la Televisión en México*. Mexico City: Editores Asociados, 1972.

Redd, Lawrence N. *Rock Is Rhythm and Blues (The Impact of Mass Media)*. East Lansing, Mich.: Michigan State University Press, 1974.

Roark, Garland. *The Coin of Contraband*. Garden City, N.Y.: Doubleday, 1964.

Rosen, Philip T. *The Modern Stentors: Radio Broadcasters and the Federal Government, 1920–1934*. Westport, Conn.: Greenwood Press, 1980.

Smith, J. Harold. *The Time of My Life*. Orlando, Fla.: Radio Bible Hour, 1981.

Tosches, Nick. *Country*. New York: Charles Scribner's, 1977.

Townsend, Charles R. *San Antonio Rose: The Life and Music of Bob Wills*. Chicago: University of Illinois Press, 1976.

Turner, Dallas. *Cowboy Slim Rinehart's Folio of Country Song Hits*. Reno, Nev.: Dallas Turner Publications, 1983.

Ward, Ed, Geoffrey Stokes, and Ken Tucker. *Rock of Ages: The Rolling Stone History of Rock and Roll*. New York: Rolling Stone Press/Summit

Books, 1986.

Weaver, A.F. *Time Was in Mineral Wells . . . A Crazy Story But True.* Mineral Wells, Tex.: Mineral Wells Heritage Association, 1975.

Weisman, Alan. *La Frontera.* New York: Harcourt, Brace, Jovanovich, 1986.

Winston, Alvin G. *Doctors, Dynamiters, and Gunmen.* Muscatine, Iowa: Baker Sales Co., 1936.

————. *The Throttle: A Fact Story of Norman Baker.* Muscatine, Iowa: Baker Sales Co., 1934.

Wood, Clement. *The Life of a Man.* Kansas City: Goshorn Publishing Co., 1934.

Woolery, D. R. *The Grand Old Lady of the Ozarks.* Hominy, Okla.: Eagle's Nest Press, 1986.

UNPUBLISHED MANUSCRIPTS

Hoffer, Thomas. "Norman Baker and American Broadcasting." Master's Thesis, University of Wisconsin, Madison, 1969.

Jackson, James Barton. "Federal Regulation of Radio Broadcasting," Master's Thesis, University of Texas, Austin, 1940.

Kahn, Ed. "The Carter Family: A Reflection of Changes in Society." Ph.D. dissertation, University of California, Los Angeles, 1970.

Price, John A. "Tijuana Ethnology: The Cultural Nature of an International Border." Department of Anthropology, San Diego State College, 1969.

Resler, Ansel Harlan. "The Impact of John R. Brinkley on Broadcasting in the United States." Ph.D. dissertation, Northwestern University, Evanston, Ill., 1958.

Saragoza, Alex. "Behind the Scenes: Media Ownership, Politics, and Popular Culture in Mexico, 1930–1958. University of California, Berkeley, 1986.

ARTICLES

Ahrens, Pat. "The Role of Crazy Water Crystals in Promoting Hillbilly Music." *JEMF Quarterly,* 17, no. 19 (Autumn 1970): 107.

Bailey, Richard Hughes. "Dr. Brinkley of Kansas." *Nation,* September 21, 1932.

Biffle, Kent. "Doc Brinkley Put a Kink in Texas History." *Dallas Morning News,* February 3, 1985.

Blau, Eleanor. "Harlem Preacher Stresses Power of Money and Prayer." *New York Times,* July 26, 1972.

Brammer, Billie Lee. "Salvation Worries? Prostate Trouble?" *Texas Monthly,* March 1973.

Brinkley, J. R. "Dr. Brinkley Finds Mexico Land of Many Delights." *Wichita Beacon,* February 22, 1931.

Budd, Millie. "Fred Cannata: The Man Who Helped Bring Talking Movies to Houston." *Houston Business Journal,* 9, no. 51 (June 16, 1980): 5.

Caldwell, Louis G. "Developments in Federal Regulation of Broadcasting." *Variety Radio Directory,* 1938–39.

Carmack, George. "The Doctor Heard Round the World." *San Antonio Express-News,* December 13, 1975.

Casey, Robert J. "Radio With a Sombrero." *Nation,* January 1, 1939.

————— . "Strumming Those Symptoms—The Doc's (Mex.) on the Air." *Chicago Daily News,* March 12, 1937.

Cochran, Mike. "Spanish Replaces Faded Echoes of the X." *San Antonio Light,* May 25, 1986.

Copper, Donald. "Dr. Brinkley's Own Story." *Radio Stars,* August 1933.

Cramp, Arthur J. "Norman Baker vs. the American Medical Association." *Hygeia,* May 1932.

Davenport, Walter. "Gland Time in Kansas." *Collier's,* January 16, 1932.

————— . "Where's Them Biscuits, Pappy?" *Collier's,* (January 6, 1940): 21.

"Doomsday, Salvation and XERF." *Southwest Scene,* November 29, 1970.

Drummond, Hugh, M.D. "The Ultimate Erector Set." *Mother Jones,* March 1987.

Evans, Derro. "The Twilight of Minerva Brinkley." *Sunday Magazine, Dallas Times Herald,* Sept. 2, 1973.

Fishbein, Morris. "Modern Medical Charlatans." *Hygeia,* January and February, 1938.

Ford, Dan. "Wolfman Jack, From Cub to Howling Success." *Los Angeles Times,* December 3, 1972.

Furnas, J. C. "The Border Radio Mess." *Saturday Evening Post,* September 23, 1948.

————— . "Country Doctor Goes to Town." *Saturday Evening Post,* April 20, 1940.

Germani, Clara. " 'Border Blasters' Blitz U.S. Airwaves With Offbeat Programming From Mexico." *Christian Science Monitor,* September 16, 1983.

"Goat Glands and Sunshine." *Time,* November 16, 1931.

Goodyear, Russell. "Historians Hear Paper on Dr. Brinkley." *Del Rio* (Tex.) *Guide,* April 1984.

Gould, Jack. "Reform, With Mountain Music." *New York Times,* February 1, 1942.

Hale, Leon. "The House Where Dr. Brinkley Lived." *Houston Post*, June 4, 1978.

Harper, Jim. "Gordon McLendon: Pioneer Baseball Broadcaster." *Baseball History*, Spring 1986.

Hedgepeth, William. "Brother A. A. Allen on the Gospel Trail: He Feels, He Heals, and He Turns You On With God." *Look*, October 7, 1969.

Heinl, Robert D. "Mexico Menaces American Radio." *Tower Radio*, May 1934.

Herman, John R., M.D. "Rejuvenation: Brown-Sequard to Brinkley." *New York State Journal of Medicine* 82 no. 12 (November 1982) 1731.

Hill, Dick. "Tuning the Dial." *Tune in to Old Time Radio*, April 1986.

Ike, Reverend. "Evangelism in the Church." *New York Amsterdam News*, Summer 1976.

Kahn, Ed. "International Relations, Dr. Brinkley, and Hillbilly Music." *JEMF Quarterly* 95, part 2, no. 30 (Summer 1973): 47.

———. "Tapescript: Interview With Charlie, Bubb, and Lucille Pickard." *JEMF Quarterly*, n.d.

———. "Tapescript: Interview With Don Howard." *JEMF Quarterly*, n.d.

Krehm, William. "Love and Hair-Goo on the Air." *Saturday Evening Post*, October 9, 1943.

Ladwig, Craig. "New Chance to Assess Goat-Gland Doc." *Kansas City Star*, March 6, 1977.

Lifsher, Marc. "Border Station Against Making Radio Waves." *Dallas Times Herald*, January 2, 1982.

Martin, William C. "The God-Hucksters of Radio." *Atlantic*, August 1970.

———. "This Man Says He's the Divine Sweetheart of the Universe." *Esquire*, June 1974.

McEvoy, J. P. "I've Got That Million Dollar Smile." *American Mercury*, October 1938.

McFarland, Keith D. "Brinkley . . . . He Nearly Became Governor." *Kanhistique*, September 1977.

"The Mexican Air." *Newsweek*, August 19, 1940.

Morthland, John. "A Blast From the Past." *Westward Magazine, Dallas Times Herald* March 17, 1985.

Motavalli, John. "Burning the Midnight Snake Oil." *Channels*, November 1986.

Murphy, Vi. "Elegance Returning to Baja Hotel." *San Diego Union*, August 16, 1974.

"Norman Baker Dons Federal Prison's Garb." *Des Moines Register*, March 23, 1941.

"O'Daniel Plans Own Paper to Sass Back at Texas Foes." *Newsweek*, April 8, 1940.

Ord, Paul. "Not So Crazy Water." *Texas Parade*, February 1940.

Paris, Mike. "The Jesse Rodgers Story." *Old Time Music*, Winter 1974–75.

Parson, Chuck. "Yodeling Cowboy." *True West*, August 1986.

Patoski, Joe Nick. "Rock 'n' Roll's Wizard of Oz." *Texas Monthly*, February 1980.

Paz-Martinez, Eduardo. "Home of the Wolfman—Ciudad Acuña's XERF Is Junkyard of Legends Now." *Houston Post*, March 30, 1986.

Peeler, Tom. "Healing Waters—Jim Collins' Father's Magic Elixir." *D*, November 1983.

Perry, Charles. "Wolfman Comin' at Ya, Babe-ey!" *Rolling Stone*, October 1, 1970.

"The Platter Spinner Is Radio's New Hero." *Business Week*, January 28, 1956.

Prather, Alfred. "Radio Racketeer." *Master Detective*, December 1943.

Price, John D. "Superpowers and Borderblasters." *Broadcast Programming and Production*, May 1979 and July 1979.

Robins, Sam. "Waves That Cross the Rio Grande." *New York Times*, February 6, 1938.

Robinson, Elsie. "O'Daniel 'Captures' Texas—How 'Miracle Man' Outwits Politicians." *Los Angeles Examiner*, August 21, 1938.

Ruff, Ann. "Burnhams Restoring Showplace Mansion." *Del Rio* (Tex.) *Guide*, April 1984.

Russell, C. Allyn. "J. Frank Norris: Violent Fundamentalist." *Southwestern Historical Quarterly* 75, no. 3, 271.

"Salesman: 'Doctor's' Border Programs Cause Formal Protest." *Newsweek*, February 13, 1933.

Schneider, Albert J. " 'That Troublesome Old Cocklebur': John R. Brinkley and the Medical Profession of Arkansas, 1937–1942." *Arkansas Historical Quarterly* 30, no. 1 (Spring 1976): 27.

Schruben, Francis W. "Who Speaks for Brinkleyism?" *Kanhistique*, November 1978.

Smith, Randy. "Remembering Pappy." *Dallas Times Herald*, July 13, 1980.

Smith, Warren B. "Norman Baker—King of the Quacks." *Iowan*, January–February 1959.

Strout, Richard Lee. "The Radio Nostrum Racket." *Nation*, July 17, 1935.

Szilagyi, Pete. "Mighty XERF Born Again." *Onward, Austin American Statesman*, September 13, 1983.

Taylor, Frank J. "Latin America's Big Voice." *Reader's Digest*, July 1944.

Thornton, William M. "Curb Sought on Radio Use Across Border." *Dallas Morning News*, February 24, 1940.

"Thousands Lured by Promised Cure." *Quad City Times*, April 17, 1977.

Tolbert, Frank X. "Doc Brinkley's Grand Estate." *Dallas Morning News*, June 26, 1966.

————. "Here's Background on 'Home of Crazy'" *Dallas Morning News*, June 22, 1956.

"The Top 40 Story: Gordon McLendon." *Radio and Records*, 1973.

Tribe, Ivan. "The Economics of Hillbilly Radio: A Preliminary Investigation of the 'p.i.' System in the Depression Decade and Afterward." *JEMF Quarterly*, n.d.

"Twenty-Seven Candidates Seek Senate Seat in Screwy Texas Race." *Life*, June 30, 1941.

Waddell, Ross. " 'The Diamond Man' Uses Powerful Station." *Del Rio* (Tex.) *Guide*, December 1984.

Wardlaw, Frank. "The Goat-Gland Man." *Southwest Review*, Spring 1981.

Weber, Josie. "The Santa Claus Houston Forgot." *Texas Sunday Magazine, Houston Post*. December 24, 1967.

Welsome, Eileen. "Fascination With Infamous Brinkley Lives After Death." *San Antonio Light*, November 6, 1982.

Westheimer, David. "The Not-New Art of Rejuvenation." *Houston Post*, April 2, 1986.

————. "Some Have Fond Memories of Will." *Houston Post*, April 9, 1986.

Whitman, Arthur. "Big Noise From the Border." *Texas Magazine, Houston Chronicle*, October 13, 1968.

Wolfe, Joseph G. "Norman Baker and KTNT." *Journal of Broadcasting*. 12, no. 4 (Fall 1968): 389.

Young, Roland. "Lone Star Razzle Dazzle." *Nation*, June 21, 1941.

Other periodicals we consulted include *Eagle Pass* (Tex.) *Daily Guide, Southwest Advertising, Waco* (Tex.) *Tribune-Herald, McAllen* (Tex.) *Daily Press, Variety, Arkansas Democrat, Del Rio* (Tex.) *Evening News, Del Rio* (Tex.) *News-Herald, Wichita* (Kansas) *Eagle, Clark's Country Music News, Del Rio* (Tex.) *Press, Broadcasting, Country Song Roundup, Texas Weekly, Texas Centennial, Kansas City Journal-Post, Family Altar News, Miracle Magazine, Kansas Teacher, Laredo* (Tex.)

Times, Kansas Historical Quarterly, McAllen (Tex.) *Monitor, Good News Herald, Billboard, Country Music Reporter, Journal of the American Medical Association, San Angelo Standard-Times, W. Lee O'Daniel News, Journal of the Kansas Medical Society,* and the *Wall Street Journal.*

ARCHIVAL COLLECTIONS

Texas Medical Foundation, Austin; Country Music Foundation, Nashville; Barker Texas History Center, Austin; Kansas Museum of History, Topeka; Carnegie Public Library, Eureka Springs, Ark.; Eureka Springs Historical Museum, Eureka Springs, Ark.; Val Verde County Library, Del Rio, Tex.; San Antonio Public Library; Texas Room, Houston Public Library; Dallas Public Library; Southwest Collection, Texas Tech University, Lubbock; American Medical Association, Chicago; Muscatine Public Library, Muscatine, Iowa; Library of Congress, Washington, D.C.; Texas State Library, Austin; Fort Worth Public Library; Iowa State Historical Department, Iowa City; National Museum of Communication, Las Colinas, Tex.; Texas Collection, Baylor University, Waco; Benson Latin American Collection, Austin, Tex.; Special thanks to William C. Martin for access to his amazing collection of border radio evangelists' materials.

INTERVIEWS

People interviewed by Gene Fowler and/or Bill Crawford: Hank Thompson, Webb Pierce, Patsy Montana, Wayne Raney, Paul Kallinger, Wolfman Jack, Nestor Cuesta, James Weldon, Hawley Pettit, Arturo González, Bob Pinson, Wilbur L. Matthews, Max Churchill, Stan Baker, Lloyd Richardson, Horace Fohn, Sam Morris, Sam Morris, Jr., Jim Collins, Dick Reavis, Sr., Arnaldo Ramirez, Norman Fischer, Bess Bradley, Bob France, Chuck McCassen, Juan Raul Rodríguez, Eduardo Villanueva, Willie Lopez, Marvin "Smokey" Montgomery, and Bruce "Roscoe" Pierce. Special thanks to Dallas Turner for generously sending us eight cassette tapes filled with his insightful reminiscences of the history of border radio.

People interviewed by Rachel Maurer: Bess Bradley, Ruth Pickard, Chris Strachwitz, Wolfman Jack, Paul Kallinger, J. C. Bishop, Bill Callahan, Gerald Carson, Sleepy La Beef, and Red Wassinich.

AUDIO AND FILM SOURCES

Lyndon Baines Johnson Library, Austin, Tex.; record collection of Cary Ginnell; border radio transcription collection of Ed Kahn, curated by Gene Earle; Murry and Jolene Burnham, Marble Falls, Tex.; Kansas

Museum of History, Topeka; UCLA Film·Archives; Dick Hill, Hastings, Nebr.; *Goat Gland Doctor,* television documentary, KTWU, Topeka, Kans., 1986; *The Quack Who Cured Cancer,* documentary film, Realidad Productions, Santa Fe, N.Mex., 1987; *When They Let the Hammer Down,* record album, the Delmore Brothers and Wayne Raney, Bear Family Records LC 5197, 1984; *The Carter Family on Border Radio,* record album, Arhoolie Records/JEMF 101, n.d., liner notes by Archie Green and William H. Koon; *Classic Country Western, the Rarest Radio Recordings of All Time!,* record album, Radiola 4MR-2, 1984; *The Voice of Temperance,* record, Sam Morris, San Antonio, n.d.; and *Ballad of an Unsung Hero,* documentary film, produced by Paul Espinosa, KPBS-TV, San Diego, 1983, Bob Pinson, Country Music Foundation, Nashville, Tenn.

ADDITIONAL ACKNOWLEDGMENTS

In addition to the persons and institutions named above, we wish to acknowledge the assistance of James Andrews, Henry Hubben, David Stansbury, the Del Rio Chamber of Commerce, Tom Munnerlyn, Mardema Ogletree, Brian Robertson, Cary Ginnell, Frank Cotolo, Leslie Ernst, J. Harold Smith, Rupert "Slim Hawkins" Daugherty, Jesse Herrera, Bill Malone, Charles Wolfe, Joe Nick Patoski, Tom Miller, Ginny Burnett, Murry and Jolene Burnham, Dave King, Ken Ausubel, Amelia Crawford, Barbara Farmer, Guillermo Margadant, Maria del Carmen Carmona, Rena Fraden, Dave Kendall, Tim Hamblin, Joe McDermott, Américo Paredes, Ricardo Romo, Don Stadtner, and Anne Norman for the index.

Photo Sources

1. *San Antonio Light* Collection, Institute of Texan Cultures
2. *San Antonio Light* Collection, Institute of Texan Cultures
3. Kansas State Historical Society, Topeka, Kansas
4. Kansas State Historical Society, Topeka, Kansas
5. Border Radio Research Institute
6. The Throttle
7. *Del Rio News Herald*
8. Warren's Studio, Del Rio, Texas
9. Border Radio Research Institute
10. Border Radio Research Institute
11. Kansas State Historical Society, Topeka, Kansas
12. *Eagle Pass Daily Guide,* Barker Texas History Center
13. Border Radio Research Institute
14. The Throttle
15. The Throttle
15. John B. "Roscoe" Pierce
16. Cary Ginnell
17. Border Radio Research Institute
18. Border Radio Research Institute
19. Border Radio Research Institute
20. *W. Lee O'Daniel News,* Barker Texas History Center
21. Border Radio Research Institute
22. Texas State Library
23. Austin History Center, Austin (Texas) Public Library, Austin, Texas

24. Austin History Center, Austin (Texas) Public Library, Austin, Texas
25. Kansas State Historical Society, Topeka, Kansas
26. Texas State Library
27. Texas State Library
28. New York Times
29. Border Radio Research Institute
30. Border Radio Research Institute
31. Warren's Studio, Del Rio, Texas
32. Warren's Studio, Del Rio, Texas
33. Border Radio Research Institute
34. Warren's Studio, Del Rio, Texas
35. Nestor Cuesta
36. *San Antonio Light* Collection, Institute of Texan Cultures
37. *San Antonio Light* Collection, Institute of Texan Cultures
38. Nestor Cuesta
39. Arnaldo Ramirez
40. KDRY, San Antonio, Courtesy Sam Morris
41. *Saturday Evening Post*
42. Dallas Turner
43. William C. Martin Collection, from Reverend Ike press kit
44. *Miracle Magazine*, Courtesy William C. Martin
45. William C. Martin Collection
46. William C. Martin Collection
47. Publicity still, Universal Studios
48. Bill Crawford

Song Title Index

Index